Contents

Introduction to Local Area Networks

Understanding Client-Server Communications in a Local Environment

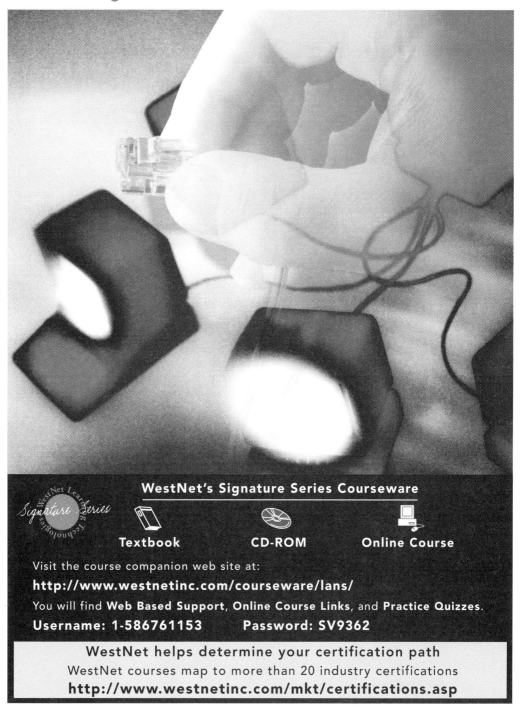

WestNet's Signature Series Courseware

Textbook   **CD-ROM**   **Online Course**

Visit the course companion web site at:

http://www.westnetinc.com/courseware/lans/

You will find **Web Based Support**, **Online Course Links**, and **Practice Quizzes**.

Username: 1-586761153   **Password: SV9362**

WestNet helps determine your certification path

WestNet courses map to more than 20 industry certifications

http://www.westnetinc.com/mkt/certifications.asp

CREDITS

Author and Development Editor: Kenneth D. Reed

Editorial and Production Manager: Marilee E. Aust

Book Design and Composition, and Copy Editor Manager: D. Kari Luraas, Clairvoyance Design

Illustrator: Lynn Siefken

Proofreader: Larry Beckett

Technical Writer and Editor: Kathy Russell

Indexer: Amy Casey

Copy Editor: Sheryl Shapiro, Clairvoyance Design

Cover Design: David Jones

Printer: Johnson Printing

Revised edition © 2001 by WestNet Learning Technologies
Copyright © 1994–2000 by WestNet Learning Technologies

ISBN: 1-58676-115-3

Printed in the United States of America

Reed, Kenneth D.
Introduction to LANs
576 pp., includes illustrations and index

1. Review of LAN Fundamentals 2. Connecting Computers 3. Ethernet LANs 4. Token Ring and FDDI LANs
5. ATM LANs 6. LAN Networking Software 7. The Novell NetWare Client/Server System
8. Network OS Software—Windows NT 9. Analysis of LANs

WB27.0

For instructor-led training, self-paced courses,
turn-key curricula solutions, or more information contact:

WestNet Learning Technologies (dba: WestNet Inc.)
5420 Ward Road, Suite 150, Arvada, CO 80002 USA
E-mail: Info@westnetinc.com

To access the WestNet student resource site, go to
http://www.westnetinc.com/student

Overall Course Evaluation Survey

INTRODUCTION

The prerequisite to the *Local Area Networks* course is the *Introduction to Networking* course. In *Local Area Networks*, we explain the basic principles and technologies of local area networks (LANs). These principles are also used in other types of networks. However, we will concentrate on how those concepts apply to common local networking technologies such as Novell NetWare, Microsoft Windows NT, and Windows 2000.

OVERVIEW

In Units 1 and 2, we review the fundamental concepts that you learned in the *Introduction to Networking* course. We recall the general classifications of networks and the basic types of network topologies. We then review the characteristics of the transmission media that create those topologies.

Both topologies and media are closely related to media access method, thus the next few units examine the popular Data Link protocols such as Ethernet, Token Ring, and Fiber Distributed Data Interface (FDDI). These concepts were introduced in *Introduction to Networking*, but this course will examine each in much greater detail. We will also discuss Asynchronous Transfer Mode (ATM) in depth, because this popular wide area protocol is gradually moving to the LAN environment.

When you have a firm understanding of the lower layers of a LAN, we move on to consider the specialized software applications called network operating systems (NOSs). We then examine the details of the dominant LAN operating systems (OSs): Windows NT/2000 and Novell NetWare.

Finally, we take a look at the factors a network administrator must consider when maintaining or expanding a LAN. We introduce the most common methods and tools you will need to keep a local network working smoothly.

Unit 1
Review of LAN Fundamentals

This unit reviews the most important networking principles that were presented in the "Introduction to Networking" course. A solid understanding of these concepts is necessary before you move on to more detailed study of local area networks (LANs).

Lessons

1. Network Classifications and Topologies
2. Programs, Processes, Protocols, and Layers
3. The OSI Model

Terms

adapter—An adapter is a computer card that fits into the computer bus. One type of adapter is a NIC. A NIC provides a connection (interface) to the networking media for sending information across a network.

client—The client portion of a client/server architecture is any node or workstation used by a single user. If multiple users share resources on the same workstation, it becomes a server. Examples of clients are a Microsoft Windows NT Workstation and a PC running Windows 98.

client/server—Client/server (or client server) is a model in computer networking where individual PCs can access data or services from a common high-performance computer. For example, when a PC needs data from a common database located on a computer on a LAN, the PC is the client and the network computer is the server.

Domain Name System (DNS)—DNS is an Internet service that translates domain names into IP addresses. Because domain names are alphanumeric, they are easier to remember. The Internet however, is really based on IP addresses. Every time you use a domain name, a DNS service must translate the name into the corresponding IP address. For example, the domain name www.example.com might translate to 198.105.232.4.

Ethernet—Ethernet technology, originally developed in the 1970s by Xerox Corporation in conjunction with Intel and DEC, is now the primary medium for LANs. The original Ethernet has 10-Mbps throughput and uses the CSMA/CD method to access the physical medium. Fast Ethernet (100-Mbps Ethernet) and Gigabit Ethernet (1,000-Mbps Ethernet) are later technologies based on the original approach.

frame relay—A frame relay is essentially an electronic switch. Physically, it is a box that connects to three or more high-speed links and routes data traffic between them. Frame relay is intended only for data communications, not voice or video. Transmission errors are detected but not corrected (the frame is discarded).

Hypertext Transfer Protocol (HTTP)—HTTP is an application-level protocol that can be used for many tasks, such as name servers and distributed object management systems, through extension of its request methods (commands). A feature of HTTP is the typing of data representation, allowing systems to be built independently of the data being transferred. HTTP has been used by the Web global information initiative since 1990.

Internet Protocol (IP)—IP is a Network Layer protocol responsible for getting a datagram through a network.

Medium Access Control (MAC)—MAC is one of the media-specific IEEE 802 standards (802.3, 802.4, and 802.5) that defines the protocol and frame formats for Ethernet, Token Bus, and Token Ring. It is the lower sublayer of the Data Link Layer of the OSI model.

network interface card (NIC)—A NIC is an expansion board that is inserted into a computer so the computer can be connected to a network. Most NICs are designed for a particular type of network, protocol, and media, although some can serve multiple networks.

network operating system (NOS)—NOS is the software that manages server operations and provides services to clients. The NOS manages the interface between the network's underlying transport capabilities and the applications resident on the server.

Open Systems Interconnection (OSI)—OSI began as a reference model, that is, an abstract model for data communications. However, now the OSI model has been implemented and is used in some data communications applications. The OSI model, consisting of seven layers, falls logically into two parts. Layers 1 through 4, the "lower" layers, are concerned with the communication of raw data. Layers 5 through 7, the "higher" layers, are concerned with the networking of applications.

peer-to-peer—Two programs or processes that use the same protocol to communicate and perform approximately the same function for their respective nodes are referred to as peer processes. With peer processes, in general, neither process controls the other, and the same protocol is used for data flowing in either direction. Communication between them is referred to as "peer-to-peer."

point-to-point—A network connects nodes, some of which are hosts to which terminal nodes attach, in two different ways: point-to-point and broadcast. Point-to-point networks fall into two classes: circuit-switched networks, in which a connection is formed between the nodes, as in a telephone network; and packet-switched or connectionless networks, in which packets of data, or datagrams, are passed from node to node until they reach their destination, like telegrams.

protocol—Data communications involves the transfer of data between computer programs. Just as humans must share a common language to communicate, programs must have a common protocol. A protocol defines the format and meaning of the data that programs interchange.

Request for Comment (RFC)—An RFC is one of the working documents of the Internet research and development community. A document in this series may be on essentially any topic related to computer communication, and may be anything from a meeting report to the specification of a standard.

topology—Topology refers to the specific physical configuration of a network or a portion of a network. Ring and star are examples of different network topologies.

Transmission Control Protocol (TCP)—TCP is a Transport Layer protocol used to send messages reliably across a network. It is usually paired with IP.

Lesson 1—Network Classifications and Topologies

Two of the most important characteristics of a network are size and shape. Both of these factors influence the transmission technologies and communication protocols that the network uses. This lesson reviews the terms and concepts that network professionals use to describe the broadest, most fundamental aspects of a network's design.

Objectives

At the end of this lesson you will be able to:

- Name and describe the major classifications of computer networks

- Explain the factors that distinguish the major network classifications

- Draw examples of the most common computer network topologies

Network Classification

Networks are classified according to the area over which they extend. The smallest networks consist of two nodes connected by a cable in the same room. The largest networks include millions of nodes around the world. The size and extension of a network depend on the number of nodes that need to communicate, and where these nodes are in relation to each other.

 Key Point

Networks are classified by the distance separating communicating computers.

LANs

A LAN can consist of a few nodes, as depicted on the LAN Diagram, or up to several hundred nodes. However, a LAN is typically confined to a single building.

A segment is a portion of a LAN in which all nodes are directly connected. For example, all nodes may be connected by a single bus cable, or, as shown on the LAN Diagram, connected to a central hub. A LAN can consist of many segments linked together in certain ways to form a larger, but still local, network.

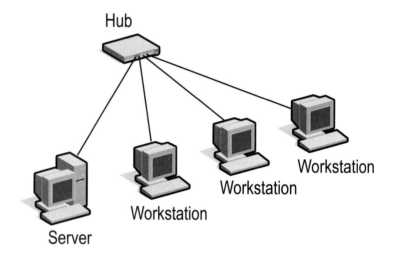

LAN

Campus Networks

When computers are connected across multiple buildings, the entire collection of computers is often referred to as a campus network. A campus network consists of several LANs tied together in some way to form a larger network.

Campus networks are built by connecting LANs to other LANs with an organization's networking infrastructure. In other words, the networking equipment used to connect LANs to form a campus network is owned and operated by the people within the organization. When all of the networking equipment and transmission systems belong to the organization that uses them, that infrastructure is called private facilities. The Campus Network Diagram illustrates a typical campus network.

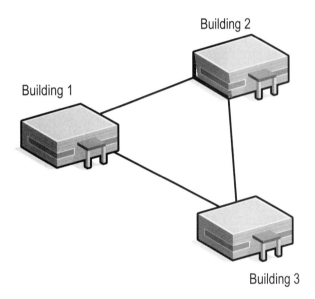

Campus Network

MANs

A metropolitan area network (MAN) interconnects two or more LANs across a city-wide area. The MAN Diagram illustrates a typical MAN. For example, a business might interconnect several branch offices.

One of the primary differences between a MAN and campus network is that a campus network uses private facilities for interconnecting individual LANs, and a MAN uses public or shared facilities leased from a local telephone company. These leased services include point-to-point lines such as T-carriers (fractional T1, T1, or T3), or switched services such as Integrated Services Digital Network (ISDN), frame relay, or Asynchronous Transfer Mode (ATM).

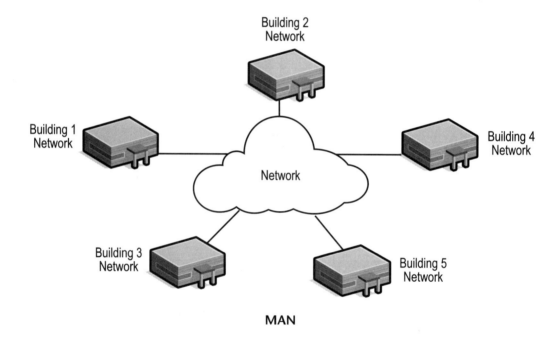

MAN

WANs

Wide area networks (WANs) are formed by connecting LANs across a region or the world. As you can see on the WAN Diagram, both local and long-distance public facilities are typically used to connect LANs across multiple cities. WANs can be built using the same transmission technologies as MANs.

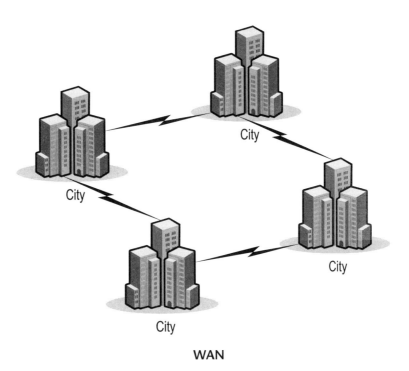

WAN

Within each city, we may have LAN, campus, and MAN connectivity. The WAN portions of the network are the connections that provide communication between cities. Information travels across the WAN portion of the network only when it is destined for another computer in another city.

Network Topologies

A topology is a generalized geometric configuration of some class of objects that join together. With respect to networks, topologies describe different ways computers can be connected to make networks.

 **Key Point**

Star, ring, and bus are the most common LAN topologies.

Networks can have several different arrangements of links. The choice of topologies is often a matter of the technology being used for the network, or geographic considerations.

Bus Topology

A bus is a single electrical circuit to which all devices in the network are connected (although the bus might be made up of many individual pieces of wire). The Bus Topology Diagram illustrates this type of network layout.

A bus topology is a broadcast network. When a node transmits data, the signal travels down the bus in both directions. Each node connected to the bus receives the signal as it passes that connection point. However, a node ignores any signal that is not specifically addressed to it.

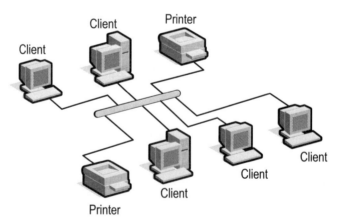

Bus Topology

When the signal reaches the end of the bus cable, a terminator (resistor) prevents the signal from reflecting back from the end of the wire. If a bus network is not terminated, or if the terminator has the wrong level of resistance, each signal may travel across the bus several times instead of just once. This problem increases the number of signal collisions, degrading network performance.

If the bus cable breaks, the entire network may be disabled. In addition, it can be difficult to change the number and position of nodes on a bus network

Star Topology

By far, the most common network topology is the star topology. In a star network, individual computers are connected to a central device, such as a hub or switch, as illustrated on the Star Topology Diagram. When a computer sends information to another computer, it is transmitted through the central device.

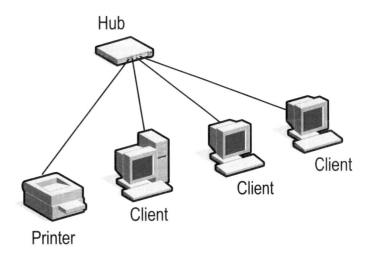

Star Topology

Like the bus topology, a hub-centered star topology is a broadcast network, because the hub copies each signal to all other computers attached to it. And, like a bus, the entire network may go down if the central hub fails.

Ring Topology

A "pure" ring topology is a collection of separate point-to-point links, arranged to make a ring. Each node's network interface card (NIC) has one input and one output connection, so each node is connected to two links.

When a node receives a signal on its input connection, its repeater circuitry retransmits that signal, immediately and without buffering, to its output connection. Thus, in many rings, data flows only in one direction, as illustrated on the Ring Topology Diagram.

To send a message, a node transmits new bits onto the ring. If a message is addressed to a node, that node copies bits off the ring as they go by. If a node receives a message that is not addressed to it, it repeats the message without copying it.

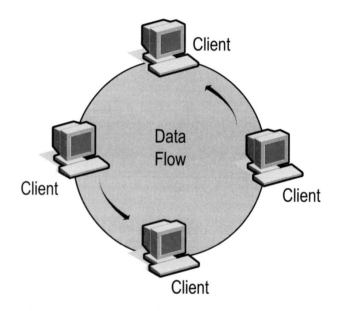

Ring Topology

If a ring node malfunctions or is shut down, the ring is broken, and data transfer stops until the failed node is restored or removed from the ring. The ring can also be broken if any cable between nodes is damaged or broken. Therefore, some ring topologies such as Fiber Distributed Data Interface (FDDI) use a dual-ring structure. If one cable link fails, the other can immediately take over.

Ring topologies are often used as network backbones. A ring backbone often connects the floors of a multistory building or buildings in a campus network or MAN.

Star Ring Topology

A star ring topology combines a physical star configuration with a logical ring of information flow. The Star Ring Topology Diagram illustrates a typical star ring, such as a Token Ring LAN. In a star ring topology, wires run from each node to a central ring wiring concentrator, also called a multistation access unit (MAU). The star ring is a physical star configuration, but information travels from node to node in a logical ring as the MAU copies each signal to each of its nodes in turn. The MAU performs two other important functions:

- It detects when a node is not responding and automatically "locks it out" so that the ring can continue to operate when a node fails.

- It provides a "bridge" to other rings, sending messages addressed to nodes on other rings across the connection to those rings, and accepting messages from other rings for its nodes. Rings joined in this manner effectively become a single ring. By connecting wiring concentrators, ring size is effectively unlimited.

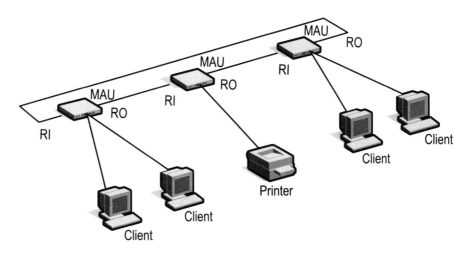

Star Ring Topology

Mesh Topology   In a mesh topology, point-to-point links directly connect every site to every other site. Mesh networks are usually built over time as new sites are added to the overall network. The Mesh Network Topology Diagram provides an example of a mesh configuration. A mesh topology is often used for MAN or WAN networks.

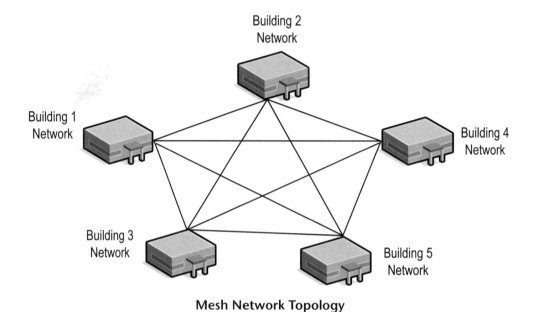

Mesh Network Topology

The number of point-to-point links increases sharply with the number of locations. Thus, if a network must connect more than a few sites, a mesh topology is usually too expensive.

Network Cloud
When an organization must connect more than a few sites over a metropolitan or wide area, a cloud network is usually more economical and flexible than a mesh of point-to-point links. The network cloud, shown on the Network Cloud Topology Diagram, represents a public mesh network of switching devices, often owned by a telephone company. Common types of cloud networks include the public telephone system, the Internet, or switched transmission services such as frame relay or ATM.

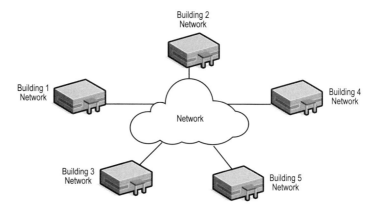

Network Cloud Topology

To use the services of a cloud network, a company subscribes to the service, then sets up a point-to-point connection between each location and a device at the edge of the cloud. The network provider is responsible for moving each message across the cloud to its destination.

Activities

1. A group of computers are connected in a multistory building. This would be considered what type of network?

    a. WAN

    b. MAN

    c. LAN

    d. None of the above

2. A group of computers in the south side of a city are connected to another group of computers downtown. This would be considered what type of network?

    a. WAN

    b. MAN

    c. LAN

    d. LAN and MAN

3. A group of computers in Denver are connected to another group of computers in San Francisco. This would be considered what type of network?

    a. WAN

    b. MAN

    c. LAN

    d. None of the above

4. Which of the following best describes a LAN?

    a. It is confined to only a few buildings and maintained by long-distance carriers

    b. It is confined to a single building or a single floor of a building

    c. It spans multiple cities and possibly multiple countries

    d. It spans a single city and uses local telephone company facilities for connectivity

5. Which of the following best describes a WAN?

    a. It is confined to only a few buildings and maintained by long-distance carriers

    b. It is confined to a single building or single floor of a building

    c. It spans multiple cities and possibly multiple countries

    d. It spans a single city and uses local telephone company facilities for connectivity

6. Which of the following best describes a MAN?

    a. It is confined to only a few buildings and maintained by long-distance carriers

    b. It is confined to a single building or single floor of a building

    c. It spans multiple cities and possibly multiple countries

    d. It spans a single city and uses local telephone company facilities for connectivity

7. A hub (or MAU) is used to provide connectivity in both a star and star ring network. True or False

8. A mesh topology is commonly found in LANs and provides connectivity between computers in a small network. True or False

9. The most common topology being implemented in LANs today is star topology. True or False

10. An organization may use more than one type of topology in a single network. True or False

11. Does the star topology have an advantage over a pure ring?

    _____

    _____

12. Describe how a company might grow and require the four different types of networks described in this lesson.

    _____

    _____

    _____

13. Discuss the primary differences between the types of networks described in this lesson. Describe the type of network used at your organization.

14. Why do different LANs require different topologies?

15. Draw networks that consist of six computers connected using each of the configurations discussed in this lesson.

Extended Activities

1. Using a Web search engine, find at least one definition for a LAN, MAN, and WAN. Contrast and compare these definitions.

    _____

    _____

    _____

    _____

    _____

    _____

2. Using the Web or an equipment catalog, research hubs and MAUs. List the prices, features, and capacity of each device. Compare their similarities and differences.

    _____

    _____

    _____

    _____

Lesson 2—Programs, Processes, Protocols, and Layers

In the previous lesson, we reviewed the various ways that computers and networks can be physically connected. However, network communication relies on more than simple hardware connections. Several layers of software components are also necessary to exchange data between applications on different linked computers. This lesson reviews the principles that allow those software components to communicate.

Objectives

At the end of this lesson you will be able to:

- Describe the difference between a program and a process

- Name the two ways that most computers communicate in a LAN

- Explain the relationship between protocols and services

- Describe the relationship between a communication process and its corresponding header

- Explain how different address types are used to transmit information from one computer application to another

 **Key Point**

Peer-to-peer and client/server are the most common methods of communicating in a LAN.

Programs, Processes, and Protocols

The terms "program," or "application," means a complete set of routines that provide a high-level function of some sort. For example, a word processing application performs the general task of creating documents. However, that broad task is composed of many subprocesses, such as opening files, saving files, copying and pasting text, or deleting data. Therefore, we use the term "process" instead of "program" to refer to some subset of functions (still possibly quite complex) that fits into a larger program or is part of a large system.

This distinction is important because some processes within a program are designed to communicate and cooperate with other processes over a network. The term process is used especially when talking about a program when it is executing (in operating systems [OSs], an executing program is a process).

Protocols

A protocol is a set of communication rules that give meaning to the signals exchanged by two nodes. Two devices or processes can exchange information when they both use the same protocol. Each type of process may use a different protocol, even when multiple processes are running on the same computing device.

A communication protocol typically adds "administrative" data to the beginning of a message. That nonmessage data is called a protocol header. A protocol header functions like an envelope or a packing label to describe the content of a message, its length, the identity of its sender or recipient, the time of day it was sent, and any other information that the communicating processes need to know about the message itself.

Communication Between Processes

Computers and processes generally cooperate using three methods of communication:

- Master/slave

- Peer-to-peer

- Client/server

In a LAN, peer-to-peer and client/server communication are the most common.

Master/Slave Communication

Master/slave communication occurs when one node has much greater computing capacity than another. For example, a typical master/slave relationship occurs in mainframe environments where a powerful central computer runs all the applications, stores all the data, and does all the processing. Simple "dumb" terminals function as slaves to this master, because they have no real processing or data storage capability. Individual terminals may not initiate an interaction, but must wait for the master mainframe to command it to send information. The slave merely displays text received from the master and sends information to the master in the form of the operator's keystrokes.

Peer-to-Peer Communication

When two processes have roughly the same power and can perform approximately the same services for each other, we call them "peer" processes. When processes use peer-to-peer communication, neither one controls the other.

A peer-to-peer computer network allows various combinations of workers to share files, folders, applications, and printers. No single computer sets the rules for these interactions, as seen on the Peer-to-Peer Traffic Diagram. However, each computer's user can decide what resources to make available to other peer users. Most popular desktop OSs, such as Windows 2000 or the Mac OS, have built-in software for creating peer-to-peer networks.

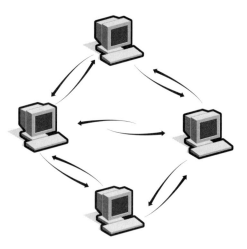

Peer-to-Peer Traffic

Client/Server Communication

Another way that processes can communicate is for one process to assume the role of client and the other that of server. The client process makes requests for the server process to perform some task. Client/server communication is typically used to allow sharing of centralized resources, such as data, applications, peripheral devices, or storage space. A typical client/server network is illustrated on the Client/Server Diagram.

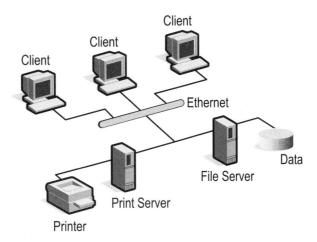

Client/Server

Typically, a client process is found on a lower capability, end-user node, such as a workstation or personal computer (PC). The server process runs on a node with larger capacity or greater power, such as a network file server.

A client/server network is implemented with a specialized network operating system (NOS) such as Novell NetWare, Windows NT Server, or Windows 2000 Server. UNIX and Linux also provide client/server features.

Both client and server processes are dedicated to their respective tasks, and those roles never reverse. However, the same computing machine can run multiple processes. Some of those processes can be servers of some functions, and some can be clients of other servers. Thus it is important to remember that "server" refers to a process, not necessarily a particular machine.

Client and server processes interact with each other by transmitting request/reply pairs. The client process initiates an interaction by issuing a request to the server. The server process responds with a reply satisfying the request. This request/reply communication essentially divides a task into two parts and executes each part on a different system on the network.

Also, peer-to-peer communication can still occur on a client/server network. If servers have been established for shared functions such as file sharing or printing, two computers may still exchange data as peers.

Client and server processes share a common protocol. However, the protocol defines entirely different conventions for communications originating from the client and those originating from the server. This is in contrast with peer-to-peer communication, in which the protocol is more or less the same in both directions.

Comparing Communication Methods

The Communication Comparison Table summarizes the common trade-offs between peer-to-peer and client/server networking.

Communication Comparison

Peer-to-Peer Advantages	Peer-to-Peer Disadvantages	Client/Server Advantages	Client/Server Disadvantages
Simplicity	Not practical in large networks	Access to common resources	Complexity
Low cost	Most OSs limit number of nodes connected	Scalable to very large environments	High cost for small networks
Easy to manage in small networks	No single point for backup and administration	Dedicated shared resources and administration points	Often requires trained personnel
Easy to troubleshoot			Harder to troubleshoot

Layers of Protocols and Services

Each program or process provides a service to the end user or to another program or process. For example, a World Wide Web (Web) browser provides a service to the user by retrieving Web pages from a Web server, then displaying them on the user's monitor.

But many different protocols may need to cooperate to provide a single service to a user. For example, when a Web server sends data to a Web browser, it uses Hypertext Transfer Protocol (HTTP) in conjunction with Transmission Control Protocol (TCP) and Internet Protocol (IP). Each of these protocols is a separate entity with its own specific functions. They provide services to each other, not directly to the end user. IP provides a service to TCP, TCP provides a service to HTTP, and so forth. The service relationships are often described as the underlying services, as presented on the Layers and Services Diagram.

Layers and Services

These interactions between processes and protocols form a layered hierarchy or protocol stack. In a protocol stack, each process uses the service of the process in the layer below it, and provides a service to a process in the layer above it.

Logical and Physical Addresses

Each protocol may use a different type of address to direct a message to the correct process on the intended destination device. These addresses fall into two general categories:

- Physical address
- Logical address

Physical Addresses   A physical address is a unique identifier hard-coded into the NIC of each node. Its other common names are:

- Hardware address
- NIC (or adapter) address
- Medium Access Control (MAC) address
- Data Link address

25

The designers of the most popular MAC-layer protocols (Ethernet, Token Ring, and Fiber Distributed Data Interface [FDDI]) have allocated 48 bits for the hardware address. Each NIC comes with a hardware address preconfigured from the factory. NIC manufacturers register hardware addresses with a worldwide central authority to guarantee the numbers they assign do not conflict with those of any other manufacturer. This guarantees each hardware address is globally unique.

It would be natural to want to associate the term "physical address" with the Physical Layer. However, the Physical Layer is only concerned with transmitting and receiving bits from the physical medium, and does not "see" bits as organized into meaningful patterns, such as an address. The physical address, or hardware address, is actually processed by OSI Layer 2, the Data Link Layer. We review the OSI model in the next lesson. This hardware address is the address ultimately required for frames to be delivered to a destination network node.

Logical Addresses

Logical addresses are symbolic identifiers. These are assigned by software and are used by processes operating at OSI Layer 3 and above. There are two primary types of logical addresses:

- Network addresses, such as an IP address (144.25.54.8)

- Port or process addresses, such as a port number (Port 23)

Data often starts out (at the higher layers) addressed to some symbolic name, such as the host name in the command Telnet Serverhost. The name "serverhost" is the logical address of the destination the user is attempting to contact using the telnet (TCP/IP) application and protocol. But if the message is actually to be delivered to this host, the sending computer must somehow discover the destination's physical address. In this case, an intermediate logical address (the IP address) will first be derived from the symbolic name using some sort of a name service process, such as Domain Name System (DNS). Then a protocol such as Address Resolution Protocol (ARP) can find the hardware address that corresponds to that IP address. When the sending node knows all of these addresses, it can finally transmit the data to its destination.

The most important fact to remember about logical addresses is that a logical address will not get the information "into the box." Only a hardware address used by the Data Link Layer, whether a broadcast address, multicast (group) address, or unicast (individual) address, can physically deliver a frame to the destination device.

Layers of
Addresses

Physical and logical addresses work together to transmit information from source to destination within a segment of a network. As an example, consider how a Web server returns data in response to a client request. The server responds by sending a frame of information across an Ethernet network to the client that made the request. This response is shown on the Web Page Response Diagram.

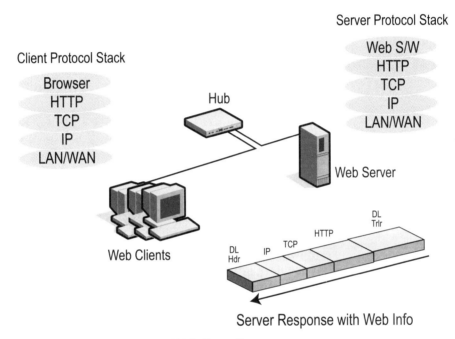

Web Page Response

This diagram demonstrates the correlation between clients, client applications and client processes, client protocols and corresponding servers and server applications, server processes, and server protocols. On the server side of the diagram, the computer is running some type of Web server software such as Apache or Internet Information Server (IIS). The software consists of not only the application, but the protocols needed to send Web documents to the client. The application interfaces with HTTP, which is responsible for responding to the client with the appropriate information.

The HTTP process running on the server creates an HTTP header that contains protocol information used to communicate with the peer HTTP process running on the client. HTTP on the server uses TCP to establish a connection with the client, and reliably transfer the HTTP response to the client software. Thus, the TCP process running on the Web server communicates with the TCP process running on the client.

TCP on the server communicates with IP on the server to transmit the TCP message across the network, packet by packet. IP on the Web server indirectly communicates with its IP peer on the client. IP on the Web server also communicates with the Web server's Ethernet driver. The Ethernet driver is responsible for transmitting a frame of information, consisting of the packet and message, to the next node in the network across a physical link. It does this by relying on the services of the Ethernet NIC and the Physical Layer (the cables and connectors). On the Web Page Response Diagram, both the Web server and client NICs are located on the same physical segment.

In this scenario, three addresses are used by the sending and receiving computers to communicate between application processes. At the lowest level, the Ethernet processes, located on the NICs of the server and client, use Ethernet physical addresses to transmit a frame from NIC to NIC. Each frame contains an IP packet, or portion of a packet.

IP addresses indicate which host on the network should get each packet located inside the Ethernet frame. Each packet contains a TCP message, or portion of a message. As the receiving IP process receives all packets that make up the TCP message, it passes the messages or fragments up to TCP.

TCP reassembles the original message, then passes it to the destination software process address (port). In this case, the data is addressed to the HTTP process at Port 80.

Activities

1. List services that might be more common in a client/server network than a peer-to-peer network.

    _____

    _____

    _____

    _____

2. How does a client/server environment differ from a peer-to-peer environment?

    _____

    _____

3. Does peer-to-peer communication have any advantage over client/server communication?

    _____

    _____

4. List advantages and disadvantages of both peer-to-peer and client/server networks.

Peer-to-Peer Advantages	Peer-to-Peer Disadvantages	Client/Server Advantages	Client/Server Disadvantages

5. Describe the relationship between a computer, computer program, computer process, protocol, and protocol layer.

_____

_____

_____

_____

_____

_____

6. Is an IP address a physical or a logical address?

_____

Extended Activities

1. Build a peer-to-peer network using a Windows desktop such as Windows 98 or Windows 2000. Each user should be able to share files between computers by mapping drive letters to at least two other computers. See your instructor for directions on WestNet labs.

2. Using a Web search engine, find information (such as RFCs) about the following protocols:

   a. HTTP

   _____

   _____

   b. TCP

   _____

   _____

   c. IP

   _____

   _____

Lesson 3—The OSI Model

The OSI reference model describes a theoretical protocol stack that consists of seven layers of services and protocols. At the bottom, the concrete Physical Layer contains protocols that transmit bits over physical media. At the top, the abstract Application Layer contains programs such as electronic mail (e-mail).

The OSI model is not a protocol, but an abstract structure that describes the functions and interactions of various data communication protocols. It provides a conceptual framework that helps us discuss and compare network functions and components.

Objectives

At the end of this lesson you will be able to:

- Describe the primary function of each layer of the OSI model

- List the two main types of addresses found in most computer networks

- Understand why three types of addresses are used to move information from source to destination

 **Key Point**

Each layer of the OSI model uses the services of the layer below it and provides services to the layer above.

Protocols and Layers

As you recall, multiple protocols and processes work together in a layered arrangement. In computer networking terms, a layer is a process (or set of processes) that provides services to the next higher layer and uses the services of the next lower layer. Cooperating layers of protocols are called a "protocol stack" or a "protocol suite."

In a protocol stack, the services offered by each layer progress from abstract, higher level services in the top layers, to more concrete, transmission-oriented services in the bottom layers. Thus, a program that resides at the highest layer typically provides many sophisticated services to the user. However, most of these services are actually implemented, directly and indirectly, by the lower layers.

Because a program provides services only to the layer above it and uses services only of the layer below it, a change to any given layer affects only the layer above it. Layering breaks a single large program into parts isolated from one another according to function, making the program easier to write and change. Layering does, however, extract a performance penalty. There is some overhead associated with moving data through multiple layers of protocols; however, the benefit is generally worth the performance price.

Layering applies to protocols as well as services. In a system that has a layered architecture, each process communicates only with its peer process.

Otherwise, as with services, a change to one process would affect many other processes. Each pair of peers communicates with a common protocol that is appropriate to the services they provide. Therefore, each layer of processes uses a corresponding layer of protocols.

For example, in a Web interaction, TCP on the client communicates with TCP on the server. HTTP on the client communicates with HTTP on the server, and so forth.

When different layers of protocols work together, they use the following basic techniques:

- Encapsulation—On the sending node, each protocol adds its own header to a message as it moves downward through the stack. Each header contains information that is useful to the receiving process. Thus, peer processes communicate through their respective protocol headers.

- Segmentation—If a layer receives a message that is too long, it divides the message into manageable fragments.

- Decapsulation—On the receiving node, each protocol removes its own protocol header before passing the encapsulated message up to the layer above.

- Reassembly—If a message was segmented, one of the processes on the receiving end reassembles the segments into their correct order, then passes the restored message up to the layer above.

Primary Functions of OSI Model Layers

Each layer of the OSI model describes the services that a protocol provides, but it does not specify exactly how a protocol must do that. For example, several different protocols provide the functions of OSI Layer 3 (the Network Layer), and a developer can create a new one at any time.

The OSI Model Layers Table provides an overview of the primary functions of each layer of the OSI model. It also presents the unit of information and address type where appropriate.

OSI Model Layers

OSI Model Layer	Layer Function	Unit of Information	Address Type
Application	User functionality	Program	
Presentation	Character representation Data compression Security	Characters and words	
Session	Establishing, conducting, and ending sessions		
Transport	Transmitting messages from sending computer process to receiving computer process	Message	Process to process between applications
Network	Transmitting individual packets across a network	Packet	Packet address identifying receiver's network and host location
Data Link	Transmitting frames containing packets across a link en route to final destination	Frame	NIC (next node in network)
Physical	Transmitting bits in the form of signals across physical media	Bit	

Physical Layer

The Physical Layer provides the service of transmitting a signal, across a physical communication medium, that represents binary bits. That medium can be a copper cable (coaxial or twisted pair), a fiber optic cable, or a radio channel. Thus, the Physical Layer includes the following types of hardware devices that send and receive signals over each type of physical medium:

- NICs
- Fiber optic transceivers
- Radio transceivers
- Modems

Physical Layer processes are concerned only with the physical signals that represent data bits. Thus, they are only "aware" of signals over the medium, and are not concerned with any device that may be at the other end of the wire or channel. This also means that Layer 1 processes cannot detect errors in data transmission. Most error detection, and all error correction, are the responsibility of higher layers.

Data Link Layer

The Data Link Layer addresses groups of bits to a device located across a single physical transmission path, called a link. Each group of bits that the Data Link Layer transmits is called a frame.

To form a frame, the Data Link Layer encapsulates a Network Layer packet within a header and trailer. The header contains the hardware address of the destination node. The trailer contains a Frame Check Sequence (FCS) value that the receiving node uses for error detection. The Data Link Layer is the only OSI layer that adds a trailer to the data it transmits.

Each frame carries a packet of data across a single physical link. The encapsulated packet does not change, but a new frame is built around the packet for the trip across each link. Thus, we often say that the Data Link Layer is concerned with transmitting data to the next node in the network.

Popular Data Link protocols include:

- High-Level Data Link Control (HDLC)
- Synchronous Data Link Control (SDLC)
- Link Access Procedure for D channel (LAPD), used in ISDN
- LAN protocols such as Ethernet, Token Ring, and FDDI
- WAN protocols such as frame relay, ATM, and ISDN

Network Layer

The Network Layer is responsible for transmitting data packets between source and destination nodes that may not be connected by the same physical link. The Network Layer addresses a data packet to the logical description of a computer that may be located several links away from the source. If the source and destination nodes are not directly connected, then the Network Layer must use intermediate nodes, when necessary, to get a packet to its destination.

Unlike a Data Link address, which is globally unique, a Network Layer address is a logical identifier. Each Network Layer address is only unique within a single network. If a packet's source and destination are in different networks, the Network Layer may have to resolve different addressing conventions and duplicated node addresses used in different types and versions of networks.

The Network Layer also moves packets to and from node types that may use different Data Link protocols. For example, when a router forwards a packet from an Ethernet LAN to a frame relay network, it removes the Ethernet header and trailer and builds a new frame formatted for the frame relay network.

Common Network Layer protocols include:

- X.25—X.25 is an older packet switching protocol that has been largely replaced by faster protocols based on the same basic approach.

- IP—IP is the primary Layer 3 protocol used across the Internet and in many LANs.

- Internetwork Packet Exchange (IPX)—IPX is Novell NetWare's proprietary Network Layer protocol.

Transport Layer

The Transport Layer, or Layer 4, addresses data to a particular process running on a destination computer. Peer software processes at either end of a connection use the Transport Layer to carry on a conversation. Processes in the Transport Layer act as if their nodes are adjacent. They rely on lower layers to handle the details of passing data through intermediate nodes across the network. Thus, Layer 4 insulates the higher levels from all concerns about the transportation of data.

Basic services provided by the Transport Layer include:

- Addressing

- Connection management

- Flow control and buffering

- Multiplexing and parallelization
- Reliable and sequenced delivery
- Service quality management

The most common Transport Layer protocols are:

- TCP—TCP works in conjunction with IP, in the widely used TCP/IP protocol stack.
- Sequenced Packet Exchange (SPX)—SPX is Novell NetWare's Transport Layer protocol. It works in conjunction with IPX.

Upper Layers: Session, Presentation, and Application

The job of the upper layers, taken collectively, is to provide user-oriented services through a set of widely available standard applications, and through specialized applications written for the users by programmers. The Session Layer, and the Presentation Layer above it, provide reusable services for the applications that reside in the Application Layer.

The Session Layer facilitates a step-by-step interaction between two entities. It establishes the session, manages the dialog to prevent simultaneous transmission, and ends the session gracefully. A single session may continue across one or more connections. Similarly, a single connection may support one or more sessions.

The Presentation Layer deals with the format, or representation, of computer information. It resolves differences between different types of character encoding systems, such as Extended Binary Coded Decimal Interchange Code (EBCDIC) and the American Standard Code for Information Interchange (ASCII) character code. It provides security by encrypting and decrypting data. It also compresses data before transmitting it, to use the communication channel more efficiently.

The Application Layer contains programs that invoke the underlying services of the network. Some of these applications are written specifically for one network, while others are widely used standard applications. When these applications need to communicate with peers over the network, they can use their own protocols, plus the services of the lower layers.

Application Layer programs include:

- User applications, such as e-mail or file transfer, provide standard services directly to the user. Each of these applications has its own standard protocol at the Application Layer level.

- Application services, such as virtual filestores, provide services to other applications, but not directly to the user. These facilities simplify application development by allowing programmers to use a common service rather than duplicating the same features in every application.

Activities

1. Draw a protocol stack of a computer that can access the Internet.

2. Name the OSI layers, and describe the purpose of each layer.

   _____

   _____

   _____

   _____

   _____

   _____

3. Name a Data Link Layer protocol.

   _____

   _____

4. Name a Network Layer protocol.

   _____

   _____

5. Name a Transport Layer protocol.

_____

_____

6. Describe the difference between a logical address and physical address.

_____

_____

_____

_____

_____

7. Why are two logical addresses needed in computer networking?

_____

_____

_____

_____

_____

Extended Activities

1. On a Windows PC that is part of a LAN, open the Control Panel. Select Network (on Windows 98) or Network and Dial-Up Connections (on Windows 2000). Select your LAN connection, then choose Properties.

   View the properties of each of your installed network components, and write down as much information as you can find about the network configuration of this computer (do not make any changes). Arrange these notes according to the OSI model.

2. The terms processes, programs, layers, and protocols can be challenging to keep separate and distinct. Break into focus groups of no more than three people and discuss with each other what these terms mean.

Summary

This unit reviewed the basic concepts that underlie all networks.

Networks fall into one of four broad classifications, according to their size and the distance between their nodes:

- LANs link computers within one building or floor.

- Campus networks link several LANs in adjacent buildings.

- MANs link LANs across a city-wide area.

- WANs link LANs across a region, nation, or the world.

Networks can also be described in terms of the physical arrangement of their internal connections. Six main types of topologies are common in networks:

- Bus networks link nodes to a single shared electrical cable. This approach has largely been replaced by star networks.

- Star networks link nodes to a shared wiring device, such as a hub or switch. This arrangement is flexible and easy to manage.

- Ring networks link each node to two others, forming a physical ring. If one station fails, the ring is broken. Thus, some ring networks (such as FDDI) use two parallel rings.

- Star ring networks are physically wired in a star topology, but data moves from node to node in a logical ring pattern.

- Mesh networks link each node to every other. These are more common in MANs and WANs, and become expensive and hard to manage when the network grows to more than a few nodes.

- Cloud networks are privately owned systems that provide transmission services for a fee. The actual structure of the cloud may use any of the topologies above, but those details are invisible to the user of the network's services. The telephone system and the Internet are two widely used network clouds.

We also looked at the difference between programs, processes, and protocols. A network uses many specialized programs and processes to move data, rather than a few complex components. Because these elements interact in a hierarchical pattern, we call a set of cooperating processes a protocol stack. The OSI reference model describes an idealized protocol stack, in which each layer provides a service to the layer above, and uses the services of the layer below.

Each layer of the stack uses its own protocol to communicate, and each protocol uses its own type of address. Thus, several types of addresses, both physical and logical, are needed to transmit a data message between applications on different nodes.

Unit 1 Quiz

1. Which of the following is the lowest layer?

    a. Data Link Layer

    b. Physical Layer

    c. Network Layer

    d. Transport Layer

2. Which of the following layers deals with bits?

    a. Data Link Layer

    b. Physical Layer

    c. Network Layer

    d. Transport Layer

3. Which of the following is a Data Link Layer protocol?

    a. Binary

    b. IP

    c. TCP

    d. Ethernet

4. What is the primary purpose of a Data Link Layer protocol?

    a. Transmit bits across a physical link

    b. Transmit frames across a physical link

    c. Transmit packets across a network

    d. Transmit messages from process to process

5. What is the primary purpose of a Transport Layer protocol?

    a. Transmit bits across a physical link

    b. Transmit frames across a physical link

    c. Transmit packets across a network

    d. Transmit messages from process to process

6. What is the primary purpose of a Physical Layer protocol?

    a. Transmit bits across a physical link

    b. Transmit frames across a physical link

    c. Transmit packets across a network

    d. Transmit messages from process to process

7. What is the primary purpose of a Network Layer protocol?

    a. Transmit bits across a physical link

    b. Transmit frames across a physical link

    c. Transmit packets across a network

    d. Transmit messages from process to process

8. What is an example of a Network Layer protocol?

    a. Ethernet

    b. IP

    c. TCP

    d. RS-232

9. What is an example of a Transport Layer protocol?

    a. Ethernet

    b. IP

    c. TCP

    d. RS-232

10. When an application is sending data to a distant computer, what process occurs on the sending node?

    a. Encapsulation

    b. Decryption

    c. Decapsulation

    d. Translation

11. Match the list below with the appropriate corresponding letter.

    a. Format and meaning of transmitted information

    b. Subset of a computer program

    c. Cable

    d. Bits

    e. Devices connected across a large geographic area

    f. Devices connected within a single building

    g. Messages

    h. Frames

    i. Packet

    Physical Layer _____

    Data Link Layer _____

    Network Layer _____

    Transport Layer _____

    Binary information _____

    Protocol _____

    Process _____

    LAN _____

    WAN _____

12. By the time a message is transmitted across a cable, where will you find an IP packet?

    a. Inside a TCP message

    b. Inside a frame

    c. Inside the IP header

    d. Encapsulating a frame

13. What three addresses are needed to move data from one application to another across a network?

    a. Ethernet address, Data Link address, IP address

    b. Port address, process address, IP address

    c. Logical address, network address, NIC address

    d. Network address, NIC address, process address

14. If segmentation occurs on the sending node, what must occur on the receiving node?

    a. Reassembly

    b. Encapsulation

    c. Parallellization

    d. Resolution

15. The Presentation Layer is concerned with which of the following?

    a. How bits are represented by electrical signals

    b. How characters and numbers are represented by bits

    c. How data looks to the user

    d. How applications are represented by icons

16. Encapsulation means that each layer on the sending node does which of the following?

    a. Adds a trailer to the data

    b. Removes its protocol header from the data

    c. Adds its protocol header to the data

    d. Adds a header to each bit

17. What is the OSI model?

    a. A protocol stack developed by Microsoft

    b. A set of regulations for program development

    c. An obsolete system that is not widely used

    d. An abstract conceptual framework that describes network interactions

18. What is the main advantage of a layered communication architecture?

    a. It increases system flexibility, and simplifies software development and maintenance

    b. It improves network performance by reducing transmission overhead

    c. It increases network security by requiring intruders to penetrate many layers

    d. It improves network reliability by providing redundant functions

19. Many networks use TCP and IP, but SPX and IPX are only used by which of the following?

    a. Windows NT and Windows 2000

    b. Novell NetWare

    c. UNIX and Linux

    d. Internet Service Providers

20. What is the purpose of a port address?

    a. It identifies one port of a hub, switch, bridge, or router

    b. It identifies the device that connects a LAN to the Internet

    c. It identifies a software process

    d. It identifies a Web server

Unit 2
Connecting Computers

In this unit we review the Physical Layer components that we first covered in *Introduction to Networking*. We also move on to explain the deeper technical details of these media. Because unshielded twisted pair (UTP) cable is the dominant medium in most new networks, Lesson 5 explains the technical details of the connector cables that link devices in a UTP-based network.

Each type of transmission medium (copper cable, optical fiber, or radio) has its own particular strengths and weaknesses. Thus, there is no single best way to connect computers. Lesson 4 presents some of the main factors to consider when choosing a network's transmission medium.

Lessons

1. NICs
2. Review of Cable Properties
3. WLANs
4. Media Selection and Installation
5. UTP Patch Cables and Connectors

Terms

American National Standards Institute (ANSI)—ANSI is a national voluntary organization that develops and publishes standards for data communications, programming languages, magnetic storage media, the OSI model, office systems, and encryption.

bandwidth—Bandwidth is the amount of data that can be transmitted in a fixed amount of time. For digital devices, the bandwidth is usually expressed in bps or bytes per second. For analog devices, the bandwidth is expressed in cycles per second, or Hz.

baseband—Baseband is a form of modulation where signals are placed directly on the transmission media and take up the available bandwidth of the entire communication channel.

broadband—Broadband is a type of communication in which multiple signals are simultaneously carried on the same physical medium, each on a separate range of frequencies.

cable categories—There are several cable categories used to describe the different types of twisted pair networks as follows:

- Categories 1 and 2 are used for low-speed data transmission and voice.

- Category 3 is the most common type of network cabling in use today. It is used for 4-Mbps Token Ring and 10BaseT networks.

- Category 4 is used for voice and data transmission rates of 16 Mbps.

- Category 5 is used for voice and data transmission rates up to 100 Mbps. It is the most popular type of network cabling being used in new installations. Category 5E (enhanced) provides data rates up to 200 Mbps through more precise manufacturing techniques.

Carrier Sense Multiple Access with Collision Detection (CSMA/CD)—CSMA/CD is set of rules determining how network devices respond when two devices attempt to use a data channel simultaneously (called a collision). Standard Ethernet networks use CSMA/CD. This standard enables devices to detect a collision. After detecting a collision, a device waits a random delay time and then attempts to retransmit the message. If the device detects a collision again, it waits twice as long to try to retransmit the message. This is known as exponential backoff.

central processing unit (CPU)—A CPU controls the operation of a computer. It interprets and executes instructions to carry out computer-related tasks.

crossover cable—A crossover cable is a UTP cable with RJ-45 connectors at both ends, designed to directly connect the NICs of two computers. The pins on each connector are attached to different wires, thus signals flow from the output of one NIC to the input of the other, and vice-versa. See patch cable.

daisy chain—A daisy-chain network is created by linking multiple devices by means of a cabling system. In an AppleTalk network, the daisy-chain topology is created using PhoneNet connectors and twisted pair wiring (regular phone wire). A daisy-chain configuration must be terminated at both ends using terminating resistors.

detector—A detector is a device that receives optical signals and converts them into electrical signals.

direct memory access (DMA)—DMA is the type of memory access that does not involve the main processor in a computer to transfer data directly from memory to a peripheral device, such as a hard drive or NIC.

Electronic Industries Association (EIA)—EIA is a national trade organization that publishes hardware-oriented standards for data communications. EIA-232-D is an example (corresponds to RS-232).

Extended Industry Standard Architecture (EISA)—EISA is a 32-bit computer bus specification introduced in 1988. It provides additional features beyond that of the ISA bus standard.

feeder—A cable that connects a single-floor network segment to a building backbone or multistory trunk is referred to as a feeder.

index of refraction—The index of refraction is the ratio of light velocity in a vacuum to its velocity in another transmission medium. See refraction and total internal reflection.

Industry Standard Architecture (ISA)—ISA is a PC expansion bus for modems, video displays, speakers, and other peripherals.It is also called an AT bus.

input/output (I/O)—I/O is the process of moving data to and from a computer CPU to a peripheral device. Input devices include such things as keyboards and mice. Output devices include monitors and printers. Some devices are used for both input and output, such as a disk drive or NIC.

insertion loss—Insertion loss is the reduction in signal strength caused by cutting an optical fiber cable to attach a node or monitoring device.

insulation displacement connector (IDC)—An IDC is a type of electrical connection device that strips away a wire's insulation as the wire is pressed down (punched down) into an electrical contact point. Punchdown blocks, patch panels, and RJ-45 connectors are types of IDC.

interference—Interference is any energy that interferes with the clear reception of a signal. For example, if one person is speaking, the sound of a second person's voice interferes with the first. See noise.

light-emitting diode (LED)—An LED is a device that converts electrical signals into light pulses.

mode—A mode is an independent light signal traveling through an optical fiber.

multidrop—Multidrop refers to a data communication configuration where multiple terminals, printers, and workstations are located on the same media, and only one can communicate with the "master" at a given time. Multidrop is a form of unbalanced communication.

multiplexer (MUX)—A MUX is a device that allows multiple signals to travel over the same physical medium.

multistory trunk—A multistory trunk is a bundle of cables installed vertically in a multistory building to provide a medium for network backbones that connect network segments on multiple floors.

noise—Noise is any condition, such as electrical interference, that destroys signal integrity. Noise can be caused by many electromagnetic sources, such as radio transmissions, electrical cables, electric motors, lighting dimmers, or bad cable connections.

operating wavelength—The wavelength of an optical signal (mode) is referred to as an operating wavelength. Wavelength determines the color of visible light, although network signals in optical fiber use infrared wavelengths that are invisible to the human eye.

patch cable (patch cord)—A patch cable is a UTP cable with RJ-45 connectors at both ends, designed to connect a computer's NIC to a port of a hub or switch. On both connectors, each pin is attached to the same wire, thus signals flow straight through the cable. See crossover cable.

Peripheral Component Interconnect (PCI)—PCI was introduced by Intel to define a local bus system for a computer. PCI allows up to 10 expansion cards to be installed in a computer. PCI technology is capable of transferring data across a PC bus at very high rates.

photodiode—A photodiode is a semiconductor device that converts light into electrical signals.

plenum—A plenum is a duct for building heating or air conditioning, often found above suspended ceiling tiles or in raised floors. Plenum-grade cable meets fire codes because the cable coating is fire-resistant and does not emit toxic fumes when burned.

pulse code modulation (PCM)—PCM is a method of converting an analog voice signal to a digital signal that can be translated accurately back into a voice signal after transmission. The device that converts an analog signal to PCM is a codec (coder/decoder). A codec first samples the voice signal at several thousand samples per second. Each sample is converted to a binary number that expresses the amplitude of the sample in a very compact form. These binary numbers form the digital bit stream that comes out of a codec. The receiving codec reverses the process, using each successive binary number to control a digital/analog circuit that generates the required analog wave form on the voice output channel.

random access memory (RAM)—RAM is the memory of a computer that can be read from or written to by computer hardware components such as a CPU.

refraction—Refraction is the tendency of a light ray, or electromagnetic signal, to be deflected from a straight path when it passes obliquely from one medium into another medium that has a different index of refraction. See index of refraction and total internal reflection.

RJ-45 connector—RJ-45 is a snap-in connector for UTP cable, similar to the standard RJ-11 telephone cable connector. The RJ-45 connector can terminate up to eight wires.

Thicknet—Thicknet is also known as 10Base5 or Yellow Wire. Thicknet can carry a signal 500 m before a repeater is required. The maximum number of nodes allowed in a trunk segment is 100. The maximum number of trunk segments allowed in an Ethernet network is five, of which only three may be populated with nodes. Thicknet is no longer installed in computer networks.

Thinnet—Thinnet (or 10Base2) can carry a signal 185 m before a repeater is required. The maximum number of nodes that can be connected to a Thinnet trunk segment is 30.

total internal reflection—Total internal reflection occurs when a light ray traveling in one material hits another material and reflects back into the original material without any loss of light. In optical fiber, total internal reflection occurs for two reasons. First, the core has a higher index of refraction than the cladding; this difference causes the light to refract, or bend. Second, the light signals enter the cable at a shallow angle; an overly steep light angle will cause some or all of the light to enter the cladding instead of reflecting back into the core. See refraction and index of refraction.

transceiver—A device that can both transmit and receive optical signals is referred to as a transceiver.

twisted pair—In twisted pair cabling, pairs of conductors are twisted together to randomize possible cross-talk from nearby wiring. Inadequate twisting is detectable using modern cable testing instruments.

unshielded twisted pair (UTP)—UTP is the most common type of network cabling, and is used extensively in telephone networks and many data communication applications. UTP can carry a 100-Mbps digital signal 100 m using twisted pairs of cable without requiring that the signal be repeated.

Lesson 1—NICs

A network interface card (NIC) provides the link between a computer and the physical hardware of a network. A NIC is the hardware component inserted into the personal computer (PC) or workstation that allows it to be connected to the network. If the network contains a dedicated server, internetworking device, or peripheral device, that hardware also contains a NIC.

Objectives

At the end of this lesson you will be able to:

- Explain how computers attach to a network that uses UTP cable

- Describe the basic characteristics of a NIC

- Describe the performance improvements a PCI bus offers

Key Point   *NICs provide the interface between a computer and a network.*

NIC Connectivity

There are many ways to connect NICs to a network. The NIC Connectivity Diagram shows the method commonly used in twisted pair networks. Each NIC attaches to a network wall outlet by means of a twisted pair cable with RJ-45 connectors.

On the other side of the wall, a separate twisted pair cable leads to a wiring closet, where it is terminated on a punchdown block or patch panel. Punchdown blocks and patch panels are types of insulation displacement connectors (IDC). That term simply means that the wire insulation is stripped away from the copper wire when the wire is punched down into an electrical contact point. An IDC both simplifies installation and makes secure connections.

Punchdown blocks and patch panels make it simpler to manage many separate workstation cables. A patch cord links each terminated wire to a port on a hub, switch, or multistation access unit (MAU). To move a workstation to a different segment of the network, we simply reconnect the patch cord to a different port or device. However, in many small networks, each workstation's twisted pair cable may be attached directly to a hub that forms the central point of a network.

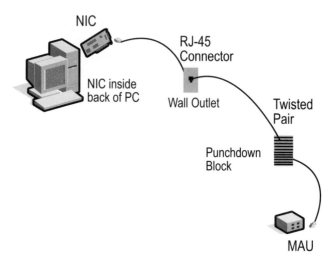

NIC Connectivity

NIC Considerations

The NIC Options Table shows characteristics to consider when choosing a NIC.

NIC Options

LAN protocol	Ethernet, FDDI, Fast Ethernet, ATM, Token Ring, AppleTalk, etc.
Computer bus supported	MCA, ISA, EISA, PCI, NuBus, VME
RAM buffer size	8 KB, 16 KB, 32 KB, etc.
I/O bus width	8 bit, 16 bit, 32 bit, 64 bit, etc.
Data rate	10 Mbps, 4 Mbps, 16 Mbps, 100 Mbps
Media type supported	Coaxial, UTP, STP, Fiber, Wireless
O/S supported	NetWare, Windows NT/2000, UNIX/Linux, Mac OS, etc.
Processor Capability	386, 486, Pentium, Pentium II, Pentium III, etc.

NIC Connectivity in a PC

The NIC fits into a slot on the motherboard that is connected to the computer bus (also referred to as the input/output [I/O] or expansion bus). This bus connects adapter cards, such as NICs, to the central processing unit (CPU) and random access memory (RAM). The speed at which data is transferred to and from the NIC is a key factor in NIC performance. The wider the bus, the more data can be transferred simultaneously. Another key factor in NIC performance is the method used to transfer data to and from the NIC.

The NIC should use as little of the computer CPU as possible when transferring data. There are four types of data transfer techniques used in NICs as follows:

- Direct memory access (DMA)—Allows transfer of information to and from memory without involving the CPU; the system DMA controller performs the transfer. DMA is also referred to as standard DMA.

- Bus mastering DMA—This mode is supported by Peripheral Component Interconnect (PCI) NICs. The PCI card actually takes control of the system bus prior to the transfer.

- Shared memory—A NIC stores data on shared RAM. The CPU also has access to the shared memory space.

- Programmed I/O—A NIC stores data in I/O registers. This is usually the slowest method because the CPU has to wait.

NIC Bus Architectures

Until recently, the most commonly used PC bus was an Industry Standard Architecture (ISA) bus. Newer PCs use a PCI bus. The PCI bus offers superior throughput for NICs and other peripheral devices in desktop systems. PCI NICs (used for Ethernet local area network [LAN] connections) are becoming the NICs of choice in networked desktops and servers. The high performance, ease of use, and enhanced reliability of PCI NICs make their widespread adoption in standard Ethernet networks inevitable.

A desktop's bus architecture determines how quickly data is exchanged between the CPU, memory, and peripheral devices. Buses should match the capabilities of their microprocessors to obtain optimal system performance. ISA and Extended Industry Standard Architecture (EISA) buses, once the standards for desktops, were designed for earlier generations of microprocessors and applications.

Today, however, much faster processors such as the Intel Pentium II and Pentium III series are commonplace, and bandwidth-intensive applications such as Microsoft Windows-based programs, multimedia, and imaging applications are proliferating. Buses now must support multitasking operating systems (OSs) as well as small computer systems interface (SCSI) devices, LAN NICs, and powerful video cards.

As an example, a Pentium processor accepts 32-bit data paths, and processes up to 500 megabytes per second (MBps). With its maximum throughput of 528 MBps, the PCI bus is designed to keep up with Pentium-based machines. The ISA bus, on the other hand, offers data paths no wider than 16 bits, and a maximum transmission rate of only 16.5 MBps. Designed for either 32- or 64-bit data paths, the PCI bus was developed to provide the faster throughput that today's technologies demand. PCI can provide clock speeds up to 66 megahertz (MHz). ISA and EISA run no faster than 8.25 MHz. In addition, the next highest level of PCI specifications, which calls for 64-bit data paths, matches even better the performance of Pentium-grade microprocessors.

A key factor in any system's overall performance is the CPU utilization required by the various tasks being performed. PCI has a clear advantage over older technologies, because PCI components are designed as bus master devices. With bus mastering, a PCI device can request control of the bus to initiate data transfers into system memory with no system CPU intervention. As a result, the CPU is free to focus on other computing tasks during network transfers, providing faster and more responsive system performance. Because ISA-based devices are not bus master devices, they require the host CPU to perform data transfers. This is a disadvantage in multitasking operating environments, which require more CPU cycles due to the number of application tasks being performed in parallel.

Although Fast Ethernet (100-Mbps) NICs have advantages in advanced network installations, there will continue to be a strong demand for high-performance, reliable 10-Mbps PCI NICs for standard 10-Mbps Ethernet connections.

Activities

1. Why it is important not to interrupt a computer's CPU when sending data to and from a NIC?

   _____

   _____

   _____

   _____

2. Discuss what makes the speed of a bus important.

   _____

   _____

   _____

   _____

Extended Activity

Using the Web or a catalog, find Ethernet 10-Mbps NICs and 10/100 NICs from three separate vendors. Compare prices and functionality.

_____

_____

_____

_____

_____

_____

Lesson 2—Review of Cable Properties

The cabling of a network must meet the network's basic requirements for speed, security, flexibility, and LAN protocol. This lesson reviews the key properties of both copper and fiber cables.

Objectives

At the end of this lesson you will be able to:

- Describe the physical properties of coaxial cable, twisted pair, and optical fiber
- List the advantages and limitations of twisted pair networks
- Describe how fiber cabling carries a data signal
- Explain the most appropriate use of fiber cabling in a computer network

Coaxial Cabling

Coaxial cabling is still widely used in computer networks. Although it is not commonly installed in new network implementations, it may be installed in networks where a large coaxial cable network already exists.

 **Key Point**

> *Coaxial cables are not widely used in new installations of computer networks.*

Physical Properties

Coaxial cable was the dominant transmission medium for LANs for many years, however, it has lost ground to UTP and fiber optic cable in the past several years. 10Base5 (Thicknet) is no longer installed, and 10Base2 coaxial (Thinnet cable) is installed only in networks that already contain this type of cable.

Coaxial cable is composed of two conductors. Solid wire forms the inner conductor, and the outer conductor serves as a shield and is usually grounded. Between the two conductors is a plastic insulator. A plastic outer jacket surrounds the cable assembly. There are many different forms of coaxial cable; however, they are usually divided into two classifications—those used for baseband transmission, and those used for broadband transmission. The Coaxial Cable Diagram illustrates the construction of coaxial cables.

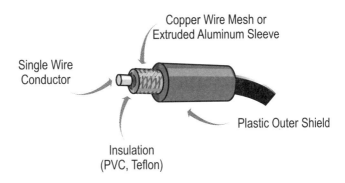

Single Wire Conductor

Copper Wire Mesh or Extruded Aluminum Sleeve

Plastic Outer Shield

Insulation (PVC, Teflon)

Coaxial Cable

Baseband cable has a center conductor of solid or stranded copper. This conductor is surrounded by a plastic insulator and contained in a braided aluminum or copper shield or outer conductor. The entire package is encased in an outer cover, typically made of polyvinyl chloride (PVC) or plenum-grade plastic.

Transmission Method

In baseband coaxial systems there is no modulation of the signal. The digital signal occupies the entire bandwidth of the cable. Thus, baseband cables have only one channel in operation at any moment. In broadband coaxial systems, multiple channels operate on a single cable simultaneously.

Coaxial Cable Transmission Span

The Institute for Electrical and Electronics Engineers (IEEE) 802.3 (Ethernet) LAN standard specifies a maximum distance of 1.8 kilometers (km) for broadband cabling.

Baseband systems, such as data networks, can typically cover distances of between 1 and 3 km. However, for an Ethernet network, the maximum distance between any two devices is 2.8 km. The primary reason for this limitation is not the physical cable construction, but the timing considerations in the Medium Access Control (MAC) layer framing protocol and the Ethernet send and receive algorithm.

Coaxial Cable Bandwidth

Bandwidth is another variable that differs significantly between broadband and baseband systems. Many baseband implementations operate in the range of 10 Mbps. Others operate at higher rates, such as Token Ring at 16 Mbps. Newer Ethernet installations operate at still higher rates: 100 Mbps and 1 gigabit per second (Gbps). Broadband systems, on the other hand, offer increased bandwidth capabilities because there are multiple channels on each cable.

Coaxial Cable Topology

Coaxial cable can be used in both point-to-point and broadcast mode. In bus architectures, such as Ethernet 10Base2, multiple devices are usually "dropped" from a single cable. Depending on the application and required data rates, a broadband system may support thousands of connections. Baseband systems can support up to 100 devices for a single cable, segmenting some implementations. The Coaxial (Bus) Topology Diagram illustrates this type of network layout.

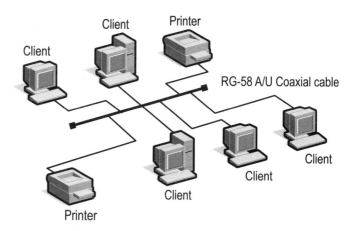

Coaxial (Bus) Topology

Coaxial Cable Security

Tapping or intercepting a signal from a remote point is difficult with coaxial cabling systems. Any attempt to tap into the coaxial bus will break or interrupt network traffic.

Coaxial Cable Noise Immunity

Coaxial cable provides excellent noise immunity compared to UTP installations. The outer braided shield effectively conducts all outside electrical signals to the ground, protecting the signal on the inner conductor.

Coaxial Cable Installation Considerations

Coaxial cable is significantly more difficult to install than twisted pair cables. This contributes to UTP's growing popularity and coaxial cable's lack of popularity.

Twisted Pair Cabling

By far, the most popular communications medium is twisted pair cabling. As the name implies, the wires are twisted, which reduces noise and adjacent interference for the entire length of the cable. Twisted pairs are available with braided or foil electrostatic shielding (shielded twisted pair [STP]), which further enhances the noise reduction properties of the medium.

 **Key Point**

Twisted pair is the predominantly used medium in new LANs.

Twisted Pair Properties

Twisted pair cables usually consist of four to eight wires. Multi-pair cable consisting of 25-pair cables is often used to consolidate many twisted pair cables for easier cable routing. UTP is the primary cabling type for most local network computing systems, as well as the medium of choice for high-speed data transmission applications.

Twisted Pair Transmission Method

Twisted pairs support both analog and digital transmission using a wide variety of encoding and modulation techniques. Digital transmission on twisted pairs often uses pulse code modulation (PCM) when used for integrated voice and data applications.

Twisted Pair Transmission Span

Twisted pair installations are frequently limited to 100 m per segment, without repeaters. Using repeaters to compensate for attenuation (signal loss over distance), the line can be extended to meet most practical application requirements. However, as the length of a segment increases, its data rate decreases. The higher the bit rate, the shorter the span.

Twisted Pair Bandwidth

As with many other media, the bandwidth and distance of twisted pairs are interrelated. Using repeaters at relatively short intervals in a LAN environment can enhance the maximum bandwidth, and enable transmission rates on the order of 10 Mbps to greater than 100 Mbps.

Twisted Pair Topology

Twisted pairs are generally used in point-to-point environments: however, it is possible to use them in configurations that simulate multipoint broadcast capabilities. This is achieved using a technique known as daisy-chaining. The device itself (as opposed to a central hub) is responsible for forwarding the information. Star topologies, using hub devices, have become the most popular implementation of twisted pair technology. The Hub and Daisy-Chain Configurations Diagram illustrates this popular setup.

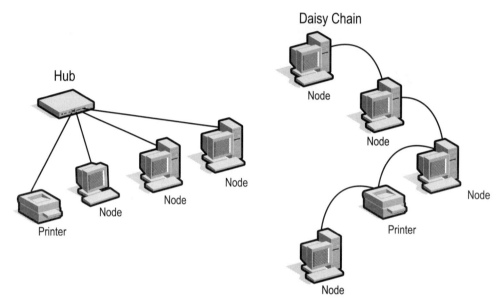

Hub and Daisy-Chain Configurations

Twisted Pair Security

Twisted pair is the least secure of the common LAN media types. This is because of its unshielded nature, and the fact that it is easy to plug into a UTP hub where signals are broadcast. Encryption can add a higher level of data protection as opposed to limiting access to the network.

Twisted Pair Noise Immunity

Twisted pairs provide the least immunity to noise of all physical conductors. The medium both emits and absorbs noise and is sensitive to electromagnetic interference (EMI) and radio frequency interference (RFI). Reasonably good noise immunity can be achieved if the twist length is significantly shorter than the effective wavelength of the signal.

Twisted Pair Installation Considerations

Twisted pairs are easy to install. In most installations, the twisted pair is routed from desktops to a central wiring closet. Twisted pair cabling typically uses RJ-45 connectors at the ends of the cable, which makes the cable easy to snap in and out of the ports of patch panels or hubs.

UTP Cable Categories

There are five levels (or categories) of UTP cable. All are constructed of four unshielded pairs of either 22- or 24-gauge solid conductors. Higher category UTP cable can support applications in lower levels. The six UTP cable categories are defined below:

- Category 1 cable supports applications such as voice communications and very low-speed data applications. There are specific upper limits of use, however, Category 1 cable is not suited for LANs.

- Category 2 cable supports Integrated Services Digital Network (ISDN), T1 (a digital wide area network [WAN] carrier facility), and LANs operating at 1 Mbps or less.

- Category 3 cable supports LANs at speeds up to 10 Mbps and in some cases, such as 100VG-AnyLAN and 100BaseT4, speeds up to 100 Mbps.

- Category 4 cable supports LANs at speeds up to 16 Mbps (for example, Token Ring).

- Category 5 cable supports LAN speeds of 100 Mbps and greater.

- Category 5E (enhanced) cable supports LAN speeds up to 200 Mbps.

Factors such as environment, cable length, quality of installation, number of connections, and equipment type can vary the capabilities of a cabling system on a case-by-case basis. Although lower grade cabling may support some higher speed applications, attenuation and crosstalk problems increase.

Most new networks install Category 5 cabling and components to ensure proper network operation, and accommodate higher speed applications like Fast Ethernet (100 Mbps) and Asynchronous Transfer Mode (ATM) (155 Mbps). However, Category 5 cabling alone will not guarantee effective transmission, because it requires compatible connectors and patch panels. In other words, if Category 5 cable is installed with lower grade components or poor workmanship, the resulting network will likely be certified as only Category 3 or 4.

Category 5 cabling and components not only make operational sense, but economic sense as well. When components are installed that implement higher speeds, such as Fast Ethernet, the cabling infrastructure can remain in place. An example of Category 5 wiring and components is shown on the Wiring Closet Diagram.

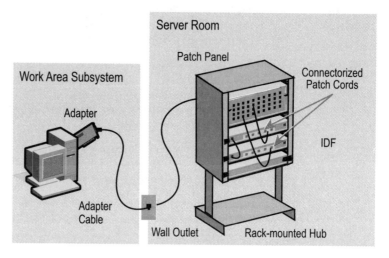

Wiring Closet

Fiber Optic Cabling

High immunity to noise and increasing bandwidth has increased the implementation of fiber optic cable over the past several years. Standards such as Fiber Distributed Data Interface (FDDI), along with fiber optic cable's increased use as a backbone technology, have helped increase the popularity of fiber optic media.

Key Point

Fiber optic cabling provides high bandwidth over long distances.

Optical Fiber Properties

Signaling on optical fiber is accomplished by sending a signal-encoded beam of light through a glass or plastic fiber called a waveguide. Each fiber has a center core of highly refractive glass or plastic. Surrounding this core is a cladding material with a lower index of refraction. The outside of a fiber bundle is covered with a reinforced protective coating.

When light traveling down the core reaches the boundary between the core and cladding, the change in refractive index causes the light to completely refract, or bend, back into the core. This effect is called total internal reflection. The cladding of each fiber completely contains light signals within each core; therefore, preventing crosstalk.

The Fiber Optic Cable Diagram illustrates optical fiber construction.

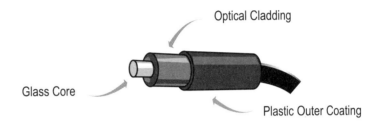

Fiber Optic Cable

Different types of optical fibers are available. The two most common types are as follows:

- Single-mode fiber is characterized by an extremely small core diameter (on the order of 8 microns). Lasers are used to transmit light representing the binary information.

- Multimode fiber has a larger core and uses light emitting diodes (LEDs) to transmit the light signal.

In multimode fibers, the diameter of the core (usually 62.5 microns) is sufficiently large to allow light to travel on different paths and send multiple signals. Each of these paths is considered a mode of propagation. The photons that constitute the light pulse all have the same operating wavelengths; however, depending on where the first reflection occurs, the photons take different paths through the waveguide. In contrast, single-mode fiber is characterized by a core diameter of approximately 8 microns. The photons are only permitted one route through the waveguide.

Optical fiber cables may contain multiple fibers. Some cables have steel or composition stress materials among the glass fibers to provide support when the cables are suspended overhead. Other cables contain fibrous material (Kevlar) of very high pulling strength, to permit pulling the cable without stressing the optical fibers.

Optical Fiber Transmission Method	Both lasers and LEDs are used as light sources for transmission. LEDs are predominantly used in data transmission environments on multimode fiber, and lasers are ideal for voice transmission on single-mode fiber. LEDs are less expensive, not as sensitive to temperature, and offer a longer operational life than lasers. The detectors, which function as transceivers on the other end of the fiber, convert light pulses into an electrical signal. Two photodiode devices are used. Transmission on an optical fiber is usually unidirectional, although recent developments enable transmission of multiple signals on a single fiber in either direction simultaneously. LANs generally require the use of two fibers.

Optical Fiber Transmission Span

Several variables affect the range of optical fibers:

- Bandwidth

- Repeater placement

- Single- or multimode fiber use

Multimode fibers without repeaters can be extended to 5 to 10 km. In this range, the fiber can support transmission rates of up to 100 Mbps. For shorter distances of perhaps 1 km, up to 1 Gbps has been demonstrated. Single-mode fiber, although not used very often in short-range data applications, performs well in excess of 100 km. These larger geographic ranges are coupled with data rates of 200 Mbps.

A concern with this type of medium, however, is the signal loss that occurs at taps, connectors, patch panels, and splices. This will vary with the nature of the tapping/splicing technology.

Optical Fiber Topology

Optical fibers are most often connected in a point-to-point or ring fashion. Multidrop configurations are possible, but the cost and reduction of topologic flexibility make this less practical. Implementations most commonly encountered in office buildings today use optical fiber cable for multistory trunks and sometimes for feeders on a single floor, as illustrated on the Multifloor Wiring Diagram. Distribution to the less stable workstation environment is usually accomplished using multiplexers and hub connectivity to twisted pair or coaxial cable.

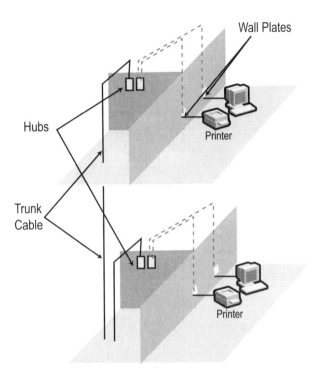

Multifloor Wiring

Optical Fiber Security

Optical fibers are generally secure from intrusions or tapping. Difficulty in tapping and minimizing the insertion loss prevents most intruders from successfully penetrating the security of a fiber optic cabling system.

Optical Fiber Noise Immunity

One of the most significant advantages of optical fiber is that it is virtually immune to noise. Light is not affected by radio waves or magnetic fields.

Fiber Optic Installation Considerations

Optical fiber exhibits a number of positive attributes with regard to installation. The danger of electrical short circuits between conductors is not an issue, and the cable can even be totally immersed in water without affecting the signal. The cable itself is lighter than other media, which also facilitates installation. On the other hand, fiber optic cabling is expensive and difficult to correctly install and terminate, thus requiring specialized installation training and extensive post-installation testing.

Activities

1. Fiber optic cabling provides a high degree of immunization to noise. True or False

2. Optical cladding is used to reflect light as it travels down a glass core in a fiber optic cable. True or False

3. A glass core is used to generate light signals for transmission of digital information. True or False

4. Multimode cabling has a larger glass diameter than single-mode cabling. True or False

5. Multimode cabling is capable of carrying information over longer distances than single-mode cabling. True or False

6. LEDs are the light source for single-mode cabling. True or False

7. Fiber optic cables often carry more than one signal at a time. True or False

8. Fiber optic cables often have several glass fibers to increase the speed that light travels across a physical network. True or False

9. Why has twisted pair gained such widespread acceptance?

   _____

   _____

   _____

   _____

10. What does the statement "the higher the bit rate the shorter the span" mean?

    _____

    _____

    _____

    _____

11. What is the function of a hub in a UTP-based network?

_____

_____

_____

_____

12. List three characteristics of twisted pair cabling.

_____

_____

_____

13. Draw a Thinnet Ethernet network that consists of 10 workstations and 2 printers.

14. Draw a network that consists of a fiber optic backbone that connects four workgroups. Each of the workgroups has four users that use Ethernet and UTP cabling.

Extended Activities

1. Obtain samples of Thinnet, Thicknet, STP, UTP, and fiber cables, and discuss the characteristics of each.

   _____

   _____

   _____

   _____

2. Using the Web or a catalog, find the cost per foot of Thinnet coaxial cable, fiber optic cabling, UTP, and STP.

   _____

   _____

   _____

   _____

Lesson 3—WLANs

As the globally recognized LAN authority, the IEEE 802 committee has established the standards that have driven the LAN industry for the past two decades, including 802.3 Ethernet and 802.5 Token Ring. In 1997, after seven years of work, IEEE published 802.11, the first internationally sanctioned standard for wireless LANs (WLANs).

Like all IEEE 802 standards, 802.11 focuses on the bottom two levels of the ISO model: the Physical Layer and Data Link Layer. Any LAN application, network operating system (NOS), or protocol, including TCP/IP and Novell NetWare, will run on an 802.11-compliant WLAN as easily as they run over Ethernet. The standards-based technology allows administrators to build networks that seamlessly combine more than one LAN technology to best fit their business and user needs.

Objectives

At the end of this lesson you will be able to:

- Describe the MAC method used by wireless networks, and explain why it is different than cabled networks

- Explain the difference between 802.11a and 802.11b wireless networks

- Name some of the key constraints on the speed and operating distance of a wireless LAN.

 **Key Point**

Many aspects of WLAN operation are strictly controlled by government regulations.

802.11 Equipment and Operating Modes

802.11 defines two basic pieces of equipment:

- A wireless station is usually a PC equipped with a wireless NIC. Wireless end stations can be 802.11 PC Cards, PCI, or ISA NICs, or embedded solutions in non-PC clients (such as an 802.11-based telephone handset).

- An access point (AP) acts as a bridge between the wireless and wired networks. An access point usually consists of a radio, a wired network interface (e.g., 802.3), and bridging software conforming to the 802.1d bridging standard. The access point acts as the base station for the wireless network, aggregating access for multiple wireless stations onto the wired network.

The 802.11 standard also defines two operating modes:

- Infrastructure mode describes a wireless network that consists of at least one access point connected to the wired network infrastructure, plus a set of wireless end stations. This configuration is called a Basic Service Set (BSS). An Extended Service Set (ESS) is a set of two or more BSSs forming a single subnetwork. Since most corporate WLANs require access to the wired LAN for services (file servers, printers, Internet links), they will operate in infrastructure mode.

- Ad hoc mode (also called peer-to-peer mode or an Independent Basic Service Set, or IBSS) is simply a set of 802.11 wireless stations that communicate directly with one another without using an access point or any connection to a wired network. This mode is useful for quickly and easily setting up a wireless network anywhere that a wireless infrastructure does not exist or is not required for services. For example, ad hoc mode is appropriate for hotel rooms, convention centers, or airports, or where access to the wired network is barred (such as for consultants at a client site).

The 802.11 Physical Layer

The three physical layers originally defined in 802.11 included two spread-spectrum radio techniques and a diffuse infrared specification. The radio-based standards operate within the 2.4-gigahertz (GHz) ISM band. These frequency bands are recognized by international regulatory agencies, such as the Federal Communications Commission (FCC) (USA), ETSI (Europe), and the MKK (Japan) for nonlicensed radio operations. As such, 802.11-based products do not require user licensing or special training.

Spread-spectrum techniques, in addition to satisfying regulatory requirements, increase reliability and boost throughput. Most important, they allow many unrelated products to share the spectrum without explicit cooperation and with minimal interference.

The original 802.11 wireless standard defines data rates of 1 Mbps and 2 Mbps by means of radio waves using frequency hopping spread spectrum (FHSS) or direct sequence spread spectrum (DSSS). It is important to note that FHSS and DSSS are fundamentally different signaling mechanisms and will not interoperate with one another.

FHSS

Using the frequency hopping technique, the 2.4-GHz band is divided into 75 1-MHz subchannels. After the sender and receiver agree on a hopping pattern and set of usable subchannels, data is sent over each of the subchannels in turn. In effect, both sender and receiver are retuning their radios to a different channel at pre-arranged times (though at an extremely fast rate). Each conversation within the 802.11 network occurs over a different hopping pattern, and the patterns are designed to minimize the chance of two senders using the same subchannel simultaneously.

FHSS techniques allow for a relatively simple radio design, but are limited to speeds of no higher than 2 Mbps. This limitation is driven primarily by FCC regulations that restrict subchannel bandwidth to 1 MHz. These regulations force FHSS systems to spread their usage across the entire 2.4-GHz band, meaning they must hop often, which leads to a high amount of hopping overhead.

DSSS　　　　In contrast, the direct sequence signaling technique divides the 2.4-GHz band into 14 22-MHz channels. Adjacent channels overlap one another partially, with 3 of the 14 being completely nonoverlapping. Data is sent across one of these 22-MHz channels without hopping to other channels. To compensate for noise on a given channel, a technique called "chipping" is used. Each bit of user data is converted into a series of redundant bit patterns called "chips." The inherent redundancy of each chip (each data bit is represented by a multibit signal), combined with spreading the signal across the 22-MHz channel, provides for a form of error checking and correction. Even if part of the signal is damaged, it can still be recovered in many cases. This minimizes the need for retransmissions.

The 802.11 Data Link Layer

The Data Link Layer within 802.11 consists of two sublayers: Logical Link Control (LLC) and MAC. The 802.11 standard uses the same 802.2 LLC and 48-bit addressing as other 802 LANs, allowing for very simple bridging from wireless to IEEE wired networks. However, the MAC method is unique to WLANs.

The 802.11 MAC is very similar in concept to 802.3, in that it is designed to support multiple users on a shared medium by having the sender sense the medium before accessing it. For 802.3 Ethernet LANs, the Carrier Sense Multiple Access with Collision Detection (CSMA/CD) protocol regulates how Ethernet stations establish access to the wire and how they detect and handle collisions that occur when two or more devices try to simultaneously communicate over the LAN.

An 802.11 WLAN cannot use the CSMA/CD method, because of two problems that are unique to radio transmission:

• The near/far problem

• The hidden node problem

The Near/Far Problem

The "near/far" problem means that a nearby radio signal is significantly stronger than a signal from farther away. To use CSMA/CD, a station must be able to transmit and listen on the same medium at the same time. But the near/far problem means that a station's own transmission is much more powerful than any other node on the same channel. Thus, when a node is transmitting, it cannot "hear" a collision.

To solve the near/far problem, 802.11 uses a slightly modified protocol known as Carrier Sense Multiple Access with Collision Avoidance (CSMA/CA) or the Distributed Coordination Function (DCF). CSMA/CA attempts to avoid collisions by using explicit packet acknowledgment (ACK).

CSMA/CA works as follows. When a station is ready to transmit, it first senses the channel. If no activity is detected, the station waits an additional, randomly selected period of time and then transmits if the medium is still free. If the packet is received intact, the receiving station issues an ACK frame that, once successfully received by the sender, completes the process. If the ACK frame is not detected by the sending station, either because the original data packet was not received intact or the ACK was not received intact, a collision is assumed to have occurred. The sending station waits another random amount of time, then transmits the data packet again.

CSMA/CA thus provides a way of sharing access over the air. This explicit ACK mechanism also handles interference and other radio-related problems very effectively. However, it does add some overhead to 802.11 that 802.3 does not have, so that an 802.11 LAN will always have slower performance than an equivalent Ethernet LAN.

**The Hidden
Node Problem**

Another MAC-layer problem specific to wireless networks is the "hidden node" issue. This describes a situation in which two stations on opposite sides of an access point can both "hear" activity from the access point, but not from each other, usually due to distance or an obstruction.

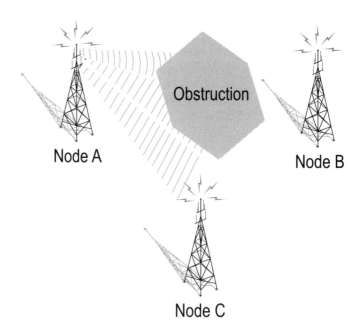

Hidden Node Problem

To solve the hidden node problem, 802.11 specifies an optional Request to Send/Clear to Send (RTS/CTS) protocol at the MAC layer. When this feature is in use, a sending station transmits an RTS and waits for the access point to reply with a CTS. Since all stations in the network can hear the access point, the CTS causes them to delay any intended transmissions, allowing the sending station to transmit and receive a packet acknowledgment without any chance of collision.

Since RTS/CTS adds additional overhead to the network by temporarily reserving the medium, it is typically used only on the largest-sized packets, for which retransmission would be expensive from a bandwidth standpoint.

Error Correction and Reduction

Finally, the 802.11 MAC layer provides for two other robustness features:

- CRC checksum—Each packet has a CRC checksum calculated and attached to ensure that the data was not corrupted in transit. This is different from Ethernet, where higher level protocols such as TCP handle error checking.

- Packet fragmentation—Large packets can be broken into smaller units when sent over the air, which is useful in very congested environments or when interference is a factor, since larger packets have a better chance of being corrupted. This technique reduces the need for retransmission in many cases and thus improves overall wireless network performance. The MAC layer is responsible for reassembling fragments received, rendering the process transparent to higher level protocols.

Enhancements to the 802.11 PHY Layer

Two new Physical Layer technologies have been developed to improve the basic 802.11 data rate of 1–2 Mbps:

- 802.11b delivers up to 11 Mbps using direct sequence spread spectrum in the 2.4-GHz band

- 802.11a delivers up to 54 Mbps using frequency division multiplexing in the 5-GHz band

Since these are both Physical Layer technologies, they both support the existing 802.11 MAC layer. Both can operate up to several hundred feet. However, actual working distances and data rates depend on a combination of factors, such as transmitter power, physical obstructions in the line of sight, and the presence of interfering signals. In general, the data rate of a WLAN falls as the distance between transmitter and receiver increases.

802.11b

In September 1999, IEEE ratified the 802.11b "High Rate" amendment, which added two higher speeds (5.5 and 11 Mbps) to 802.11. The basic architecture, features, and services of 802.11b are defined by the original 802.11 standard. The 802.11b specification affects only the Physical Layer, adding higher data rates and more robust connectivity. At this writing, the 802.11b standard is the dominant technology used in WLANs.

The key contribution of the 802.11b addition to the WLAN standard was to standardize the Physical Layer support of two new speeds, 5.5 Mbps and 11 Mbps. To accomplish this, DSSS had to be selected as the sole Physical Layer technique for the standard since, as noted earlier, frequency hopping cannot support the higher speeds without violating current FCC regulations. The implication is that 802.11b systems will interoperate with 1-Mbps and 2-Mbps 802.11 DSSS systems, but will not work with 1-Mbps and 2-Mbps 802.11 FHSS systems.

802.11a

Despite its number, the 802.11a standard was developed after 802.11b. The numbering seems out of sequence because the 802.11a committee was formed first, but the 802.11b group released its standard sooner.

The 802.11a standard is assigned to 300 MHz of the 5-GHz range. This 300 MHz of bandwidth is divided into three nonlicensed "domains" that each have different maximum power levels:

- 5.15 GHz to 5.35 GHz (200-MHz total bandwidth)—In this domain, the maximum transmission power is 50 milliwatts (mW).

- 5.25 GHZ to 5.35 GHz (100-MHz total bandwidth)—In this domain, transmission power may be as high as 250 mW.

- 5.725 GHz to 5.825 GHz (100-MHz total bandwidth)—This domain is intended for outdoor applications, with a maximum transmission output of 1 watt.

802.11b networks may legally output up to 1 watt as well, but typically transmit at only 30 mW to reduce heat and conserve battery power. 802.11a networks require these higher power levels because a higher frequency needs more power to travel the same distance as a lower frequency.

Higher Data Rates

802.11a can theoretically deliver a raw data rate of 54 Mbps. There are two key reasons why it is so much faster than 802.11b:

- Higher frequency—High frequencies can carry more data because each cycle is a signal change that provides an opportunity to represent a bit. All 802.11 wireless networks use a type of modulation called "phase shift keying," which represents a bit by inverting a radio wave from positive to negative, or negative to positive. Sophisticated variations on this technology can squeeze 8 to 10 bits into each cycle, yielding 1.125 Mbps. However, for a receiving node to detect such complex and subtle signals, the sending node must transmit them at higher power levels than typically used by 802.11b networks.

- Parallel channels—802.11a transmits data over a "carrier" band that is 20 MHz wide. That carrier band is divided into 52 subchannels, each about 300 KHz wide. Data is transmitted in parallel over 48 of these subchannels, with 4 subchannels used for error correction. If the network is using the most intense form of phase shift keying, each subchannel can deliver 1.125 Mbps. Thus, the total data rate = 1.125 Mbps x 48 = 54 Mbps.

More Bandwidth, Less Interference

802.11a has been assigned about four times more bandwidth than 802.11b. Furthermore, the ISM band used by 802.11b is heavily used by many other technologies, particularly cellular phones and Bluetooth devices. These sources of potential interference can reduce the effective data rate of an 802.11b WLAN. There is less competition for the spectrum assigned to 802.11a, at least for now.

No Common Ground

Because both of these standards operate at the Physical Layer, they can support existing 802.11 MAC protocols. However, because 802.11a and 802.11b each use a different part of the spectrum and a different method of spread spectrum transmission, they are incompatible with each other.

Activities

1. Describe the near/far problem, and explain how the 802.11 MAC method overcomes it.

   _____

   _____

   _____

   _____

2. A small office uses an 802.11b wireless bridge to link laptops to the wired network. Can it move up to the faster 802.11a standard by simply replacing its wireless access point?

3. Give two reasons why 802.11a is faster than 802.11b.

   _____

   _____

   _____

   _____

4. What is the hidden node problem, and how does the 802.11 MAC solve it?

   _____

   _____

   _____

   _____

Extended Activity

If your class has access to wireless network equipment, install a wireless access point and at least one wireless end station. Measure the time required to transfer a large file while the end station is near the wireless bridge. Now move the end station farther away from the access point, and time the same file transfer again. Continue moving the end station farther away until it cannot connect to the network.

If you can equip a laptop computer with a wireless NIC, test the effect of different physical obstructions. For example, is your operating distance longer, or data rate higher, when the computer has a clear line of sight back to the wireless bridge, or when they are separated by walls or floors?

Lesson 4—Media Selection and Installation

Selecting and implementing cable is an important consideration in the overall design, implementation, and maintenance of a LAN. Recent trends in cabling affect installation decisions. These trends include:

- High use of Category 5 UTP

- Increased use of optical fiber cabling

- Reduced cost of network cabling

This lesson reviews some of the common points to consider when choosing and installing cable. It is important to understand the environment that the network will operate in so proper planning can be performed before installation of the physical plant.

Objectives

At the end of this lesson you will be able to:

- Explain the purpose and function of a site survey

- Describe where each type of cabling is best suited

- List the points to consider when choosing media

- Explain the relationship between bandwidth and distance

- Name the major standards that apply to LAN cabling and installation

 **Key Point**

The physical medium chosen is extremely important to the operation of a network.

TIA/EIA Cable Standards

The Telecommunications Industry Association (TIA) and Electronic Industries Association (EIA) have developed standards that have proven valuable to users faced with making cabling decisions for their networks. Because TIA and EIA are composed largely of manufacturers and distributors that produce and sell systems, components, and cabling, their representation on the standards committees ensures the standards provide for the requirements of existing and future systems.

ANSI

The American National Standards Institute (ANSI) has adopted the standards listed below. Some of the initial standards include:

- Commercial Building Telecommunications Wiring Standard (TIA/EIA-568)

- Commercial Building Standard for Telecommunications Pathways and Spaces (TIA/EIA-569 and subsequent enhancements)

- Residential and Light Commercial Telecommunications Wiring Standard (TIA/EIA-570 and subsequent enhancements)

- Administration Standard for the Telecommunications Infrastructure of Commercial Buildings (TIA/EIA-606 and subsequent enhancements)

Some of the more common standards are described in the following sections.

TIA/EIA-568 Intrabuilding Wiring Standard

This standard defines a generic telecommunications wiring system for commercial buildings that will support a multiproduct, multivendor environment. It also provides direction for the design of telecommunications products for commercial enterprises. The purpose of this standard is to enable planning and installation of building wiring with little knowledge of the telecommunications products that subsequently will be installed. Installation of wiring systems during building construction or renovation is significantly less expensive and less disruptive than after the building is occupied.

83

This standard establishes performance and technical criteria for various wiring system configurations for interfacing and connecting their respective elements. To attain a multiproduct wiring system, a review of performance requirements for most telecommunications services was conducted. The diversity of services currently available, coupled with the continual addition of new services, means there may be cases where limitations to desired performance occur. The user should consult standards associated with the desired services to understand any such limitations.

TIA/EIA-569 Commercial Building Standard for Telecommunications Pathways and Spaces

The purpose of this standard is to standardize specific design and construction practices within and between (primarily commercial) buildings in support of telecommunications media and equipment. Standards are provided for rooms or areas and pathways into and through which telecommunications equipment and media are installed. Part of the expected usefulness of this standard is that it can be referenced in documents such as bid requests, specifications, and contracts leading up to construction of facilities. TIA/EIA-569 should also prove useful to contractors responsible for delivering a well-designed facility to a client.

TWSS Standard

This standard includes detailed specifications on all aspects of the Telecommunications Wiring System Structure (TWSS) as follows:

- Horizontal wiring—from the work area telecommunications outlet to the telecommunications closet

- Backbone wiring—interconnection of telecommunications wiring closets

- Work area wiring—from the telecommunications outlet to the station equipment

- Telecommunications closet—area set aside to house TWSS equipment, such as patch panels and hubs

- Equipment room—similar to telecommunications closet, but usually centralized and housing more complex equipment, such as routers and bridges

- Entrance facilities—telecommunications service entrance, including safety devices

The TIA/EIA 568 standard contains detailed specifications on the electrical and physical characteristics of each of these cable types. Connector specifications are included for all media.

For more information on this subject, visit the following Web site: **http://www.anixter.com**.

NEC

The National Electrical Code (NEC) is a set of safety standards and rules for the design and installation of electrical circuits, including network and telephone cabling. The NEC is developed by a committee of ANSI, and published by the National Fire Protection Association. New versions of the NEC are published every three years and are dated by their year of publication.

The NEC is concerned with the safe physical installation of electrical circuits, not their function. Its rules and standards are intended to prevent electrical fires and accidental electrocutions. For example, the NEC specifies different cable installation methods, depending on whether the cable must be run through walls, under carpets, underground, or over outside poles. Thus, a single run of network cable may require several different combinations of conduit or supporting hardware as it travels through different physical environments.

In addition, the NEC specifies that certain types of devices and network circuits must be electrically grounded. Again, this requirement is intended to prevent electrical injuries by providing a safe path for excess electrical current caused by internal sources (such as malfunctioning equipment) or external sources (such as lightning).

The NEC has been adopted as law by many states and cities, and is usually enforced by the local building department. Each local area may require compliance with a different version of the NEC. However, the NEC does not have the force of law until it is formally adopted by a local government. Any new network installation in such an area must pass an electrical inspection similar to that required for a building's power distribution wiring.

Copies of the NEC are available from ANSI, the IEEE Standards Office, or your public library.

FCC

The spectrum of radio frequencies is a finite natural resource. Improvements in technology continue to expand the usable number of radio bands, by making it possible to use higher and lower frequencies. However, each newly available frequency is still unique.

In the United States, the Federal Communications Commission (FCC) licenses the use of radio frequencies, to ensure that the limited available bandwidth is properly allocated among potential users. For example, FCC regulates microwave LANs and requires a license to operate them. FCC also regulates interstate communications. It sets the rules that determine which telecommunications companies may offer what services, and in what areas.

Cable Properties

The properties of each type of cable must be considered when deciding which physical media should be used for a given implementation:

- Physical properties—The medium's physical construction includes characteristics such as the number of conductors, conductors' composition, and type of insulation used to protect the conductor.

- Transmission method—The transmission method describes the way information is transferred between source and destination computers in a LAN.

- Transmission span—This describes the maximum feasible distance between two nodes. These limitations cannot be considered alone, because transmission span is related to bandwidth.

- Bandwidth—The amount of data that can be transmitted in a fixed amount of time. For digital devices, which are by far the most common in LANs, bandwidth is expressed in bits per second (bps) and sometimes bytes per second (Bps).

- Topology—Topology focuses on whether the media is generally used for point-to-point or broadcast transmission. Due to specific physical characteristics and implementation constraints, some transmission media lend themselves to certain topologies.

- Security—Depending on the application requirements, different levels of security are built into a network, such as access to the facilities, network, and data. At the Physical Layer, the concern is with unauthorized access to the network media by tapping. Copper media can be tapped fairly easily, while fiber is difficult to tap without detection.

- Noise immunity—In networking, noise immunity is the interference (static) that destroys the integrity of signals on a physical cable. Noise can come from a variety of sources, including radio waves, nearby electrical wires, lightning, and bad connections.

- Installation considerations—Each media type should be evaluated in terms of its suitability for intrabuilding wiring, focusing on such characteristics as ease of installation, tapping and splicing, and connectors.

- Cost—Cost is probably the most difficult element to evaluate. Keep in mind that the cable itself is a small part of the total cost. Labor costs associated with installation, as well as ongoing management and maintenance costs, can be significant. Also, the range of installation costs varies so widely for different implementations and sites that it is almost impossible to establish any benchmarks. The best approach is to obtain the latest price quotes from the cable supplier(s) per job.

Site Surveys

The first activity that must be performed in planning cable installations is a site survey. The network designer should physically walk through the site with the construction supervisor and user personnel, and identify the locations of all equipment, host computers, workstations, PCs, telephones, and any other devices that may require access to the cable plant. Special attention should be given to the locations and layout of floor troughs and inaccessible areas. All cable routes and tap locations should be clearly identified on the floor plans or blueprints. The following form can be used to guide a consultant or designer through a site survey:

Site Survey Form	Notes
How many sites need to be connected?	
How far apart are the sites?	
Where are the nodes located within a site?	
Can the floor troughs or conduit handle additional cable?	
Do users move frequently?	
Are there sources of electromagnetic interference?	

After performing the site survey and designing the cable layout, whether coaxial cable, twisted pair cable, or optical fiber, you are ready to begin the process of estimating the material and labor costs of the installation.

87

Cable Applications

The most common types of cables used in computer networks are best suited for certain applications. This section reviews where these types of cables are normally found and applications that commonly use each type.

Coaxial Cable Applications

Coaxial cabling is typically found in older networks. Although coaxial cable is seldom implemented in new LAN installations, there is a significant amount of installed coaxial cable in computer networks. It is becoming less popular for connecting devices in the work area primarily because of the increased performance attributes of high-quality twisted pair cable and the availability of fiber optic options.

Optical Fiber Applications

Optical fiber has been used primarily for LAN backbones, wide area computer topology, and voice communications. However, progress in the development of taps, splitters, and couplers has resulted in increasing use for intrabuilding and LAN desktop implementations. Optical fiber alternatives are offered as part of most proprietary cabling systems, but the specifications of these optical fibers should be evaluated against industry standards.

Twisted Pair Cable Applications

UTP has become the medium of choice in LAN installations. Whether connected through a hub or switch, UTP cabling is generally used. Private branch exchanges (PBXs) and conventional telephone systems also use twisted pair cable.

WLAN Applications

The relatively low data rate of 802.11b WLANs usually makes them less attractive than cabled networks. However, wireless transmission is often the best choice when it is difficult (expensive) or impossible to install fixed cabling. For example, wireless connections between closely spaced buildings can eliminate the high cost of installing cable under streets. WLANs are also good solutions for older buildings that have no inside network wiring, such as most public schools. The increased cost of wireless equipment is more than offset by eliminating the need to install new cable.

Comparing Media

The Physical Layer options considered in this lesson are summarized in the Media Comparison Table.

Media Comparison

Characteristics	Twisted Pair	10Base2 Thinnet	10Base5 Thicknet	Fiber Optic	Wireless
Distance	Short to Moderate	Moderate	Moderate	Moderate to Long	Short to Moderate
Resistance to noise	Low (UTP) Moderate (STP)	Moderate	Moderate	Very high	Low to moderate
Ease of installation	Generally easy to install and maintain	Easy to install	Requires trained or professional installer	Requires specialized installer	Generally easy to install and maintain
Installation costs	Low	Low to Moderate	Low to Moderate	High	Moderate to High
Topology	Star, Ring, or Bus (daisy chain)	Bus	Bus	Star, Ring, or Mesh	Mesh or Star

General Installation Guidelines

As LAN data rates steadily increase, good craftsmanship in the network physical plant has never been more important. A 100-Mbps Fast Ethernet network can be slowed to a crawl by flaws as simple as poorly made patch cables. LAN performance depends on a quality cable installation that takes into account the following considerations:

- Install enough cable for future needs, especially in a new building. It is almost always more expensive to incrementally add cable within completed walls, ceilings, or floors.

- Follow local building codes and be aware of state and federal guidelines. NEC specifies many aspects of fire safety for cable installation. Study and understand all aspects of the appropriate structured wiring plan, if you use one.

- Hire an experienced and reputable cabling contractor familiar with all applicable building codes, your desired network specification, and your chosen structured wiring plan. Because fiber optic cable requires well-trained, experienced installation technicians, many organizations hire specialists to install fiber networks.

- Test the cabling plant to ensure it meets your performance criteria.

- Do not cut corners on material quality. Use the correct grade of cable and connectors for your LAN type. Do not use untwisted (telephone) cables for twisted pair installations. Use plenum-grade cable for cable runs through environmental air-spaces (plenum area), such as the area above suspended ceilings, and the return-air cavities used for heating, ventilating, and air conditioning (HVAC) systems. Plenum-grade cable has a special jacket that is fire-resistant and does not produce toxic smoke.

- Label all cables and maintain a wiring plan that identifies all cables, devices, and connectors.

- When making connections in twisted pair cable, do not unwrap any more of the cable jacket than necessary. Also, do not untwist the end of each pair more than absolutely necessary (about one half inch). Either of these can create excessive crosstalk and degrade performance.

- To reduce EMI and RFI, run data cables perpendicular to power lines whenever possible. Do not run copper cable parallel to electrical power lines at a distance of less than 6 to 8 inches. Keep data cables several feet away from high-capacity power lines.

- Use cable hangers to support the weight of cables in ceiling areas.

- Bundle cables neatly, but do not squeeze them tightly. Excessive pressure on a cable can change the transmission characteristics of both copper and fiber.

- Do not bend a cable tighter than its specified minimum bending radius. A kink in a twisted pair cable will deform the twist patterns, which increases interference. A too-tight bend in a fiber optic cable can break the fiber, or create strain that changes the cable's refractive index and causes signal attenuation.

- Keep copper patch cables as short as possible so that they do not pick up noise.

- Make sure every system is properly grounded, has voltage surge and lightning protection, and has an uninterruptible power supply (UPS).

Activities

1. Discuss how each standard might be necessary in the installation and maintenance of LANs.

   _____

   _____

   _____

   _____

   _____

   _____

2. List at least three common cable standards.

   _____

   _____

   _____

3. Rank the top three cable characteristics from most important to least important for the following situations:

   a. New installation of a small network for a startup business

      _____

      _____

   b. Installation of a network in a machine shop

      _____

      _____

   c. Installation of a network at a military facility

      _____

      _____

Extended Activities

1. Review Web sites of vendors that supply LAN cabling such as those listed below. Discuss the types of cabling offered by these companies.

   a. **http://www.lucent.com**

   _____

   _____

   _____

   b. **http://www.anixter.com** (Review and discuss the structured cabling guide.)

   _____

   _____

   _____

   c. **http://www.amp.com**

   _____

   _____

   _____

   d. **http://www.belden.com**

   _____

   _____

   _____

   e. **http://www.3com.com** (Review and discuss the school wiring guide.)

   _____

   _____

   _____

2. Review Web sites of standards organizations such as:

   a. American National Standards Institute at
      http://www.ansi.org

   b. Electronic Industries Association at **http://www.eia.org/**

   c. Telecommunications Industry Association at
      http://www.tiaonline.org/

   d. International Telecommunications Union at
      http://www.itu.ch/

3. Research the bandwidths and maximum distance per bandwidth for each of the following types of media:

   a. UTP Category 5 cabling

   b. 10Base2 coaxial cabling (RG-58 A/U)

   c. Multimode fiber optic cabling

   d. Single-mode fiber optic cabling

   e. 802.11b WLANs

4. Bring to class NICs (Ethernet and Token Ring) and a variety of different types of cabling, such as Thicknet, Thinnet, UTP, and fiber (both single-mode and multimode). Pass these around so that everyone will have an opportunity to see what various cables actually look like.

Lesson 5—UTP Patch Cables and Connectors

In most offices, UTP cabling is installed within walls, under floors (in channels called wiring troughs), and above suspended ceilings. This cabling becomes part of the invisible infrastructure of a building, and a network administrator rarely needs to deal with it.

Thus, most of the physical configuration of a UTP network is done with individual patch cables. These cables are used to connect computers to a building's permanent network wiring, or to devices such as hubs or switches. This lesson introduces two different types of UTP cables, and explains when to use each one.

Objectives

At the end of this lesson you will be able to:

- Diagram the 568A and 568B patterns for UTP connectors

- Name the wire pairs in a UTP cable, in the order specified by TIA/EIA

- Explain the difference between a patch cable and a crossover cable

- Identify the wire pairs used in an Ethernet LAN

 **Key Point**

Patch cables connect computers to hubs or switches. Crossover cables connect computers directly to each other.

UTP Wire Pairs

A UTP cable contains four pairs of wires. Each pair is twisted to cancel out the effect of electromagnetic interference from other wires and devices. A pair of wires works together to transmit the same signal, so you can think of the pair as a single conductor.

All of the eight wires are physically identical. The only difference between them is the number of twists in each pair and the color of their insulation. Each pair consists of a solid-colored wire, and a white wire striped with the same color. The TIA/EIA wiring standards assign each pair a number, as follows:

- Pair 1: Blue and White-Blue

- Pair 2: Orange and White-Orange

- Pair 3: Green and White-Green
- Pair 4: Brown and White-Brown

To remember this order, wiring installers use the nonsense words BLOGB or BLOGBR, which mean: **BL**ue, **O**range, **G**reen, **BR**own

RJ-45 Connectors

UTP cables are terminated on a snap-in connector called an RJ-45, shown on the RJ-45 Connector Diagram. The "RJ" means "Registered Jack," which simply means that it has been registered with the FCC.

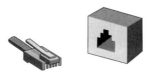

RJ-45 Connector

An RJ-45 connector is very similar to the RJ-11 connectors used on telephones. The RJ-45 is bigger, because it has eight connector pins, one for each of the eight wires in a UTP network cable. As you will see shortly, each of these eight wires is assigned a particular pin position.

Two Types of UTP Cables

A UTP-based LAN can use two types of movable cables:

- Crossover cables connect two NICs directly to each other.
- Patch cables (patch cords) connect a device to a permanently installed cable, or to a hub or switch.

Crossover Cables   A crossover cable directly connects two computers. In effect, the cable uses a length of UTP to form the world's simplest bus network. These are not generally used in most LANs, but are useful for small home office networks or for temporary connections between two computers.

If one computer is to send a signal directly to the other, then the output of the sender's NIC must be connected to the input of the receiver's NIC. And that's exactly what a crossover cable does; one wire pair "crosses over" from the output of NIC A to the input of NIC B. Likewise, a second wire pair crosses over from the input of NIC A to the output of NIC B. This arrangement is shown on the Crossover Cable Diagram. For clarity, this diagram has been simplified to only show two wires.

Crossover Cable

As you can see on this diagram, each wire must be terminated on a different pin on each connector. Otherwise, a wire would link the two inputs, or the two outputs, which would make communication impossible. Thus, each connector of a crossover cable must use a different "pinout" configuration.

Patch Cables

Patch cables are simpler, because they connect a computer to a hub or switch (or to another cable that is connected to a hub or switch). The crossover function is built into these networking devices, so the cable does not need to do that job. You can see this difference on the Patch Cables Diagram. Thus, each connector of a patch cable uses the same pinout pattern.

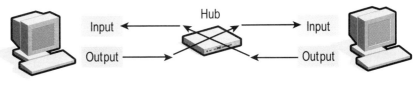

Patch Cables

Connector Pinout Patterns

TIA/EIA specifies two RJ-45 pinout configurations, called 568A and 568B. These patterns are shown on the RJ-45 Pinout Patterns Diagram.

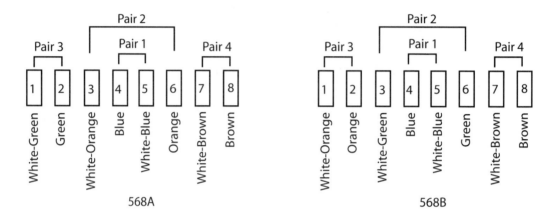

RJ-45 Pinout Patterns

An Ethernet network uses only two wire pairs: green and orange. However, the TIA/EIA standard also specifies the positions of the blue and brown pairs because they may be used by another system, such as a telephone.

If you look carefully at the two pinout diagrams, you will see that the positions of the green and orange pairs are opposite in each specification. This explains the way these configurations are used to build cables:

- On a crossover cable, one connector uses the 568A pattern, and the other connector uses the 568B pattern.

- On a patch cable, both connectors use the same pattern; both ends are 568A, or both ends are 568B. A cable may use either A or B, as long as both ends use the same pattern.

As you can see, crossover cables and patch cables are incompatible. You cannot use a patch cable to directly connect two NICs. You cannot use a crossover cable to connect a computer to a hub or switch.

Activities

1. What wire colors are used for Ethernet signaling?

   _____

2. How many individual wires and pairs make up a Category 5 UTP cable?

   _____

3. What wire pair is considered to be #3?

   _____

4. Why do the connectors of a crossover cable use two different wiring patterns?

   _____

   _____

5. In the grids below, write the color of the wire that connects to each pin:

   TIA/EIA 568A Standard

Pin 1	Pin 2	Pin 3	Pin 4	Pin 5	Pin 6	Pin 7	Pin8

   TIA/EIA 568B Standard

Pin 1	Pin 2	Pin 3	Pin 4	Pin 5	Pin 6	Pin 7	Pin8

Extended Activity

If a cabling kit is available, construct a small patch cable and a small crossover cable, using Category 5 cabling and RJ-45 connectors. Follow the TIA/EIA-568 specification on wire colors and pins. If a working LAN is available, test both cables by transferring a file.

Summary

This unit discussed the properties of the three main physical transmission media used for networks today: copper cabling, optical fiber cabling, and WLANs. By now, it should be apparent that there is no one best type of physical transmission medium.

Most LANs use UTP copper wiring, because of its attractive combination of low cost, simple installation, and high reliability. However, fiber optic cable and wireless transmission offer their own unique benefits that can often solve connection problems in challenging physical locations, or give users greater mobility. Thus, the choice of a physical medium must always balance operational requirements, such as speed, security, flexibility, and simplicity, against cost.

Unit 2 Quiz

1. What is a patch cable NOT used for?

    a. To link a computer to a hub port

    b. To link a computer directly to another computer

    c. To link two hubs by their uplink ports

    d. To link a hub to a patch panel

2. What makes a crossover cable different from a patch cord?

    a. A crossover cable uses the TIA/EIA 568A pinout pattern on both jacks, but a patch cord uses the TIA/EIA 568B pinout pattern on both jacks.

    b. A crossover cable uses the 568A pattern on one jack, and the 568B pattern on the other. A patch cord uses the same pinout pattern on both jacks.

    c. A crossover cable uses two connectors at each end, one for input signals and one for output. A patch cord uses one connector at each end.

    d. A crossover cable terminates all four pairs on each RJ-45 connector, but a patch cord terminates only two pairs on each connector.

3. In a UTP cable, why is each pair of wires twisted?

    a. To cancel out interference

    b. To clearly identify which two wires form a pair

    c. To simplify installation

    d. All of the above

4. Plenum cable is required in airspaces because:

    a. It's lighter

    b. The jacket is tougher to withstand sharp edges of ducts

    c. Its performance does not change when chilled or heated

    d. It does not produce toxic fumes when burned

5. What signaling method does the 802.11a WLAN standard use?

    a. Direct sequence spread spectrum

    b. Frequency division multiplexing

    c. Frequency hopping spread spectrum

    d. Orthogonal time division multiplexing

6. What is the key reason that smart LAN administrators demand well-made cable connections?

    a. The neat appearance helps justify expensive systems to upper management.

    b. Good cable connections are more durable.

    c. Bad cable connections degrade a network's performance.

    d. Good cable connections boost a network's data rate higher than the normal maximum for a LAN protocol.

7. A network administrator wants to upgrade from 10-Mbps Ethernet to Fast Ethernet. Half the computers use 10-Mbps NICs, and half use 10/100-Mbps NICs. The network is wired with Category 5 UTP. What is necessary to make this upgrade?

    a. Change the cabling to Category 5E

    b. Replace the 10-Mbps hub with a 100-Mbps hub

    c. Replace the 10-Mbps NICs with 100-Mbps NICs

    d. Replace the hub and NICs with 100-Mbps or 10/100-Mbps devices

8. An executive uses a laptop that is equipped with an 802.11b wireless NIC. The wireless access point is installed near her office. This user's network performance is good when she works at her desk, but is degraded when she attends meetings in the conference room across the building. What might be the cause?

    a. The conference room is too far from the access point.

    b. There are too many obstructions between the access point and conference room.

    c. There is a source of radio interference between the access point and conference room.

    d. Any of the above.

9. An ISA bus is faster than a PCI bus. True or False

10. Fiber cabling is not as secure as STP. True or False

11. Data transfer rates (internal to the PC) are inversely proportional to clock speed. True or False

12. An ISA NIC uses bus mastering. True or False

13. Category 3 cabling cannot support 100-Mbps Ethernet. True or False

14. WLAN equipment based on the 802.11a standard is fully backward compatible with 802.11b equipment.
True or False

15. Why has Category 5 UTP cabling gained such widespread acceptance in LANs?

_____

_____

16. If you were installing cabling in a building that had a significant amount of electrical noise, which cabling option would be best?

_____

_____

17. If you needed to connect a computer to a network but the distance between the hub and computer was longer than the specification would allow, what could you do?

_____

_____

18. What type of connector is used to connect Category 5 UTP to wall outlets?

_____

19. Name the color of each individual wire in a Category 5 twisted pair cable.

_____

_____

20. The TIA/EIA 568 standard specifies two wiring patterns for an RJ-45 connector on a twisted pair cable. What is the difference between them?

_____

_____

Unit 3
Ethernet LANs

When the first "personal" computers (PCs) were networked at Xerox Palo Alto Research Center (PARC) in the 1970s, the available networking technology was inadequate in many respects. To provide better data and resource sharing, Ethernet was developed by Xerox Corporation, in conjunction with Intel and Digital Equipment Corporation.

As workstations proliferated in the early 1980s, so did Ethernet, which spread to the networked PC environment. Ethernet has emerged as the local area network (LAN) technology of choice in a majority of networks. It is estimated that over two-thirds of all current LANs are Ethernet, the majority of which use twisted pair cabling. Standard Ethernet equipment is now very inexpensive. Network interface cards (NICs,) hubs, and cabling have become commodities.

The speed of Ethernet continues to increase. The original version of Ethernet delivers 10 megabits per second (Mbps), and is still widely used. Later versions provide 100-Mbps and 1,000-Mbps (1 gigabit per second [Gbps]) throughput, using the same carrier sense multiple access with collision detection (CSMA/CD) method to access the physical media.

Lessons

1. Review of Ethernet
2. Ethernet Frame Format
3. Fast Ethernet
4. Gigabit Ethernet
5. Switched Ethernet Configurations
6. VLANs

Terms

Address Resolution Protocol (ARP)—ARP is the protocol used by IP (as in TCP/IP) for address resolution. Address resolution refers to the ability of a station to resolve another station's MAC (hardware) address given its IP address.

attempt counter—An attempt counter is a value that records the number of times an Ethernet NIC has attempted to transmit the same frame. The NIC discards a frame after 16 consecutive collisions occur for the same transmission attempt.

attempt limit—An attempt limit is the maximum number of times (16) that an Ethernet NIC will attempt to retransmit a frame after a collision.

backbone—The backbone of a network is the portion that carries the most significant traffic. It is also the part of the network that connects many LANs or subnetworks together to form a network. Bridges are often used to form network backbones. In this configuration, bridges often limit local traffic from the backbone to reduce congestion and isolate problems.

backoff time—When a collision occurs on an Ethernet segment, all transmitting nodes "back off" and do not transmit for a random length of time before attempting to transmit again. This is referred to as the backoff time. This random time interval reduces the likelihood that both stations will attempt to retransmit at the same time.

bridge—A bridge is a hardware device that connects LANs. It can be used to connect LANs of the same type, such as two Token Ring segments, or LANs with different types of media such as Ethernet and Token Ring. A bridge operates at the Data Link Layer of the OSI reference model.

broadcast—The term broadcast is used in several different ways in communications and networking. With respect to LANs, the term refers to information (frames) sent to all devices on the physical segment. For example, a bus topology, in which a common cable is used to connect devices, is considered a broadcast technology.

Another common use of the term broadcast relates to frames. Broadcast frames contain a special destination address that instructs all devices on the network to receive the frame.

carrier sense multiple access with collision detection (CSMA/ CD)—CSMA/CD is set of rules determining how network devices respond when two devices attempt to use a data channel simultaneously (called a collision). Standard Ethernet networks use CSMA/CD. This standard enables devices to detect a collision. After detecting a collision, a device waits a random delay time and then attempts to retransmit the message. If the device detects a collision again, it waits twice as long to try to retransmit the message. This is known as exponential backoff.

checksum—The number of bits in a transmitted unit of data is referred to as the checksum. A checksum is appended to the data unit as a simple error-detection method. The receiving node counts the data bits and compares the result to the checksum, to see whether all bits have arrived. If the numbers match, the transmission was probably complete.

collapsed backbone—A collapsed backbone is a network topology that uses a multiport device, such as a switch or router, to carry traffic between network segments or subnets. This is in contrast to a traditional backbone which, in the case of Ethernet, originally consisted of a single common bus cable to which nodes and subnets were connected.

collision—A collision occurs in an Ethernet network when two frames are put onto the physical medium at the same time and overlap fully or partially. When a collision occurs, the data on the physical segment is no longer valid.

Copper Distributed Data Interface (CDDI)—CDDI is a version of FDDI that runs on copper wiring such as twisted pair.

Ethernet—Ethernet technology, originally developed in the 1970s by Xerox Corporation in conjunction with Intel and DEC, is now the primary medium for LANs. The original Ethernet has 10-Mbps throughput and uses the CSMA/CD method to access the physical medium. Fast Ethernet (100-Mbps Ethernet) and Gigabit Ethernet (1,000-Mbps Ethernet) are later technologies based on the original approach.

Fibre Channel—Fibre Channel is a very high-speed fiber optic data transfer interface based on the ANSI FCS. FCS can carry multiple existing protocols, including IP and SCSI.

frame—A frame is a unit of information transmitted across a data link. Ethernet frames, for example, are frames generated by an Ethernet NIC.

frame check sequence (FCS)—FCS is a 4-byte CRC value used to check for damaged frames. CRC is a mathematical process used to check the accuracy of data being transmitted across a network. When a block of data is about to be transmitted, the sending station performs a calculation on the data block and appends the resulting CRC value to the end of the data block (frame). The receiving station performs the same calculation on the data. If the CRC values match, the data was transmitted without errors.

interframe gap—An interframe gap is the minimum time interval between Ethernet frames. After a node detects the end of a frame, it must wait this amount of time before attempting to transmit.

Logical Link Control (LLC)—LLC is a Data Link Layer protocol used to control the flow of information across a physical link. LLC is often used in Ethernet networks that use the IEEE frame type, which does not include a type field.

Medium Access Control (MAC)—MAC refers to the Data Link Layer framing and access protocol used to transmit frames between NICs.

multimode fiber—Multimode fiber is a fiber optic cable thick enough to transmit several different optical signals simultaneously. Each signal is separated by the others by being reflected at different angles within the fiber. See single-mode fiber.

nanometer (nm)—A nanometer is one billionth of a meter, or 10^{-9}. See wavelength.

noise—Any condition, such as electrical interference, that destroys signal integrity is referred to as noise. Noise can be caused by many electromagnetic sources, such as radio transmissions, electrical cables, electric motors, lighting dimmers, or bad cable connections.

Peripheral Component Interconnect (PCI) Bus—PCI bus is a newer 64-bit local bus technology for PCs. A bus connects the central processor of a PC with the video controller, disk controller, hard drives, and memory.

random backoff—See backoff time.

signal reflection—Signal reflection refers to the situation where part, or all, of an electrical signal bounces back from an improperly made cable connection. This effect creates signal noise that can be misinterpreted as frame collisions.

single-mode fiber—Single-mode fiber is a thin fiber optic cable that can transmit only one optical signal. Because there is no chance the signal can interfere with any other signal, single-mode fiber can transmit signals over much longer distances than multimode fiber. See multimode fiber.

Simple Network Management Protocol (SNMP)—SNMP is a network management protocol based on the manager/agent model, in which a complex central manager directs simple device-based agents to supply information or change configurations. The original version of SNMP was derived from SGMP, and was published in 1988.

start of frame delimiter (SOFD) —An SOFD is a byte that ends with two consecutive bits, which serve to synchronize the frame-reception portions of all stations on a LAN.

wavelength—The distance between one crest of a wave and the next is referred to as the wavelength. Light wavelengths are measured in nanometers (nm), or billionths of a meter. Each nanometer is 10^{-9} meter.

Lesson 1—Review of Ethernet

Ethernet is a Data Link specification for Medium Access Control (MAC). In other words, the Ethernet specification defines how multiple network nodes can use the same shared medium to transmit signals to each other. This lesson reviews the basic operation and configuration of Ethernet networks.

Objectives

At the end of this lesson you will be able to:

- Describe how Ethernet frames are transmitted across a physical link

- Describe how Ethernet frames are received by a NIC

- Understand the concept of "collisions"

- Draw 10Base2, 10Base5, and 10BaseT Ethernet network configurations

 **Key Point**

Ethernet, in a star topology, is the most common LAN protocol used today.

MAC: CSMA/CD

The inventors of Ethernet chose a technology called CSMA/CD as their technique for controlling access to the shared media (the logical bus). An Ethernet node must have the ability to listen to the bus and transmit simultaneously:

- CS—Carrier sense (each device can detect the signal)

- MA—Multiple access (devices attach to the same physical medium)

- CD—Collision detection (each device knows when signals overlap)

Sending a Frame   The Ethernet Send Algorithm Diagram illustrates the logic used to transmit a frame.

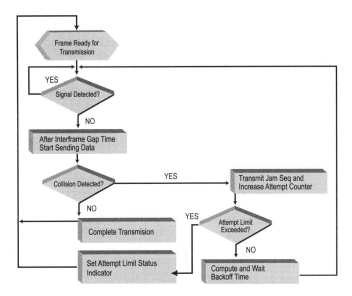

Ethernet Send Algorithm

Each node follows these steps to transmit a message:

1. Listen to the bus (the shared medium) to see whether any other node is transmitting (sensing the carrier signal does this). If a transmission is detected, continue listening until the channel is idle.

2. When no signal is detected, start transmitting the message.

3. While transmitting, listen to the bus. Compare the received message to what was transmitted. As long as they are the same, continue transmitting.

4. If the message received is not what was transmitted, assume a collision. Stop transmitting.

Note: The transceiver simply watches for a voltage threshold violation. Consequently, signal reflections and noise often appear as collisions.

5. Transmit a jam sequence to warn all other stations that a collision has been detected, and to ensure that all network devices stop transmitting. The jamming sequence takes the form of 96 bits of alternating 1s and 0s.

6. Wait a random time and then start over with Step 1.

An important aspect of the CSMA/CD algorithm is the random-length interval (a few milliseconds [ms]) that a node waits before trying to retransmit when a collision occurs. Because the probability of two nodes waiting the same length of time is very small, a second collision is unlikely to occur. This ensures that nodes do not just keep "butting heads," with none able to access the bus.

On a heavily used network, collisions will occur, and time will be wasted each time this happens. This is one reason that performance of an Ethernet network decreases as the load increases.

Note that the node stops transmitting as soon as a collision is detected—that is the significance of the "CD" in CSMA/CD. Other similar protocols do not require a node to stop transmitting until the end of its message, thus a significant amount of time is lost when any of the colliding nodes is transmitting a long message.

A potential problem with CSMA/CD is the time it takes for an electrical signal to travel from one point on the bus to another. This is called propagation delay. In a large network, if two Nodes, A and B, are at opposite ends of the bus, and both start transmitting at the exact same moment, Node A might transmit the last bit of its message before the first bit has had time to reach Node B, and vice versa. Neither node would detect a collision, yet the signal would be garbled. One way of solving this problem is to require that frames be at least long enough to prevent this situation, which is how Ethernet works.

Receiving a Frame

The Ethernet Receive Algorithm Diagram presents the sequence for receiving a frame.

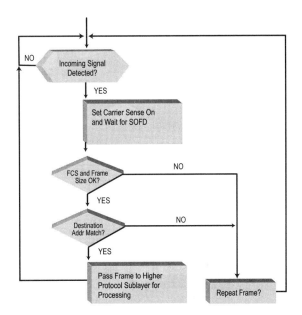

Ethernet Receive Algorithm

Older Bus Configurations

Ethernet began as a bus solution using coaxial cabling at 10 Mbps. The most straightforward Ethernet configuration consists of several Ethernet workstations connected onto a single cable segment.

In general, coaxial cable has been overtaken by twisted pair and fiber optic cable installations. Although it has good resistance to electromagnetic interference (EMI) and radio frequency interference (RFI), it is bulky and relatively difficult to install through the wire ducts and other spaces within a building. However, many of these older configurations may still be found in LANs.

**Thinnet
Configuration**

A typical Ethernet bus network is shown on the 10Base2 Ethernet Configuration Diagram, consisting of four network nodes and a single server.

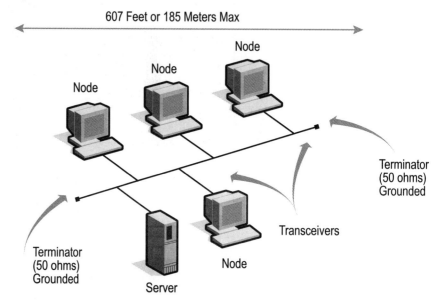

10Base2 Ethernet Configuration

A 10Base2 configuration typically uses Thinnet (Cheapernet) coaxial cabling. The NIC normally contains the transceiver, and the Thinnet cable is attached to the NIC by means of a T-connector as shown on the 10Base2 Adapter and Cable Diagram.

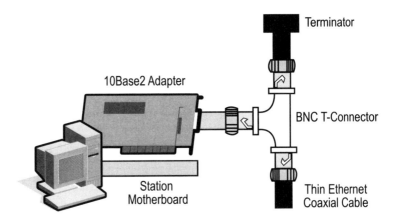

10Base2 Adapter and Cable

A transceiver is a device that takes the digital signal from the workstation and converts it to a format suitable for the physical cabling. Thinnet connectivity is simple, and provides a low-cost alternative for Ethernet networks. The following specifications apply to 10Base2 Ethernet networks:

- RG-58A/U coaxial cabling is normally used.

- The Ethernet 5/4/3 rule applies:

  – Up to *five* segments can be connected in a series between transmitter and receiver.

  – Up to *four* repeaters may be used to connect segments.

  – A maximum of *three* segments can contain Ethernet nodes.

- A maximum of 30 nodes can be attached to each segment.

- Minimum distance between drops (node connections) is 1.64 feet.

- Each segment must be terminated at both ends, with one end using a grounded terminator.

**Thicknet
Configuration**

- Another example of an Ethernet network is shown on the 10Base5 Ethernet Configuration Diagram. 10Base5 cabling is also referred to as Thicknet or Yellow Wire (because the outer cover is often yellow). An external transceiver is normally used in Thicknet applications. The NIC attaches to the transceiver with a special cable called an attachment unit interface (AUI). The transceiver then attaches to the physical network cabling.

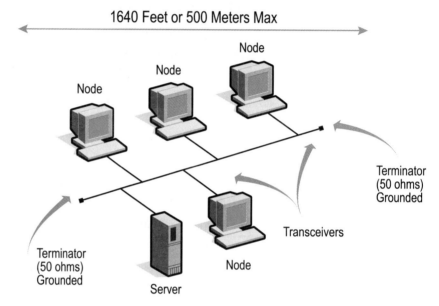

10Base5 Ethernet Configuration

The following specifications apply when reviewing a coaxial Ethernet network configuration:

- Transceivers should be placed at 8.5-foot intervals or multiples thereof.

- Each segment must be no greater than 500 meters (1,640 feet).

- The Ethernet 5/4/3 rule applies:

  - Up to *five* segments can be connected in a series between transmitter and receiver.

  - Up to *four* repeaters may be used to connect segments.

  - A maximum of *three* segments can contain Ethernet nodes.

- There can be a maximum of 100 nodes per segment.

- RG-8 coaxial cable is normally used.

- Each segment must be terminated at both ends, with one end using a grounded terminator.

Star Configurations

Newer Ethernet networks use star configurations as the primary method of connectivity. New installations of Ethernet have NICs with unshielded twisted pair (UTP) cable ports that connect to a central device such as a hub. Like a coaxial bus, a hub is a logically passive device. In other words, it simply repeats the bits it receives, without evaluating or changing them.

An example of an Ethernet network is shown on the 10BaseT Ethernet Configuration Diagram. This configuration consists of an Ethernet hub (also referred to as a wiring concentrator) connecting eight workstations. The cables use RJ-45 connectors that connect directly to the NIC on the device end and the hub on the other end. Category 5 UTP cabling is commonly used to wire these types of networks.

10BaseT star-wired networks provide the following advantages over 10Base2 and 10Base5:

- Nodes are easily added to, and removed from, a network.

- Network problems are easier to troubleshoot because suspect nodes can easily be disconnected from the hub.

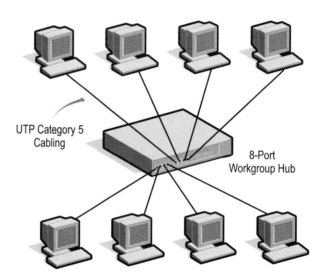

10BaseT Ethernet Configuration

Hub-to-Hub Connectivity

After an Ethernet hub fills to capacity, additional computers cannot be connected to the hub. As a network grows and more nodes are needed, hubs can be added to provide more physical ports for additional device connectivity. The Ethernet Hub-to-Hub Diagram illustrates this principle.

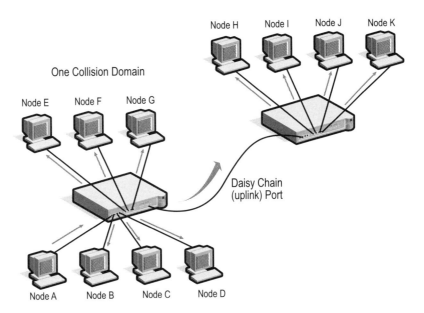

Ethernet Hub-to-Hub

Many hubs include an uplink port that can be used for either device connectivity or hub connectivity. A switch, mounted under this port, is put in one position for attaching a computer, and the opposite position when attaching to another hub.

When two or more hubs are linked, this configuration also represents a single collision domain. If a frame is generated from Node A to the hub, the hub will repeat the frame out each port. This includes the uplink port that attaches to the second hub. The second hub will then take this frame and repeat it out each of its ports as well.

As networks grow, more and more hubs may be added to increase the number of nodes attached to a network. At some point in time, servers must be added to provide options not available in a strictly peer-to-peer network. This is shown on the Ethernet Client/Server Configuration Diagram, where the server is connected to one of the hub ports in the same manner (by means of NIC and UTP cabling) that desktop computers attach to a hub.

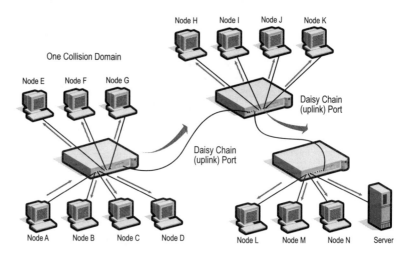

Ethernet Client/Server Configuration

Note that on this diagram, all nodes are connected in the same collision domain. Regardless of where the information is going to or coming from, each node receives the frame transmission. As traffic increases in the network, there will be a point where performance is unacceptable. In other words, the 10-Mbps bandwidth shared by all devices in this broadcast network will no longer be adequate. In this scenario, Ethernet switches are often used to increase performance by isolating traffic within separate collision domains. We review the principles of traffic isolation later in this unit.

Activities

1. List the three properties of CSMA/CD and write a brief description of each.

   _____

   _____

   _____

   _____

   _____

   _____

2. Why is a random backoff important in an Ethernet network?

   _____

   _____

   _____

   _____

3. Describe the Ethernet transmission sequence.

   _____

   _____

   _____

   _____

4. If a frame is sent between two clients attached to the same hub, how many total devices in this network will detect this frame?

   _____

5. What is the purpose of the central hub?

   _____

6. Why is a minimum Ethernet frame size necessary?

7. Using 12-port hubs, draw an Ethernet network consisting of 50 computers.

8. How many collision domains are there in this network?

9. Draw a Thinnet network diagram that consists of three segments. The first and last segments contain 10 nodes. The middle segment does not contain any nodes and is only used for network extension.

Extended Activities

1. Using a Web search engine, find information that relates to the 5/4/3 rule and coaxial Ethernet. List your findings.

    _____

    _____

    _____

2. Using the Web or a catalog, research Ethernet hubs and list three vendor products. Summarize your findings and include the cost per port and functionality of each product.

    _____

    _____

    _____

    _____

    _____

3. Go to the Web site **http://www.ots.utexas.edu/ethernet/** and research the history and current state of Ethernet.

4. Review the brief tutorial found at this Web site.

Lesson 2—Ethernet Frame Format

As you will recall from your study of the Open Systems Interconnection (OSI) model, the Data Link Layer is responsible for transmitting frames across a single link in a network. There are different frame types, each associated with specific technologies. This lesson describes the format and function of an Ethernet frame.

Objectives

At the end of this lesson you will be able to:

- Describe the difference between frame formats of Ethernet version 2 and Institute for Electrical and Electronics Engineering (IEEE) 802.3

- Diagram the structure of an 802.3 Ethernet frame

- Explain the purpose of each frame field

Key Point

Ethernet frames provide transfer of information between Ethernet NICs.

Ethernet Version 2 Frame

Ethernet Version 2 is the protocol originally developed by Xerox, DEC, and Intel. The format of the version 2 Ethernet frame is presented on the Ethernet Frame Format Diagram.

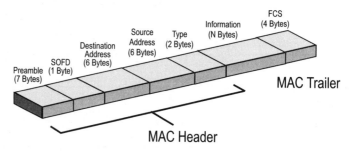

Ethernet Frame Format

An Ethernet frame header and trailer consists of 18 bytes (144 bits) divided into groups, called fields. Each field contains a particular type of information that the receiving Data Link process needs to process the frame. An Ethernet frame contains the following fields:

- Preamble (7 bytes)—7 bytes of "10101010" to synchronize with all other stations on the LAN.

- Start of Frame Delimiter (SOFD)(1 byte)—10101011.

- Destination address (DA) (6 bytes)—The 48-bit address of the receiver's NIC.

- Source address (6 bytes)—The 48-bit address of the sender's NIC.

- Type (2 bytes)—The type of packet contained in the frame.

- Data—The packet data passed down from the Network Layer. The length of this data may range from 46 to 1,500 bytes. If the encapsulated data is less than 46 bytes, "padding" bits are added to bring the data length up to 46 bytes.

- Frame check sequence (FCS) (4 bytes)—A checksum used for error detection. This field forms the MAC trailer.

Minimum and Maximum Frame Sizes

Padding the frame ensures that the frame is long enough so the DA field gets to the farthest node before the end of the frame is transmitted. Thus, measuring from the start of the DA field to the end of the FCS field, the total minimum frame size is 64 bytes, and the maximum frame size is 1,518 bytes.

Padding may have big implications for network traffic, depending on the type of data being transmitted. Some very heavily used applications, such as the UNIX Visual Editor (vi), are character oriented, so that a single character is transmitted each time a key is pressed. So, in a worst-case scenario, each one-byte character is not only carried within a separate frame, but the data field is padded with 45 additional bytes. Applications such as File Transfer Protocol (FTP) usually transmit blocks of data, so padding is not a problem.

Broadcast and Multicast Addresses

An Ethernet frame can be addressed to a group of nodes by setting one of the control bits in the DA. This allows "multicasting" frames to a group of nodes, or "broadcasting" frames to all nodes. Any Ethernet node in the world can be addressed in this way, although the Network Layer must handle the routing of frames addressed to destinations not on the LAN.

IEEE Ethernet Frame

IEEE developed its own CSMA/CD protocol called 802.3, which used a slightly different frame format than Ethernet version 2. Since then, the 802.3 MAC approach has been widely adopted, and the term "IEEE 802.3" is now equivalent to "Ethernet."

The IEEE Ethernet frame format is defined by the 802.2 Logical Link Control (LLC) standard and is presented on the IEEE Ethernet Frame Format Diagram. This frame format differs from the standard Ethernet frame format in that a Length field replaces the Type field. The Type field function is performed, in this case, by an LLC header field that follows the Length field.

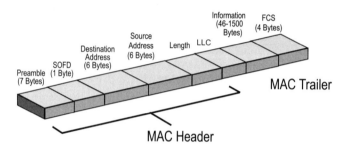

IEEE Ethernet Frame Format

Activities

1. What does the SA field of an Ethernet frame contain?

    _____

    _____

    _____

2. What different types of information can the DA field of an Ethernet frame contain?

    _____

    _____

    _____

3. What is the difference between Ethernet version 2 and IEEE Ethernet formats?

    _____

    _____

    _____

4. What is the purpose of the FCS field?

    _____

    _____

    _____

5. What is the preamble used for?

    _____

    _____

    _____

Lesson 3—Fast Ethernet

Fast Ethernet is identical to 10-Mbps Ethernet, only it is 10 times faster. Fast Ethernet, also referred to as 100BaseT, uses UTP to send Ethernet frames at 100 Mbps. The frame format of Fast Ethernet is the same as 802.3 Ethernet.

Objectives

At the end of this lesson you will be able to:

- Describe why faster technologies are necessary

- Explain the relationship between standard Ethernet and Fast Ethernet

 **Key Point**

Fast Ethernet is identical to 10-Mbps Ethernet, only faster.

The Need for Speed

In some cases, 10-Mbps Ethernet networks may not provide enough bandwidth for an organization. As new network applications are implemented using high-resolution graphics, video conferencing, and other rich media data types, pressure is growing at the desktop, server, hub, and switch for increased bandwidth. The Network Applications Table summarizes typical high-bandwidth applications and their impact on the network.

Network Applications

Application	Data Type/Size	Network Traffic Impact	Network Requirements
Scientific modeling	Gigabytes	Increase in large files Large bandwidths required	Higher bandwidth desktop, server, backbone
Publications Imaging	100s of megabytes	Increase in large files Large bandwidths required	Higher bandwidth desktop, server, backbone

Network Applications (Continued)

Application	Data Type/Size	Network Traffic Impact	Network Requirements
Internet Intranet Extranet	Audio, video 1–100 megabytes	Increase in large files Large bandwidths required Low latency necessary	Higher bandwidth desktop, server, backbone low latency
Data warehousing Network backup	Terabytes	Increase in large files Large bandwidths required Fixed time of transmission	Higher bandwidth desktop, server, backbone low latency
Desktop Conferencing Whiteboarding	1.5–4 Mbps	Class of service required High volume of data	Higher bandwidth desktop, server, backbone low latency

Many of these applications transmit large files over the network. Scientific applications demand ultra-high bandwidth networks to communicate three-dimensional visualizations of complex objects, ranging from molecules to aircraft. Magazines, brochures, and other complex, full-color publications prepared on desktop computers are transmitted directly to digital-input printing facilities. Many medical facilities are transmitting complex images over LAN and wide area network (WAN) links, enabling sharing of expensive equipment and specialized medical expertise. Engineers are using electronic and mechanical design automation tools to work interactively in distributed development teams, sharing files in the hundreds of gigabytes.

Many companies are now using Internet technologies to build private intranets. This enables users in an organization to go beyond electronic mail (e-mail) and access critical data through familiar Web browsers, opening the door to a new generation of multimedia client/server applications. Although intranet traffic is currently composed primarily of text, graphics, and images, it is expected to expand rapidly to include streaming audio, video, and voice.

Data warehousing has become popular as a way of making enterprise data available to decision makers for reporting and analysis without sacrificing the performance, security, or integrity of production systems. These warehouses may contain gigabytes or terabytes of data distributed over hundreds of platforms and accessed by thousands of users. The warehouses must be updated regularly to provide users near-real-time data for critical business reports and analyses.

Network backup of servers and storage systems is common in many industries that require enterprise information to be archived. Such backups usually occur during off-hours and require large amounts of bandwidth during a fixed amount of time (four to eight hours). Backups involve gigabytes or terabytes of data distributed over hundreds of servers and storage systems throughout an enterprise.

As these applications proliferate and require ever greater shares of bandwidth at the desktop, and as the total number of network users continues to grow, organizations will need to migrate critical portions of their networks to higher bandwidth technologies.

Fast Ethernet Over Twisted Pair

An example of a 100BaseT network is shown on the 100BaseT Network Diagram. This configuration is identical to a star configuration used in 10-Mbps Ethernet LANs. The devices connected to each of the 100BaseT hubs share the 100-Mbps bandwidth.

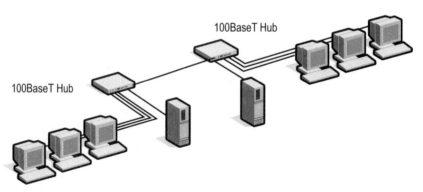

100BaseT Hub

100BaseT Hub

100BaseT Network

100BaseTX is the specification that describes how to run 100-Mbps Fast Ethernet over Category 5 UTP. The MAC frames of 100BaseT and 10-Mbps Ethernet are identical. Therefore, equipment used to bridge 10-Mbps Ethernet with Fast Ethernet need only be concerned with the data rate, and not the content or format of the frame. Other key points regarding Fast Ethernet are:

- All equipment—such as hubs, switches, and NICs—must support the 100 Mbps data rate.

- The maximum UTP cable length is 100 meters.

- Category 5 cabling must be used, so an upgrade to Fast Ethernet sometimes requires a cable replacement.

- The maximum number of repeater hops is two.

Fast Ethernet Over Fiber

The 100BaseFx standard allows Fast Ethernet to run over fiber optic cable. The use of fiber optic cabling extends the maximum segment length to 325 meters.

Mixed Ethernet Networks

It is possible to combine Ethernet LANs that use both 10-Mbps and 100-Mbps technology. This is illustrated on the 10/100BaseT Network Configuration Diagram.

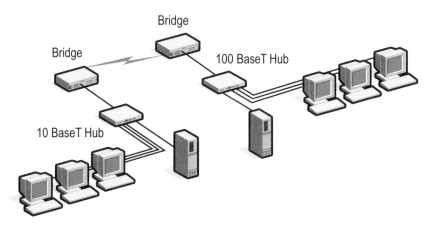

10/100BaseT Network Configuration

In this configuration, the nodes on one hub share 10 Mbps of bandwidth, while the other hub's nodes share 100 Mbps. Since both portions of the network use the same frame format and MAC method, data passes seamlessly between the regular Ethernet switch and the Fast Ethernet switch. Thus, this approach is often used to connect 10 Mbps workgroups to a Fast Ethernet backbone.

Activity

What is the difference between the frame formats of 10 Mbps Ethernet and 100-Mbps Ethernet?

_____

_____

Extended Activities

1. What products are currently available for these newer technologies?

    _____

    _____

    _____

2. A typical quote from a LAN implementation vendor is shown below. This estimate contains the cost of installing a 16-station Fast Ethernet network using Category 5 twisted pair cabling and a 100BaseT hub.

    Draw a diagram of this network and discuss in class.

Quantity	Description	Unit	Price	Extended Price
1	16-port Fast Ethernet hub	each	$480.00	$480.00
16	Ethernet PCI 32-bit 100-Mbps NIC	each	$60.00	$960.00
1,200	4 pair UTP plenum 24 gauge Category 5 cable (75′ per drop)	feet	$0.29	$348.00
1	24-port Category 5 patch panel and wall mount bracket	each	$165.00	$165.00
16	Wall mount faceplates with Category 5 jacks	each	$6.50	$104.00
16	4-foot Category 5 patch cords	each	$3.10	$49.60
16	Installation/drop charge	each	$125.00	$2,000
	Total			$4,106.60

Lesson 4—Gigabit Ethernet

In a relatively short time, network connections have evolved from shared or switched Ethernet (10 Mbps) to shared or switched Fast Ethernet (100 Mbps) to accommodate rising bandwidth demand. Business applications are now advancing to embrace high-resolution graphics, video, and other rich media types that exceed the capacity of even Fast Ethernet performance. Furthermore, Internet and intranet applications create unpredictable any-to-any traffic patterns. Switching at the network edge puts a tremendous load on the network backbone where traffic aggregates.

Gigabit Ethernet (1,000 Mbps) offers a new level of performance scalability that can use much of the installed base of Ethernet equipment, while taking advantage of the historical cost effectiveness of Ethernet switching equipment.

Ethernet is the dominant and most ubiquitous LAN technology today, and the most widely understood. Because Gigabit Ethernet adheres to fundamental Ethernet principles, network staffs can continue to build on their existing training and skills. This extension of basic Ethernet technology reduces the total cost of ownership of an Ethernet network.

Objectives

At the end of this lesson you will be able to:

*   Identify the common features shared by both Fast Ethernet and Gigabit Ethernet, as well as features that differ between the two standards

*   Describe some of the problems Gigabit Ethernet may solve, as well as problems it may create

*   Discuss how much of a network's existing Ethernet technology might be preserved in a migration to Gigabit Ethernet

 **Key Point**

Gigabit Ethernet preserves the existing Ethernet frame format and CSMA/CD media access.

The Gigabit Ethernet Standard

The goal of the IEEE 802.3z Task Force, which developed the Gigabit Ethernet standard, was to deliver 10 times the performance of Fast Ethernet at very affordable prices. As the Ethernet Compatibility Table shows, Gigabit Ethernet uses existing Ethernet technologies, taking advantage of Ethernet's fiercely competitive pricing.

Ethernet Compatibility

Variable	Fast Ethernet	Gigabit Ethernet
Speed	100 Mbps	1,000 Mbps
Frame Format	802.3 Ethernet	802.3 Ethernet
MAC Layer	802.3 Ethernet	802.3 Ethernet
Flow Control	802.3x Ethernet	802.3x Ethernet
Primary Mode	Full duplex	Full duplex
Physical Signaling	FDDI	Fibre Channel

The 1000BaseX (IEEE 802.3z) Gigabit Ethernet standard was ratified in June 1998, after more than two years of intense effort within the IEEE 802.3 Ethernet committee. The key objective of the 802.3z Gigabit Ethernet Task Force was to develop a Gigabit Ethernet standard that accomplished the following:

- Allowed half- and full-duplex operation at speeds of 1,000 Mbps

- Used the 802.3 Ethernet frame formats

- Used the carrier sense multiple access/collision detect (CSMA/CD) access method with support for one repeater per collision domain

- Addressed backward compatibility with 10BaseT and 100BaseT technologies

Because the fundamental features of the 802.3z specification have been stable during the last stages of the standardization process, network vendors have been able to build and deliver quality, mature Gigabit Ethernet products for some time now. In addition, numerous interoperability demonstrations have been sponsored by the Gigabit Ethernet Alliance and other independent organizations, giving customers confidence to use Gigabit Ethernet products in their production networks.

Gigabit Ethernet Cabling and Distance Specifications

As illustrated on the Gigabit Ethernet Layers Diagram, the Physical (PHY) Layer is a crucial part of the Gigabit Ethernet specification. It provides the interface between the MAC layer and the transceivers in Gigabit Ethernet hardware. The Physical Layer performs encoding, decoding, carrier sense, and link monitor functions.

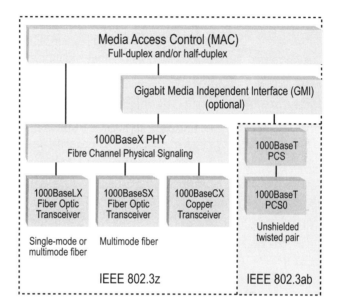

Gigabit Ethernet Layers

The IEEE 802.3z Gigabit Ethernet standard includes three Physical Layer specifications: two for fiber optic media (1000BaseSX and 1000BaseLX), and one for shielded copper media (1000BaseCX). Another working group, the IEEE 802.3ab Task Force, is also defining the Physical Layer to run Gigabit Ethernet over the installed base of Category 5 UTP cabling. This 1000BaseT standards effort is still in progress.

The above diagram shows the various layers of Gigabit Ethernet and the distinction between the 802.3z and 802.3ab specifications. A fourth transceiver type, 1000BaseLH (not shown on the diagram), is a multivendor specification that defines optical transceivers that support distances greater than the 1000BaseLX specification.

Fiber Cabling Specifications

The Gigabit Ethernet standard includes three specifications for fiber cabling:

- 1000BaseSX ("S" for short wavelength) defines optical transceivers or Physical Layer devices for laser fiber cabling. The wavelength of SX lasers is 770 to 860 nanometers (nm), and is commonly referred to as 850 nm. 1000BaseSX is based on the Fibre Channel physical signaling specification. Targeted for multimode fiber only, 1000BaseSX transceivers are less costly than those found in products implementing the long wavelength specification described below.

- 1000BaseLX ("L" for long wavelength) defines optical transceivers or Physical Layer devices for laser fiber cabling. The wavelength of LX lasers is 1,270 to 1,355 nm, and is commonly referred to as 1,350 nm. 1000BaseLX is also based on the Fibre Channel physical signaling specification. 1000BaseLX is specified for use on either multimode or single-mode fiber.

The Gigabit Ethernet Distances for Fiber Optic Media Table shows the distance specifications for 1000BaseSX and 1000BaseLX fiber optic media. Note that the distance Gigabit Ethernet can reach depends on the bandwidth (measured in megahertz multiplied by kilometers [MHz × km])—the greater the bandwidth of the fiber, the further the distance supported. It is also important to note that IEEE specifies minimum rather than maximum ranges. Under average operating conditions, the minimum specified distance can be exceeded by a factor of three or four. However, most network managers are conservative when they design networks, and use the IEEE specifications as the maximum distances.

Gigabit Ethernet Distances for Fiber Optic Media

Transceiver	Fiber Diameter (microns) MM = Multimode SM = Single-Mode	Bandwidth (MHz*km)	Minimum Range (meters)
1000BaseSX	MM 62.5	160	2 to 220
	MM 62.5	200	2 to 275
	MM 50	400	2 to 500
	MM 50	500	2 to 550

Gigabit Ethernet Distances for Fiber Optic Media (Continued)

Transceiver	Fiber Diameter (microns) MM = Multimode SM = Single-Mode	Bandwidth (MHz*km)	Minimum Range (meters)
1000BaseLX	MM 62.5	500	2 to 550
	MM 50	400	2 to 550
	MM 50	500	2 to 550
	SM 9	NA	2 to 5,000

- 1000BaseLH ("LH" for long haul) is a multivendor specification that defines optical transceivers that support distances greater than the 1000BaseLX specification; each vendor has a set of transceivers designed to cover different distances. Although it is not an IEEE standard, many vendors are working to interoperate with IEEE 1000BaseLX equipment, and are using the gigabit interface connector (GBIC) multivendor specification to provide greater flexibility.

The Gigabit Ethernet Distances for 1000BaseLH Fiber Optic Media Table lists specific wavelength distances recently qualified by 3Com; this list will grow as more GBIC distances undergoing qualification testing are approved. The appearance of these long distance devices has sparked the interest of carriers in offering Gigabit Ethernet-based metropolitan area network (MAN) services. There are implementation caveats, however. Network planners must provide sufficient cabling attenuation to ensure that a 40-km transceiver does not overdrive a 10-km transceiver on the receiving end.

Gigabit Ethernet Distances for 1000BaseLH Fiber Optic Media

Transceiver	Single-Mode Fiber Diameter (microns)	Wavelength (nm)	Minimum Range (km)
1000BaseLH (Extended distance)	9	1310	1 to 49
1000BaseLH (Extended distance)	9	1550	50 km to 100

Copper Cabling Specifications	Gigabit Ethernet also includes two copper cabling specifications:

- 1000BaseCX ("C" for copper) defines transceivers or Physical Layer devices for shielded copper cabling. 1000BaseCX is intended for short-haul copper connections (25 meters [m] or less) within wiring closets. This physical interface uses Fibre Channel physical coding, a different driver on shielded copper, and 150 ohm balanced cable. It supports wiring distances up to 25 m. (Note: IBM Type 1 cable is specifically mentioned in the IEEE 802.3z standard as not recommended.)

- 1000BaseT ("T" for twisted pair) is the specification for Gigabit Ethernet over four-pair Category 5 UTP copper cabling for distances up to 100 m, enabling network managers to build networks with diameters of 200 m. Extensive signal processing required on the 1000BaseTX transceiver itself.

Implementing Gigabit Ethernet in a Network

To assess a new technology like Gigabit Ethernet, you must compare it to other technologies and evaluate its impact on existing network topology and equipment. In this section, we consider both the advantages and limitations of Gigabit Ethernet.

Gigabit Ethernet and Link Aggregation	Link or port aggregation, also called trunking, often comes up in discussions of Gigabit Ethernet migration. Link aggregation is the ability to support multiple, point-to-point, parallel active links between switches, or between a switch and server. The advantages of link aggregation are higher bandwidth, redundant links, and load sharing.

If the business requirement is simply to add more bandwidth between devices, and the devices can be upgraded to Gigabit Ethernet, Gigabit Ethernet is the right choice. If the business requirement includes the need for resilient and redundant links with load balancing, then link aggregation (aggregating multiple links into one logical connection) is the right choice.

Link aggregation and Gigabit Ethernet are complementary technologies, because Gigabit Ethernet links can themselves be aggregated with link aggregation technology. The primary application of link aggregation technology in the near future will be to build resilient, redundant links between Layer 2 and Layer 3 Gigabit Ethernet switches. Many vendor-specific link aggregation implementations exist in the industry today.

Optimizing Servers to Handle Gigabit Ethernet

Although Gigabit Ethernet relieves the bottleneck at the server, server environments are not yet fully optimized to handle the entire available gigabit bandwidth. The good news is that server systems and their software and hardware components are rapidly evolving to ensure the server system bandwidth capacity can handle the Gigabit Ethernet data rate. In addition, Gigabit Ethernet NICs currently under design will overcome some of the server system bottlenecks and be optimized for the upcoming evolution in server architecture. Critical server system improvements are discussed in the following sections.

PCI Bus Bandwidth

The Peripheral Component Interconnect (PCI) bus is the predominant bus in x86 platforms, and is also available in some non-x86 systems. Although the original PCI bus in earlier server systems had insufficient bandwidth to carry gigabit-speed input/output (I/O) traffic, newer buses are quickly becoming wider and faster, and are not a bottleneck for the Gigabit Ethernet network connection.

The PCI Bus Bandwidth Matrix shows that PCI buses support gigabit rates today, but the real bandwidth of the PCI bus is slightly lower than the maximum bus bandwidth, due to the PCI bus overheads involved. In full-duplex mode, Gigabit Ethernet provides 2 Gbps bandwidth; therefore, at a minimum, the wider 64-bit bus at 33 MHz is required to support Gigabit Ethernet. However in a 64-bit, 33-MHz PCI server, bus overhead means that the PCI bus is still slower than the full-duplex Gigabit Ethernet line rate.

Bus Width	Bus Speed	Maximum Bus Bandwidth
32 Bit	33 MHz	1 Gbps
64 Bit	33 MHz	2 Gbps
64 Bit	66 MHz	4 Gbps

PCI Bus Bandwidth

To solve the slowdown, a Gigabit Ethernet NIC uses onboard NIC memory to buffer incoming frames while the PCI bus is busy or catching up. In the newest 64-bit 66 MHz PCI servers, the PCI bus is faster than the line rate, so the NIC's onboard memory is used to buffer outgoing frames while the network is busy. NIC memory can thus have an important impact on performance. This memory is typically carved into receive and transmit buffers. The NIC's onboard memory also serves to improve performance by storing and buffering frames on a heavily loaded bus with devices contending for access to the bus.

Flow control capability, available on some Gigabit Ethernet NICs, also helps prevent buffer overflows: flow control signals the sender to pause if the receive buffer is about to overflow. This controlled slowdown in transmission provides better performance overall by eliminating costly timeouts and subsequent retransmissions.

Better techniques for efficiently using the PCI bus are also being engineered. These techniques and innovations allow the PCI NIC to better interact with the bus, and improve performance and PCI bus utilization in next-generation servers.

NOS

The history of networking has always involved moving bottlenecks from one part of a network to another. With the development of Gigabit Ethernet, Ethernet frames travel at speeds of 1 billion bits per second (bps). With the PCI bus developments described above, an I/O bus on the end station can support speeds of 1 billion bps or faster. Therefore, the bottleneck has moved from the network to inside the host itself; the challenge is now to increase the performance of the network operating system (NOS) and host.

The performance of the server connection depends heavily on the NOS and underlying protocols. UNIX operating systems appear better adapted to handle Gigabit Ethernet speeds. The Transmission Control Protocol/Internet Protocol (TCP/IP) protocol, running under Microsoft Windows NT 4.0, still has much room for improvement, because TCP/IP is a complex connection-oriented protocol that requires high central processing unit (CPU) bandwidth to process packets at Gbps rates.

CPU Utilization at Gigabit Speeds

At gigabit speeds, routine networking tasks such as TCP/IP checksum calculations can easily tie up the processor, resulting in 100 percent CPU utilization that leaves no processing power for other applications. Therefore, well-designed Gigabit Ethernet NICs offload such tasks from the host processor, performing them in the NIC hardware. These Gigabit Ethernet NICs also consolidate interrupts, interrupting the CPU less frequently and for multiple tasks each time. This results in lower CPU utilization for better application performance.

To overcome some of the bottlenecks caused by the host, a few vendors have supported a proprietary solution known as "jumbo frames" to provide a better data payload-to-packet overhead ratio. A jumbo frame has a non-Ethernet standard maximum transmission unit (MTU) that exceeds 1,518 bytes. For example, one jumbo frame size is 9 kilobytes (KB). Although jumbo frames provide some performance benefits, their major drawback is their proprietary frame format. Any switch or NIC that supports jumbo frames cannot interoperate directly with other standards-based Ethernet switches and NICs on the network.

Memory Subsystems

Memory subsystem performance also affects overall server performance and network connection throughput. Memory with zero-wait states is typically better suited for servers, because frequent access to large contiguous data stores is usually required. Although the initial latency is typically higher for such memory, the server throughput could reach a high peak sustained level during large contiguous data accesses.

Cache memory holds data that is accessed often or is expected to be accessed next. This data is available for the NIC much faster than data off a disk storage subsystem. Cache memory and system memory help improve performance by reducing the impact of storage access time. While a large amount of cache memory is beneficial to performance, the optimum amount of cache memory for the server varies based on the frequency and type of cache accesses. Look for flexibility in the server's cache size configuration.

The system bus speed between the processor and external (L2) cache is also important. The system bus speed (not to be confused with the PCI I/O bus speed) has been 66 MHz until recently. Server throughput has improved markedly in newer servers with processors that support a 100-MHz system bus.

Storage Subsystems

Storage is typically the slowest component of the server. It usually uses rotating media (disk) technology with mechanical limitations. Fast and Wide Small Computer System Interface (SCSI), Fibre Channel, and disk arrays bring high performance to this area; however, storage still remains the slowest link in the server performance chain. Fortunately, system memory and cache can be used to increase storage performance.

Gigabit Ethernet Migration Scenario

Gigabit Ethernet is best suited for unclogging network bottlenecks that occur in three main areas:

- Switch-to-switch connections

- Connections to high-speed servers

- Backbone connections

Initial Configuration

The following scenario details a network migration to Gigabit Ethernet. As shown on the Starting Point Diagram, the initial building backbone is 10-Mbps Ethernet. Several Ethernet segments or workgroups are collapsed into a 10/100-Mbps switch, which in turn has several 10-Mbps Ethernet server connections.

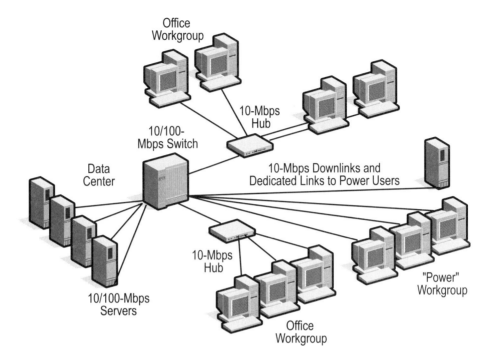

Starting Point

In this scenario:

- Power users are experiencing bottlenecks from their 10-Mbps links.

- Users on the shared segments are experiencing slow response times.

- All new desktops are equipped with 10/100-PCI NICs.

Phase 1 Upgrade The Phase 1 Diagram shows how the first upgrade phase is implemented in three areas:

- Upgrading the network backbone to 100-Mbps Fast Ethernet

- Upgrading the power workgroup to 100-Mbps Fast Ethernet connections between the end stations and switch

- Implementing 10-Mbps switching in other workgroups that need dedicated bandwidth

The result? Power users immediately acquire 100-Mbps connection speeds, and other workgroups that need it enjoy dedicated 10-Mbps bandwidth. The speed of the backbone increases tenfold to accommodate the overall increase in network bandwidth demand. Meanwhile, the investment in existing switches and NICs is preserved.

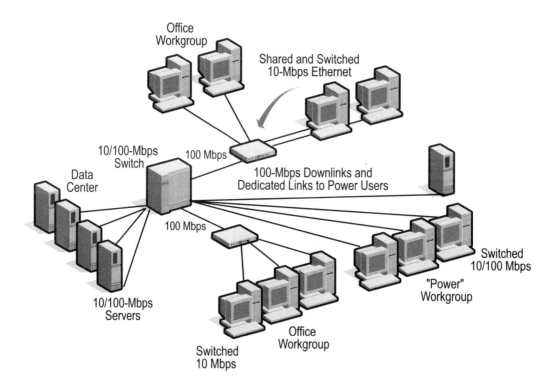

Phase 1

Phase 2 Upgrade
The Phase 2 Diagram shows how the riser downlinks are upgraded to Gigabit Ethernet to increase backbone bandwidth even further. To accomplish this, the switches in the wiring closets that support power users or large workgroups are upgraded with Gigabit Ethernet downlink modules, the basement switch is upgraded to 100/1,000-Mbps capability, and key servers are upgraded with Gigabit Ethernet NICs. A key point to notice is that upgrades of the backbone to Gigabit Ethernet support the extension of switching to the edges. Both office workgroups now support switched 10 or switched 10/100 Ethernet to the desktops.

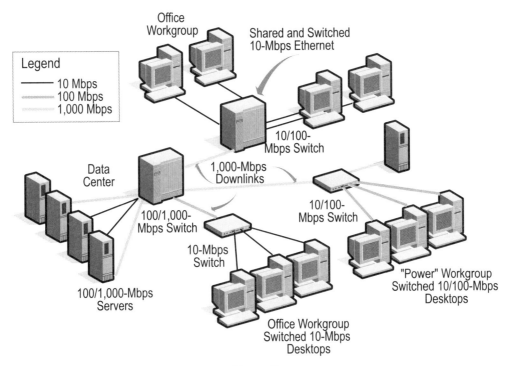

Phase 2

Also in this Phase 2 upgrade, the Fast Ethernet backbone switch that aggregates multiple 10/100 switches is upgraded to a Gigabit Ethernet switch that supports multiple 100/1,000 switches. Gigabit full-duplex repeaters are installed, as needed, to aggregate servers or build Gigabit Ethernet support for workgroups that manipulate very large multimedia and graphics files. In addition, after the backbone is upgraded to a Gigabit Ethernet switch, farms of high-performance servers with Gigabit Ethernet NICs can be connected directly to the backbone, increasing throughput to the servers for users with high-bandwidth application files, or for bandwidth-intensive data warehousing and backup operations.

After the Phase 2 upgrade, the overall network now supports a greater number of segments and more bandwidth per segment.

Activities

1. How does Gigabit Ethernet compare with Fast Ethernet in terms of similar technology?

   _____

   _____

   _____

   _____

2. List the characteristics of Gigabit Ethernet fiber cabling specifications.

   _____

   _____

   _____

   _____

   _____

   _____

3. What are the characteristics of Gigabit Ethernet copper cabling specifications?

   _____

   _____

   _____

   _____

4. Contrast link aggregation with Gigabit Ethernet in terms of solutions to provide additional bandwidth.

   _____

   _____

   _____

   _____

5. Discuss the problems of delivering Gigabit Ethernet to servers and workstations with PCI buses.

_____

_____

_____

_____

6. What would logically be the first area in an enterprise network that would benefit from migration to Gigabit Ethernet?

_____

7. Would most users benefit from Gigabit Ethernet to the desktop or should the existing Ethernet technology be preserved? Explain.

_____

_____

_____

_____

Extended Activity

Research information on the latest 10-Gbps Ethernet standards and compare these to the Fibre Channel standard.

Lesson 5—Switched Ethernet Configurations

As networks grow and traffic increases, standard Ethernet networks no longer provide the performance necessary to meet growing user demands. Ethernet switches provide performance improvements over hub-based solutions.

Objectives

At the end of this lesson you will be able to:

- Describe how switches work

- Explain why network performance often improves when a hub is replaced by a switch

- Explain the difference between a collision domain and a broadcast domain

- Explain why broadcast traffic should be minimized.

 **Key Point**

> *A switch improves network performance by dividing the network into separate collision domains.*

Review of Collision Domains and Traffic Isolation

All nodes attached to an Ethernet hub share the same bandwidth. Thus, each hub (or group of interconnected hubs) forms a single collision domain. In a small network, this means every node in the network receives every frame transmitted. The Ethernet Collision Domain Diagram illustrates this principle.

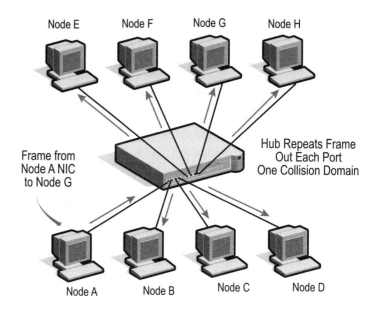

Ethernet Collision Domain

As shown on this diagram, Node A wants to send information to Node G. A frame is sent from Node A to the hub. The hub repeats the frame out every port. Each node attached to the hub receives the frame. However, only the node that has a NIC address (in this case Node G) that matches the frame address will process the frame and pass its contents to the next highest layer.

Switch Operation

An Ethernet switch (also called a switching hub) provides connectivity between any two attached Ethernet devices (or segments) on a frame-by-frame basis. As a result, switches can isolate traffic within individual workgroups.

This approach increases overall performance as long as some of the traffic remains local to the individual workgroups. If all of the traffic is destined for other workgroups, the switch will forward it, and overall network performance is not improved.

There are two common types of Ethernet switches:

- Store-and-forward switches read the entire frame, check each frame for accuracy, then direct the frame to the destination.

- Cut-through switches (also called cross-point or fast-forward switches) do not error-check the frame, but merely direct it to the appropriate destination as soon as they read the destination address. Cut-through switches are much faster than store-and-forward switches.

In Ethernet switching, the MAC-layer address determines the hub or switch port to which the frame will travel. Because no other ports are aware of the frame's existence, the stations do not have to be concerned with whether their frames will collide with data from other stations as they transmit toward the switch. In Ethernet switching, a virtual connection is established between the sending and receiving ports. This dedicated connection remains in place only long enough to transmit the frame between the sending and receiving stations.

If a station has frames for a busy switch port, that station's port momentarily holds them in its buffer. (Ethernet frames are 1,518 bytes; the size of port buffers differs by vendor from a few hundred to thousands of frames.) When the busy port becomes free, the frames are released from the buffer and sent to the newly freed port. This mechanism works well unless the buffer gets filled, in which case frames may be lost. The Standard Hub vs. Switching Hub Diagram compares Ethernet LANs implemented by a standard hub versus a switching hub.

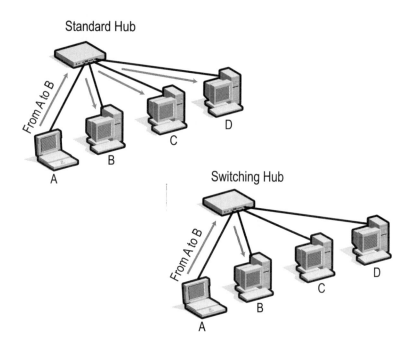

Standard Hub vs. Switching Hub

By using a switch, network performance is increased when traffic is sent between different nodes attached to the switch. For example, if client A sends information to client C at the same time client B sends information to client D, the performance of the network is doubled. In other words, the full bandwidth is potentially available to every device attached to the switch, instead of being shared among multiple stations. If the Ethernet network is based on 10 Mbps, each port has 10-Mbps bandwidth available. Similarly, if the network is based on 100 Mbps, each port has 100-Mbps bandwidth available and so forth.

Switched Ethernet Backbone

The Switched Workgroups Diagram illustrates how performance can be improved by adding a switch instead of a new hub. On this diagram, each hub connects to a switch port. Users are logically arranged into workgroups on a hub-by-hub basis. When information is being sent between users in the same workgroup (attached to the same hub), the transmission of the frame is isolated to that workgroup. The switch does not forward the frame to the other hubs.

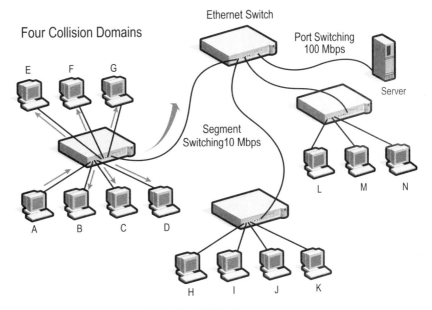

Switched Workgroups

Note on the diagram that the server has been given its own port. This illustrates another important technique, called "port switching" (or device switching). When a hub is attached to a switch port, multiple users are attached to the same switch port because they are all attached to the same hub. We call this "segment switching."

When multiple segments need access to the same device, such as a server or shared printer, that device should be attached to its own port. If the server was left on a hub, the heavy traffic to that computer would degrade performance for the other devices attached to that hub.

Many switches offer ports with different speeds, and 10/100-Mbps Ethernet switches are common. In the example above, the server is given a 100-Mbps port, while the workgroups share 10-Mbps bandwidth. The decision to put a server on one port and workgroups on another is dependent on the traffic flow in the network. Keep in mind that if a majority of the workgroup traffic travels through the switch, performance will be less than when traffic is isolated to each workgroup. Even though the workgroups are in separate collision domains, traffic destined for a computer in another workgroup may affect the performance of the computers in that workgroup. This is demonstrated on the Workgroup-to-Workgroup Traffic Diagram.

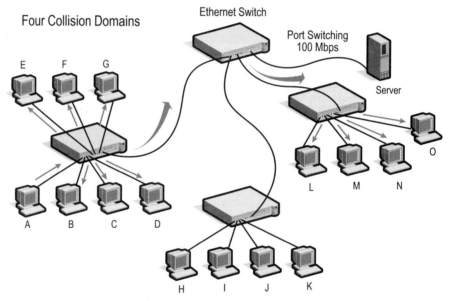

Workgroup-to-Workgroup Traffic

Note that the Ethernet switch may have an overall bandwidth limitation that prevents it from operating at its theoretical limit. This should be considered when purchasing switch hardware. For example, if there are 24 ports that can each operate at 100 Mbps, and the 25th port can operate at 1 Gbps, the switch hardware would need to be capable of handling 3.4-Gbps rates.

Switched Ethernet Backbone and Router Connectivity

Most networks need connectivity to the outside world. Whether we need to connect to another network or many networks, devices such as bridges and routers can be used to make the connection. The Ethernet Switch and Router Diagram illustrates one possible configuration for connecting a switched network to another network.

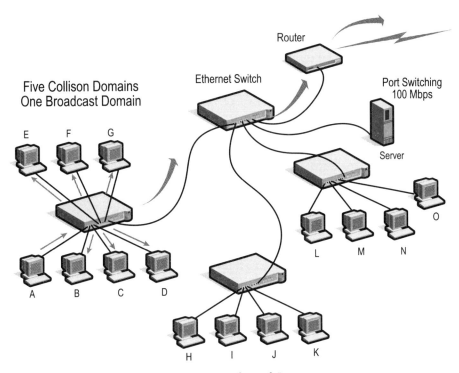

Ethernet Switch and Router

As shown on this diagram, Node A is transmitting data to a destination outside the network. The frame it sends is addressed to the router's NIC. Before construction and transmission of the frame, the sending computer determines the NIC address of its default router (the router assigned to forward traffic beyond the LAN). The frame is sent to the hub and broadcast out each hub port. The switch, based on the Ethernet destination address (NIC address), sends the frame to the router NIC. The router receives the frame, processes the packet inside the frame, and sends the information to the appropriate network.

Broadcast Domains

As we explained earlier, a frame can contain a special "broadcast" address, which tells every node to process the frame. Broadcast frames are sent out for several reasons. For example, if a node has a packet to send and knows the packet address but not the frame (NIC) address, it will broadcast a message asking for the node with the matching packet address for its frame (or MAC) address. In a Transmission Control Protocol (TCP)/Internet Protocol (IP) network, this is performed by the Address Resolution Protocol (ARP).

Broadcast frames differ from frames that have a specific NIC address. When a switch sees a frame with a specific NIC address, it makes a switching decision. When a typical Layer 2 switch sees a frame with a broadcast address, it has no choice but to send the frame out every port.

A broadcast domain is the portion of a network through which a broadcast frame will be forwarded. Though a switch divides a network into separate collision domains, all ports of a switch form a single broadcast domain. This is illustrated on the Ethernet Broadcast Domain Diagram.

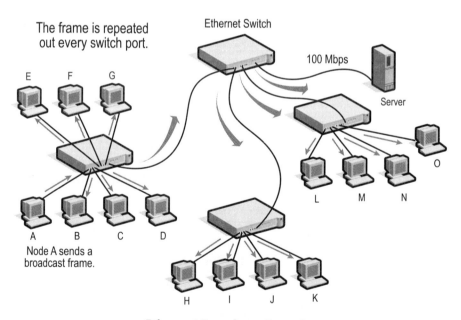

Ethernet Broadcast Domain

Broadcast traffic can significantly decrease the available bandwidth in a LAN, so administrators work to minimize it wherever possible. A common approach is to use a router to divide a network into separate broadcast domains. A router can do this because it does not forward broadcast frames to all ports. However, another emerging technique for broadcast containment is the use of virtual LANs (VLANs). We examine this method in the next lesson.

Activities

1. What is the difference between a switch and a hub?

    _____

    _____

    _____

    _____

2. For each of the referenced diagrams, how many collision domains and broadcast domains are in each configuration:

    a. For the first diagram, use the 10BaseT Ethernet Configuration Diagram from the lesson called "Review of Ethernet."

        _____

    b. For the second diagram, use the Ethernet Hub-to-Hub Diagram from the lesson called "Review of Ethernet."

        _____

    c. For the next diagram, use the Switched Workgroups Diagram from Lesson 5.

        _____

3. Draw a diagram that contains three collision domains and one broadcast domain.

Extended Activities

1. Research the current implementation costs of an Ethernet LAN.

2. Perform the lab exercise entitled "Hubs and Switches in Networks."

3. Perform the hands-on exercises to demonstrate the difference between hubs and switches.

4. Observe the instructor's demonstration of LAN features/functions (in lab or classroom).

Lesson 6—VLANs

VLANs were created to reduce broadcast traffic in a LAN. However, LANs also offer efficient and flexible ways to form logical groups of users in what is normally a single broadcast domain. Using special switches and software, without moving users to new desks, VLANs can create the appearance of a private LAN for every virtual workgroup. In addition, when users choose to move to new physical locations, some VLANs can simplify the administrative tasks necessary to accomplish those moves.

Objectives

At the end of this lesson you will be able to:

- Describe what a VLAN does

- Explain the need for broadcast containment

- Explain how VLANs contain broadcast traffic

Key Point

VLANs provide broadcast containment and form virtual workgroups.

Switched VLANs

A VLAN consists of many nodes connected by a single bridging domain. A bridging domain is a portion of a network that consists of end nodes and Layer 2 devices, such as bridges and switches. An example of a VLAN is shown on the VLAN Diagram. In this diagram, end nodes are grouped logically, although they may be physically separated.

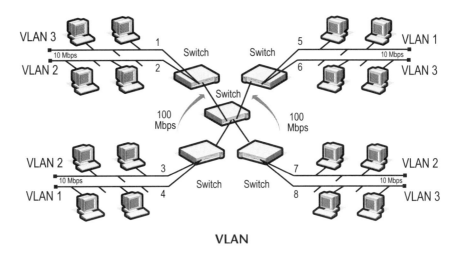

VLAN

Three VLANs are shown on this diagram (VLAN 1, VLAN 2, and VLAN 3). VLAN 1 consists of the nodes on Ports 4 and 5. VLAN 2 consists of the nodes on Ports 2, 3, and 7. VLAN 3 consists of the nodes on Ports 1, 6, and 8.

The switches are tied together through high-speed links: in this case 100-Mbps Fast Ethernet. VLANs are normally established as a set of related user groups, such as departments dispersed over multiple floors of a large building. The primary reason to build VLANs is to isolate broadcast traffic by grouping segments to form logical traffic patterns. In the configuration shown, individual VLANs do not connect to other VLANs. A router is necessary to provide VLAN-to-VLAN communications.

Routed VLANs

The Routed VLAN Configuration Diagram demonstrates the configuration normally used to segment switched networks into VLANs, while maintaining widespread communication using a routed backbone. In this configuration, VLAN 1 can communicate with VLAN 3 by "going to Layer 3" in the router.

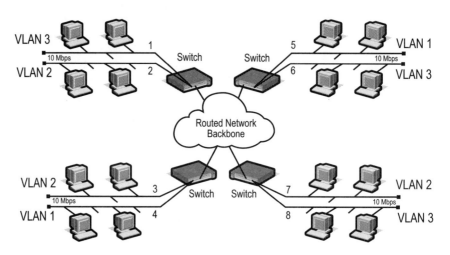

Routed VLAN Configuration

If a node on VLAN 1 wants to communicate with another node on VLAN 1, the router isolates local traffic to this segment of the network. However, if a node on VLAN 1 wants to communicate with a node on another VLAN, such as VLAN 3, it must be routed across the network backbone.

VLANs have recently developed into an integral feature of switched LAN solutions offered by every major LAN equipment vendor. Although end-user enthusiasm for VLAN implementation is just taking off, most organizations have begun to look for vendors that have a well-articulated VLAN strategy, as well as VLAN functionality built into their products. One of the reasons for the current attention placed on VLAN functionality is the rapid deployment of LAN switching that began in 1995.

VLANs for Broadcast Containment

One of the primary purposes for implementing VLANs is broadcast containment, which is the practice of limiting the amount of broadcast traffic on a network.

Routers, by their very nature, contain broadcast traffic because they analyze packet and frame addresses. They only pass traffic destined for remote Layer 3 addresses networks. But a disadvantage to router processing is the time it takes to process both frames and packets. A router must remove each frame header, analyze the packet address, then rebuild the frame to forward it to its destination. In contrast, switches are faster, because they can forward frames by simply inspecting the frame's destination addresses.

Switched VLANs provide broadcast containment by assigning devices, workgroups, or ports a VLAN number. When broadcast frames are received by a switch, they are only sent out ports that are a part of the sender's VLAN.

The shift toward LAN switching as a replacement for local/departmental routers—and now even shared media devices (hubs)—will only accelerate in the future. With the rapid decrease in Ethernet and Token Ring switch prices on a per-port basis, many more ambitious organizations are moving quickly toward networks featuring private port (one user per port) LAN switching architectures. A desktop switching architecture like this is ideally suited to VLAN implementation. To understand why private port LAN switching is so well suited to VLAN implementation, it is useful to review the evolution of segmentation and broadcast containment in networks over the past several years.

In the early 1990s, organizations began to replace two-port bridges with multiport, collapsed backbone routers to segment their networks at Layer 3, and thus also contain broadcast traffic. In a network using only routers for segmentation, segments and broadcast domains correspond on a one-to-one basis. Each segment typically contained between 30 and 100 users.

With the introduction of switching, organizations were able to divide the network into smaller Layer 2-defined segments, enabling increased bandwidth per segment. Routers could now focus on providing broadcast containment. In addition, broadcast domains could now span multiple switched segments, easily supporting 500 or more users per broadcast domain. However, the continued deployment of switches, thereby dividing a network into more and more segments (with fewer and fewer users per segment), does not reduce the need for broadcast containment. Using routers, broadcast domains typically remain in the 100 to 500 user range.

The Future of VLANs

VLANs represent an alternative solution to routers for broadcast containment, because VLANs allow switches to also contain broadcast traffic. With the implementation of switches in conjunction with VLANs, each network segment can contain as few as one user (approaching private port LAN switching), while broadcast domains can be as large as 1,000 users or more. In addition, if implemented properly, VLANs can track workstation movements to new locations without requiring manual reconfiguration of IP addresses, as would be necessary in a network using a router to contain broadcasts.

Why have not more organizations deployed VLANs? For the vast majority of end-user organizations, switches have yet to be implemented on a large enough scale to necessitate VLANs. But this situation is changing.

There are, however, other reasons for the lukewarm reception VLANs have received from network users until recently. Despite the frequently quoted numbers illuminating the hidden costs of networking, such as administration and moves/adds/changes, customers realize that VLANs have their own administrative costs, both straightforward and hidden.

In addition, VLANs have been, and still are, proprietary, single-vendor solutions. History has shown that customers prefer the multivendor/open systems policies that have developed in the migration to LANs and the client server model. However, this may also be changing.

In December 1998, IEEE published its open specification for VLANs: 802.1Q. This open standard promises to give the communications industry a clear definition of VLANs and their use in switched networks. Having a standard for robust multivendor VLAN functionality will allow companies to reassess their VLAN strategies to take advantage of new capabilities.

Activities

1. VLANs are typically implemented using which type of device?

   a. Bridge

   b. Gateway

   c. Repeater

   d. Switch

2. Which of the following best describes the functionality of a VLAN?

   a. Grouping nodes logically that may be physically separated

   b. Grouping nodes physically in one single routing domain

   c. Replacing passive hubs for performance purposes

   d. Providing performance improvements over traditional routed networks

3. What is the primary reason to build a VLAN?

   a. Separate servers from workstations

   b. Minimize broadcast traffic

   c. Increase reachability of broadcast traffic

   d. Provide for increased segment-switching capabilities

4. VLANs can be created using a variety of switch vendor products in the same network. True or False

5. Each VLAN can be roughly equated to a broadcast domain. True or False

Extended Activity

Configure a switch to act as a VLAN in a network.

Summary

This unit reviewed today's predominant LAN technology: Ethernet. We reviewed older Ethernet configurations as well as current configurations. We discussed how Ethernet uses a technology called CSMA/CD to control access to the shared medium (bus or logical bus). We also studied the format of Ethernet LAN frames as they move data from NIC to NIC.

Two issues involving Ethernet networks require special configurations and devices. The first issue is performance. As networks grow and traffic increases across networks, Ethernet performance tends to degrade. Performance is typically increased by replacing hubs with switches. The added intelligence of a switch boosts overall network performance by isolating traffic within workgroups.

Another issue is broadcast containment. In many networks, broadcast containment is provided by devices that reside above the Data Link Layer, such as routers. Many LANs today are based on switches, which inherently do not provide broadcast traffic containment. VLANs provide broadcast containment at the Data Link layer, while simplifying the process of assigning users to workgroups.

Unit 3 Quiz

1. What does NIC stand for?

   a. Network interface control

   b. Network interface card

   c. National Institute for Communications

   d. Network interface carrier

2. Which of the following best describes the function of a MAC layer address?

   a. Transmits a frame to the next destination NIC

   b. Transmits a packet to the correct port

   c. Transmits a frame to the final destination

   d. Transmits a frame to the correct socket

3. Why would you replace a hub with a switch?

   a. Increase WAN connectivity

   b. Increase Internet connectivity

   c. Increase LAN performance

   d. All of the above

4. What is the most widely installed LAN technology?

   a. Ethernet

   b. Token Ring

   c. ARCnet

   d. FDDI

5. Why is a jamming message sent out over an Ethernet?

   a. Warn other stations that a collision has been detected

   b. Corrupt the preamble of the incoming MAC frame

   c. Resynchronize all stations on the local Ethernet

   d. Ensure that all remote stations have received the previous frame

6. Most organizations replace standard 10-Mbps Ethernet with:

   a. 100-Mbps Ethernet

   b. 100-Mbps FDDI

   c. Gigabit Ethernet

   d. 622-Mbps ATM

7. What layer of software is normally loaded on the NIC?

   a. Physical

   b. Data Link

   c. Network

   d. Transport

8. What is the maximum length of a Fast Ethernet UTP segment?

   a. 100 meters

   b. 1,000 meters

   c. 10 kilometers

   d. 200 meters

9. What is the difference between the Ethernet version 2 frame format and IEEE 802.3 frame format?

   a. Length of the frame

   b. Length field in the frame

   c. Length of the padding

   d. Length of the cabling

10. Which of the following statements is not true regarding Ethernet?

    a. Ethernet is the predominant MAC standard being used in LANs.

    b. The Ethernet frame type is the same for Fast Ethernet and 10-Mbps Ethernet.

    c. Ethernet speeds range from 10 to 1,000 Mbps.

    d. Ethernet can only be used with Category 5 UTP.

11. How is Fast Ethernet similar to standard Ethernet?

    a. The same frame format is used.

    b. Cat 5 cabling can be used for both.

    c. Star configurations are used in both types.

    d. All of the above.

12. Which is not a MAC layer standard?

    a. Ethernet

    b. Token Ring

    c. CDDI

    d. UTP

13. The Ethernet standard is:

    a. IEEE 802.5

    b. IEEE 802.2

    c. IEEE 802.3

    d. IEEE 800.X

14. How are store-and-forward switches different than cut-through switches?

    a. Cut-through switches work at Layer 1, but store-and-forward switches work at Layer 2.

    b. Store-and-forward switches are more accurate, but cut-through switches are faster.

    c. Cut-through switches forward one frame at a time, but store-and-forward switches move frames in large batches.

    d. Store-and-forward switches are faster, but cut-through switches are more accurate.

15. Gigabit Ethernet uses a different frame format than 10-Mbps Ethernet and Fast Ethernet. True or False

16. Why do administrators want to contain broadcast traffic?

17. Where are Ethernet frames processed?

18. What is the advantage of a switch over a standard hub?

19. What is the primary method (cabling and components) for implementing Ethernet LANs today?

20. According to the Ethernet 5/4/3 rule, how many 10Base2 segments may have nodes attached?

Unit 4
Token Ring and FDDI LANs

In addition to Ethernet, Token Ring and Fiber Distributed Data Interface (FDDI) are popular local area network (LAN) protocols found in computer networks today. Although not as predominant as Ethernet, they are both commonly used in LANs. However these ring-based networks use a fundamentally different method of Medium Access Control (MAC) than Ethernet.

There are three main types of ring network technologies:

- IBM Token Ring (IEEE 802.5 standard) is a LAN protocol that delivers 4 or 16 megabits per second (Mbps) throughput over unshielded twisted pair (UTP) cabling.

- FDDI is a high-speed ring protocol based on fiber optic transmission. FDDI is often used for network backbones, because it provides throughput of up to 100 Mbps.

- Copper Distributed Data Interface (CDDI) implements the basic approach of FDDI, using copper wiring instead of optical fiber.

This unit reviews the basic features of a Token Ring network, explains the details of Token Ring framing, and briefly covers FDDI.

Lessons

1. Token Ring Framing and MAC
2. Token Ring Configurations
3. Review of FDDI

Terms

channel—Channel refers to the physical link that provides connectivity between communicating devices. Channel and link are often used interchangeably.

cluster controller—A cluster controller is an IBM device used to control communications between an IBM mainframe and a terminal device (IBM 3270 or ASCII terminal). It is also referred to as a communications controller.

Data Link Control (DLC)—DLC is a generic term that refers to a protocol (such as Token Ring or Ethernet) used to transfer information across a single link.

Fiber Distributed Data Interface (FDDI)—A LAN standard specifying a 100-Mbps token-passing network using fiber optic cable.

front-end processor (FEP)—A FEP is a device used in IBM mainframe networks that provides connectivity between networking devices and a mainframe. A FEP is also referred to as a communications controller.

IBM 3172—An IBM 3172 is a type of protocol converter (gateway) that translates traffic between a LAN (Token Ring or Ethernet) and an IBM mainframe. It is also referred to as a LAN gateway.

Internetwork Packet Exchange (IPX)—IPX is NetWare's proprietary Network Layer protocol.

multistation access unit (MAU)—A MAU is a device used in Token Ring networks to provide connectivity between individual workstations. It is also referred to as a Token Ring hub.

NetWare Core Protocol (NCP)—NCP is the proprietary protocol used by the NetWare OS to transmit information between clients and servers. NCP messages are transmitted by means of IPX.

Lesson 1—Token Ring Framing and MAC

A Token Ring network avoids collisions by passing a token from one node to the next. A node may transmit only when it has the token. The token circulates around the network at a steady rate. Applications can reliably predict the next time they will be able to transmit or receive data. This quality of a network is called "deterministic" response, and it makes Token Ring a good choice for real-time applications, such as computer-aided manufacturing.

Objectives

At the end of this lesson you will be able to:

- Describe the purpose of each part of a Token Ring header
- Explain the difference between a Token Ring frame and a token
- Describe how a Token Ring network operates

 **Key Point**

A Token Ring node may not transmit unless it controls a free token.

Token Ring Frame Format

A Token Ring frame is more complex than an Ethernet frame because it provides more functionality.

The Token Ring Token and Frame Format Diagram presents the Token Ring frame format. The top portion of the diagram shows the format when data from an upper layer is being encapsulated by the Token Ring MAC header and trailer. The bottom portion of the diagram shows the format of a free token.

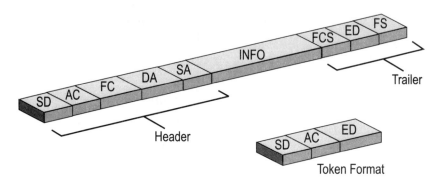

Token Ring Token and Frame Format

The Token Ring frame contains the following fields:

- Starting Delimiter (SD) (1 byte)—Indicates the start of the Token Ring Frame. Its encoded values are JK0JK000. "J" and "K" are special bit positions; their values (1 or 0) allow the receiving station to consistently identify the start of the frame.

- Access Control (AC) (1 byte)—The format of this byte is PPPT-MRRR. P and R are priority bits that indicate the priority of a frame. M is a monitor bit, used by a ring monitor station to determine if a frame is circulating endlessly on the ring. T is a token bit that differentiates a free token from a frame.

- Frame Control (FC) (1 byte)—The format of this byte is FFZZZZZZ. The F bits indicate whether the frame contains information from layers above. The Z bits contain Data Link Layer control information.

- Destination Address (DA) (6 bytes)—The physical address of the node(s) to receive the data. The DA can be 16 or 48 bits long. The 16-bit address is used commonly on FDDI rings, while the 48-bit address is used on both FDDI and Token Ring networks. The first bit in the address is set to one if the frame is addressed to a group of nodes. The first bit is not set if the frame is intended for an individual station.

- Source Address (SA) (6 bytes)—The physical address of the node(s) to send the data. The SA can be 16 or 48 bits long. The 16-bit address is used commonly on FDDI rings, while the 48-bit address is used on both FDDI and Token Ring networks.

- Information (INFO) (variable length, up to 17,800 bytes)—Contains either data from an upper layer, or additional control information beyond that contained in the FC field.

- Frame Check Sequence (FCS) (4 bytes)—A value used for error control. The source computer runs the frame's data through a mathematical algorithm, and stores the resulting 32-bit value in the FCS field. The destination computer repeats the calculation, then compares its result to the FCS. If the two values match, then it is likely that the frame has no errors.

- Ending Delimiter (ED) (1 byte)—This signals the end of the frame. The format of the byte is JK1JK1IE. The J and K bits allow the receiving station to consistently identify the end of the frame. The I bit (intermediate bit) indicates whether the frame is the last in a sequence of frames, and the E bit indicates whether an error was detected by the receiving (or repeating) station.

- Frame Status (FS) (1 byte)—Indicates whether the frame has been received. The format of the FS byte is ACXXACXX. If the A bit is set, it indicates the receiving station has recognized the address. If the C bit is set, it indicates the receiving station(s) has copied the frame.

Token Ring MAC

On a ring network, a 3-byte token circulates continuously around the ring, and a node may not transmit a frame until it receives the token. Each node's NIC contains a repeater that receives bits from one of the two links and transmits them on the other. It receives frames simply by copying bits as they go by.

The MAC question regarding a ring LAN is, "When can the node insert bits onto the ring?" The answer lies in the token passing protocol, as illustrated on the Token Ring Flow Diagram and described below.

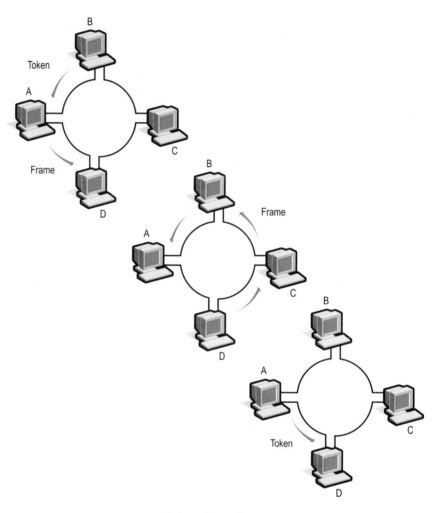

Token Ring Flow

Token passing consists of several elements:

- On an inactive LAN, a 3-byte token circulates endlessly.

- The token is like a frame, except that bit 4 in the second byte indicates the network is free. A node may transmit only when it has a free token.

- Three priority bits indicate whether the station can grab the token after the current transmission. If the priority of the token is higher than the frame waiting to be transmitted, the token is passed on to a node with higher priority traffic.

- A node transmits its frame after it gains control of the token.

- Each successive node retransmits the frame until the frame arrives at the source node.

- Only one frame can circulate on a 4-Mbps Token Ring (IEEE 802.5), or an IEEE 802.4 Token Bus. Multiple tokens can circulate on 100 Mbps FDDI networks, and on 16-Mbps Token Rings that use Early Token Release.

Transmitting a Frame

When a node needs to transmit a frame, several actions occur, as presented on the Token Ring Send Algorithm Diagram:

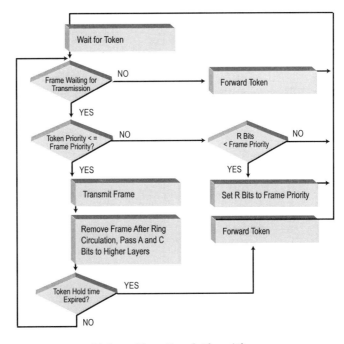

Token Ring Send Algorithm

- A 3-byte token circulates endlessly around the ring, even when the network is idle. Only one token and, at most, one message can circulate on the ring at one time, although different parts of the token and message are simultaneously received and retransmitted by different nodes.

- A node may transmit a frame when it receives a free token. It first receives and repeats the starting delimiter. The node then checks the token priority in the access control field to make sure a higher priority task on the ring is not waiting for the token. If the priority is okay, the node appends the remaining header information, inserts its data frame after the token, then adds the trailer. It then sets bits in the token to mark it as "busy," and retransmits both token and frame to send them around the ring. If a node has more data to send, it must stop transmitting after 10 milliseconds (ms) and wait for the token to come around again.

- When the token and frame return to the node that originally transmitted them, that node reads the trailer's Frame Status bits to see that its frame was successfully received. The sending node then resets the token's bits to indicate that the token is free, and repeats the free token to the next node. It does not retransmit the data frame, thus removing that message from the ring.

- The node must stop transmitting after a certain period of time. If it has more data to send, it must wait for the token to come around again. The token will circulate around the ring, passing through the destination node, until it returns to the source node. As it passes through the destination node, that node copies the data into its own memory. It then sets the "A" and "C" bits in the trailer's Frame Status byte to show the sending node that the address has been recognized ("A" bit is set) and the frame has been copied ("C" bit is set).

- When the source node receives the frame it originally sent, it does not retransmit it; this removes the frame from the ring. The node then transmits a free token.

Receiving a Token Ring Frame

The Token Ring Receive Algorithm Diagram illustrates the general process required for a node to receive a frame:

- When a node receives a busy token and its data, it checks the frame address.

- If the token is not addressed to this station, this station will pass it on to the next. However, before forwarding the frame, this station checks the priority bits in the frame header. If this station is waiting to send a transmission with a priority higher than the current frame, it sets the R bits to its own priority. This ensures that this station will receive the freed token (assuming no other station bumps this one with a higher priority). Finally, the node repeats the token and frame to the next node on the ring.

- When a node receives a frame addressed to it, it copies the data frame. It then sets the A and C bits in the trailer's Frame Status field to indicate that the data has been received, and repeats the token and frame to the next node.

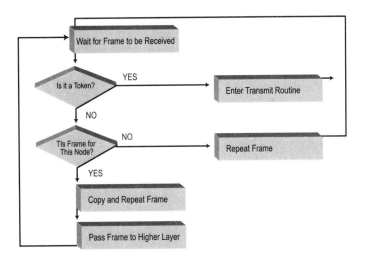

Token Ring Receive Algorithm

Activities

1. What does the source address of a Token Ring frame indicate?

    _____

    _____

2. What does the destination address of a Token Ring frame indicate?

    _____

    _____

3. What is the purpose of a Token Ring trailer?

    _____

    _____

4. If a frame contains information destined for the Internet, what would the contents of the Token Ring INFO field most likely be?

    _____

    _____

5. What is the purpose of an FC byte?

    _____

    _____

Extended Activities

1. Perform the LAN paper lab exercise.
2. Go to the IBM Web site **http://www.ibm.com** and research the latest developments in Token Ring and Token Ring products.

Lesson 2—Token Ring Configurations

There are many ways to configure Token Ring networks. Most use a star ring topology, in which each node connects to a multistation access unit (MAU) at the center of the star wiring pattern. Information travels from node to node in a logical ring as the MAU copies each signal to each of its nodes in turn. The star ring topology is easy to set up and manage, and the central MAU can bypass a malfunctioning node.

Objectives

At the end of this lesson you will be able to:

- Draw network diagrams consisting of Token Ring LAN configurations

- Describe the basic operation of a Token Ring bridge

 **Key Point**

There are many ways to configure Token Ring networks.

Token Ring MAU Connectivity

The Simple Token Ring Diagram illustrates how several ring segments are connected by means of MAUs.

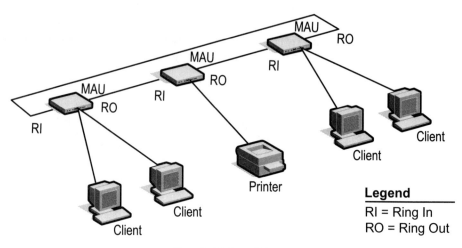

Simple Token Ring

In most cases, Token Ring networks are found in networks that also contain an IBM host (mainframe). The Token Ring and IBM Host Connectivity Diagram illustrates three traditional Token Ring configurations used to access an IBM host. Token Ring nodes can access host resources by means of front-end processors (FEPs), cluster controllers, or through LAN gateway devices such as IBM 3172s.

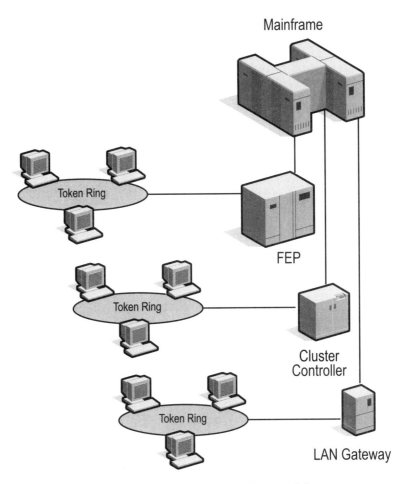

Mainframe

FEP

Token Ring

Token Ring

Cluster
Controller

Token Ring

LAN Gateway

Token Ring and IBM Host Connectivity

Token Ring Bridges

The Token Ring Bridge Diagram shows how Token Ring networks can be joined using bridges. The purpose for using a bridge is to isolate traffic on one ring from the other ring. The rings should be arranged so that most of the traffic on one segment of the network remains on its own ring rather than crossing the bridge. Adding a second bridge provides redundancy and higher levels of availability. The IBM 8230 and 8228 rings on the diagram are IBM MAU products commonly found in Token Ring networks.

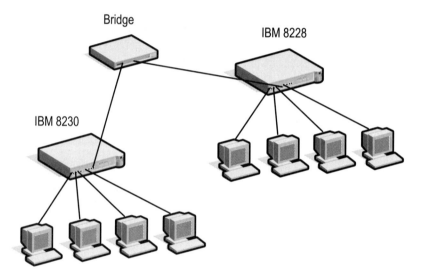

Token Ring Bridge

The Token Ring Backbone Configuration Diagram shows how to form a backbone configuration using Token Ring networks and bridges. This configuration allows for any-to-any communication between network nodes across several rings. When networks are large enough to have multiple rings, the backbone configuration provides the shortest average path between any two nodes on the network.

Shared devices, such as printers and file servers, can be placed on the backbone to provide quick access to all nodes on the network. A typical implementation for this type of configuration is connecting multiple floors in a multistory office complex. Each floor may contain a separate ring, and all rings (floors) can be connected by means of the backbone.

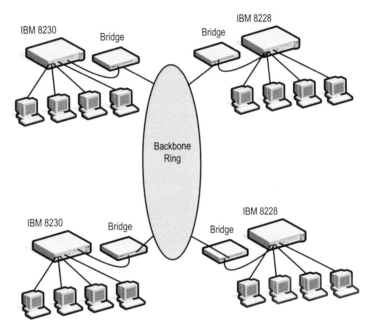

Token Ring Backbone Configuration

In many networks, fiber optics are used as the ring backbone. This eliminates problems associated with different ground potentials found in separate buildings, and other environmental hazards. Differing ground potentials can cause devices to ground through the data network versus the building electrical system, causing data interference and shock hazards. The use of nonconducting fiber to carry interbuilding signals avoids these problems. Additionally, environmental hazards such as corrosion are eliminated through the use of fiber optics.

The Token Ring and FDDI Diagram shows how Token Ring networks can be connected to a FDDI backbone. This is a very typical configuration in today's LAN environments. Token Ring and Ethernet LAN segments connect to high-speed backbones by means of bridges or routers for connectivity to other segments or across wide area networks (WANs).

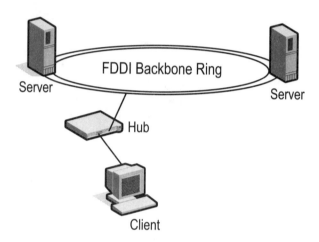

Token Ring and FDDI

Activities

1. What does the term star ring refer to in a Token Ring network?

   _____

   _____

   _____

   _____

   _____

   _____

2. What is the purpose of the RI and RO ports in a Token Ring MAU?

   _____

   _____

   _____

   _____

   _____

3. How many tokens can be circulating in the Token Ring and IBM Host Connectivity Diagram at the same time?

   _____

   _____

4. How many tokens can be circulating in the Token Ring Bridge Diagram?

   _____

   _____

5. How many tokens can be circulating in the Token Ring Backbone Configuration Diagram?

   _____

   _____

6. Draw a two-ring bridged token ring network.

Extended Activities

1. Using a Web search engine, research the other devices shown in this lesson but not described, including:

   a. Front-end processors (IBM 3745)

   b. Cluster controllers (IBM 3174)

   c. LAN gateways (IBM 3172)

   d. Mainframes

2. Build a small Token Ring network or visit a site that contains a Token Ring network.

Lesson 3—Review of FDDI

Because fiber optic cable supports higher transmission speeds than copper wire, it is easy to see how we can speed up a network by simply replacing twisted pair cable with optical fiber. The FDDI, (pronounced "fiddee") protocol does this; however, it uses more than just a faster medium to achieve its 100-Mbps throughput.

FDDI is a token-passing ring protocol, based on the Token Ring standard. A FDDI ring can be combined with Token Rings or Ethernet buses to provide a high throughput backbone for a network. In 1990, FDDI was adopted by the American National Standards Institute (ANSI) as the high-speed standard for backbone networks that provide connectivity between workgroups in a LAN. This lesson reviews the major features of the FDDI protocol.

Objectives

At the end of this lesson you will be able to:

- Describe the basic operation of a FDDI network
- Explain the features and benefits of FDDI

 **Key Point**

FDDI is a fiber optic, highly redundant LAN technology that is primarily used for network backbones.

FDDI has found its niche as a reliable, high-speed backbone for mission-critical and high-traffic networks. FDDI can transport data at a rate of 100 Mbps and support 500 stations or more on a single network. FDDI was designed to run through fiber cables, transmitting light pulses to convey information back and forth between stations. FDDI can also run on copper using electrical signals; also known as CDDI. The FDDI Diagram illustrates a typical FDDI being used as a backbone for a network.

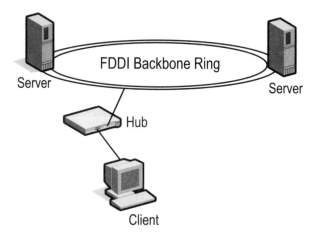

FDDI

Key FDDI Features

Although FDDI is a Data Link technology similar to Token Ring, three important differences make the technology and protocols of FDDI more complicated:

- Dual-ring topology—A FDDI network consists of two rings, each one rotating in a different direction.

- Multiple tokens and messages—Multiple tokens and messages can circulate on a FDDI ring.

- Flexible use of channels—When necessary, some of the ring's capacity can be used for nondata transmission such as telephone service.

Dual Ring Topology	The FDDI standard specifies dual channels, running in opposite directions. (In contrast, a Token Ring has only one physical link between each pair of adjacent nodes.) This double-ring design provides much greater reliability and recoverability, a highly desirable goal for a standard aimed at network backbones. The dual-channel architecture is implemented as follows:

- A node can communicate on one or two of the channels. The standard does not require communication on both channels, so lower cost, single-channel machines can be built. The two types of FDDI stations are called dual-access stations (DAS) and single-access stations (SAS).

- A dual-access station has at least two ports—an A port, where the primary ring comes in and secondary ring goes out, and a B port where the secondary ring comes in and the primary ring goes out. A station may also have a number of M ports, which are attachments for single-attachment stations. Stations with at least one M port are called concentrators.

- If the node communicates on both channels and one channel fails, the node often will still be able to communicate on the other.

- When a break occurs in both channels on the ring, either because of a node failure or because a link is damaged, the nodes on either side of the break connect the two channels together, effectively turning them into one longer ring. This allows operation to continue until the problem is resolved.

- Each dual-access station on a double-ring network, whether it communicates on one channel or on both, must still connect to both and provide shunt circuits to handle recovery.

Multiple Tokens and Messages	Consider a single message transmitted from a node around a ring, and back to the sending node. If transmission were truly instantaneous, the node would see the first bit of the message on its input connection the moment it transmitted it on its output connection.

But it takes time for a token to make its way around a ring, because each node's repeater must copy each bit from its input to its output. In a Token Ring network, this time is wasted, because a single token serves the entire ring; the token must come all the way around and be freed by the originating node before any other node can transmit.

However, a FDDI backbone ring may contain as many as 1,000 nodes and up to 200 kilometers (km) of optical fiber; there can be a long delay from the time a node transmits the final bit of a message until it receives the first bit of the returning token. Therefore, the FDDI standard allows many tokens and messages to circulate on a single FDDI ring.

When a FDDI node has finished transmitting a message, and is not receiving anything, it immediately transmits a new free token. That token can then be used by the next node on the ring that needs to transmit, and that transmission will occur simultaneously with the transmission of data for other busy tokens on the ring.

Flexible Use of Channels

A portion of a FDDI ring's data transmission capacity can be given up for synchronous traffic, such as telephone service. This essentially layers one or more high-speed communication channels onto the ring.

For example, imagine a FDDI ring that serves as the backbone for a large network. If network traffic is lower at night than during the day, a significant portion of the backbone capacity goes unused during those hours. Thus, the FDDI standard allows a portion of its 100-Mbps bandwidth to be used to emulate a T1 or T3 (E1 and E3 in Europe) communication channel for either voice or data.

FDDI MAC

FDDI's media access is similar to that used by Token Ring. A station generates a special signaling sequence called a token that controls the right to transmit. This token is continually passed around the network from one node to the next. When a station has something to send, it captures the token, sends the information in a well-formatted FDDI frame, and then releases the token. The header of these frames includes the address of the station(s) that copy the frame.

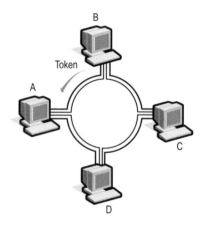

All nodes read a frame as it travels around the ring to determine whether they are the recipient of the frame. The destination node copies the data, resets the Frame Status bits in the frame trailer, and retransmits the frame to the next station on the ring. When the frame returns to the originating station, this station strips the frame and retransmits the freed token. This access scheme thus allows all stations to share the network bandwidth in an orderly and efficient manner.

CDDI

CDDI is a version of FDDI designed to run on either shielded twisted pair (STP) or UTP copper wire. A major reason for the development of CDDI is that STP and UTP are relatively inexpensive and widely used. Using existing copper wire is an attractive alternative to fiber optic cabling, which can be an expensive proposition for bulk implementations.

The operation of CDDI follows the same rules as FDDI. However, the maximum segment length for CDDI over UTP is only 100 meters (m).

Activities

1. Why has FDDI found its niche as a corporate backbone solution? Give at least two answers.

   _____

   _____

   _____

   _____

2. Why would FDDI be used in an environment where noise is an issue?

   _____

   _____

3. What is the purpose of the two FDDI rings?

   _____

   _____

   _____

   _____

4. Which other LAN protocol does FDDI have the most in common with?

   _____

   _____

5. Draw a network that contains a FDDI backbone connecting four workgroups by means of routers.

6. Briefly describe how a FDDI network operates.

_____

_____

_____

_____

7. How does CDDI compare to FDDI?

_____

_____

_____

_____

Extended Activity

Using a Web search engine or a catalog, research FDDI and CDDI products. Find examples of NICs and devices used to build FDDI and CDDI backbones.

Summary

The choice of a Data Link LAN protocol depends on the needs of an organization and particular installation requirements. A LAN architecture should be chosen to fit the environment, and many factors play a role in the decision.

Each LAN protocol uses a different frame format that is appropriate to its operation. As you saw in this unit, a Token Ring frame is more complex than an Ethernet frame, because Token Ring provides features that Ethernet does not.

When you compare Ethernet to Token Ring and FDDI, two main differences are apparent.

First, Ethernet performance degrades severely under heavy load, because its effective throughput drops off due to collisions. In contrast, FDDI and Token Ring handle heavy loads gracefully, while providing very high effective throughput. On the other hand, Ethernet performance increases as the load decreases, while ring network performance is constant even if very few users are on the network. This makes Ethernet a better choice for non-real-time applications that can benefit from the faster speed of a lightly used network.

Second, ring networks are deterministic, which means that their performance is steady and predictable. Ethernet allows nodes to compete for access to the shared medium, which means that a node cannot rely on being able to transmit or receive at a regular pace. This difference makes ring networks better choices for real-time applications such as streaming video or industrial controls.

Unit 4 Quiz

1. What does MAU stand for?

   a. Multistation Access Unit

   b. Multinode activity and usage

   c. Media access usage

   d. Media activity unit

2. Where are MAUs normally found?

   a. Token Ring networks

   b. Ethernet networks

   c. FDDI networks

   d. Almost all LANs contain MAUs

3. Which of the following is not a MAC layer protocol?

   a. FDDI

   b. Ethernet

   c. Token Ring

   d. IPX

4. When a Token Ring frame returns to the node that sent it, what does that node do?

   a. Removes the data and transmits a free token

   b. Sends an acknowledgement to the recipient

   c. Transmits an "all clear" message to other nodes

   d. Removes the frame, and lets the next sending node generate a token

5. What is FDDI commonly used for in a corporate network?

   a. Wireless configurations

   b. Router connectivity

   c. Bridge connectivity

   d. Backbone connectivity

6. What is the most widely installed LAN technology?

    a. Ethernet

    b. Token Ring

    c. ARCnet

    d. FDDI

7. What are ring LAN protocols, such as Token Ring and FDDI, best suited for?

    a. Large late-night data backups

    b. Robotics control

    c. Database report generation

    d. Large corporate intranets

8. What common information is found in both Ethernet and Token Ring frame headers and trailers?

    a. Source and destination addresses

    b. Port numbers

    c. IP addresses

    d. Socket numbers

9. The RI port of a Token Ring MAU provides:

    a. Connection from the monitor

    b. Connection from another MAU

    c. Connection to a router

    d. Connection to a bridge

10. Which is not a MAC layer standard?

    a. FDDI

    b. Token Ring

    c. CDDI

    d. UTP

11. What is a token?

    a. Four bytes of all "1"

    b. A 3-byte message

    c. Two bytes of alternating "1" and "0"

    d. A "clear to send" message from all other nodes

12. Once a node gains control of the token, it may keep the token until it has finished transmitting. True or False

Unit 5
ATM LANs

With each new application version, software developers add sophisticated features that enhance the user's experience and erase the effect of distance between coworkers. Unfortunately, each one of these slick interfaces and powerful client/server operations puts additional demands on limited network resources. Just as a user can never have too much hard drive space, it seems a network can never have enough bandwidth.

This demand for capacity is increasing so fast that traditional network design solutions are becoming inadequate to meet it. Proven shared-media local area network (LAN) technologies such as Ethernet, Token Ring, and Fiber Distributed Data Interface (FDDI) are gradually failing to meet the challenges posed by bandwidth-intensive applications such as interactive multimedia, video conferencing, and Internet audio.

Asynchronous Transfer Mode (ATM) technology has emerged as one solution to the bandwidth crunch. ATM is a high-speed, connection-oriented, cell-switching and multiplexing technology that can transmit voice, video, and data across LANs, metropolitan area networks (MANs), and wide area networks (WANs). It offers the potential to create high-speed networks that use the same basic technology in the office LAN and the global WAN.

Lessons

1. Introduction to ATM
2. The Need for ATM
3. ATM Architecture
4. LAN Emulation
5. ATM Devices
6. ATM Deployment

Terms

100VG-AnyLAN—100VG-AnyLAN is a 100-Mbps Ethernet technology standard that directly competes with 100BaseT Ethernet. The IEEE 802.12 committee is currently investigating this technology. The access method used by this standard is different than the CSMA/CD method used by 10-Mbps Ethernet and Fast Ethernet; however, the MAC frame format is the same. The new access method is called "demand priority."

Address Resolution Protocol (ARP)—ARP is a protocol that allows a host to use a logical (network) address to obtain the hardware (NIC, MAC) address for a remote station.

ATM Forum—The ATM Forum is an international industry organization that promotes the use of ATM by facilitating a rapid convergence of interoperability specifications.

backplane—The backplane is the "motherboard" of a device that provides the device's basic functionality. The backplane's design determines the basic features of a hub, switch, bridge, or router. Modules plug into the backplane to provide port interfaces or additional features. If the backplane architecture is Ethernet, Token Ring, or FDDI, it is referred to as a shared-bus backplane, because Ethernet, Token Ring, and FDDI are all shared-media protocols.

bridge/router (Brouter)—A brouter is an internetworking device that combines the functions of both a bridge and a router. See router.

Broadband-Integrated Services Digital Network (B-ISDN)—
ISDN line rates are available in two basic varieties: basic (primary) and broadband. Basic, primary, or "narrow" ISDN consists of two bearer (B) channels and a data (D) channel. Each bearer channel can carry one voice conversation or data at a transmission rate of 64 Kbps. The ISDN-PRI is similar to T1 signaling, and consists of 24 channels, including 23 channels (64 Kbps each) that carry voice, data, and video; and 1 data channel that carries signaling information. B-ISDN (also called wide ISDN) offers multiple channels above the primary rate (A, C, and H series of channels).

circuit switching—Circuit-switched networks establish a physical connection between two nodes, and all packets in one transmission are passed between the same nodes by "switching" them through intermediate points (other nodes or a host computer). Circuit switching guarantees that all packets in the same transmission will sequentially travel over the same physical transmission path. However, each transmission is limited to one path, and cannot achieve greater transfer speed by using multiple parallel paths.

class of service (CoS)—In general, CoS (also called quality of service, or QoS) measures different characteristics of a transmission service. In the context of the OSI reference model, users of the Transport Layer specify QoS parameters as part of a request for a communication channel. These parameters define different levels of service based on the requirements of an application. For example, an interactive application that requires good response time would specify high QoS values for connection establishment delay, throughput, transit delay, and connection priority. However, a file transfer application requires reliable, error-free data transfer more than it needs a prompt connection, thus it would request high QoS parameters for residual error rate/probability.

coder/decoder (codec)—A codec is a hardware/software device that takes an analog video signal and converts (codes) it to digital format for compression and transmission. On the receiving end, the digital signal is put back (decoded) into the original analog signal. See PCM.

collapsed backbone—Collapsed backbone is a network topology that uses a multiport device, such as a switch or router, to carry traffic between network segments or subnets. This differs from the original Ethernet backbone, which consisted of a single common bus cable to which nodes and subnets are connected.

cross-connect—The term cross-connect refers to a high-speed switch that does not error check frames, but simply passes them to the appropriate destination.

Data Exchange Interface (DXI)—DXI is an ATM interface that converts variable-length network frames to fixed-length ATM cells. ATM DXI converts LAN frames to the variable-length DXI frame format. The ATM CSU/DSU then converts the DXI frames to fixed-length ATM cells. This two-step conversion simplifies processing on the ATM CSU/DSU, because it only needs to convert one type of frame.

data service unit/channel service unit (DSU/CSU)—The hardware required to connect a common carrier connection (leased line) to a router is referred to as the DSU/CSU. Frame relay service requires one DSU/CSU, whereas private line service requires two DSU/CSUs.

datagram (packet)—A datagram is a unit of information processed by the Network Layer of the OSI reference model. The packet header contains the logical (network) address of the destination node. Intermediate nodes forward a packet until it reaches its destination. A packet can contain an entire message generated by higher OSI layers, or a segment of a much larger message.

Distributed Queue Dual Bus (DQDB)—DQDB is the IEEE 802.6 standard for MANs. See SMDS.

FDDI II—FDDI II is an incompatible extension to FDDI that provides better support for constant bit-rate applications such as voice and video transmission. FDDI II divides its 100-Mbps bandwidth into 16 circuits that can be allocated to various types of traffic; those circuits can be further divided into 96 channels per circuit.

FDDI Follow-On LAN (FFOL)—FFOL is a proposed 2.4-Gbps standard that could eventually replace FDDI.

flat address space—Flat address space refers to a system of one-part, unique addresses, not arranged into a hierarchical organization.

frame relay—Frame relay is a technology designed to move data across a WAN. Frame relay normally operates at speeds of 56 Kbps to 1.5 Mbps.

hub—Also referred to as a wiring concentrator, a simple hub is a repeater with multiple ports. A signal coming into one port is repeated out the other ports.

Institute of Electrical and Electronic Engineers (IEEE)—IEEE is a professional organization composed of engineers, scientists, and students. Founded in 1884, IEEE publishes computer and electronics standards, including the 802 series that defines shared-media networks such as Ethernet and Token Ring.

intelligent hub (smart hub)—An intelligent hub is a hub that has been enhanced with additional hardware to support multiple media types and media access methods (Data Link protocols), such as Ethernet, Token Ring, and FDDI. Smart hubs can provide additional internetworking functionality through plug-in bridge and router modules and network management.

International Telecommunication Union-Telecommunications Standardization Sector (ITU-TSS)—ITU-TSS is an intergovernmental organization that develops and adopts international treaties and telecommunications standards. ITU was founded in 1865 and became a United Nations agency in 1947. ITU-TSS was formerly the Consultative Committee for International Telephony and Telegraphy (CCITT).

Internet Engineering Task Force (IETF)—IETF is a large, open, international community of network designers, operators, vendors, and researchers concerned with evolution of the Internet architecture and smooth operation of the Internet.

Internet Protocol (IP)—IP is a Network Layer protocol responsible for getting a packet (datagram) through a network. It is the "IP" in TCP/IP.

latency—The transmission delay created as a device, such as a bridge or router, processes a packet or frame is referred to as latency. It is the duration from the time a device reads the first byte of a packet or frame, until the time it forwards that byte.

microsegmentation—Microsegmentation is the practice of increasing usable bandwidth by subdividing networks into smaller and smaller segments.

multiplexer (MUX)—A MUX is a device that allows multiple signals to travel over the same physical medium. See TDM and STDM.

optical carrier (OC)—OC is one of the optical signal standards defined by the SONET digital signal hierarchy. The basic building block of SONET is the STS-1 51.84-Mbps signal, chosen to accommodate a DS3 signal. The hierarchy is defined up to STS-48; that is 48 STS-1 channels, for a total of 2,488.32 Mbps capable of carrying 32,256 voice circuits. The STS designation refers to the interface for electrical signals. The corresponding optical signal standards are designated OC-1, OC-2, etc.

permanent virtual circuit—A path through a packet-switching or cell-switching network that behaves like a dedicated line between source and destination endpoints is referred to as a permanent virtual circuit.

pulse code modulation (PCM)—PCM is a method of converting an analog voice signal to a digital signal that can be translated accurately back into a voice signal after transmission. The device that converts an analog signal to PCM is a codec. The codec first samples the voice signal at several thousand samples per second. Each sample is converted to a binary number that expresses the amplitude of the sample in a very compact form. These binary numbers form the digital bit stream that comes out of a codec. The receiving codec reverses the process, using each successive binary number to control a digital/analog circuit that generates the required analog wave form on the voice output channel.

quality of service (QoS)—See class of service.

repeater—A repeater is a Physical Layer device that connects one cable segment of a LAN to another, possibly connecting two different media types. For example, a repeater can connect a thin Ethernet cable to a thick Ethernet cable. It regenerates and boosts electrical signals, thus a repeater can be used to lengthen a network segment. Because a repeater reproduces exactly what it receives, bit by bit, it also reproduces errors. However, it is very fast and causes very little delay.

router—A router is a Layer 3 device with several ports that can each connect to a network or another router. The router examines the logical network address of each packet, then uses its internal routing table to forward the packet to the routing port associated with the best path to the packet's destination. If the packet is addressed to a network that is not connected to the router, the router forwards the packet to another router that is closer to the final destination. Each router, in turn, evaluates each packet and then either delivers the packet or forwards it to another router.

server farm—A server farm is a collection of departmental servers located in a data center, where they can be provided with consolidated backup, uninterrupted power supply, and a secure operating environment.

statistical time-division multiplexing (STDM)—STDM is a multiplexing technology in which each port competes for access to the bus based on need. Bandwidth is not wasted on unused time slots, which sometimes happens in TDM. STDM is good for bursty traffic. See MUX and TDM.

super server—A super server refers to large-capacity computing hardware that handles huge transaction loads or giant databases, and functions as a server in a client/server architecture. Some organizations, such as those hosting heavy e-commerce traffic, are converting mainframe systems to function as super servers.

switch—A switch is a device that operates at the Data Link Layer of the OSI reference model. A switch can connect LANs or segments of the same media access type. A switch dedicates its entire bandwidth to each frame it switches.

switching hub—See switch.

Switched Multimegabit Data Service (SMDS)—SMDS is a connectionless service used to connect LANs, MANs, and WANs to exchange data. SMDS is cell oriented and uses the same format as the ITU-T B-ISDN standards. ITU-T has standardized a connectionless Broadband Network Service (I.364) that will primarily be offered by local telephone companies as a MAN service. Internal SMDS protocols are referred to as SMDS Interface Protocol-1, -2, and -3 (SIP-1 through -3). They are a subset of the IEEE 802.6 standard for MANs, also known as DQDB.

synchronous—Synchronous refers to data communication that is controlled by the microprocessor clock; signals are permitted to start and stop at particular times. To use synchronous communication, the clock settings of the sending and receiving systems must match.

Synchronous Digital Hierarchy (SDH)—SDH is an international standard for synchronous data transmission over fiber optic cables; SONET is the U.S. implementation. The standard SDH transmission rate, referred to as STM-1, is 155.52 Mbps. This is equivalent to SONET's OC-3.

Synchronous Optical Network (SONET)—SONET is the U.S. optical transmission standard that is part of the international SDH. The basic building block of SONET is the STS-1 51.84-Mbps signal, chosen to accommodate a T3 signal.

Synchronous Transport Signal (STS)—STS is a term that describes a SONET data transfer rate. For example, STS-1 is 51.84 Mbps, STS-3 is 155.52 Mbps, STS-12 is 622.08 Mbps, and STS-48 is 2.488 Gbps. The STS designation refers to the interface for electrical signals. The optical signal standards are correspondingly designated OC-1, OC-2, etc.

T3, E3—T3 is one of the T-carrier multiplexing standards. It operates at 44.736 Mbps, the equivalent of 672 voice circuits. E3 is the European equivalent of T3, operating at 34.368 Mbps.

T-carrier—T-carriers are one of several hierarchical systems for multiplexing digitized voice signals. The first T-carrier was installed in 1962 by the Bell system. The T-carrier family of systems now includes T1, T1C, T1D, T2, T3, and T4 (and their European counterparts E1, E2, etc.). T1 and its successors were designed to multiplex voice communications. Therefore, T1 was designed such that each channel carries a digitized representation of an analog signal that has a bandwidth of 4,000 Hz. It turns out that 64 Kbps is required to digitize a 4,000-Hz voice signal. Although current digitization technology has reduced the requirement to 32 Kbps or less, a T-carrier channel is still 64 Kbps.

time-division multiplexing (TDM)—TDM is multiplexing technology that guarantees each port a fixed amount of bandwidth on a rotating basis. TDM is suited to constant bit-rate traffic. See MUX and STDM.

transparent bridging—Transparent bridges enable frames to move back and forth between two network segments running the same MAC-layer protocols. This type of bridging is referred to as "transparent" because the source station transmits a frame to the destination station as if it were on the same physical network segment; that is, the bridge is "invisible." Transparent bridges typically connect Ethernet network segments. However, transparent bridging may also be used with Token Ring and FDDI networks.

virtual channel connection (VCC)—VCC refers to the endpoints of a one-directional ATM VC. A VCC is a point at which the ATM cell payload is passed to, or received from, a VC.

virtual LAN (VLAN)—A VLAN is a group of computers in a large LAN that behave as if they are connected to their own small private LAN. VLANs are created using special switches and software, so computers can be assigned to different VLANs without changing their physical configuration.

X.25—X.25 is a packet-switching network, public or private, typically built upon the facilities of public telephone networks (leased lines). In the United States, X.25 is offered by most carriers and VARs, such as AT&T, US Sprint, Ameritech, and Pacific Bell. The X.25 interface lies at OSI Layer 3, rather than Layer 1. X.25 defines its own three-layer protocol stack.

Lesson 1—Introduction to ATM

ATM is an emerging technology that can transmit voice, video, and data across LANs, MANs, and WANs. ATM is an international standard defined by the American National Standards Institute (ANSI) and International Telecommunication Union-Telecommunications Standardization Sector (ITU-TSS). ATM implements a high-speed, connection-oriented, cell-switching and multiplexing technology.

Many in the telecommunications industry believe ATM will revolutionize the way networks are designed and managed, because ATM combines the best features of two common transmission methods. Its connection-oriented nature makes ATM a reliable service for delay-sensitive applications, such as voice, video, or multimedia. Its flexible and efficient packet switching provides quick transfer of other forms of data.

In a relatively short period of time, ATM has gained a worldwide reputation as the ultimate means of solving end-to-end networking problems. The popularity of ATM has grown such that virtually every LAN hub vendor, router vendor, and service provider is racing to develop ATM-based products.

Objectives

At the end of this lesson you will be able to:

- Describe the three switching technology transfer modes

- Describe the key features of ATM, and explain how they allow ATM to transport a variety of data types

- Compare and contrast ATM and traditional networking technologies

 **Key Point**

ATM performs well for both delay-sensitive audio/video traffic and bursty data transfers.

ATM Defined

A transfer mode specifies a method of transmitting, multiplexing, and switching data in a network. Three transfer modes are commonly used in networks:

- Synchronous Transfer Mode (STM)
- Packet Transfer Mode (PTM)
- ATM

STM

STM technologies, such as T1, divide each transmission frame into a series of time slots and then allocate particular time slots to each user. STM is ideal for transmission of voice and video, because it provides a constant bit-rate service. Voice and video require predictable and guaranteed network access, or the quality of the transmission degrades rapidly. But STM is inefficient for bursty data communications because the same time slot in each frame is reserved for a particular user, regardless of whether the user has data to transmit.

PTM

PTM networks, such as the 802-series LAN protocols, break data into variable-size units (packets, datagrams, or frames). Each unit contains both user data and a header that provides information for routing, flow control, and error correction. Instead of establishing a dedicated physical connection between the source and destination station, the network relays packets from one node to another, often in multiple parallel paths, until they reach their final destination.

PTM is excellent for bursty data applications because a station only consumes bandwidth when it needs to transmit data. However, PTM does not provide the guaranteed network access required by constant bit-rate applications such as voice or video.

ATM

ATM combines the strengths of STM (constant transmission delay and guaranteed capacity) and PTM (flexibility and ability to handle intermittent traffic) in a single transfer mode that meets the needs of voice, video, and data applications.

In computing, the term "asynchronous" usually means that data transmission is coordinated through start and stop signals, without the use of a common clock. However, ATM networks use "asynchronous" to describe how network bandwidth is assigned to user applications. ATM assigns network access to users based on demand, which means that locations in the synchronous data stream are assigned to users in a random, or asynchronous, pattern. These concepts are illustrated on the ATM Diagram.

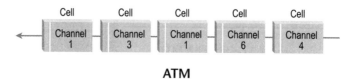

ATM

Summary of Transfer Modes

The Comparison Matrix for STM, PTM, and ATM Table provides a comparison of the three transfer modes.

Comparison Matrix for STM, PTM, and ATM

Capability	STM	PTM	ATM
Switching unit	Groups of bits	Variable-length packets	Fixed-length cell
Mode of operation	Connection-oriented	Connectionless	Connection-oriented
Addressing	Time slot position	Packet addressing	Connection identifier
Multiplexing	Time-division	Statistical	Cell asynchronous
Bandwidth	Dedicated	Flexible	Flexible and scalable
Network delay	Low	Lower	Lowest
Applications	Voice and video	Data	Voice, video, and data

Comparing ATM and Traditional Networking Technologies

ATM is very different from traditional shared-media networking technologies such as Ethernet, Token Ring, and FDDI. Some of the major differences are summarized in the ATM and Traditional Networks Comparison Table, and are discussed in detail below.

ATM and Traditional Networks Comparison

Feature	ATM	Traditional Networks
Available bandwidth	Extremely flexible and scalable	Fixed
Media access	Switched parallel point-to-point	Shared (CSMA-CD or token passing)
Mode of operation	Connection-oriented	Connectionless
Data transfer unit	Fixed-length cells	Variable-length frames
Error correction and flow control	None	Frame by frame

Scalable Bandwidth

ATM was developed to support scalable bandwidth. Unlike traditional LAN and WAN standards, ATM is designed to be independent of the transmission technology over which it runs. To provide flexible and scalable access, ATM is designed to operate at different speeds, over different media types, using different transport technologies.

ATM was initially offered over existing T3 (45 megabits per second [Mbps]), E3 (34 Mbps), and multimode fiber (100 Mbps). ATM is currently available at Synchronous Optical Network (SONET) speeds, at rates of 155 Mbps, 622 Mbps, 1.2 gigabits per second (Gbps), 2.4 Gbps, and higher.

Switched Parallel Point-to-Point Access

When new users are added to a traditional shared-access LAN such as Ethernet or FDDI, the amount of bandwidth available to each user is reduced. For example, assume you have an Ethernet LAN with five workstations and a 10-Mbps hub. In this situation, each workstation is provided with approximately one-fifth (2.0 Mbps) of the available bandwidth. If the LAN grows and the number of workstations is doubled, each workstation is now provided with approximately one-tenth (1.0 Mbps) of the available bandwidth. The Traditional Shared-Access LAN Diagram illustrates this type of setup.

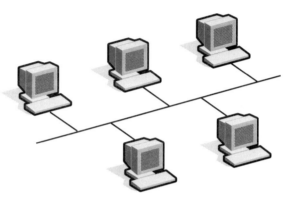

Traditional Shared-Access LAN

An ATM network is designed in a star-wired topology that provides a dedicated access line to connect each network node to a separate port of an ATM switch. This offers several improvements over traditional shared-access technologies:

- The star topology allows each ATM switch to support a wide range of access speeds, because the speed of each switch interface can be tailored to meet the needs of its attached network node. This allows low-speed users to share the same switch with bandwidth-intensive applications. The star topology can provide expensive, high-capacity links to connect high-performance routers and servers, while offering less expensive links to connect client workstations.

- The more sophisticated ATM switches use a new form of parallel or "busless" switching, rather than traditional bus-based architectures. In a bus-based switch, all cells pass across a shared internal bus from the switch's input interface to the output interface. This requires that all cells pass through a single point that has a fixed amount of bandwidth. In a parallel (busless) switch, multiple switching elements simultaneously switch traffic across a switching fabric between the input and output ports. As a result, each cell can pass through an ATM switch without contention in the same amount of time. The ATM's Parallel Point-to-Point Access Diagram presents parallel switching.

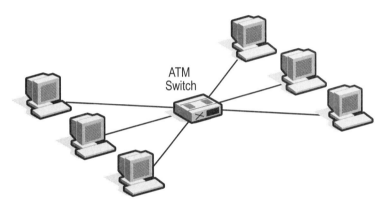

ATM's Parallel Point-to-Point Access

ATM's use of a parallel architecture helps reduce contention for scarce network resources. Network nodes do not have to compete with other network nodes for access to the switch, because each device has a dedicated access line. In addition, traffic within the switch does not have to compete with other traffic for access to the internal bus, because the switch is based on a busless architecture. This parallel architecture effectively multiplies the available network bandwidth, instead of dividing it among all nodes.

Connection-Oriented Mode

Traditional PTM technologies operate in a connectionless mode. In a connectionless network (sometimes called a datagram service), a predefined end-to-end connection between the source and destination nodes is not required for data transmission. As a result, data packets flow across the network along the best available path, rather than over a predefined path. Packets in the same transmission often travel over multiple parallel paths.

ATM operates in a connection-oriented mode. A pair of source and destination nodes establishes a virtual connection before the source begins transmitting data. All cells transmitted between a pair of source and destination nodes follow the same virtual connection or virtual path (VP) (through a network of ATM switches) during the transmission. A later transmission between the same source and destination may follow a different VP, but the path will not change for the duration of the transmission. The Virtual Connections Diagram illustrates this type of connection.

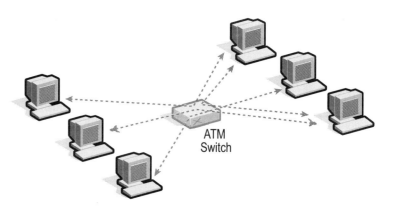

ATM
Switch

Virtual Connections

Connection-oriented networks trade greater complexity required in end nodes to support signaling and connection setup, for much greater simplicity in intermediate (switching) nodes. A connection-oriented network has several advantages over a connectionless network when attempting to support real-time, high-speed applications:

- A connection-oriented network allows the network to guarantee a minimal level of service. If the network does not have sufficient resources to accept a connection request, the network simply refuses to establish the connection. This guarantees that the network will have sufficient resources to support all active connections and queue (buffer) overflows will not occur.

- A virtual connection between users means switching delay is virtually eliminated because signals travel over the same logical path for the duration of the connection. This is important because both voice and video applications are extremely sensitive to variations in transmission delay.

- The devices at each end of a virtual circuit may operate at different speeds because an end-to-end physical connection is not established. This allows data to be transmitted at one speed by the source node while it is received at a different speed by the destination node.

- The utilization of the connection is relatively high while the connection is established. When there is no more data to be transmitted, the connection is terminated and the previously allocated network resources may now be used by another connection.

Fixed-Length Data Cells

ATM formats data into fixed-size units called cells. Each cell contains 53 bytes that are divided into a 48-byte payload (data) field and a 5-byte header. The fixed length makes it simpler and faster for an ATM switch to process cells. ATM's cell-switching approach also makes efficient use of network bandwidth for bursty data transfers, by allocating cells to applications only as needed. The ATM Cell Diagram illustrates the basic format of an ATM cell.

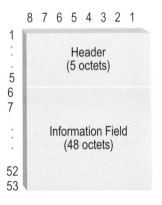

ATM Cell

The major function of the 5-byte ATM header is to identify the virtual connection to which the cell belongs. The use of a small information field reduces the number of internal buffers a switch must support, while reducing the queuing delay for the switch's buffers. This allows an ATM switch to process cells very quickly, which reduces latency and increases throughput.

Elimination of Link-by-Link Error Correction and Flow Control

ATM does not support error correction or flow control on a link-by-link basis. The traditional functions of packet headers, such as sequence numbers for error correction and flow control, and discard eligible bit, are eliminated. This means an ATM switch can process a cell very quickly, eliminating queuing delays while increasing switch throughput.

If a physical link introduces a bit error, or is temporarily overloaded, resulting in the loss of a cell, an ATM network does not request retransmission of lost or corrupted cells from the node at the other end of the physical link. This concept is presented on the Elimination of Link-by-Link Error Correction and Flow Control Diagram.

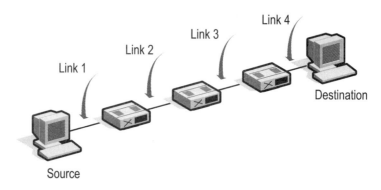

Elimination of Link-by-Link Error Correction and Flow Control

There are two reasons why it is unnecessary for an ATM network to support error correction or flow control:

- The introduction of fiber-based digital transmission facilities has created a relatively error-free transmission environment. In the 1970s, transmission facilities typically had bit error rates of 10^{-4} (one error for every 10,000 bits). Today's fiber optic digital transmission facilities have bit error rates less than 10^{-6} (less than one error for every 1,000,000 bits). Fewer transmission errors means less need for the network to perform error correction.

- Over the years there has been a tremendous increase in the amount of computing power available to user workstations. Today, workstations run higher level protocols such as Transmission Control Protocol (TCP)/Internet Protocol (IP) that perform error correction and retransmission procedures traditionally performed by the transmission network. Because an ATM network can concentrate on just switching cells and not worry about error correction, the cell throughput at each switching node is significantly increased.

Activities

1. ATM is a subset of the B-ISDN standard. True or False

2. Both PTM and ATM are connection-oriented. True or False

3. An ATM network is not designed to support error correction. True or False

4. Briefly describe the basics of ATM in terms of what it was designed to do.

   _____

   _____

   _____

   _____

5. List the three transfer modes that compose switching technologies.

   _____

   _____

   _____

6. Contrast ATM with STM.

   _____

   _____

   _____

   _____

7. Why is it difficult to send voice and video over a PTM network?

   _____

   _____

   _____

   _____

8. List at least three differences between ATM and other net-working technologies.

_____

_____

_____

9. Describe what is meant by a virtual connection.

_____

_____

_____

10. List one advantage of using fixed-length cells.

_____

_____

Extended Activity

Using your favorite Internet search engine, locate information on B-ISDN standards. Summarize some of the characteristics and services offered.

_____

_____

_____

_____

_____

_____

_____

Lesson 2—The Need for ATM

Today's networks carry levels of traffic that no one could have anticipated 10 years ago. As a result, network administrators are discovering that many time-honored principles of network design cannot provide the bandwidth and performance demanded by sophisticated applications and multimedia systems.

Many network professionals and vendors are embracing ATM technology because it offers both high throughput for data transfers, and predictable performance for real-time applications.

Objectives

At the end of this lesson you will be able to:

- Discuss the factors driving the growth of ATM
- Compare and contrast the benefits and limitations of ATM

Key Point

As a method of increasing bandwidth, ATM is superior to traditional solutions such as network segmentation.

Factors Driving the Growth of ATM

The demand for bandwidth is rising dramatically, particularly among workgroup users in distributed environments. Although this demand may currently be restricted to just a few users or workgroups, it will almost certainly spread in the future. There are several reasons for this projected growth:

- Continuing growth in the overall number of network nodes
- Increasing power, memory, and storage capacity of desktop platforms
- Increasing popularity of graphical user interfaces (GUIs)
- Development of bandwidth-intensive network applications such as graphics, imaging, and multimedia
- Distributed, shared-database applications running on new client-server technology rather than traditional host-based systems

- Increasing need to provide high-speed access to large volumes of data for anyone in any location in an organization

- Popularity and increasing use of the Internet

Within the next few years, the current generation of shared-access LAN technologies, such as Ethernet, Token Ring, and FDDI, will not be able to provide the bandwidth required to support these growing challenges. This is because on a shared-access LAN, only one station can transmit data at a time. As a result, the transmission rate of the LAN technology limits the capacity of the LAN. This limitation can cause two potential problems:

- As more users are added to a shared-access LAN, the bandwidth available to each user is reduced. Each user gets a smaller slice of a fixed-sized pie.

- As bandwidth demands of desktop applications increase, the bandwidth available to each user on a shared-access LAN is reduced, because each station requires more. Each user demands a larger slice of a fixed-sized pie.

What happens when there is no longer enough pie to meet each user's demands? The network will collapse.

Segmentation—A Solution for Today's Problems?

As bandwidth requirements and the number of users grow, network managers have two possible solutions: install a LAN technology that supports a higher data rate, or divide the existing LAN into smaller segments. Because the cost of installing a new technology is high, segmentation is the most common and cost-effective solution. If the number of users on each LAN segment is reduced, the amount of bandwidth available to each user increases because fewer users must compete for the same bandwidth. Network designers currently use four strategies or combination of strategies to segment their networks:

- Conventional switching hubs

- Port-switching hubs

- Distributed backbones

- Collapsed backbones

Conventional Switching Hubs

Conventional switching hubs implement high-speed frame switching to deliver significant improvements within installed Ethernet and FDDI LANs. A conventional switching hub is a chassis equipped with multiple high-speed backplanes. Each backplane accepts multiple port modules, each of which typically connects 8 to 12 nodes. The chassis also accepts other modules such as power supplies, internal bridges, and network management units.

The Conventional Switching Hub Architecture Diagram illustrates the architecture of a conventional switching hub. In this architecture, subsegments are first formed by attaching groups of nodes to individual port modules (cards). On the diagram, each of the five port modules forms a subsegment that contains eight user ports. The subsegments (port modules) are then combined to create complete segments by connecting each port card to one of the hub's backplanes. All port modules attached to the same backplane become members of the same physical segment or collision domain.

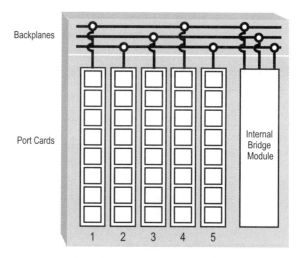

Conventional Switching Hub Architecture

On this diagram, nodes attached to Port Cards 1 and 4 are members of the same physical segment. Similarly, nodes attached to Port Cards 2 and 5 are members of the same segment, and nodes attached to Port Card 3 are members of the same segment.

An internal bridge module provides communication between segments. A dedicated external bridge/router may also be used to provide connectivity between backplane segments. The key benefit of a conventional switching hub is that it is simple to assign nodes to several different segments by connecting each one to a particular port card.

Port-Switching Hubs

Port-switching hubs provide all the benefits of conventional switching hubs in addition to allowing the creation of virtual LANs (VLANs). VLANs permit nodes to be members of the same logical segment regardless of their physical port connection. The LAN segments reside on the backplanes of the hub, rather than port modules, which makes it possible for a VLAN to span multiple port modules.

The Port-Switching Hub Architecture Diagram illustrates the architecture of a port-switching hub. In a port-switching hub, segmentation is performed by assigning each user port, rather than all users attached to a port card, to one of the hub's backplanes. On the diagram, each of the five port cards contains eight user ports. Each user port contains a number that indicates the backplane to which the port is assigned. Communication between nodes assigned to different segments (backplanes) is provided by an internal bridge module. An external bridge/router may also be used to provide connectivity between backplane segments.

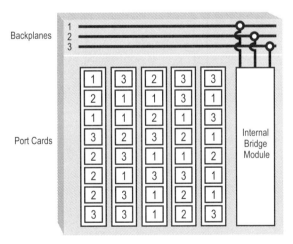

Port-Switching Hub Architecture

To reassign a node from one VLAN to another, the network manager does not have to manually disconnect a user's workstation from one port and reconnect it to another port. Port-switching hubs allow a manager to reconfigure segments and relocate users through software on a central management console.

Distributed Backbones

One common architecture used to construct building and campus backbones is based on a distributed routing approach. In a typical distributed backbone, LAN segments on each floor are connected to a hub through routers, as shown on the Distributed Backbone Architecture Diagram. Similar to the solutions above, the members of each LAN segment compete for bandwidth with each other.

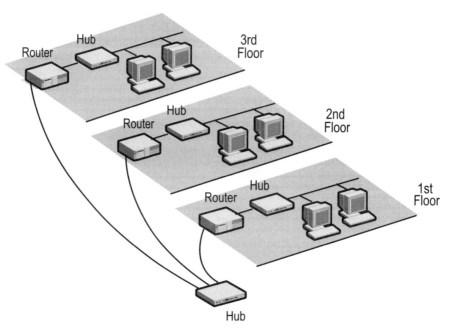

Distributed Backbone Architecture

FDDI is sometimes used to create building and campus backbones because of its 100-Mbps capacity. As illustrated on the FDDI Distributed Backbone Architecture Diagram, routers attached to the FDDI ring provide connectivity to department LANs linked to hubs.

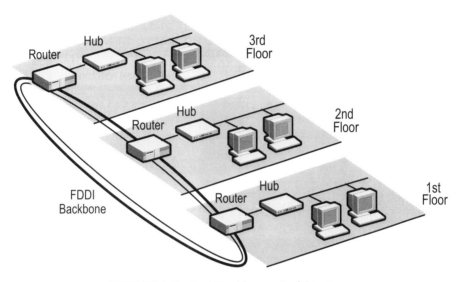

FDDI Distributed Backbone Architecture

A distributed backbone provides the required connectivity; however, there are two important disadvantages to using a distributed backbone architecture:

- The bandwidth provided by a shared-media backbone is restricted to the data rate of the technology running on it. In most cases, this is Fast Ethernet or FDDI. The use of a shared-access technology can result in reduced performance as the demand for backbone bandwidth increases.

- The distribution of routing equipment throughout the building is costly and complicates management by decentralizing it.

For these reasons, many administrators are replacing distributed backbones with collapsed backbones.

Collapsed Backbones

A collapsed backbone eliminates the router on each floor, and concentrates all connections in a single device. In a collapsed backbone, each floor-level hub is connected, using a dedicated line, to a single multiport router or switch. As illustrated on the Collapsed Backbone Architecture Diagram, this architecture effectively "collapses" the distributed backbone onto the high-speed backplane of the central router or switch. The central device's backplane functions as the network's backbone. The backplane can move data much faster than the shared-access technology of a distributed backbone.

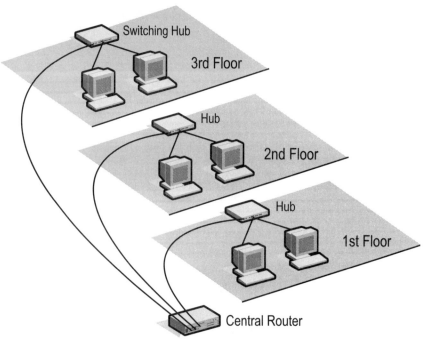

Collapsed Backbone Architecture

As the demand for bandwidth grows, having all resources on one floor share a single LAN can quickly lead to a performance bottleneck. The answer to this problem is to further segment each floor LAN into multiple LANs. In this way, the network manager can leverage the collapsed backbone architecture by extending the segmentation provided by the building backbone down to the floor level. The Collapsed Backbone with Multiple LANs on the Third Floor Diagram presents such a configuration, with three LAN segments deployed on the third floor.

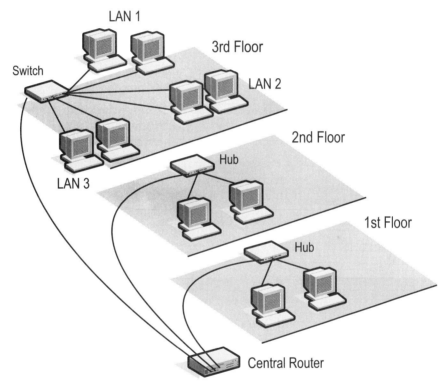

Collapsed Backbone with Multiple LANs on the Third Floor

A collapsed backbone gives network managers the connectivity of a distributed backbone, plus the following additional benefits:

- Lower equipment costs because only a single router port is needed for each floor instead of an entire router

- Higher performance because the router's backplane is much faster than a shared-media backbone

- Easier network management because all configuration, trouble-shooting, and upgrading is accomplished at one central location

- Simpler connections and hardware management using a single connection point for all network media

- Improved ability to expand the building connectivity system in the future (scalability)

However, there are still some disadvantages to a collapsed backbone architecture:

- A collapsed backbone supports only a single type of traffic (data traffic), because the router introduces transmission delays that degrade the performance of voice, video, or multimedia.

- The backplane of the router (or switch) is still a shared-access technology that provides a fixed amount of bandwidth. This means a collapsed backbone has limited scalability.

Segmentation— Only a Short-Term Solution

In the near future, the current solution of segmentation and microsegmentation will continue to support existing LAN technologies for two important reasons:

- Segmentation immediately improves performance because the fixed amount of network bandwidth is shared by fewer users.

- Segmentation does not require changes to end-user's software or hardware.

Unfortunately, in the long term, segmentation is not a complete solution to the bandwidth problem. Today's shared-access technologies are simply running out of bandwidth because users are demanding support for an increasing number of complex applications.

To illustrate this bandwidth crunch, in the late 1980s an Ethernet LAN was considered adequate to support 200 to 300 workstations. Today, that number has dropped to less than 30 workstations. In certain cases, network managers are placing as few as three or four workstations on a single Ethernet segment. If this trend continues, each workstation will eventually require a private LAN segment to provide sufficient bandwidth to satisfy its networking demands. The cost to support this type of network architecture would be prohibitive.

There are several other reasons why segmentation and microsegmentation can provide only a short-term solution:

- Segmentation is successful only if frequently communicating nodes share the same network segment. Unfortunately, this is not always possible on large corporate networks, because employees' locations have very little to do with their projects or coworkers. Segmentation can actually make performance and congestion worse if traffic must leave the local segment. If a client accesses a server on another segment, the transmission consumes bandwidth on the client's segment, the remote server segment, and any intervening segments. In addition, each device that processes the traffic, such as a router, adds processing time that may cause sluggish response times and application time-outs.

- Segmentation can be very expensive due to the number of routers or switches required to segment the network. This expense increases dramatically as the number of LAN segments increases.

- The costs of managing a large router-based network can be very high. Every time an existing LAN is segmented, the Network Layer address of each device on the new segment must be changed.

- Collapsed backbones offer a limited solution because the router or switch backbone provides only a fixed amount of bandwidth. As the number of LANs and amount of traffic increases, the backbone of the router or switch may not be able to provide enough bandwidth to support all of its attached LANs. The collapsed backbone cannot scale infinitely in a cost-effective manner.

- Software-based switching is not as fast as hardware-based switching. Routers use software-based switching, which introduces some delay as a packet passes through a router. As the number of routers increases, so does processing delay.

- Emerging technologies, such as Fast and Gigabit Ethernet, can increase the capacity of a LAN; however, each workstation must be equipped with a new network interface card (NIC).

- There is no guarantee that, once segmented, a LAN will not have to be segmented again.

ATM—A Scalable Solution for the Future

As we have seen, ATM is not a shared-access technology. As a result, ATM does not face the same challenges and limitations as Ethernet, Token Ring, and FDDI. This section presents the benefits and limitations of ATM.

Benefits of ATM

In many ways, ATM is perfectly suited to meet the challenges data networks will face:

- ATM provides a high-bandwidth transport service for bursty applications. ATM over SONET and SDH allows ATM to be deployed at data rates of 622 Mbps, 1.2 Gbps, 2.4 Gbps, and higher.

- The connection-oriented nature of ATM provides the benefits of circuit switching's minimal delays for voice and video applications. An ATM network guarantees delay-sensitive applications the bandwidth needed to provide an adequate quality of service (QoS).

- The connection-oriented operation of ATM provides inherent security to protect user data.

- ATM's parallel point-to-point access design allows each ATM switch to support a wide range of access speeds. This means the speed of each switch interface can be tailored to meet the needs of its attached network node.

- ATM's parallel point-to-point access design eliminates contention among end nodes for access to the ATM switch. Each node is provided with a dedicated point-to-point link to the ATM network.

- The use of fixed-length cells permits extremely fast switch processing that can be performed in silicon. This eliminates queuing delays, increases switch throughput, and reduces overall network delay.

- The development of scalable ATM switch architectures means the capacity of a typical ATM switch expands as new interfaces are added. Unlike a traditional collapsed backbone architecture, with fixed bandwidth, the capacity of an ATM switch can scale up as more bandwidth is needed.

- ATM allows the creation of a single integrated network that supports all communication services. ATM is designed to provide a satisfactory QoS to support audio, video, data, fax, still images, and multimedia applications on the same network. It appears ATM will be able to handle all perceived communications needs, both present and future, across a single integrated network.

- ATM is the first technology that can be deployed in LAN, MAN, and WAN environments. When public ATM services are available, an ATM LAN switch could, in theory, seamlessly connect to a WAN. ATM has the potential to blur the boundaries between LANs, MANs, and WANs.

- ATM can be selectively deployed in the parts of a network that can most benefit from ATM's advantages (such as backbones). This allows managers to implement ATM in comfortable steps that provide significant benefits at minimal cost.

- ATM is being used across the computing and communications environment in a wide variety of products that include telephony, internetworking, and computing applications. Eventually, each of these separate switching fabrics may be integrated into a single fabric that provides universal connectivity for all applications.

- ATM is based on internationally accepted standards. Although some standards are still being developed, the ATM Forum is playing a key role in getting vendors to implement certain standards that will enable users to build ATM networks. The standards-based approach to ATM should result in a variety of interoperable devices and imaginative applications from many vendors. This competition translates into lower costs for users.

- Virtually every vendor and telecommunications carrier supports ATM, and is anxious to get ATM-based products to market.

Limitations of ATM

Despite ATM's many advantages, there are still some drawbacks at this stage in ATM's development:

- The complete set of ATM standards is still under development. However, the key standards that permit the deployment of private building and campus backbone networks have been approved.

235

- There is a lack of real-world experience with ATM in large data networks. Computer modeling has been performed; however, ATM has not been deployed on the same scale as Ethernet, Token Ring, FDDI, X.25, or frame relay.

- ATM requires new hardware before it can be deployed. ATM switches must be purchased, and ATM interfaces are required for workstations and routers directly connected to the ATM switch.

- ATM does not support wireless communication.

Activities

1. List five factors driving the growth and adoption of ATM technology and provide an example of each.

    _____

    _____

    _____

    _____

    _____

    _____

    _____

    _____

    _____

    _____

2. What are the four current segmentation strategies network managers are using to solve their bandwidth problems?

    _____

    _____

    _____

    _____

3. Describe three potential drawbacks of relying on segmentation to address bandwidth issues.

    _____

    _____

    _____

    _____

    _____

    _____

4. List some benefits and limitations of ATM.

_____

_____

_____

_____

Extended Activity

1. Break into focus groups of no more than three to five people, depending on class size. Each person in the group will then choose one of the following items to informally present/ describe to the other group members:

   a. Distributed versus collapsed backbone architecture

   b. Growth factors driving ATM

   c. Segmentation strategies

   d. ATM benefits

Lesson 3—ATM Architecture

ATM corresponds to the Data Link and Physical Layers of the Open Systems Interconnection (OSI) reference model. However, the ATM architecture includes its own set of protocols, which create a separate layered ATM reference model.

This lesson presents the layers of the ATM reference model and describes how ATM protocols work together to provide data transfer service tailored to the needs of different applications.

Objectives

At the end of this lesson you will be able to:

- Describe the standard interfaces to an ATM network

- Explain the limitations of network segmentation as a method of increasing bandwidth

- Diagram the ATM protocol stack, and show how it relates to the OSI reference model

- Discuss the basic operation of an ATM network

- List the ATM Physical Layer standards

- Describe the operation and features of the ATM layer

Key Point

Although ATM standards are incomplete, enough vendors agree on the key specifications to make ATM a practical technology.

ATM Standards Groups

There are three major organizations responsible for developing the standards that define ATM:

- ITU-TSS

- ATM Forum

- Internet Engineering Task Force (IETF)

ITU-TSS, formerly Consultative Committee for International Telephony and Telegraphy (CCITT), developed the original standards that define the fundamental ATM protocols and interfaces. These specifications include ATM cell size, cell structure, User-Network Interface (UNI), Physical Layer protocols, and data rates.

The ATM Forum is an industry consortium composed of vendors and carriers. It was founded in late 1991 because its members became frustrated by the slow rate of specification by ITU-TSS. The primary goal of the ATM Forum is to develop a subset of ITU-TSS standards that its members agree to implement and support. The ATM Forum hopes to develop its specifications more rapidly than ITU-TSS, and thus facilitate multivendor interoperability and deployment of ATM into production networks. The ATM Forum bases its work on existing ITU-TSS specifications and drafts; however, it does not wait for completion of the ITU-TSS standards process before releasing its own specifications.

IETF is responsible for solving short-term and medium-term engineering problems on the Internet. The Internet is a large international network composed of universities, government facilities, research institutions, and some private corporations. The primary goal of the IETF "IP-over-ATM" Working Group has been to develop standards that support transmission of IP and the Address Resolution Protocol (ARP) over ATM.

ATM Network Interfaces

The ATM standards defined by these groups specify two types of interfaces for ATM networks:

- User-Network Interface (UNI)

- Network-to-Network Interface (NNI)

The ATM UNI and NNI Diagram illustrates the differences between these two types of interfaces.

UNI

UNI defines the interface between a user and a network. A private UNI defines the interface between an ATM user device and a private ATM switch. A public UNI defines the interface between an ATM user device or a private ATM switch, and an ATM switch deployed in a public service provider's network.

NNI

NNI defines a switch-to-switch interface. NNI is known as an Inter-Switching System Interface (ISSI). A private ISSI defines an interface between private ATM switches. A public ISSI defines an interface between public switches. It is important to note that NNI does not include the interface between a private switch and a public switch. This interface is considered part of a public UNI.

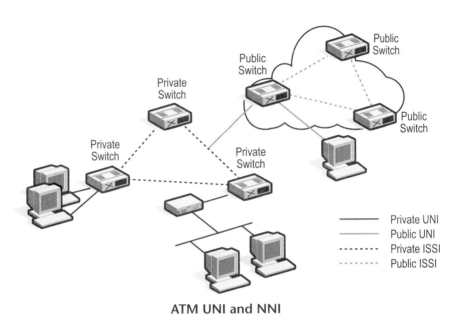

ATM UNI and NNI

How an ATM Network Operates

An ATM network provides a connection-oriented transport service. This means one ATM device must establish a connection with another ATM device before it can transmit information.

All ATM connections are virtual in the sense that bandwidth is not permanently assigned to the connection. Rather, the network agrees to provide the required bandwidth when the user has cells to transmit. These virtual connections, or virtual circuits, may be established as permanent virtual circuits (PVCs), or on demand as switched virtual circuits (SVCs) using a signaling protocol.

Different types of applications require different levels of service from a network. For example, voice and video applications are very sensitive to delay and variations in delay, but they are insensitive to minimal cell loss. On the other hand, data applications are insensitive to delay or variations in delay, but they are extremely sensitive to cell loss.

To meet the specific service requirements of each application, the node requests a connection with particular characteristics (we will discuss these in detail later). Some of the information in a connection request includes:

- Called party number
- Average bandwidth requirements
- Peak bandwidth requirements
- Maximum acceptable percentage of cell loss
- Maximum acceptable variation in network delay

The Virtual Circuits and ATM Network Diagram illustrates virtual circuit connections.

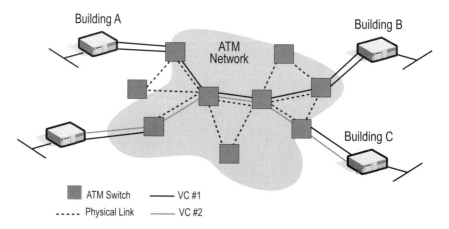

Virtual Circuits and ATM Network

The network uses the connection request to select the individual physical links to support the virtual circuit across the network. For example, when selecting a specific physical link, the network ensures it can support all virtual circuits assigned to the physical link and still maintain the service requirements for each individual virtual circuit. When the network and user agree on the characteristics of the connection, the network establishes the virtual circuit across the network. If the network cannot support the desired class of service for a connection request, it is required to reject the connection request.

After the connection is established, the nodes at each end of the connection exchange information by transmitting cells across the UNI. The cells are relayed from switch to switch until they eventually arrive at the UNI of the destination node.

VCs and VPs

All cells that form a single transmission from a source to a destination are referred to as a virtual channel (VC). A VC is a stream of ATM cells flowing between two or more endpoints. The endpoints of a VC may be a user-to-user connection, user-to-network connection, or network-to-network connection. The point at which an ATM cell is passed to or from a higher layer is considered the endpoint of a VC.

When two or more VCs are traveling from the same source to the same destination, ATM groups them into one virtual path (VP). The VCs and VPs Diagram illustrates the relationship between VCs and VPs.

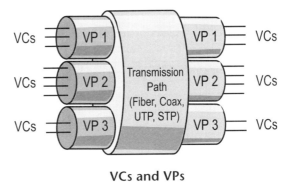

VCs and VPs

A VC is not required to be part of a VP; if only one VC needs to travel between a particular pair of ATM switches, the switches will negotiate a virtual circuit for the one VC.

In this regard, ATM is like travel. Each data cell of each VC is like a single car in a convoy that shares the same purpose, origin, and destination. Each VP is like a stretch of road that transports many unrelated convoys that happen to be sharing the same path.

Individual ATM cells do not need to include any addressing information to help them move from one ATM switch to another; the switches themselves keep track of that by maintaining each virtual circuit connection. However, because ATM can multiplex data among many different sources and destinations, ATM switches need a way to distinguish one VC from another. To do that, each ATM cell header includes two fields:

- VC identifier (VCI) uniquely identifies one VC. Each VC is one data transmission from a source node to a destination node.

- VP identifier (VPI) identifies a group of VCs moving from the same source to the same destination.

ATM Network Architecture

ATM has been selected as the transport technology for B-ISDN. In this context, transport refers to the use of ATM switching and multiplexing techniques at the Data Link Layer of the OSI reference model to convey traffic between two devices on a network. The OSI Reference Model and ATM Diagram illustrates the relationship.

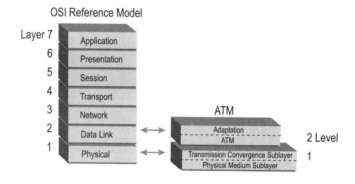

OSI Reference Model and ATM

ATM networking requires more than just implementation of the ATM protocol. The ATM protocol operates over a Physical Layer and requires protocols immediately above the ATM layer to adapt various services to ATM. In addition, higher layer protocols that provide network management and signaling for switched virtual connections are also required. These additional ATM-specific protocols create an ATM protocol reference model.

ATM Protocol Reference Model

The ATM protocol reference model is similar to the OSI reference model in that communications from higher layers occur through three layers:

- ATM Adaptation Layer (AAL) contains two sublayers:
  - Convergence sublayer (CS)
  - Segmentation and reassembly (SAR) sublayer
- ATM Layer
- Physical Layer contains two sublayers:
  - Physical medium (PM) dependent sublayer
  - Transmission convergence (TC) sublayer

In addition to the three main protocol layers, the reference model also contains three planes:

- The user plane (U-plane) allows the transmission of user information. It contains the Physical Layer, ATM layer, and multiple AALs for different service users.

- The control plane (C-plane) is responsible for call control and connection control functions. It shares the Physical Layer and ATM layer with the U-plane, as well as AALs and higher layer signaling protocols.

- The management plane (M-plane) includes layer management and plane management. Layer management is responsible for functions related to the management of each layer of the ATM reference model. Plane management is responsible for the coordination of management between planes and management of the whole system.

The ATM Protocol Reference Model Diagram illustrates this type of model.

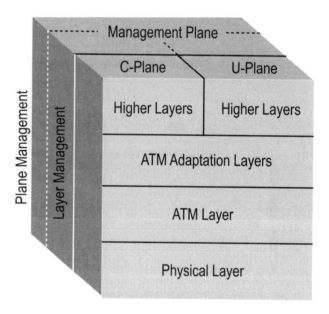

ATM Protocol Reference Model

The following sections describe the layers of the ATM reference model, beginning with the Physical Layer and moving up to the higher layers.

Physical Layer

The Physical Layer defines how cells are transported over a network. This includes physical interfaces, media, and information rates. The Physical Layer also defines how cells are converted to a line signal depending on the media type.

ATM is media-independent in that it is not tied to any particular transmission medium. No new, ATM-specific Physical Layers have been defined. Rather, existing Physical Layers are proposed for ATM. The ATM Forum UNI Specification provides specifications for Physical Layer interfaces for both the public and private UNIs, as illustrated on the Public and Private ATM UNIs Diagram.

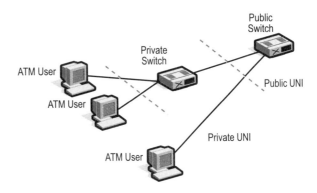

Public and Private ATM UNIs

Public and Private UNI

A public UNI defines the interface between a user device (workstation, hub, bridge, router, or private ATM switch) and an ATM switch deployed in a public service provider's network. A private UNI defines the interface between a user device and a private ATM switch.

The ATM Forum UNI includes support for the following Physical Layer protocols at the UNI:

- 44.736 Mbps (Unchannelized Digital Signal [DS]3, Public UNI)

- 100 Mbps (FDDI Multimode Fiber Interface—4B/5B Encoding, Private UNI)

- 155.52 Mbps (SONET STS-3c, Public and Private UNI)

- 155.52 Mbps (Multimode Fiber Interface, Private UNI)

- 155.52 Mbps (Shielded Twisted Pair [STP]—8B/10B encoding, Private UNI)

In the near future, additional Physical Layer specifications over twisted pair wire are needed because potential users are demanding support for ATM over their installed cable plants. To meet this demand, the ATM Forum has begun work for interfaces over Category 3 unshielded twisted pair (UTP) (at the Synchronous Transfer Signal [STS]-1 rate of 51 Mbps) and Category 5 UTP (at the STS-3 rate of 155 Mbps). It is expected the Category 3 UTP specification will scale to lower speeds to support fractional STS-1 (STS-.5, STS-.25, and others). When these standards are completed, it is expected that ATM's acceptance as a desktop connection technology will accelerate because existing cabling plants can be used and the cost for each connection will decrease.

Physical Layer Sublayers

The ATM Physical Layer protocols are divided into two sublayers:

- PM-dependent sublayer supports functions that are specific to the transmission medium selected

- TC sublayer supports functions that are independent of the characteristics of the transmission medium

Some of the functions performed by the TC and PM sublayers are shown on the ATM Physical Layer Functions Diagram.

TC	Generation/verification of header checksum (HEC) Creating cell boundaries within the physical payload Adapting cells to fit within the transmission system Transmission frame generation/recovery
PM	Bit timing and line coding Physical Medium

ATM Physical Layer Functions

ATM Over a Synchronous Transmission System

The Physical Layer protocols that transport ATM cells must be synchronous (clock-controlled) to provide efficiency at high data rates. ATM cells are transmitted one after the other in a regular stream, separated by a constant time interval.

The ATM Over a Synchronous Transmission System Diagram illustrates how ATM's "asynchronous" cells are transmitted over a full-duplex synchronous transmission system. The synchronous Physical Layer protocol guarantees that the time interval between the start of one cell and the start of the next cell is a constant value. However, cells are allocated to users in a random, or asynchronous, sequence. Note that empty cells are inserted in the transmission stream when a node lacks information to transmit. The empty cells are removed by the ATM switch and are not forwarded to other systems or switches.

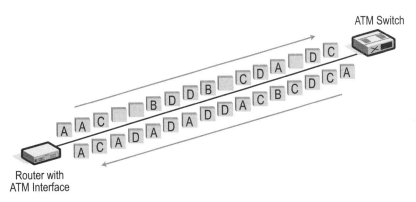

ATM Over a Synchronous Transmission System

ATM Layer

The ATM layer provides a cell relay capability using time-division multiplexing (TDM) techniques. The multiplexed information is organized into fixed-length 53-byte cells. Each cell contains a 5-byte header and a 48-byte payload (information) field.

The bytes in each cell are transmitted in increasing order, starting with byte 1. This means the cell header is transmitted first, followed by the payload field. The bits within each byte are transmitted in decreasing order starting with bit 8 (the most significant bit).

The network preserves the order of cells as they are transmitted from the source node to the destination node. The network does not detect or retransmit lost or corrupted cells (higher protocols, such as TCP, usually provide that service).

The ATM layer provides a simple transport service for many different types of telecommunications services. With the exception of the class of service (CoS) (discussed later) requested for the virtual circuit, the ATM layer is totally unaware of the type of information (voice, video, or data) it is carrying. This means that switching is the only major function an ATM network must perform. Because switching can be performed in hardware, an ATM network can operate at very high speeds.

ATM Cell Header

The primary role of the ATM header is to identify cells belonging to the same virtual circuit within the asynchronous TDM scheme. Although the structure of the ATM cell is the same everywhere within an ATM network, the structure of the cell header varies slightly between a UNI and an NNI.

The ATM Header at the UNI Diagram illustrates the structure of an ATM cell header at the UNI.

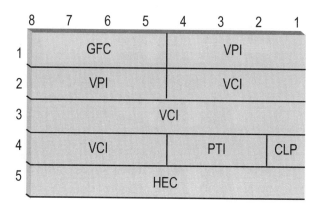

ATM Header at the UNI

The fields in the UNI cell header perform the following functions:

- Generic Flow Control (GFC) (4 bits)—Intended to allow multiple devices to use a single UNI in a shared-media configuration. Because current ATM standards support only a point-to-point configuration, neither the ITU-TSS nor ATM Forum standards define the use of this field. The default value for the GFC field is 0000 as long as these procedures remain undefined.

- Virtual path identifier (VPI) (8 bits)—The VPI identifies the cell's virtual pathway. The VPI field supports a maximum of 256 VPs across the UNI. Each ATM device may change the VPI as the cell traverses the network to its destination.

- Virtual channel identifier (VCI) (16 bits)—The VCI identifies the virtual channel to which the cell belongs. It supports a maximum of 65,536 VCs for each VP across the UNI. The VCI may also change as the cell is switched across the network. The VPI/VCI pairs tell the ATM switch how to switch a cell.

- Payload Type Indicator (PTI) (3 bits)—Indicates whether the payload data is part of the user plane, control plane, or management plane. The PTI field also indicates whether the cell has encountered congestion as it traverses the ATM network.

- Cell Loss Priority (CLP) (1 bit)—This bit is set to 1 to indicate a cell with a low priority. The default is 0 to indicate a regular-priority cell. The CLP bit may be set by either the user's AAL or the service provider. In the event of network congestion, an ATM switch discards low priority cells (CLP = 1) before discarding cells with a regular priority (CLP = 0). The CLP function is important because it allows certain types of traffic to take priority in a congested network.

It is important to note that this bit distinguishes between low and regular priority cells within a single VC. Whenever cells are discarded, the agreed-upon CoS for the VC is not violated.

- Header Error Control (HEC) (8 bits)—Provides a cyclic redundancy check (CRC) to detect errors in the cell header. Its main function is to validate the VPI and VCI fields to protect against the delivery of cells to the wrong UNI. Although this field is transmitted as part of the cell header, it is computed and used by the Physical Layer, not the ATM layer.

The ATM Header at the NNI Diagram displays the structure of an ATM cell header at the NNI.

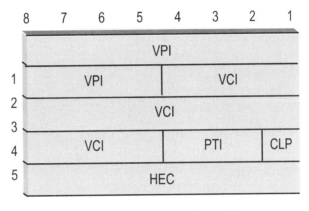

ATM Header at the NNI

The only difference between the NNI header and UNI header is in the first byte. The functions performed by the fields in the NNI header are identical to those performed by corresponding fields in the UNI header.

The NNI header eliminates the 4 bits reserved for the GFC field, thus extending the VPI field to 12 bits. Increasing the VPI from 8 to 12 bits allows the NNI to support a maximum of 4,096 VPs rather than just the 256 VPs supported at the UNI. Each VP supports a maximum of 65,536 VCs. Recall that VPs aggregate VCs to allow the trunking of VCs across transmission facilities between ATM devices.

AAL

AAL provides user-oriented functions that allow the ATM layer to transport different types of higher layer protocols and services. In other words, AAL adapts the pure transport function of the ATM layer to meet the requirements of different service users.

CoS

Voice, video, and data applications place different demands, or service requirements, on a transport service. For example, a voice application requires a constant bit-rate service to maintain a timing relationship between the source and destination; however, a voice message can remain clear despite lost cells. On the other hand, timing is not important to a data-transfer application, but it is vital that every cell arrive intact.

The ATM layer supports four distinct CoSs. Each CoS, or QoS, is defined according to three binary parameters:

- Timing between the source and destination station (required or not required)

- Bit rate (constant or variable)

- Connection mode (connection-oriented or connectionless)

The Service Classifications for AAL Table lists the four classes of service, Class A through Class D. Although eight possible combinations of these three parameters exist, only four classes of service are defined, because they are the only ones that make sense in a production network environment.

Service Classifications for AAL

Class A	Class B	Class C	Class D
Timing required	Timing required	Timing not required	Timing not required
Constant bit rate	Variable bit rate	Variable bit rate	Variable bit rate
Connection oriented	Connection oriented	Connection oriented	Connectionless

- Class A traffic includes pulse code modulation (PCM) encoded voice, constant bit-rate video, and circuit emulation (transport of a DS1, E1, or DS3 signal).

- Class B traffic includes variable bit-rate voice and video. This service class is designed to take advantage of natural variations in analog speech and video to provide an efficient transport service.

- Class C traffic includes connection-oriented data services, such as X.25, frame relay, and ISDN-D channel signaling.

- Class D traffic includes connectionless data services such as packet data carried by LANs and Switched Multimegabit Data Service (SMDS).

AAL Sublayers

The primary function of AAL is to provide an interface between user data and the ATM network. To perform this task, AAL is further subdivided into two sublayers:

- CS

- SAR sublayer

Unlike the ATM layer, AAL is usually implemented in software and not hardware. The AAL Sublayers Diagram illustrates the concepts of CS and SAR sublayer.

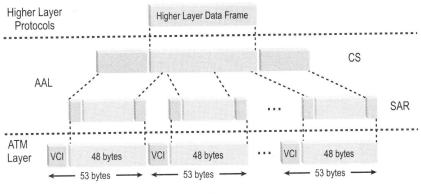

AAL Sublayers

CS is service-dependent. Depending on the supported class of service, CS detects/corrects bit errors, detects/corrects lost or misinserted cells, and maintains the timing relationship between the source and destination stations.

The SAR sublayer performs different functions depending on whether it is transmitting or receiving data. On the transmitting side, the SAR sublayer segments the higher layer protocol data units into 48-byte units for placement in the payload field of ATM cells. On the receiving side, the SAR sublayer reassembles ATM cell payload fields into the higher layer protocol data units.

253

AAL Protocols

AAL provides multiple protocols to meet the needs of different AAL service users. AAL is service-dependent, which means the functions performed by each AAL protocol depend on the specific needs of the service class it is designed to support. In addition, AAL protocols terminate in the user systems and are carried transparently by ATM intermediate systems.

The Two Traffic Types Across ATM Diagram illustrates how ATM can carry two different types of traffic, each one using a different protocol.

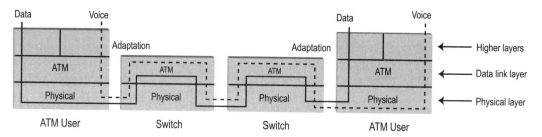

Two Traffic Types Across ATM

To meet the demands of the various service classes, several different AAL protocols have been defined. Each AAL protocol consists of a specific CS and specific SAR sublayer. AALs support error detection and framing for user information; however, they do not provide error-correction or retransmission services. If a user requires these services, they must be provided by higher layer protocols such as TCP or Transport Protocol Class (TP) 4.

Currently, there are four AAL protocols:

- AAL 1—Supports Class A traffic (voice and video), by providing constant bit-rate transmission while maintaining a timing relationship between the source and destination nodes.

- AAL 2—Transmits variable bit-rate voice and video, while maintaining a timing relationship between the source and destination nodes. AAL 2 is designed to support Class B traffic; however, its deployment is on hold pending the commercial availability of variable bit-rate coders/decoders (codecs): devices that convert motion video information into a digital bit stream.

- AAL 3/4—Transmits variable bit-rate data, either connection-oriented or connectionless, without maintaining a timing relationship between the source and destination nodes. This protocol combines two originally separate AAL protocols (3 and 4), to support both Class C and Class D traffic. AAL 3/4 has a high level of compatibility with the protocols that support SMDS. This should facilitate internetworking between SMDS interfaces and ATM interfaces that support SMDS.

- AAL 5—Provides a simple and efficient AAL (SEAL) that supports connection-oriented, variable bit-rate data communications, without maintaining a timing relationship between the source and destination nodes. Although AAL 5 provides less functionality than AAL 3/4, many equipment manufacturers have accepted it because it is easier to implement, provides better error detection, and does not consume any of the cell payload for formatting.

The Service Classes and Supporting AAL Protocols Table presents the relationship between the AAL protocols and the service classes that they are designed to support. Note that both AAL 3/4 and AAL 5 support Class C traffic.

Service Classes and Supporting AAL Protocols

Class A	Class B	Class C	Class D
AAL 1	AAL 2	AAL 3/4	AAL 3/4
		AAL 5	

The first generation of ATM equipment will support both AAL 3/4 and AAL 5, with support for AAL 1 and AAL 2 left for future software revisions. Vendors do not consider early support for AAL 1 and AAL 2 a requirement, because they see data transmission as the key initial application of ATM. Multimedia LAN applications that require transport of voice, video, and data will not appear until most workstations are equipped with native ATM interfaces.

Typical ATM Network in Action

Let us examine how ATM can support high-throughput, real-time connectivity in a typical campus environment. The ATM as a Campus Backbone Diagram presents a campus topology centered on a single ATM backbone switch. High-performance workstations, super servers, and routers with ATM interface adapters are connected to the ATM switch with dedicated access lines.

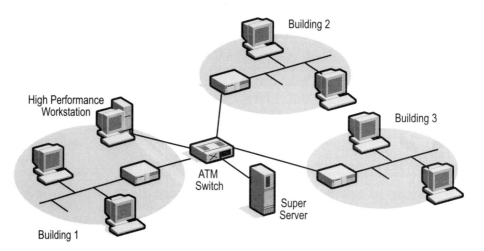

ATM as a Campus Backbone

In this example, we assume that permanent virtual circuits have already been established between each of the devices attached to the ATM switch. The virtual circuits allow each device to communicate with the other devices attached to the ATM switch.

The most popular data communications protocols, such as TCP/IP, NetWare, and AppleTalk, use variable-length packets that are almost always larger than the payload field of a single ATM cell. To exchange data from these protocols, ATM devices must segment the higher layer protocol packets to fit into cell payloads for transmission, and reassemble cell payloads into the original data packets. This process is handled by the SAR sublayer of the AAL, and is illustrated on the SAR Diagram.

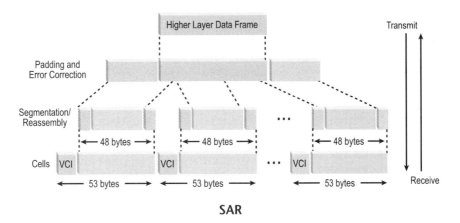

SAR

An ATM node adds overhead to each data packet it wishes to transmit across the network. This overhead pads out the data to an even number of 32-bit words and allows the receiving system to detect errors, such as lost cells.

The resulting block of data is then segmented into smaller units with additional overhead added. This overhead protects against transmission errors and indicates the beginning and end of the segments associated with the original packet.

Each segment, with overhead, is sized to fit within the 48-bit information field of an ATM cell. The appropriate VCI is placed into the cell header, and the cell is transmitted to the ATM switch.

When a cell arrives at the ATM switch, the switching process uses the VCI from the header and the inbound link number to access a switching table. The result of the table lookup is the outbound interface on which the cell should be transmitted to follow a particular PVC.

When a cell arrives at its final destination, the node's SAR sublayer reassembles the collected cells into the original data packet. It passes the packet up the stack, where a higher layer protocol examines it for errors. If an error is detected, that protocol discards the packet and initiates recovery procedures (such as requesting retransmission).

Activities

1. ATM operates at the lowest two layers of the OSI model. True or False

2. The three ATM layers are Adaptation Layer, Virtual Circuit Layer, and Physical Layer. True or False

3. The ATM layer uses TDM. True or False

4. The ATM layer knows whether it is carrying a voice, video, or data payload by examining the PTI. True or False

5. The two standard interfaces to an ATM network are UNI and NNI. Describe each interface.

_____

_____

_____

_____

_____

_____

_____

_____

_____

6. When establishing an SVC on an ATM network, what information may be included in the connection request?

_____

_____

_____

_____

_____

7. What is the difference between a VP and a VC?

   _____

   _____

   _____

   _____

   _____

   _____

   _____

   _____

8. Which ATM layer defines how cells are transported over the network?

   _____

   _____

9. List some Physical Layer protocols found at the UNI.

   _____

   _____

   _____

10. The ATM Physical Layer is divided into two sublayers. What are they?

    _____

    _____

    _____

    _____

    _____

    _____

    _____

    _____

11. Which two fields in the ATM cell header are used to determine how an ATM cell is to be routed?

_____

_____

_____

_____

12. List and contrast the four service classes for AAL in terms of traffic types.

_____

_____

_____

_____

_____

_____

_____

13. List the two sublayers of AAL and describe their function.

_____

_____

_____

_____

_____

_____

_____

_____

14. Describe how an ATM switch acts on an incoming cell.

_____

_____

_____

_____

_____

_____

15. What typically occurs when cells arrive at the final destination?

_____

_____

_____

_____

_____

_____

_____

_____

16. Why has AAL 5 gained a greater acceptance from equipment manufacturers?

_____

_____

_____

_____

17. Draw a diagram of the ATM reference model. Include planes as well as layers.

Extended Activity

1. Go to **http://www.atmforum.com** and search for additional information on topics discussed in this lesson. Like most Web sites, the ATM Forum has a search function you can use to find things such as:

   a. ATM Standards

   b. ATM Interface Specifications

   c. ATM Protocols

   d. The ATM Layer

   e. Any other topics that might be of interest

   Summarize your findings on at least two topics.

   _____

   _____

   _____

   _____

   _____

   _____

   _____

   _____

Lesson 4—LAN Emulation

ATM has the potential to solve LAN bandwidth and performance bottlenecks. However, ATM's connection-oriented architecture is incompatible with the huge installed base of connectionless LAN technology. Therefore, before the benefits of ATM can extend to the office LAN, ATM technology must offer some means of resolving the conflict between transmission styles.

In this lesson, we examine the LAN Emulation (LANE) standard. This approach allows ATM devices to coexist with Ethernet or Token Ring devices, without sacrificing the high performance that makes ATM so desirable.

Objectives

At the end of this lesson you will be able to:

- Describe how VLANs work in a LANE environment

- Briefly describe the LANE specification

- Describe the roles of LANE clients and LANE servers

 **Key Point**

LANE allows connection-oriented ATM to interoperate with existing equipment that supports connectionless LAN protocols.

Bridging the Gap between ATM and LANs

The most attractive option today for desktop connections is a LAN switch with an ATM backbone link. LAN switching boosts desktop bandwidth while protecting investments in both application software and network adapter cards. ATM eliminates bottlenecks in the backbone and provides a "fat pipe" to high-performance servers. LAN switches can be remarkably cost effective, an important benefit as the number of networked desktops continues to grow.

263

But for ATM to be successfully deployed to the desktop, it must provide LAN-like services and be able to interface with existing data communications protocols, applications, equipment, and cabling. However, the LAN protocols and equipment are based on connectionless transmission technology. Therefore, the success of ATM in backbone networks depends on effective LANE that can make a connection-oriented ATM network appear to traditional Network Layer protocols as a connectionless IEEE 802.x LAN.

To meet these goals, the LAN Emulation Technical Committee Working Group of the ATM Forum has finalized the LANE specification. The initial specification defined the procedures to convert Medium Access Control (MAC) addresses to ATM addresses and the strategy to bridge existing protocols across an ATM network.

The ATM Forum's decision to develop LANE using a bridging paradigm presents several important advantages over a routing paradigm:

- A bridging paradigm does not require modifications to the Network Layer protocols and drivers residing in network nodes.

- Bridging technology can be easily implemented in hardware, which makes it less expensive and easier to manage than routing technology, which is software-intensive.

- By supporting a standard interface between a host and its network adapter, such as the Network Driver Interface Specification (NDIS) or Open Data Link Interface (ODI), an ATM adapter appears to the host as if it is communicating over a standard IEEE 802.x shared-media LAN.

The LANE specification defined how an ATM network can emulate a significant portion of an existing IEEE 802.x MAC protocol (Ethernet or Token Ring) so that higher layer protocols (IP, Internetwork Packet Exchange [IPX], and others) can be used without modification. The goal of the LANE specification was to eliminate the need to make any changes in existing higher layer protocols.

LANE Sublayer

An IEEE 802.x LAN provides a connectionless MAC service where each node contends for access to a shared physical transmission medium. Some characteristics common to all 802.x LANs include:

- Connectionless "best effort" delivery service

- 48-bit MAC address

- Flat address space

- Support for unicast transmission using a globally unique MAC address

- Support for multicast transmission using a group address

- Support for broadcast transmission using a well-known broadcast address

- 802.2 Logical Link Control (LLC) interface to the Network Layer

- Support for transparent bridging

In contrast, ATM provides a connection-oriented communication service based on switched point-to-point media. The problem that faced the LANE working group of the ATM Forum was complex: how to make a connection-oriented ATM network appear to traditional Network Layer protocols as a connectionless IEEE 802.x LAN.

To provide a connectionless MAC service on top of ATM, a LANE sublayer is defined to emulate the operation of a connectionless LAN. The LANE sublayer is then placed on top of AAL and emulates the LAN service by making the switched point-to-point ATM network appear to the 802.2 LLC as an IEEE 802.x shared-media LAN. The LANE Sublayer Diagram illustrates this concept.

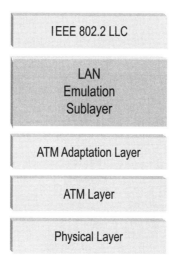

LANE Sublayer

VLANs

In a traditional IEEE 802.x LAN, traffic is transmitted to all stations on the shared physical medium; each station determines which frames it should process and which frames it should ignore. In an ATM network, a LAN segment can be emulated, using the client/server model, by allowing a select group of ATM nodes (clients) to join a LANE service (server). Each LAN is composed of all nodes that have joined the particular LANE service. An end system is configured as a member of a single LANE service, while an intermediate system such as a router belongs to multiple LANE services and provides connectivity between different emulated LANs.

Because membership in an ATM LAN segment is defined by the logical membership to a LANE service, rather than a physical connection to a LAN segment, the term VLAN often describes an ATM LAN segment. A VLAN is a group of workstations logically connected to form subnetworks, as opposed to physically connected.

The concept of VLANs provides increased flexibility in network management. Using software management tools, a network administrator can easily add or reconfigure nodes or segments of a single VLAN, even if the nodes are physically scattered.

The VLANs Using a LANE Service Diagram illustrates an ATM network composed of three separate ATM LAN segments: Segments A, B, and C. Each member of a particular LAN segment is also a member of the same LANE service.

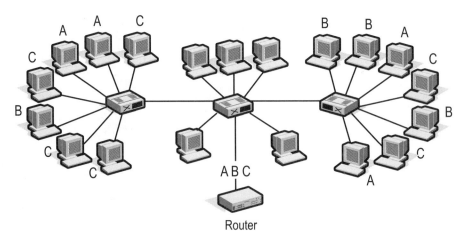

VLANs Using a LANE Service

This diagram illustrates three important concepts:

- Network nodes may be members of the same LANE service (ATM LAN segment) even if they are connected to different switches in the network, as long as the switches are interconnected.

- Traffic destined for end nodes on the same LAN segment is bridged by the LANE service. This means traffic between two native ATM nodes on Segment C is bridged.

- Traffic destined for end nodes on different LAN segments must be routed. This means each LANE service is required to forward traffic between nodes on Segments A and B to the router.

LANE Components

Each VLAN, or emulated LAN, is composed of:

- Multiple LAN Emulation clients (LE clients)

- A LAN Emulation server (LE server) for each emulated LAN

- One LAN Emulation configuration server (LECS) for the entire network

- A single broadcast and unknown server (BUS)

LE Server

A LAN Emulation server (LE server) is responsible for providing the control functions necessary for successful operation of an emulated LAN. The LE server may be implemented in an ATM-attached server, router, or switch, and may be centralized or distributed throughout the network.

An LE server manages LE clients as they attempt to join a VLAN. The LE server also registers and resolves MAC addresses to ATM addresses. When an LE client joins an emulated LAN, it registers its LAN destination with the LE server, mapping its MAC address to its ATM address.

The LE server maintains the MAC-to-ATM address mapping for all LE clients on its emulated LAN. For example, if an LE client needs to transmit unicast data, it generates a LAN Emulation Address Resolution Protocol (LE-ARP) Request to the LE server. The LE-ARP protocol resolves the destination LE client's MAC addresses to an ATM address. The LE server either responds directly to the requesting LE client by transmitting an LE-ARP Response, or forwards the query to other LE clients so they may respond directly to the requesting node. After the LE client receives the LE-ARP

Response, containing the destination ATM address, the LE client establishes a connection to the destination LE client using UNI signaling. Once the ATM connection is established, the LE client begins data transmission.

LECS

An ATM network must have one LAN Emulation configuration server (LECS) that supplies configuration information for the entire ATM network. The LECS keeps track of what LE clients are members of what emulated LANs. Each LE client (ATM node) is configured to know the identity of the LECS. After initialization, each ATM node establishes a connection to the LECS to determine the identity of its emulated LAN. In other words, after startup and initialization, each ATM node "checks in" with the LECS to learn its current VLAN membership.

LE Client

An LE client is a process, residing in an end system, that performs data forwarding, address resolution, and other control functions. Each LE client is identified by a 48-bit MAC address, and provides MAC-level emulation of an IEEE 802.3 (Ethernet) or 802.5 (Token Ring) LAN service to higher layer protocols. Each LE client implements the well-defined, peer-to-peer LANE User-to-Network Interface (LUNI) when communicating with other LE clients that are members of the same emulated LAN.

During the initialization process, each LE client performs the following procedures:

1. Establishes a connection to the LECS
2. Obtains the address of its LE server from the LECS
3. Establishes a connection to the LE server for its emulated LAN
4. Obtains the address of its BUS from the LE server
5. Establishes a connection to the BUS

BUS

The BUS is responsible for forwarding data containing multicast MAC addresses (group, broadcast, and functional addresses) or when the source LE client cannot resolve the MAC address to an ATM address. An LE client forwards all broadcast, multicast, and unresolved MAC/ATM address traffic to the BUS. The BUS emulates the broadcast capability of an 802.x LAN by unicasting the data to each LE client that has established a connection to the BUS. Recall that each LE client establishes a connection to the BUS as it joins the emulated LAN.

Activities

1. LAN protocols such as Ethernet are connectionless, and ATM is connection-oriented. True or False

2. The LANE sublayer makes an ATM network appear like a shared-media LAN. True or False

3. A LANE operates by mapping MAC addresses to/from ATM addresses. True or False

4. List two benefits of using a bridging model over a routing model for LANE.

    _____

    _____

    _____

    _____

    _____

    _____

    _____

    _____

    _____

5. Why is an ATM LAN like a VLAN?

    _____

    _____

    _____

    _____

    _____

6. Describe the function of a LECS.

    _____

    _____

    _____

    _____

    _____

    _____

7. List the functions of an LE client.

_____

_____

_____

_____

_____

_____

_____

_____

_____

_____

_____

8. Where is the LE server implemented?

_____

_____

_____

_____

_____

9. What device emulates the broadcast capability of a standard LAN?

_____

_____

_____

_____

Extended Activity

Using your favorite Internet search engine, find information on the latest LANE standard. What is the current release of the LANE specification? List some of the features the standard supports.

_____

_____

_____

_____

_____

_____

Lesson 5—ATM Devices

Standard LAN devices cannot be used to implement an ATM network, because ATM is a connection-oriented technology. ATM devices must cooperate to establish, maintain, and release virtual circuits, unlike connectionless LAN devices that are only concerned with forwarding one data frame at a time.

This lesson introduces the special features of ATM networking devices. We will focus most of our attention on the workhorse of the ATM network: the ATM switch.

Objectives

At the end of this lesson you will be able to:

- Describe the basic functions performed by products using ATM technology

- Briefly explain how an ATM switch functions

- Name and describe the three types of ATM switches

- Describe the special features of hubs and routers that Support ATM

 **Key Point**

As vendors adopt standards, ATM equipment is becoming more interoperable.

ATM Products

Market forecasts as reported by *Electronic Buyers' News* indicate that worldwide sales of ATM equipment will increase from more than $3.7 billion in 1999 to nearly $17 billion by 2003. The products offered by ATM vendors fall into five distinct categories:

- Switches
- Routers
- Intelligent hubs
- Workstation adapter boards
- ATM data service units (DSUs)

ATM Switches

Switches are the fundamental building blocks of an ATM network. Every ATM switch is required to perform three major functions:

- Direct cells from an input port to the correct output port.
- Buffer traffic before it is transmitted over an output port. If several cells arrive simultaneously at different input ports, destined for the same output port, the switch must buffer the cell(s), while one cell at a time is transmitted over the output port.
- Translate cell headers to guarantee the VPI and VCI are unique on each output port.

Types of ATM Switches

There are two functional types of ATM switches:

- VP switch—Looks for the VPI, and directs all cells with the same VPI along the same path. A VP switch is intended for MAN and WAN implementations where a multiplexed group of VCs is switched along the same route.
- VC switch—Directs individual VCs. Because VCs are sometimes contained within a VP, a VC switch must be able to demultiplex individual VCs from an inbound VP and switch them to different outbound VPs.

The basic functions performed by an ATM switch are shown on the ATM Switch Functions Diagram. A portion of the Cell Header Translation and Port Switching Table is displayed to the right of the switch block diagram.

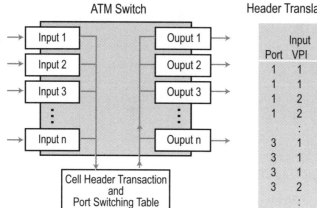

ATM Switch   Header Translation and Port Switching Table

Input			Output		
Port	VPI	VCI	Port	VPI	VCI
1	1	4	3	5	17
1	1	17	2	3	9
1	2	3	3	4	16
1	2	5	1	5	12
:			:		
3	1	3	3	5	16
3	1	5	2	5	16
3	1	7	3	2	8
3	2	5	1	5	11
:			:		

ATM Switch Functions

As illustrated, when a cell arrives at Input Port 1 with VPI = 1 and VCI = 4, it is switched to Output Port 3 and assigned VPI = 5 and VCI = 17.

It is important to note that on each input and output port the values of the VPI/VCI must be unique; the input ports cannot use the same VPI/VCI combinations as the output ports. However, identical VPI/VCI pairs may exist on different ports. For example, Input Ports 1 and 3 both contain a VPI/VCI pair where VPI = 2 and VCI = 5. In addition, Output Ports 2 and 3 both contain a VPI/VCI pair where VPI = 5 and VCI = 16.

VP Switch

Routing of VPs is performed by a VP switch. Because a VP consists of a number of VCs, a VP switch routes multiple VCs simultaneously. A VP switch is similar to a cross-connect because it switches large amounts of bandwidth consisting of many individual connections. A VP switch is designed for deployment in a metropolitan or long-haul network where a multiplexed group of VCs is switched along the same route.

The VPI uniquely defines each VP from all other VPs sharing the same transmission path in the network. A transmission path is a Physical Layer point-to-point link between two ATM devices. The

VPs and Transmission Path Diagram illustrates the relationship between VCs, VPs, and a transmission path.

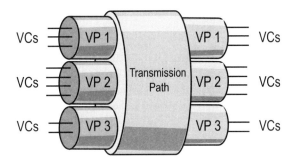

VPs and Transmission Path

In most cases, when a VP passes through an ATM switch, its cells are assigned a different VPI on the output side of the switch. This is because a given VP connection (VPC) must now be uniquely identified from the new set of VPCs sharing the output transmission path. When an ATM switch changes a cell's VPI, it notifies the other switches in that virtual circuit of the change, so those switches can reconfigure the circuit to recognize the new VPI. The Switching VPs Diagram illustrates how the VPI for a particular VPC changes as the VP passes through an ATM switch.

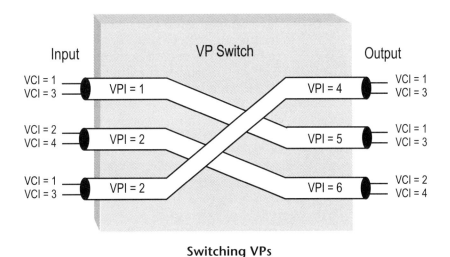

Switching VPs

On this diagram, VPI = 1 on the input port of the switch, and is changed to VPI = 5 on the output port of the switch. However, the VCI is not changed, because the VCI uniquely identifies each VC from all other VCs sharing the same VP.

A more real-world example will help clarify the most important issues concerning VP switching. On the VPC Between Two ATM Devices Diagram, an organization has three sites interconnected in a virtual private network (VPN) that carries a mixture of IP and IPX traffic. The router at each site has a VP to all other sites of the same organization. VCs are used within each VP to carry the individual IP and IPX connections.

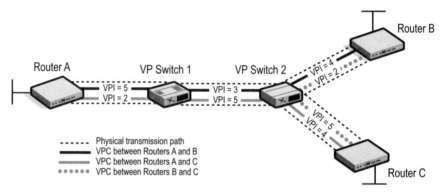

VPC Between Two ATM Devices

In this example, assume Router A has a VPC to Routers B and C. Notice that the VPC between Routers A and B is identified by VP 5 on the transmission path between Router A and VP Switch 1, by VP 3 on the transmission path between VP Switches 1 and 2, and by VP 4 on the transmission path between VP Switch 2 and Router B. The VPI on the link between VP Switches 1 and 2 must be changed from 5 to 3, because VP 5 is reserved on this physical link to identify the VPC between Routers A and C.

In this example, the routers are performing VC-based multiplexing. This means each routed protocol is carried over a separate VC within a given VP. This concept is illustrated on the VC-Based Multiplexing Diagram. Over the VPC between Routers A and B, VC 1 is dedicated to IP traffic and VC 2 is dedicated to IPX traffic. Because VCs are not modified when VPs are switched, Router A transmits IP traffic on VC 1 of VP 5, and Router B receives the traffic on VC 1 of VP 4.

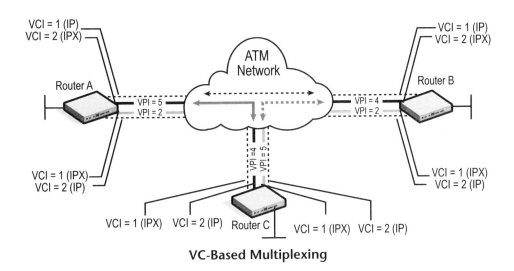

VC-Based Multiplexing

VC Switch

Routing of individual VCs is performed by a VC switch. Because VCs are contained within a VP, a VC switch must be able to demultiplex individual VCs from an inbound VP and switch them to different outbound VPs. Because VC switching is performed at a more detailed level than VP switching, a VC switch is also required to support the functions performed by a VP switch. A VC switch is designed for deployment in a building or campus network to provide local access to a WAN or MAN network composed of VP switches.

The basic functions performed by a VC switch are illustrated on the VC Switching Diagram.

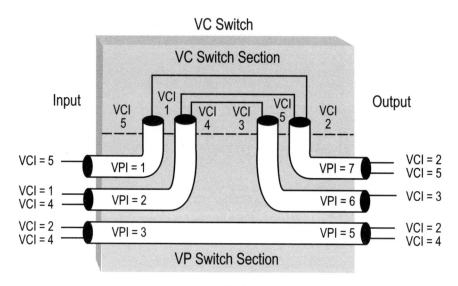

VC Switching

A VC switch may take VCs assigned to different VPs and combine them into a single VP. On this diagram, VC 5 of VP 1 and VC 1 of VP 2 are combined into VP 7. Note that VC 5 is translated to VC 2 and VC 1 is translated to VC 5.

A VC switch may take VCs assigned to a VP and switch them to several different VPs. On the above diagram, VP 2 contains VCs 1 and 4. Note that VC 1 is switched to VP 7 and assigned a new VCI of 5. Likewise, VC 4 is switched to VP 6 and assigned a new VCI of 3.

Finally, a VC switch may function as a VP switch and route all VCs of a VP to a new VP. On the VC Switching Diagram, the complete set of VCs in VP 3 is switched to VP 5 without the addition of VCs from other VPs. Notice that when a VP is switched, the VCI values are unchanged.

It is important to understand that a VC does not always have to be a member of a VP. VCs that do not belong to a VP are said to be members of the "null" VP. On the "Null" VCs and VC Switching Diagram, input VCs 1 and 4, as well as output VC 2, are members of the "null" VP. Note that there are actually two input VCs with a VCI = 1. The first is a member of VP 1, and the second is a member of the "null" VP. The switch can differentiate between the two even if their VCIs are identical.

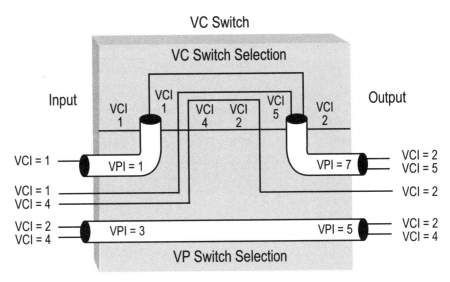

"Null" VCs and VC Switching

Interaction Between VC and VP Switches

Users can access an ATM network at either the VC or VP level. The VC Switch Providing VC- or VP-Level Access Diagram illustrates how a VC switch is deployed in a building or campus backbone to switch local traffic. The VC switch also combines traffic destined for a remote site into VPs for transmission across a MAN or WAN. In this example, the MAN or WAN is composed of VP switches.

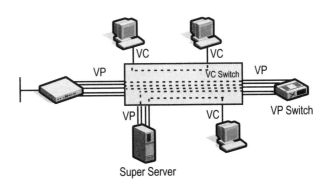

VC Switch Providing VC- or VP-Level Access

ATM Switch Designs

A number of switch designs have been developed over the past few years for both VP and VC switches. The internal architecture used by the majority of ATM switches generally falls into one of three types:

- Shared backplane switch
- High-speed memory switch
- Matrix switch

Shared Backplane Switch

In a shared backplane switch, cells are transported from the input port to the output port across a high-speed bus. The bandwidth of the bus is shared by all ports, and conflict-free transmission can be guaranteed only if the bandwidth of the bus is at least the sum of the bandwidths of all input ports. Shared backplane switches are designed for deployment in campus networks where there are a small number of ports or a relatively low-bandwidth requirement per port.

The Shared Backplane Switch Diagram illustrates the architecture of a switch that uses a shared backplane design.

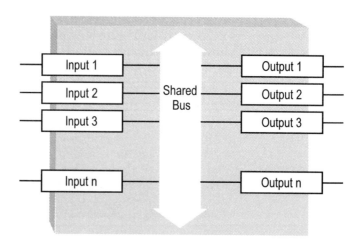

Shared Backplane Switch

The bandwidth of the bus is shared by using either TDM or statistical time-division multiplexing (STDM). TDM is suited for constant bit-rate traffic, because each port is guaranteed a fixed amount of bandwidth on a round-robin basis. STDM is better for bursty traffic because each port competes for access to the bus based on need, and bandwidth is not wasted.

*High-Speed
Memory Switch*

In a high-speed memory switch, all ports are attached to shared memory. All input ports write to this memory, and all output ports read from it. Incoming cells are read into memory, the cell header is examined to determine the output port, and the cells are either output directly to the output port or queued behind cells waiting for the same port. High-speed memory switches are designed for use in MANs and WANs where port and bandwidth requirements are high.

The High-Speed Memory Switch Diagram illustrates the architecture of a switch that uses a high-speed memory design.

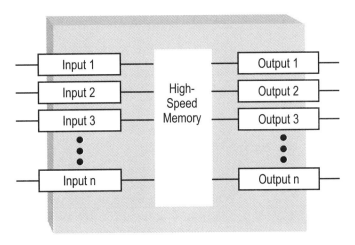

High-Speed Memory Switch

Matrix Switch

A matrix switch achieves very high-speed switching by implementing the switching function in hardware. This means the speed of a cell through a matrix switch is limited only by the speed of electrical signals through the semiconductor material. Like high-speed memory switches, matrix switches are designed for deployment in MANs and WANs where port and bandwidth requirements are high.

The Matrix Switch Diagram illustrates the architecture of a switch using a matrix design.

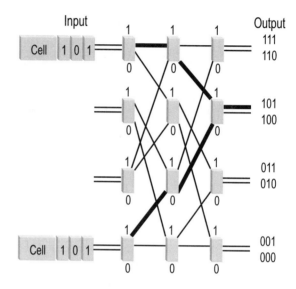

Matrix Switch

When a cell enters a matrix switch, the output port is determined by examining the cell's VPI and VCI. The output port is specified by prepending a special routing header to the cell. The routing header contains the output port address expressed in binary format.

The switch consists of a matrix of switching elements that are each responsible for interpreting only 1 bit in the routing header at a time. Each switching element reads one bit position of the address. It forwards the cell to one output if the bit is set to 1, and to another output if the bit is cleared to 0. The Matrix Switch Diagram shows the path through the switching matrix when the routing header is set to 101. Note that cells from different inputs with the same output header are switched to the same output port.

The advantage of a matrix switch is that cells from one input can be switched simultaneously with cells from all other inputs. This is because the matrix of switching elements is not a shared medium. Potential collisions within the switching matrix are avoided through the use of input buffers, cross point buffers, and output buffers.

ATM Routers

A router functions as an ATM access device, as illustrated on the Router Operating as an ATM Access Device Diagram. The router performs different functions depending on whether it is transmitting data to or receiving data from an ATM switch. On the transmission side, the router accepts a LAN frame as an input, determines the output port, and converts the frame to cells if the output port is attached to an ATM switch. On the receiving side, the router accepts cells from the ATM switch as input, reassembles the cells into a frame, determines the output port, and forwards the frame to the correct LAN segment.

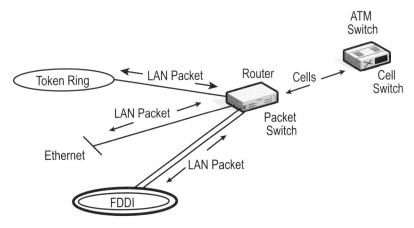

Router Operating as an ATM Access Device

It is important to note that the router switches packets and not cells. Data is reformatted to/from cells only at the interface to the ATM switch. As a result, routers function as ATM access devices that allow non-ATM LANs to connect to an ATM network.

Routers that support ATM can be classified by the type of ATM interface they implement:

- Hardware interface
- Software interface
- Frame relay interface

Hardware Interface

Routers with a hardware interface have a native ATM interface that formats LAN data frames directly into cells. With this type of interface, the router implements the AAL (cell SAR), ATM layer, and Physical Layer. A router with a hardware interface is directly connected to a port of an ATM switch, as illustrated on the Router with a Hardware Interface to an ATM Switch Diagram.

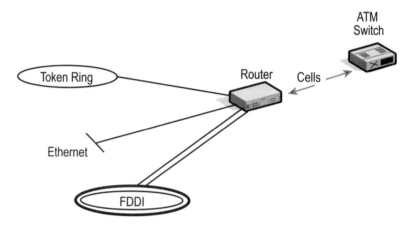

Router with a Hardware Interface to an ATM Switch

Software Interface

Routers with a software interface format LAN data frames into frames that can be recognized by ATM DSUs. The ATM Forum DXI describes how a router must format LAN frames so they can be recognized by an ATM DSU. A router that supports DXI formats each LAN frame so that the DSU knows where to find the addressing information and how to divide the packet into cells. The Router with a Software Interface to an ATM Switch Diagram illustrates this type of connection.

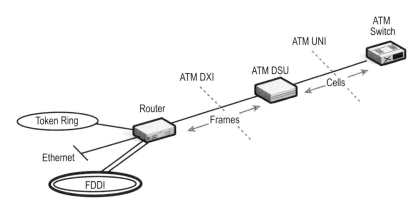

Router with a Software Interface to an ATM Switch

Frame Relay Interface

It is also possible for a router to attach to an ATM switch by way of a frame relay interface. This scenario assumes the ATM switch contains a frame relay interface. The input switch accepts frames on the frame relay interface and reformats them into cells. The cells are switched across the network until they arrive at the output switch. If the destination node is attached to an ATM interface, the cells are simply switched to the destination device. If the destination node is attached to a frame relay interface, the cells are reassembled into frames for delivery to the remote device. The Router with a Frame Relay Interface to an ATM Switch Diagram illustrates this type of connection.

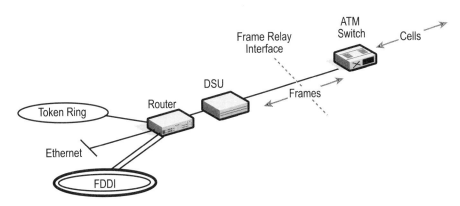

Router with a Frame Relay Interface to an ATM Switch

Intelligent Hubs

A hub permits LANs to be constructed in a star topology; nodes are attached to the central hub through point-to-point links. There are two approaches for deploying ATM in intelligent hubs:

- The hub can contain a very high-speed backplane bus that is shared by all port cards. An ATM interface module provides connectivity between the port cards attached to the high-speed bus and an ATM network.

- The hub can contain a native ATM backplane. With this approach, ATM is used across the interface between each port card and the backplane, and each port card has a dedicated ATM connection to an ATM switching module.

Local Switching Systems

For both approaches, performance of the hub may be increased by placing a switching system on each port card. The switching system operates as a MAC layer bridge in that it dynamically learns the address(es) of the device(s) attached to each port and makes a forwarding decision for each frame based on the MAC address provided by each frame. The switching system provides simultaneous communication between all ports of the card and allows data to pass through the switch at near-line speeds. The Port Card Switching System Diagram illustrates this concept.

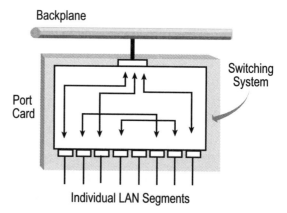

Port Card Switching System

There are two ways that implementation of a switching system on each port card can improve performance of a hub:

- The switching system reduces the amount of traffic a port card places on the backplane. If the switching system receives a frame on one of its LAN segments that is addressed to a device attached to another LAN segment of the same port card, the switching system directs the frame to the destination LAN segment but does not forward the traffic to the backplane.

- The switching system reduces the amount of traffic a port card places on each LAN segment. The switching system only forwards traffic to a given LAN segment if the switching system knows that the destination device is attached to the output LAN segment.

Ideally, each port card supports enough LAN segments so that each segment can be dedicated to a single user. The dedicated LAN segments use either Ethernet or Token Ring on each private access line, to provide each user with sole access to the LAN's bandwidth without contention. For Ethernet, this would be 10 or 100 Mbps, and for Token Ring it would be either 4 or 16 Mbps. Dedicated LAN segments reduce the immediate need for ATM to the desktop because they provide increased bandwidth without the expense of purchasing an ATM adapter for each workstation.

High-Speed Backplane with an ATM Interface Module

In the first approach, each port card is connected to a high-speed backplane that is implemented using conventional technologies. Each port card contains a local switching system that allows it to accept several dedicated LAN segments. Communication between individual port cards takes place across the high-speed backplane. An ATM interface module provides the connection between the high-speed backplane and an ATM network, as illustrated on the Intelligent Hub with a High-Speed Backplane and ATM Interface Module Diagram.

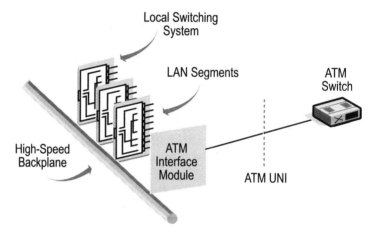

Intelligent Hub with a High-Speed Backplane and ATM Interface Module

Note that the ATM interface module provides connectivity to an ATM switch, but does not provide ATM connectivity between individual devices or LAN segments attached to the hub.

***ATM Backplane
with an ATM
Switching Module***

The second approach requires that the hub contain an ATM backplane. Each port card contains a local switching system that allows it to accept several dedicated LAN segments. Communication between individual port cards takes place across the ATM backplane. Data is transferred across the backplane from module to module in ATM cells, with the virtual circuits between modules identified by ATM connection identifiers, as illustrated on the Intelligent Hub with an ATM Backplane and ATM Switching Module Diagram.

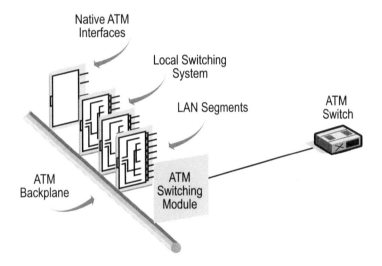

**Intelligent Hub with an ATM Backplane
and ATM Switching Module**

An interface for native ATM network adapters allows powerful workstations and servers to be directly connected to the backplane of the ATM hub. Support of both dedicated LANs and native ATM interfaces in a single platform allows users to migrate to ATM as their networks evolve over the years.

Installation of an ATM switching module provides seamless connectivity between devices attached to port cards, devices with native ATM interfaces, and private or public ATM networks.

Workstation Adapter Boards

Workstation adapter boards provide direct ATM access to the desktop, as illustrated on the Workstation Adapter Boards Diagram. Adapters are currently available for most high-speed workstations. First-generation ATM adapters could only provide connectivity with a single vendor's switch. As standards evolve, an ATM adapter should be able to connect to switches from different vendors.

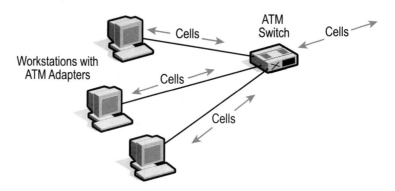

Workstation Adapter Boards

Data Service Units

DSUs convert LAN frames to cells, making it possible to connect a router (without a hardware ATM interface) to an ATM switch. This concept is illustrated on the ATM Data Service Units Diagram. DSUs can function as both access devices and local switches. First-generation ATM DSUs were limited to providing user access because they supported only one user port and a single ATM interface. Today, ATM DSUs operate as an access multiplexer (MUX)/switch in that they provide multiple user ports as well as multiple ATM interfaces. These devices switch cells from one local port to another local interface, as well as forward cells to a network switch.

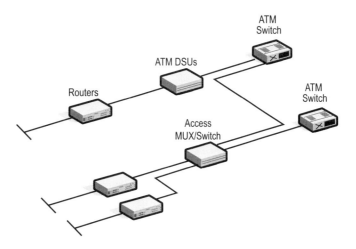

ATM Data Service Units

Activities

1. A VC switch is used to switch large amounts of bandwidth on long-haul networks. True or False

2. A VPI has end-to-end significance across an ATM network. True or False

3. A VC must always be a part of a VP. True or False

4. A high-speed memory switch can handle more traffic than a shared backplane switch. True or False

5. A router with an ATM hardware interface implements, among other layers, AAL. True or False

6. What is the fundamental building block of an ATM network?

   _____

   _____

   _____

7. List the three major functions an ATM switch must perform.

   _____

   _____

   _____

8. What is the function of a VPI?

   _____

   _____

9. How does the transmission path relate to VPs and VCs?

   _____

   _____

   _____

   _____

10. Compare a VP switch and a VC switch.

11. List the three types of ATM switch designs.

12. A router using a software ATM interface uses the ATM Forum DXI to describe:

13. What are the two approaches for deploying ATM in intelligent hubs?

14. Briefly describe the differences in the two approaches listed above.

15. What is the function of an ATM DSU?

_____

_____

_____

_____

_____

_____

_____

_____

Extended Activity

Using your favorite Internet search engine, find information on three vendors of ATM switching products. List some technical specifications you found interesting.

_____

_____

_____

_____

_____

Lesson 6—ATM Deployment

ATM technology can be used in a wide range of products across the entire computing and telecommunications environment. When ATM is fully deployed to individual desktops, it promises to merge voice, video, and data communications over a single, integrated LAN/MAN/WAN. The revolution will supposedly replace current LAN technology, and all of its shortcomings, with a new technology that will solve all of our telecommunications problems in a flash.

In reality, the revolution will be more of an evolution, and the initial changes will not be nearly as dramatic. There is simply too much money and effort invested in legacy LAN installations to instantly replace them with new ATM networks. Therefore, as a practical matter, ATM will be deployed gradually into legacy installations.

This lesson discusses the practical points to consider when gradually deploying ATM in an existing LAN. These recommendations will help you take advantage of the strengths of ATM, while getting the most value from your current installation.

Objectives

At the end of this lesson you will be able to:

- Describe plans for the initial deployment of ATM in production networks

- Discuss steps network managers can take today to prepare for the deployment of ATM products

- Discuss strategies to migrate the installed base of legacy LANs to ATM

 **Key Point**

The right choice of devices, cabling, and topology can simplify a future ATM deployment.

ATM in Building and Campus Networks

ATM initially appeared in private networks at the building/campus level, as illustrated on the ATM Deployed in a Building/Campus Network Diagram. ATM should then slowly move down to the LAN and eventually out to the WAN environment.

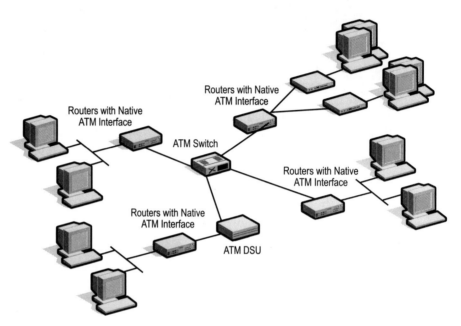

ATM Deployed in a Building/Campus Network

There are many financial and technological reasons that support the initial deployment of ATM in the building/campus environment as described below:

- Deployment at the building/campus level provides an immediate solution to one of the most pressing problems facing a network manager, the need to connect LANs in a way that combines speed, flexibility, and scalability. Installation of ATM equipment in the network backbone provides an immediate increase in bandwidth where it is needed most.

- Deployment at the campus level involves the least amount of technological risk. The initial cost is relatively low; workstation hardware and protocols do not have to be modified, a minimal set of ATM standards will suffice, and only a small portion of management information systems (MIS) staff requires training.

- The emergence of enhanced versions of conventional technologies, such as 100BaseT, Copper Distributed Data Interface (CDDI), FDDI II, FDDI Follow-On LAN (FFOL), and Switched Ethernet is bringing more bandwidth to the desktop. This slowed the demand for ATM at that level.

- Each ATM cell has a 9.4 percent overhead (5-byte header/53-byte cell). This means that only 90.6 percent of ATM bits carry user data. When compared to other technologies, which typically have a 1 or 2 percent overhead, it is clear ATM does not make efficient use of its bandwidth. As a result, ATM is not well suited for applications that run over transmission facilities with data rates less than T3 (45 Mbps) or E3 (34 Mbps), because the amount of user data throughput will be too low. Do not expect widespread deployment of ATM in WANs until very high-speed lines become the standard for point-to-point links.

- The critical issues of congestion management and flow control within an ATM network are still unresolved. The deployment of ATM in WANs requires an internationally accepted standards-based solution.

Migrating a Building/Campus Network to ATM

As part of the evolution from a single LAN per building to separate LANs on each floor or for each workgroup, many network managers have reconfigured their distributed networks to collapsed backbones. A collapsed backbone configuration concentrates all connections in a single device, along with a group of high-end servers known as a server farm. This architecture effectively "collapses" the distributed backbone onto the high-speed backplane of a central router or switch.

The migration of a collapsed backbone network to ATM can be performed in three cost-effective stages:

1. To efficiently use the current bandwidth, segment the network with VLANs and workgroups.

2. Increase overall bandwidth by installing high-speed downlinks (dedicated connections, using Fast Ethernet, FDDI, or ATM) that connect all LAN segments to the backbone device.

3. Install ATM in the backbone device itself.

Goals of an ATM Migration

When considering whether to implement ATM in an existing building/campus network, develop a migration strategy that provides the following benefits:

- Build on both current and emerging LAN technologies to meet present and future needs.

- Deploy new technology only in parts of the network where it is needed.

- Migrate the network in a series of steps at minimal incremental cost.

- Provide an economical upgrade path using currently available networking platforms and architectures.

- Implement low-latency connectivity systems in the workgroup and campus backbone for better performance.

- Implement new capabilities by building on earlier enhancements with no loss of functionality.

- Proceed in a smooth, step-by-step manner that allows integration of ATM backbones with existing "legacy" LANs to protect investment.

- Maintain seamless connectivity throughout the configuration.

- Simplify the task of managing the network.

Preparing for the Arrival of ATM

Even if your immediate plans do not include migration to ATM, you should take simple steps to prepare for the eventual arrival of ATM. These steps will both benefit your current network, and position you for the future:

- Make every effort to future-proof your cable plant by installing cable that will support ATM. For backbone applications, use multi-mode fiber, because it currently supports the 155-Mbps ATM interface. For runs to the desktop, both STP and Category 5 UTP cabling should be able to support the ATM interface.

- Design all LAN installations using smart hubs with high-capacity backplanes and a structured star wiring topology. The use of hubs and a star wiring topology provide a central point of concentration that can be used for future deployment of ATM switches.

- Purchase internetworking products from vendors committed to providing a logical and cost-effective upgrade path to ATM. This protects your investment in existing legacy LANs and network hardware.

- Select a vendor that has demonstrated expertise in routing, because routing is mandatory for a smooth transition of legacy LANs to ATM.

Activities

1. Briefly discuss two reasons for deploying ATM in building/
    campus environments.

    _____

    _____

    _____

    _____

    _____

    _____

    _____

2. ATM has an overhead of 9.4 percent for each cell. Calculate
    the overhead required to transmit an Ethernet frame carrying
    1,200 bytes of information. (An Ethernet header, not includ-
    ing the preamble, is 14 bytes: 6 bytes of Destination Address,
    6 bytes of Source Address, and 2 bytes of either type or length.
    An Ethernet trailer is 4 bytes, yielding a total of 18 bytes of
    frame overhead.)

    _____

3. List at least five benefits an ATM migration strategy should
    provide.

    _____

    _____

    _____

    _____

    _____

    _____

    _____

    _____

4. Describe the three stages for migrating from a collapsed backbone to ATM.

    _____

    _____

    _____

    _____

5. List two types of high-speed downlinks.

    _____

    _____

6. List steps a network manager can do to prepare for the eventual deployment of ATM technologies.

    _____

    _____

    _____

    _____

    _____

    _____

    _____

    _____

    _____

    _____

    _____

Extended Activity

1. Break into focus groups of no more than three to five people, depending on class size. Each group will independently discuss migration strategies as presented in this lesson. The following topics should be covered:

    a. Financial and technological reasons for deploying ATM in building/campus environments initially

    b. ATM migration strategy benefits

    c. Three-stage ATM migration plan

    d. Diagrams depicting collapsed backbones and their interpretation

    e. Future-proofing the network infrastructure

    Summarize two key points your group discussed.

    _____

    _____

    _____

    _____

    _____

    _____

Summary

In this unit, we introduced ATM and discussed the factors that are driving the growing interest in this technology as a solution to networking bandwidth problems.

ATM offers the best of two styles of network communication. Its connection-oriented service and reliable data-transfer rate provide smooth and predictable service to time-sensitive applications such as voice communications and video. Its use of fixed-length, packet-switched data cells provides efficient, high-speed data transmission using fast hardware switching.

We described the basic operation and hardware of an ATM network, and explained the technical adaptations necessary for connection-oriented ATM to coexist with connectionless LAN technology. This mixed approach to network design will become common as more organizations begin deploying ATM backbones in campus networks that use shared-media LANs.

The network engineering community, led by ITU-TSS, is working to develop international standards for ATM protocols and devices. Although these standards have not yet been formally adopted, the key vendors that compose the ATM Forum have already agreed to support some of the most fundamental of the pending standards. This commitment to a standards-based architecture should ensure that ATM technology evolves into a robust, cost-effective, and interoperable solution for next-generation networks.

Unit 5 Quiz

1. Which of the following is not used to describe ATM?

   a. Connection-oriented

   b. Cell switching

   c. Multiplexing

   d. Frame-based

2. ATM is an integral part of which of the following standards?

   a. ISDN

   b. B-ISDN

   c. Frame relay

   d. NEC

3. If SONET is used as the Physical Layer protocol for an ATM network, the speed of ATM will be which of the following?

   a. 10 Mbps

   b. 16 Mbps

   c. 155 Mbps

   d. 200 Mbps

4. What is meant by the fact that ATM is a connection-oriented protocol?

   a. A virtual circuit is established before data is sent.

   b. Frames are sent regardless of destination address.

   c. Cells are broadcast to all nodes on the bus.

   d. Each cell can take varying routes to the final destination.

5. What is the primary reason for the 5-byte header of an ATM cell?

   a. Handle error control

   b. Identify the ATM switch

   c. Identify the virtual connection

   d. Request information from the application

6. What is the purpose of an Adaptation Layer protocol used by ATM?

   a. Translating between Ethernet and Token Ring

   b. Converting between cells and frames

   c. Changing the size of ATM cells

   d. Segmenting higher layer protocol packets into cells

7. When a cell arrives at an ATM switch, the switch will use which of the following to decide the destination of the cell?

   a. Frame header

   b. Cell trailer

   c. VCI within the cell header

   d. None of the above

8. Where in an ATM network are cells reassembled into a packet?

   a. Source ATM node

   b. Each ATM switch in the network

   c. Destination ATM node

   d. All of the above

9. At what layer of the OSI model does ATM fall?

   a. Session

   b. Data Link

   c. Transport

   d. Application

10. What are the two types of ATM interfaces defined by standards bodies?

    a. UNI and NNI

    b. NNI and ISSI

    c. UNI and Data Link Layer

    d. PVC and SVC

11. Which of the following is information that might be given when an ATM connection is established?

    a. Called party number

    b. Bandwidth requirements

    c. Maximum cell loss

    d. All of the above

12. What does an ATM VC number identify?

    a. Transmission path between two switches

    b. Upper layer protocol

    c. User data

    d. None of the above

13. What is one reason LANE was created?

    a. ATM must interface with existing connectionless protocols.

    b. ATM must interface with existing connection-oriented protocols.

    c. ATM is connectionless.

    d. None of the above.

14. Which of the following is not a major ATM switch function?

    a. Route cells

    b. Buffer cell traffic

    c. Perform cell header translation

    d. Convert packet information

15. Which of the following is not an ATM switch design?

    a. Layer 3 switch

    b. Shared backplane switch

    c. High-speed memory switch

    d. Matrix switch

16. In which of the following classifications can ATM be deployed?

    a. LAN

    b. MAN

    c. WAN

    d. All of the above

17. In an ATM network, an emulated LAN is equivalent to:

    a. A VLAN

    b. A mesh network

    c. A broadcast domain

    d. A collision domain

18. What is the main technical drawback of ATM?

    a. Nondeterministic performance

    b. No error correction

    c. High transmission overhead

    d. Proprietary technologies

19. What environment would be most likely NOT consider ATM?

    a. A large telemarketing firm that carries digitized telephone calls and computer data over a single network

    b. A university that wants to deliver multimedia instruction and Internet access to classrooms and dorms

    c. An insurance company that employs 150 data entry clerks

    d. A company that specializes in computer-generated filmmaking

20. What is the main reason that ATM provides good service quality for real-time applications?

    a. It runs over fast optical fiber

    b. The small, fixed-size cells provide smooth transmission

    c. It prevents collisions

    d. It does not request retransmission of damaged cells

Unit 6
LAN Networking Software

Thus far in this course, we have reviewed the physical aspects of local area network (LAN) technologies and how network interface cards (NICs) are tied to NICs by means of cables and hubs. We have also looked at framing protocols such as Ethernet, Token Ring, and Fiber Distributed Data Interface (FDDI). These protocols are used to move frames of information across the physical structure of a LAN. We now move up from the Physical and Data Link Layer protocols to the higher layers. These layers are implemented by client software provided by desktop operating systems (OSs) such as Microsoft Windows NT, and server software implemented by means of network operating systems (NOSs).

In this unit, you will be guided through a brief description of the most important NOS solutions. We will examine how NOSs compare to the Open Systems Interconnection (OSI) model, and we will look at the key elements of each major NOS vendor's products.

Lessons

1. Review of Client/Server and NOS Fundamentals
2. RPCs
3. File Servers
4. Print Servers
5. Web Servers
6. Other Common Servers
7. Backup and Disaster Prevention

Terms

AppleTalk Filing Protocol (APF)—AFP is the protocol used in Apple networks for retrieving and storing files across a network.

application programming interface (API)—In general, an API consists of computer processes used by applications to carry out lower level tasks performed by a computer's OS. In networking, an API provides applications with a consistent method of requesting services from a network. One of the most common APIs used in networking is NetBIOS.

co-processor—A co-processor is a secondary computer processing chip that is optimized for a particular type of operation, such as graphics rendering or mathematical computation. If an application has been written to take advantage of a co-processor, then those operations can be processed there instead of the main CPU.

compiler—A compiler is a software program that takes source code from a programming language such as C++, and converts it into machine readable, executable code to be run on a computer.

Dynamic Host Configuration Protocol (DHCP)—DHCP is a proprietary approach from Microsoft that simplifies IP network management by dynamically assigning IP addresses to logical end-stations for fixed periods of time.

encryption—Encryption is the process of scrambling data by changing it in a series of logical steps, called an encryption algorithm. To increase security, an encryption algorithm uses a numerical pattern, or "key," to guide the scrambling process. Different algorithms and keys will each produce data scrambled, or encrypted, in different patterns.

error correcting code (ECC)—ECC memory tests the accuracy of data as it passes in and out of memory.

freeware—Freeware is software that does not require a license fee, because its copyright is in the public domain. In other words, the creators of the software give it away. The source code is also freely distributed, so any developer may modify or add to it (fees may be charged for those added components). Periodically, the best modifications become part of the next "official" release of the core software. Thus, freeware, or open source software, benefits from the best ideas and approaches of the worldwide software development community. The Linux OS and the Apache Web server are two of the best-known examples of freeware.

hypermedia—Hypermedia takes hypertext to another level, and includes images, sounds, and video with links that can be selected and viewed.

hypertext—Hypertext is computer information containing text that can be linked with selected phrases. The links point to other documents or files. Hypertext is basically the same as regular text, however, it contains connections within the text to other documents. The links in the text are called hyperlinks.

Hypertext Transfer Protocol (HTTP)—HTTP is the Transmission Control Protocol/Internet Protocol (TCP/IP) Application Layer protocol used to request and transmit HTML documents. HTTP is the underlying protocol of the Web.

multiprocessing—In a multiprocessing environment, multiple computers are used to process a single application.

multitasking—The ability of a computer to execute multiple processes and applications. Although a computer with a single processing unit can only execute one instruction at a time, a multitasking OS can load and manage the execution of multiple applications by allocating computer processing cycles to each application in sequence. The perceived result is the simultaneous processing of multiple applications or tasks. There are two kinds of multitasking: preemptive and cooperative. With preemptive multitasking, the OS is in charge and manages system resource allocation and task scheduling. With cooperative multitasking, applications are in charge and share resources.

multithreading—A thread is a process within an application that executes a specific operation. A computer capable of multithreading is one that supports multiple threads, essentially allowing applications to multitask within themselves.

Network Driver Interface Specification (NDIS)—The NDIS standard was developed by Microsoft and 3Com to provide a common interface between NIC drivers and networking protocols. The functionality of NDIS is comparable to ODI.

Network File System (NFS)—NFS is a file management system commonly used in UNIX-based computer systems.

open source—See freeware.

parity—Parity checking is a common error-checking method for data communications and storage devices. In parity checking, a parity bit is added to a small unit of data (usually 7 bits). The parity bit is set to 1 or 0 to make the total number of set bits in the data unit either odd or even. For example, if two devices are communicating with "even" parity, the sending device checks each data unit before transmitting it. If the 7 bits contain an even number of 1s, the parity bit is set to 0 (to maintain the even number). If the 7 bits contain an odd number of 1s, the parity bit is set to 1 (to create an even number). The receiving device then checks incoming bytes to see whether each one contains an even number of set bits. An odd number indicates a transmission or storage error.

print server—A print server is a LAN-based computer that provides users on a network access to a printer. This allows multiple users to share the printer.

remote access service (RAS)—The term RAS is normally used in the context of Windows NT, and the ability to access Windows NT and LAN services from a remote location.

remote procedure call (RPC)—RPC is a call made by an application program for services across a network connection, usually to a server.

Request for Comment (RFC)—RFC is one of the working documents of the Internet research and development community. A document in this series may be on essentially any topic related to computer communication, and may be anything from a meeting report to the specification of a standard.

semaphore—A semaphore, or a flag, is a binary bit set to indicate use of a shared system resource, such as a file. For example, if a file semaphore is set to 1, the file is in use and cannot be accessed by another user. In general, a flag can represent any value or its opposite.

source code—Source code is human-readable instructions written in a programming language, such as C++. Before an application can be run on a computer, the source code is converted to machine-readable binary codes by an application called a compiler.

Structured Query Language (SQL)—SQL is a standardized language used to retrieve data from a database.

virtual private network (VPN)—VPN is a connection, over a shared network, that behaves like a dedicated link. VPNs are created using a technique called "tunneling," which uses encryption to transmit data packets across a public network, such as the Internet or other commercially available network, in a private "tunnel" that simulates a point-to-point connection.

World Wide Web Consortium (W3C)—W3C is an independent industry organization that works to develop technically sound open standards for the Web. W3C (www.w3c.org) is the chief standards organization for HTTP, HTML, XML, DHTML, and many other Web-based technologies. It cooperates with the various Internet organizations.

Lesson 1—Review of Client/Server and NOS Fundamentals

This lesson reviews the basic concepts of client/server communication, as well as the network OSs that make that interaction possible.

Objectives

At the end of this lesson you will be able to:

- Name the typical services found in client/server networks

- Describe the primary role of a client and a server

- Name the components of a NOS

- Describe how a client communicates with a server using NOS software

- Explain the function of a redirector

 **Key Point**

A client/server network can distribute resources across a network.

Client/Server Communication

There are three architectures that applications can use to distribute functions across a network: client/server, peer-to-peer, and master/slave. However, most personal computer (PC) LANs use the client/server approach to resource sharing.

The client/server model essentially divides a task into two parts and executes each part on a different system on the network. For example, the task of creating a report can be divided into the application portion, where the report is created (client process), and the server portion, where the report is printed (server process). This concept is illustrated on the Typical Client/Server Configuration Diagram.

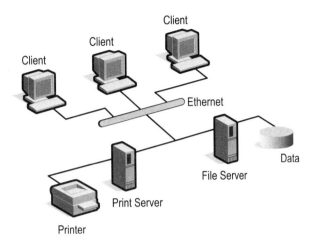

Typical Client/Server Configuration

The client and server processes interact by transmitting request/reply pairs. The client process initiates an interaction by issuing a request to the server. The server process responds with a reply satisfying the request. If a request cannot be satisfied, the server process provides an error message.

Client/server architecture has two primary advantages:

- Distributed applications—Applications can be distributed on the network based on their requirements for resources. For example, the server might provide computing-intensive services on a system with very high computing capability, while the client runs on a workstation that provides high-end graphic display capabilities. An example of this type of distributed application is a graphical client "front end," or interface, connected to a large server-based database, or "back end."

- Resource sharing—A server process typically can serve many clients, so client/server architecture is a good way to share resources such as printers, storage drives, or Internet connections.

The client process is often found on an end-user node, such as a workstation or PC, while the server process often runs on more powerful systems, such as a network file server.

As the LAN market has matured, many different client/server protocols have emerged, often competing with one another. For example, Apple's AppleTalk Filing Protocol (AFP) was designed to service Macintosh clients, and Sun Microsystems' Network File System (NFS) has emerged as the standard for servicing UNIX clients.

Client/server protocols are usually developed for a specific workstation environment, such as Apple's AFP for the Macintosh. As the LAN marketplace has matured, however, vendors have increasingly moved toward support of multiple client/server protocols.

LAN Services

Client requests and remote services provided by a server typically fall into one of the categories listed below:

- Application access—Applications can be invoked from a client to be executed remotely on a server node. Client applications use application programming interfaces *(*APIs) embedded in remote procedure calls (RPCs) to gain access to server applications. We discuss remote procedure calls in the next lesson.

- Database access—Database requests from client to server are typically made using Structured Query Language (SQL) syntax, an industry standard database query language used by many vendors.

- Print services—Clients generate print requests that are serviced by a print server. Jobs are queued by the print server, and the client is notified when the print job has been completed.

- Fax services—Clients generate fax requests that are serviced by the server similar to print requests.

- Window services—The NOS typically provides software on the client workstation to pop-up windows for status messages from remote servers.

- Network communication—Clients access a network through APIs that use communication protocols such as Internetwork Packet Exchange (IPX), Transmission Control Protocol/Internet Protocol (TCP/IP), Ethernet, Token Ring, and others. Applications can exchange files and send messages between remote applications using these services.

- World Wide Web (Web) services—Clients access Web services, such as Web pages and Web-based files, using the Internet.

NOS Components

A NOS is software that resides on a dedicated server and provides resources to clients on a network. A NOS can be divided into four components, as illustrated on the NOS Platform Diagram:

- Server platform
- Network services software
- Network redirection software
- Communication protocol software

These components work together to support the distribution of network services to users. The relationships among the components are illustrated on the NOS Platform Diagram.

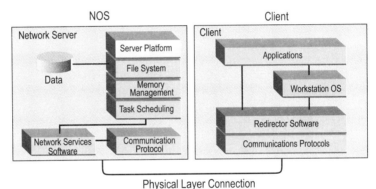

NOS Platform

NOS Platform

The server platform supports basic network operations, such as NFS, memory management, and task scheduling. The server platform typically provides:

- Preemptive multitasking—Enables tasks with higher priorities to gain access to the server processor over lower priority tasks
- Shared memory—Used for updating shared files for multiple client access
- Protected memory—Application isolation keeps applications from "stepping on each other" when an error in one application occurs

317

Network Services Software

The network services software running on a server platform provides a user with services that range from basic (file and record locking) to very complex (database queries).

Server security is another important aspect of NOSs. The server should be capable of restricting access to applications and data using login IDs or some other form of control.

Network Redirection Software

The network redirection software coexists with the OS in the user's workstation or PC. Applications access network services through this software. On the client, a redirector determines if the request from the application is for a local resource or a remote resource. If remote, the redirector software redirects the request across the network to the server.

Communication Protocol Software

The communications software provides protocols needed to transmit requests for services over the network. The server receives these requests, processes them, and sends replies back to the requesting PC or workstation using the same communications software.

Although these processes are typical of all NOSs, their functionality, reliability, and performance can vary significantly because of architecture differences.

Common NOSs

By far the most common NOS packages are Microsoft Windows NT Server, Windows 2000, and Novell NetWare. Though Windows NT Server has been replaced by the Windows 2000 family of OSs, Windows NT is still widely used. The Windows 2000 product line includes the following OSs based on Windows NT technology:

- Windows 2000 Professional is a desktop OS for individuals and businesses of all sizes. It includes improved security and enhancements for laptop computers.

- Windows 2000 Server is for Web servers or office servers in small- to medium-sized businesses.

- Windows 2000 Advanced Server is for larger business servers, especially those that host large databases.

- Windows 2000 Datacenter Server is designed for the very largest corporate databases (called data warehouses) and other applications requiring high-speed computation and large data storage.

Other NOSs include:

- Banyan Virtual Integrated Network Services (VINES)
- IBM's Warp
- Mac OS X (AppleTalk)
- LANtastic

In general, UNIX and Linux are not typically considered to be a NOS, but workstation OSs. However, UNIX contains many NOS features and is often used as a NOS providing clients access to file, print, and Web services. Thus, UNIX/Linux is considered a NOS when it is used to provide network services.

Activities

1. List the four components of a NOS.

   _____

   _____

   _____

   _____

2. Describe the function of a redirector.

   _____

   _____

   _____

   _____

3. What are the primary differences between a NOS and desktop OS?

   _____

   _____

   _____

   _____

4. What performance features does a NOS platform typically provide?

   _____

   _____

   _____

   _____

   _____

   _____

5. When does it make sense to use a peer-to-peer NOS instead of a full-blown client/server NOS? When does it make sense to use a full-blown client/server NOS instead of a peer-to-peer NOS?

_____

_____

_____

_____

Extended Activities

1. For the following applications, discuss how each could be distributed between client and server:

   a. Word processing

   _____

   _____

   b. Database

   _____

   _____

   c. Software development

   _____

   _____

   _____

   _____

2. List at least three services found in client/server networks.

   _____

   _____

   _____

3. Using a Web search engine, research the latest release levels of Microsoft and Novell NOS products and list the main features of each.

_____

_____

_____

_____

_____

_____

4. Using a Web search engine, find information about the LAN services described in this lesson. Find information on how servers are used for:

   a. Using applications that reside on a LAN server and are accessed by clients

   b. Using database programs that reside on a LAN server and are accessed by clients

   c. File and print services

Lesson 2—RPCs

As increasingly advanced network applications have been developed during the past few years, an important new programming technology has emerged to support their development: RPC. For example, RPC technology was used as a basis for Sun Microsystems' NFS. Messaging protocols, such as Server Message Block (SMB), are used in other implementations such as Microsoft Networking.

Objectives

At the end of this lesson you will be able to:

- Describe the difference between a local procedure call and RPC

- Understand the advantages of RPCs

- Understand the relationship between applications, OSs, and networks

- Describe the distinction between desktop OSs and NOSs

 **Key Point**

RPCs provide a common interface between applications and services that exist on a network.

Local Procedure Calls

Before we discuss RPCs, let us first make sure that we understand local procedure calls. The Typical Program Function Call Diagram illustrates a local procedure call.

A program, or application, consists of a sequence of instructions to a computer. As programs are developed, programmers often find that certain calculations or manipulations occur repetitively in a program. For example, a program might access a database at many different points in the program.

Rather than having to recode the database access instructions over and over again, any program language allows the programmer to collect the instructions into a reusable component called a subroutine, a function, or a procedure. The programmer can then write a short statement that executes that program component. In programming jargon, the programmer "calls a function" or "makes a procedure call."

The procedure call statement can provide parameters to the subroutine. The parameters tell the subroutine how to behave for that particular request, and also provide a place for the subroutine to store the result.

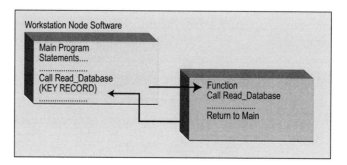

Typical Program Function Call

For example, as illustrated on the diagram, a programmer might create a subroutine called Read_Database, which is called each time it is necessary to read a record out of the database. The subroutine might accept parameters such as KEY and RECORD, with KEY providing the ID number of the record to be read, and RECORD providing space to store the record that is read from the database.

The subroutines can be part of the source code of the program, or a separate body of code referred to in the main program. When the main program is compiled (translated into machine-readable instructions), all code elements are combined, so the effect is the same.

Programs invoke most of the services of the OSs and virtually all of the services of a communication subsystem, such as Virtual Telecommunications Access Method (VTAM), through procedure calls. VTAM is an IBM API for communicating with telecommunication devices and their users.

RPCs

Suppose a programmer wants to convert the example program above into a client/server application, with the main application running on a workstation node, and the database access taking place on a network server node. How can this be done?

RPC provides a method that is very attractive from the programmer's point of view. As the name implies, RPCs allow subroutines such as Read_Database to be called remotely, that is, across the network, as illustrated on the RPC Diagram.

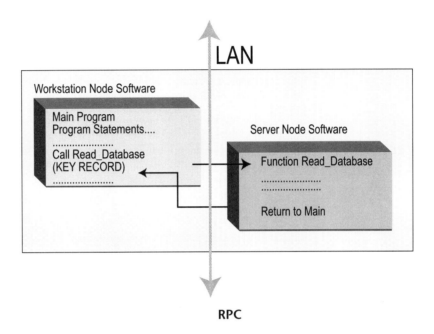

RPC

When a piece of procedure code is built into a server-based application, it does not need to be part of a corresponding client application. The client application only needs to know how to call the remote procedure. Thus, instead of sending many separate instructions over the network to the server, the client sends a short procedure call to do the same thing.

We use the same principle when we order a restaurant meal. If we want a hamburger, we don't recite the whole recipe, "First cook the meat, then find two buns..." The kitchen staff already knows how to make a burger, so we only need to make the procedure call ("One hamburger") and pass any necessary parameters ("Tomatoes and lettuce, no pickles").

Thus, RPCs offer two main advantages for the programmer:

- Simplicity—The interface to the remote database is practically identical to the interface to a local database.

- Minimal changes to the program—RPC hides much of the complexity of the network from the programmer.

Although RPC is an elegantly simple concept, its implementation is more difficult than it appears. Procedure calls to local procedures are assumed to be 100 percent reliable. If the procedure fails, so will the main program. If the workstation node has an equipment failure, both the main program and the procedure will stop. The same assumption cannot be made for remote procedures. RPC implementation must take into account the delay in sending and receiving request/reply pairs across a relatively slow communications link. For example, it's possible that a server node might fail after receiving and acknowledging a request, but before sending a reply. It is also possible to receive two replies to one request.

RPC is a programming technology that has facilitated significant advancements in data communications development. We are sure to encounter applications and network tools that employ RPC. Standards for RPC protocols continue to be developed by major vendors. RPC tools are available from a variety of sources, including Sun Microsystems and IBM.

Steps in the execution of an RPC might resemble the following:

1. Client program makes an RPC.

2. Program calls the RPC run-time library routines to establish a connection.

3. Client sends parameters and information about the remote procedure.

4. Remote procedure is executed on the remote machine.

5. Answer is assembled and returned to the client.

6. Client proceeds to the next instruction.

Application-to-Application Software Components

Several software and hardware components are necessary when making a remote procedure call from a client to server across a network. These are shown on the Client/Server Communications Diagram. The diagram illustrates the flow of information when a request is made from a client to a server. Note that after the RPC is processed at the server, the opposite flow occurs, beginning at the server and traveling across the network to the client.

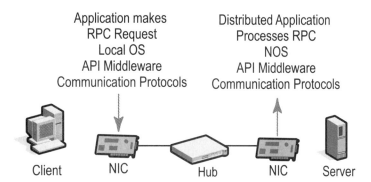

Application makes
RPC Request
Local OS
API Middleware
Communication Protocols

Distributed Application
Processes RPC
NOS
API Middleware
Communication Protocols

Client   NIC   Hub   NIC   Server

Client/Server Communications

First, an application formats an RPC to be transmitted over a network to a server that has the proper application. The RPC contains the destination server address and the requested service to be processed by the remote server. The RPC passes through an API that provides the correct formatting for the server NOS. RPCs and APIs constitute what is commonly referred to as middleware. For example, Network Basic Input Output System (NetBIOS) is a commonly used API in PC-based LANs.

The RPC is then sent across the network to the server. The NOS gives the information to the server application that processes the request. The processed results are then returned to the client in a similar fashion.

Note that there are two OSs at work here. The desktop OS is responsible for the interaction between the application and the underlying hardware of the computer. When an RPC request is made by the application, the desktop OS must bundle the request in communication protocol to be sent across a network to the appropriate server. In effect, the desktop OS is using remote hardware (and software) to process the request of the application.

On the server side of the network, the NOS is responsible for processing the client application request. The NOS must process the requests of many clients, so this type of OS must be multitasking in nature.

Activities

1. Multitasking requires more than one central processing unit. True or False

2. What is one disadvantage of using RPCs?

   _____

   _____

3. Using steps in the execution of an RPC as described in this lesson, describe how a parts database program might use an RPC to request availability and cost information for a specific part requested by the user of the parts application.

   _____

   _____

   _____

   _____

   _____

   _____

   _____

   _____

   _____

4. Describe the difference between preemptive and cooperative multitasking.

   _____

   _____

   _____

   _____

5. Describe the flow of information, including processes and protocols, between a client attached to a TCP/IP network, accessing information across the Internet from a Web server.

_____

_____

_____

_____

6. What is an API and what is it used for?

_____

_____

_____

_____

7. Compare a desktop OS with an NOS on a server.

_____

_____

_____

_____

8. What is the difference between an API and RPC?

_____

_____

_____

_____

Extended Activities

1. Using a Web search engine, research the difference between NetBEUI and NetBIOS. Find out which of these is used as an API, and how it is used by applications to send and receive information across a LAN.

    _____

    _____

    _____

    _____

    _____

    _____

2. Using a Web search engine, find and review Request for Comment (RFC) 1057 (or its updated version) that describes RPCs.

Lesson 3—File Servers

This lesson looks at one of the basic operations that a NOS performs: storing and retrieving files for multiple users. File servers contain applications software and data files that are downloaded to workstations on request.

Objectives

At the end of this lesson you will be able to:

*   Describe a file server's job in a computer network
*   Name basic functions a file server performs

 **Key Point**

File services are one of the basic functions of a NOS.

From PC to File Server

PCs become file servers because NOS software gives a PC that functionality. A file server's job is to make sure that shared resources are accessed in an orderly, nonconflicting manner. Working with the application programs, servers ensure concurrent file submission when needed, and prevent it when it should not occur. File servers control access through a variety of NOS security mechanisms, and NOSs vary in their ability to provide security as presented on the File Server Diagram.

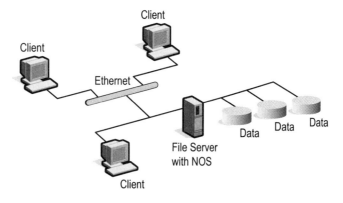

File Server

A sample screen of a Windows 98 client is shown on the Windows 98 Client and Windows NT Server Screen Diagram. This screen shot shows connectivity between a client and two servers. Westnetserver1 is a Windows NT server containing files shared by users of the network. Network drives are mapped to each client that has access to the Window's NT server.

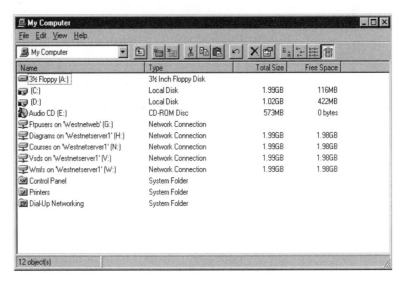

Windows 98 Client and Windows NT Server Screen

By clicking on the icon for "Courses on Westnetserver1," we see the contents of this portion of the file server as shown on the Windows NT Server for Courses Screen Diagram.

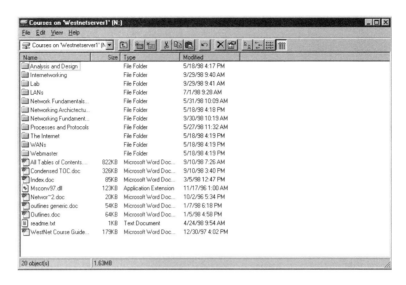

Windows NT Server for Courses Screen

Because of the heavy demands placed on file servers, they are designed for higher performance than an ordinary workstation. A powerful LAN server reduces the need for workstation power, random access memory (RAM), and disk capacity. This has a pronounced effect on direct and indirect costs such as maintenance. Concentrating processing and storage in the server may permit the use of diskless workstations, which are often used in security-conscious, dusty, or otherwise computer-unfriendly environments. Because there is no floppy diskette access, virus infection from a boot or program diskette is not possible. Internal hard disks are often replaced with RAM disks, further reducing the overall failure rate.

File Access Attributes

All files have access attributes. For example, files can be set for read only or read and write. Access attributes are usually set by the application and can be modified by the user. Network files are different from ordinary files because they may be shared by multiple users.

Attributes associated with file servers are typically:

• Exclusive—The file cannot be shared.

• Write access denied—The file can only be read by others.

• No access denied—The file can be shared, and anyone can read and write to it.

Usually, an application assigns access rights; however, users can modify them. Access control is, therefore, the first step.

Synchronization

Synchronization ensures that file updates do not occur at the same time by different users, causing a logically corrupted file. When a user wants to access a file in use by another user, the server will respond with some type of message indicating the file is in use. The File in Use Message Screen Diagram shows such a message generated by Windows NT.

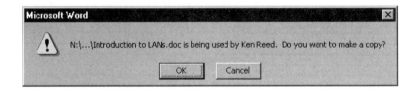

File in Use Message Screen

File locking is one synchronization technique. Multiple user updates (that is, writes to the file) are prevented by using the exclusive or write access denied file sharing attributes. The file can be shared for reading, but only one user can write to the file.

Record locking is another option. Record locking is more complex than file locking. Within record locking, two kinds of locks are used:

• Physical locks protect a record or series of records within a file by preventing access to them on the hard disk.

• Logical locks assign a lock name to the protected records. Other applications must check the lock name and its attributes and are barred from the named records.

Semaphores, or Flags

Because other devices besides disks, files, and records are shared on a file server, a procedure for organizing access to them is necessary as well. Some NOSs do this by the use of semaphores. A semaphore, or flag, is a bit that represents either a value or its opposite. For example, a particular bit can be set to 1 to indicate that a resource is shared, and set to 0 to show that it is not shared.

Each flag is a value that can be given a name, set, cleared, and tested. Unlike record or file locks, semaphores can apply more generally to files, records, record groups, or a shared peripheral, such as a modem or printer.

With more properties, semaphores are more flexible than record locks and can be used for more sophisticated control functions. Semaphores can have any assigned meaning, and are more closely related to logical locks than physical locks. Semaphores can be used in a variety of ways by different application developers and NOS vendors.

Activities

1. Describe the function of a file server.

   _____

   _____

   _____

   _____

2. Compare file locking with record locking.

   _____

   _____

   _____

   _____

   _____

3. Draw a network that contains 20 clients and 2 file servers. This network should be an Ethernet network that contains a switched backbone. The switch in this network has 12 ports: ten 10-Mbps ports, and two 100-Mbps ports. How would you configure this network?

Extended Activity

Map drives between a client and a server or between two clients. Experiment with reading and writing the same file to and from several clients to the same locations. Describe what messages appear, and what services are provided by the desktop OS or server.

Lesson 4—Print Servers

A second basic NOS function is providing print services for clients of a network. This lesson covers basic aspects of print servers in networks.

Objectives

At the end of this lesson you will be able to:

• Understand the basic operation of a print server

 **Key Point**

Print servers provide sharing of printers between multiple clients in a network.

Print Servers

A dedicated server machine can be set aside for printing, or a user's workstation can provide print services. Either way, a print server computer normally requires specialized software, such as a NOS or print server application, to manage print jobs from multiple users. Like any application, print server software requires central processing unit (CPU) cycles and memory. Thus, if a user's workstation is used as a print server, that computer will not perform as well when running other applications at the same time. If a print server is turned off, print services disappear until the machine is turned on again. The Print Servers Diagram shows different types of print servers found in a typical Novell NetWare environment.

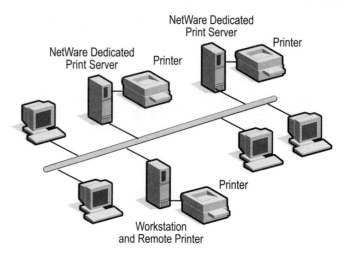

Print Servers

When users of a network want to print to a shared print device, the print server software takes the print requests and stores them until the printer is ready for printing. A print spooler is software that intercepts print requests on their way to the printer and stores the requests on its hard drive or in memory where the print jobs wait to be printed.

The job of a print server of a typical NOS or stand-alone print server is outlined as follows:

1. Requests are sent to the print server to be fulfilled.

2. If the printer is unavailable, the print server does one of the following:

    –   Buffers the print job in memory

    –   Spools the print job onto its disk until the requested printer is available

3. The print server notifies the client of the status of the print request, either by displaying how many pages are being printed, or notifying the users that the print job is complete.

4. A print queue is where print jobs wait until they can be sent directly to a printer for printing.

Activities

1. What kind of computer should be used as a print server?

   _____

   _____

2. Describe the basic operation of a print server.

   _____

   _____

   _____

   _____

Extended Activity

Using a Web search engine, research information on print servers. Find as many types of print servers as possible and describe the differences between each.

_____

_____

_____

_____

_____

_____

Lesson 5—Web Servers

Most of us are familiar with Web servers as key components of the Web. When we use a browser to access a Web page, that request is fulfilled by a distant Web server. However, Web servers are also used in private computer networks. Intranet servers are Web servers used internally by an organization. Extranets are Web servers used internally with limited outside access.

One of the reasons for the popularity of intranets and extranets is that Internet technology allows for easy interchange of hypermedia between networked environments. Some of these environments or clients can be terminal browsers, PCs running Windows, Macintoshes, or X-Windows on workstations. But all of them can use Hypertext Transfer Protocol (HTTP) to access a Web server.

Objectives

At the end of this lesson you will be able to:

- Describe the basic functions of a Web server

- Describe several hardware and software platforms used for Web services

 **Key Point**

Intranet, Internet, and extranet servers all use Web server applications.

Web Server Concepts

A Web server, also called an HTTP server or http daemon (httpd), is an application that manages Internet resources and transmits them in response to requests from Web browsers. Web browsers use HTTP to send requests for Web pages and other documents, and Web servers use HTTP to deliver the requested information.

Web servers can also be configured to provide directories and indexes, and restrict access to those directories based on user authentication. Once a user is identified, the server may also provide customized responses to errors.

The Web Server Response Diagram shows details of the protocol stacks of a typical client and server.

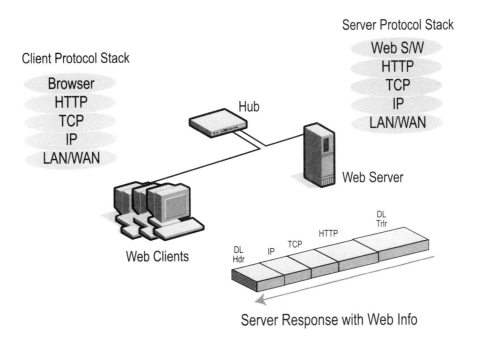

Web Server Response

On the server side of the diagram, the computer is running Web server software such as Apache or Windows NT Internet Information Server (IIS). The Web server consists of not only the application, but also the protocols needed to communicate with clients.

Web server software runs in conjunction with NOS software, to provide services to multiple clients. A Web server is typically used for both internal and external access. Access may be restricted to a select group of users, or made publicly available to millions of users across the Internet.

Basic Web servers are, despite the associated hype, relatively simple in their design. Vendors are increasingly adding more and more proprietary features to their Web servers, highlighting the need to choose a Web server wisely. In this section, we will review various Web server applications available for different platforms.

Web Server Platforms

The first decision is to choose the hardware/OS platform on which we will run our Web server. The major platform choices fall into the following categories:

- UNIX-based systems

- Microsoft Windows NT/2000

- Macintosh

UNIX-Based Systems

Because of the UNIX heritage of the Internet, more UNIX-based HTTP servers have been implemented than any other platform. There are several available HTTP servers for UNIX:

- Apache HTTP Server—The Apache HTTP server is a public domain server that serves more than 50 percent of the Web server market, according to the Netcraft Web Server Survey (**http://www.netcraft.co.uk/Survey/**).

  One of the principle strengths of Apache is that it is free. All executables, the source code, updates, patches, fixes, and documentation can be downloaded from the Apache Web site. The source code can be modified freely, so custom features can be added as necessary. The strong freeware mentality that exists in the UNIX community has helped drive the development of Apache to a level equal to or surpassing many commercial packages.

  The major disadvantage of the Apache Web server is that it is difficult to configure. Unlike products developed by Windows-oriented vendors like Microsoft and Netscape, Apache does not have a rich graphical environment in which to operate. Changes to the server must be made by modifying its configuration files. This task can be daunting to those without a strong UNIX background, and mistakes, some of which can be devastating, are easy to make.

- National Center for Supercomputing (NCSA)—The NCSA HTTP server is maintained by the NCSA at the University of Illinois at Champagne-Urbana. The Web site is **http://hoo-hoo.ncsa.uiuc.edu**. The NSCA server supports HTTP/1.0.

- World Wide Web Consortium (W3C): CERN and Jigsaw— W3C has a public domain server available, known as the CERN server. Additional information is available on their Web site at **http://www.w3.org/pub/WWW/Daemon/**.

Microsoft Windows NT/ 2000

Due to the popularity of the Windows platform, the growth of the HTTP server market for this platform has been fast. The real competition for this market consists generally of two players: Netscape and Microsoft. Their available HTTP servers are:

- Netscape Enterprise Server includes a broad range of tools in addition to the basic HTTP server. The tools provide integrated content creation and site management functionality. Also included are index and search capabilities. Netscape offers a variety of products designed to be used within the framework of the enterprise network and growing intranet niche. Enterprise Server is also supported on several major UNIX platforms.

- Microsoft IIS—Microsoft IIS is one of the easiest HTTP servers to install and maintain. It is free to all licensed users of Windows NT/2000, and the products are highly integrated. This high level of integration makes IIS a good choice for companies that already have a Windows network in operation. Companies that have enterprise networks built on UNIX may not find IIS a very good choice, because it only runs on Windows.

- Personal Web Server—Included with Windows client OSs, such as Windows 2000 or NT 4.0 Workstation, this server is good for sharing and evaluating a small Web site at the workgroup/intranet level. However, if you need powerful, dynamic content generation or electronic commerce features, you must move up to IIS.

Macintosh

If the Internet or an intranet is being installed in a Macintosh environment, a Macintosh-based HTTP server may be the best choice. With the power available in an Apple G4 processor, Macintosh servers are becoming a viable server option for many businesses. The Macintosh-based HTTP servers are also some of the easiest to install and maintain. There are several HTTP servers available for the Macintosh, including:

- WebSTAR—WebSTAR is a commercial HTTP server that features a built-in Java Virtual Machine that allows extensions to be built in Java.

- AppleShare IP—AppleShare IP is not designed to be a dedicated Web server product, but is an extension to the MacOS that provides a complete suite of Internet tools and services. A limited functionality Web server is included in the package. Although AppleShare IP is not as feature rich as many of the full-service Web servers available for Windows NT and UNIX, it does offer the ease of use common to the Macintosh.

- WebTen—WebTen from Tenon Intersystems is a full-featured Web server designed specifically for the Macintosh platform. The power and functionality of WebTen is derived from its roots: the Apache Web server. WebTen is a Macintosh-compatible version of Apache with graphic interfaces and other functionality added by Tenon. The core functionality of WebTen comes from a UNIX virtual machine running on a PowerPC-based Macintosh. The Apache Web server runs in the virtual machine, and the management modules are Web-based applications that can run on the same Macintosh as the server or be run remotely. The final piece of the WebTen package is the TCP/IP stack, which is proprietary to Tenon and does not require MacTCP.

Activities

1. What are the differences between an Internet, intranet, and extranet server?

   _____

   _____

   _____

2. List the Web servers covered in this lesson and one unique feature of each.

   _____

   _____

   _____

3. List at least two functions of a Web server.

   _____

   _____

   _____

   _____

Extended Activity

1. Using a Web search engine, research the latest products and release levels of the following Web servers. Put together a matrix of features for each product.

   a. WebStar

   b. Apache

   c. Microsoft IIS

   d. WebTen

   e. Netscape Enterprise Server

Lesson 6—Other Common Servers

On a network, almost any shared resource can be housed on its own server platform. Depending on how heavily they are used, each resource may have its own dedicated server machine, while several others may share the same server.

In this lesson, we briefly introduce some of the other types of servers commonly found in networks:

- Application servers run shared programs
- Communication servers provide multiuser access to outside network connections
- Address servers assign and manage network addresses, such as IP addresses

Objectives

At the end of this lesson you will be able to:

- Explain the technical and legal difference between single-user software and network software
- Describe the difference between a RAS and a VPN
- Explain why a Dynamic Host Configuration Protocol (DHCP) server is common in large networks

 **Key Point**

A server is a computer that hosts a shared resource.

Application Servers

As the number of LAN clients grows, there is a point where buying many stand-alone copies of application software becomes more expensive than buying a single multiuser network version. LAN-based applications are often easier to manage as well, especially when many users share a single program. When a new release is needed, it is upgraded once at the server, so each individual user does not have to upgrade software.

Application Platforms

Application server computers are optimized for a particular use, that is, they have greater processing power, disk capacity, memory, input/output (I/O) ports, and/or card slots to enhance their designated application's performance. For example, a database server should have large disk drives with very fast access times, while a financial application server needs a very fast CPU with a math co-processor.

Types of Applications

There are differences between single-user, multiuser, and network-aware (network) software. This is important when buying applications software. These three general software categories, with respect to use on a LAN are:

- Single-user—A single copy stored in a file server can be downloaded to one or more workstations, and run individually on each workstation(s). This approach can improve performance, because applications typically run faster on a client desktop than running over a network.

  Single-user software is often said to be "networkable," and some stand-alone software packages even have configurable options for network use. But other stand-alone software fits poorly into a network environment. For example, customized features may not be saved after they are set up, or they may be modified by other users with their own preferences. Files may not be properly locked for multiuser sharing, as they are in a network-aware package.

- Multiuser—Multiuser software has advantages over single-user software by allowing sharing of files created by a single-user program properly located in a user's private disk area. File or record locking allows multiple users to work with the same body of data.

- Network—Network software takes advantage of all the shared resources, such as modems, printers, and fax servers.

Application Licensing

When a single-user application operates properly over the network, it is tempting to share the software among multiple users. However, single-user software is just that; it is legally licensed for use by only one user at a time. Thus, while it may be technically possible to share a stand-alone application over the network, this practice may violate the software license.

Licensing rules are followed loosely (or ignored) by some users, to the extent that the Software Publisher's Association (SPA) estimates that over $1 billion is lost each year in the United States alone because of illegal copying. SPA has shown its willingness to sue many types of license violators, large-scale pirates, Web site operators, and careless corporations, at the request of its members.

The SPA uses civil lawsuits to seek damages against violators. However, it is also a felony under U.S. federal law to conduct commercial software piracy.

In many cases, it is up to the network administrator to ensure that an organization obeys the terms of its software licenses. Thus, the guiding rule for the use of applications is not so much technical as it is legal. We do not want to put our organizations at risk by using software, whether on a network or not, which has not been licensed properly.

Network Software Licenses

Licensing arrangements vary for network-available software. These applications are usually licensed in two ways:

- Per-seat licenses specify the number of users that may run the program at any one time. Any users may access the program (if network security allows them to), so long as the number of simultaneous users does not exceed the license limit. For example, if five users are currently using a five-user application, the sixth user who attempts to run the program will be denied access.

    One problem with this approach is that users log on to an application and forget to log off, which may prevent other users from logging on. Automatic log-off software can solve this problem and monitor application usage.

- Site licenses allow an unlimited number of users to run the program on a single network. These licenses are considerably more expensive than per-seat licenses but make good economic sense for applications that are used by everyone in a large organization.

Communication Servers

For many of the same reasons for having a print server, a separate communication server may be desirable. This type of server allows pooling of resources, only this time it is Internet connections or modems and phone lines, rather than printers. These types of servers are also called remote access servers or servers with remote access service (RAS) capabilities.

RAS Platforms

Like printing, communication carries its own set of requirements. Multiple serial ports are usually needed. Communication ports have high interrupt rates, which degrade file server performance. Buffering and management of the communication link is necessary. Communication is inherently less reliable than printer sharing, and some LAN administrators prefer to isolate this potential "problem child" onto a separate server. Security is usually enhanced. Until the communication server is satisfied, an inbound caller cannot access the LAN. The RAS Diagram illustrates such a communication server.

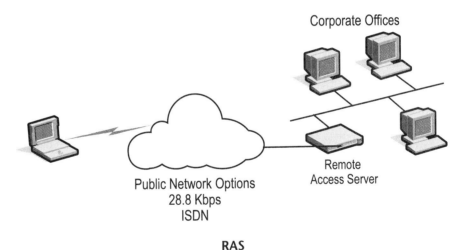

RAS

VPN

Instead of using a RAS, some organizations prefer to create a virtual private network (VPN). This service uses software encryption to create secure connections across public networks such as the Internet. VPN services are becoming more popular as the Internet is used as a wide area network (WAN) backbone alternative.

349

With VPN capability, a user at home or a remote office first connects to the Internet by means of an Internet service provider (ISP), as shown on the VPN Diagram. After establishing an Internet connection, the user can access services from their network by means of a VPN connection. After this logical VPN connection is established, the user can access resources from their own network.

The main advantage of a VPN is cost, especially if users access resources over a long distance. Because VPN includes using the Internet and dialing long distance, significant savings can be realized.

VPN

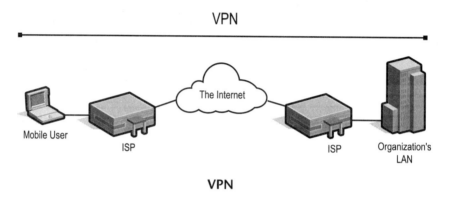

VPN

NAT

When data, such as a Web page request, is transmitted out of a LAN across the Internet, that packet contains the IP address of the source node. However, there are good reasons why network administrators usually do not want outgoing Internet traffic to identify each source node with a unique IP address.

First, the worldwide Internet community has a short supply of unique IP addresses. This means that each network often uses its own private addressing system that conflicts with the globally unique addresses used across the Internet.

Second, the practice of assigning fixed IP addresses to internal nodes is a potential security risk. A criminal hacker could use that information to penetrate the private network, just as anyone with your phone number can call you in the middle of the night.

Network Address Translation (NAT) allows a network to use one set of IP addresses for Internet communication, and a separate set for internal networking. NAT is typically installed on a company's Internet router (default gateway) and not the RAS server. However, some networks use NAT in conjunction with a communication server.

Address Servers (DHCP Servers)

In a TCP/IP network, each node's 32-bit IP address identifies both the node itself and the number of the network or subnet that contains the node. The left-most portion of the address contains the network or subnet number, and the right-most portion identifies the node.

Large networks are often divided into separate subnetworks, each identified by a different network number. Thus, when a computer must move from one subnet to another, the IP address of that device must be changed to use the network number of the new subnet. This is not much of an issue in small networks, but large networks spend a great deal of time and energy reconfiguring their internal IP addresses. To solve this problem, Microsoft developed DHCP, a TCP/IP-based solution built into the Windows client and server OSs.

DHCP, running on a server, dynamically assigns IP addresses to logical end stations for fixed periods of time. When the DHCP server detects that a workstation's physical location no longer corresponds to its allocated IP address, it simply assigns that end station a new address. By using DHCP, a network administrator can move workstations from subnet to subnet without having to manually configure each workstation's IP address.

Activities

1. Discuss advantages and disadvantages of running single-user software on a network server, versus software licensed for multiuser access.

   _____

   _____

   _____

   _____

   _____

   _____

2. What is the difference between a per-seat license and a site license?

   _____

   _____

   _____

   _____

   _____

   _____

3. How does a VPN ensure secure communication over the Internet?

   _____

   _____

   _____

   _____

   _____

   _____

4. What is the main advantage of DHCP?

_____

_____

_____

_____

_____

_____

Extended Activities

1. Research the SPA. How large is its current membership? What is its primary function?

    _____

    _____

    _____

    _____

    _____

    _____

2. Using the Web, research the similarities and differences between RAS and VPNs, and their relative advantages and disadvantages.

    _____

    _____

    _____

    _____

    _____

    _____

3. Using a Web search engine, research products available for creating a VPN. What are the features and functions? How is connectivity provided?

_____

_____

_____

_____

_____

_____

4. Find products used for creating remote access for mobile users. What are the features and functions? How is connectivity provided?

_____

_____

_____

_____

_____

_____

Lesson 7—Backup and Disaster Prevention

Many people fail to back up the data on their computers. Not only do individual users fail to back up their computers, but network servers are often not adequately backed up. It is one of the easiest tasks, yet most people do not even think of doing it on a regular basis. However, if most people lost the work on their computers, they could lose weeks or even months of work. If a company were to lose information stored on a server, it could be a disaster.

Objectives

At the end of this lesson you will be able to:

- Describe different ways to back up stored information
- List methods used to create fault-tolerant storage systems

 **Key Point**

The inability to recover from a disaster is a disaster.

Policies for Backing up Information

The first step in choosing backup policies and procedures is to assess the overall risk to the organization. This includes both the actual cost of the lost data as well as the cost of recreating the lost information. Questions we must ask include the following:

- If our organization were to have a disaster that destroyed the data, how long would it take to recover that data?
- What would this cost the organization?

Several options are available to minimize the risk of not being able to recover from a failure:

- We can establish and maintain a backup process. The backup process should include a full backup of all files on a regular basis.
- We can provide onsite storage for data that preserves backup media in the event of fire, flood, or other natural disasters. Usually, a small, fireproof safe or storage box suffices.

- We can provide offsite, secured storage facilities for backup storage. Some organizations offer offsite services where data is replicated frequently, and operations can be quickly moved to an alternate site in the event of failure.

In general, a regimented series of incremental and full backups provide security for most sites and should be the first line of defense against data loss. Many media options exist, including digital audio tape (DAT), which has a storage capability of many gigabytes (GB). Many organizations perform a full backup weekly, as well as nightly incremental backups of all servers. This whole process occurs behind the scenes, usually in the evenings, and takes anywhere from one to several hours depending on the speed of the network.

Types of Backups

In large-scale systems, backup schemes work on an incremental basis. Backup software programs usually provide backup options similar to those described below:

- Copy—Backs up specified files and does not mark them as being backed up

- Full Backup—Backs up all files in a given file system and marks them as being backed up

- Incremental—Backs up and marks specified files that have changed since the last full or incremental backup

- Daily Copy—Backs up files that have changed on that given day without marking them as backed up

- Differential Backup—Backs up files that were changed since the last full or incremental backup without marking them as backed up

These options provide most network administrators the ability to create and manage a large server with ease. Many organizations adopt a backup schedule similar to the following:

- Daily—Incremental backups of all workstations and servers occur each day. These backups are retained for one month (WestNet's system does this on one DAT).

- Weekly—Full backups of each server occur once per week. This backup is retained until the next weekly backup has been completed.

- Monthly—Full backup of all servers and workstations occurs monthly. This backup is retained until the next monthly backup has been completed.

- Annual—An annual backup of all servers and workstations is created and retained for five years.

Although this schedule may not be appropriate for every situation or site, it provides recovery options in depth. The schedule is similar to those used by many mainframe and minicomputer environments. Although this type of schedule requires a substantial number of tapes, it also provides acceptable risk management for an organization.

Most backup systems maintain logging records both on the backup system and backup media. The logs contain information such as volume names, file names, computer systems backed up, and other information relative to the site. This record keeping, along with information about storage locations, ensures a site can recover from a catastrophic failure in a timely manner.

UPS

In the event of main power failure, an uninterruptible power supply (UPS) backup power system can be installed that provides for continued operations or orderly shutdown of system resources.

Two of the most common options for UPS systems are:

- Battery power supply—Allows servers to operate long enough to shut down instead of crashing. Many OSs can be configured to shut down automatically in the event of a power failure with the assistance of a battery UPS.

- Power generators—Start up automatically in the event of a power failure, allowing systems to remain up and operating until main power is restored. Many organizations ensure that power gets to the computer room and routers to keep messages flowing until main power is restored and regular operations start up.

One of the key components to an UPS system is the ongoing maintenance and testing of resources. If a generator does not start immediately after the main power source fails, the system is worthless. There are far too many installations in which the systems have been installed at great expense, but they are not maintained. UPS system maintenance can be as easy as checking the oil of the motor that powers the generator.

An unfortunate reality is that power does and will fail — it is only a matter of when. If necessary, will the backup and power systems in your installation provide you the insurance and risk level that is acceptable to the organization? Many companies have no auxiliary power or battery backup systems, and when power fails, business stops. If this situation is acceptable, nothing else needs to be done. However, imagine a site where calls and order information are coming in from all over the world—people on the other end of the telephone are unsympathetic to the plea that "our computers are down." Again, the acceptable level of risk is a business decision that needs to be explored with all stakeholders in the process.

Fault Tolerance

Fault tolerance is the ability of a system to protect against loss of data. Backups are an example of fault tolerance. The concept of data redundancy also protects in the event of loss of original data. Two data redundancy systems are described in this section: single large expensive disks (SLED), and redundant arrays of inexpensive disks (RAID). We also focus on two primary methods used in more sophisticated fault tolerance:

- Disk striping

- Disk mirroring

SLED

The SLED model is based on the fact that the incremental cost of a disk drive is not as great as the cost of a second drive. For example, a 25 GB hard drive may cost $300, while a 40-GB hard drive costs only an additional $100, for a total of $400.

RAID

The RAID model is based on the premise that disk space is inexpensive, and replication can occur by creating intentionally redundant storage. We can create a massive storage capability for a very small amount of money compared to just a few years ago. The RAID concept is based on the premise that it is better to buy multiple disk drives and create redundancy of data on the same or different servers. Six levels of RAID have been created. Windows NT Servers support RAID levels 0, 1, and 5:

- Level 0—Disk Striping

  Disk striping divides data across several drives, which increases performance but does not provide data protection. This is illustrated on the Striping Diagram.

Striping Increases Performance

| Sp_reerc | tilesrme | rnna_fa | igcsPon |

Striping

- Level 1—Disk Mirroring and Duplexing

  Disk mirroring duplicates each drive on a mirror or backup drive, as shown on the Disk Mirroring Diagram. For example, in a four-disk RAID, two disks mirror two disks. All primary drives are mirrored, which provides a very high level of data protection. The original and mirrored disks operate on the same controller in the server.

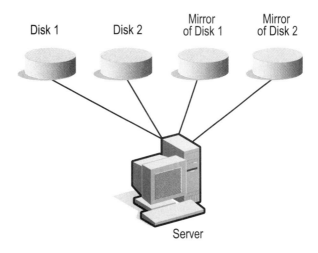

Disk 1   Disk 2   Mirror of Disk 1   Mirror of Disk 2

Server

Disk Mirroring

Duplexing is a mirroring system in which the disks use separate controllers. This setup has the advantage of providing better performance because separate data paths exist for each drive. The mirrored disk is a continual backup to the original or primary disk and it can operate automatically if the original disk fails.

Note that a file corruption or some other nonhardware-related situation can impact both disks negatively. Therefore, an efficient backup procedure is still required.

- Level 2—Disk Striping with Error Correction Code (ECC)

This level of RAID provides disk striping across all drives. ECC is stored on the drive, which uses a significant amount of disk space. In general, RAID level 2 is not implemented.

- Level 3—ECC Stored as Parity

This level is similar to RAID level 2, except that one drive is used as a storage drive for parity. Thus, in a four-drive array, three drives are used as storage and one drive is used as parity. RAID level 3 is generally not implemented.

- Level 4—Disk Striping with Large Blocks

RAID levels 2 and 3 stripe the data at the bit or byte level; RAID level 4 works with complete blocks of data. A separate disk stores parity information. As in RAID levels 2 and 3, any writes to the disk must also update the parity disk. This method is very efficient for large blocks of data; however, it is very inefficient for smaller, transaction-oriented data. In general, RAID level 4 is not implemented.

- Level 5—Disk Striping with Parity

Disk striping with parity spreads the data and parity information across the disk, as shown on the Disk Striping with Parity Diagram. This allows for faster input/output (I/O) transfers. In the event of a failure, the parity stripe block is used to recover each stripe (row) across the disk.

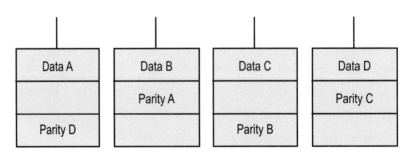

Disk Striping with Parity

Disk striping with parity is one of the most popular methods of data redundancy. It provides all the speed advantages of disk striping with none of the disadvantages of maintaining a separate parity disk.

Disaster Recovery Plan

A disaster recovery plan lists specific procedures to be performed in the event of any network failure, from a single bad component to the destruction of the entire building. Although the plan logically focuses on the network and its services, it should anticipate any problem that could compromise the network, such as fire, flood, earthquake, civil unrest, disease epidemic, security breach, or careless backhoe operators.

Furthermore, the disaster recovery plan should list critical primary and backup network resources, such as IP and MAC addresses, passwords, offsite backup locations, hardware and software systems and version numbers, as well as all baseline network statistics. The plan should also identify key individuals, teams, systems, service providers, and other personnel essential to network operations, outline their responsibilities in various types of disasters, and provide detailed contact information.

Of course, it is impossible to foresee every type of disaster. However, the process of planning for the most likely problems will create a foundation of sound systems and procedures that can be quickly adapted to unexpected events.

The network/IT disaster plan must function as one component of an overall corporate disaster plan. However, the network must have its own plan, even if the corporation does not. And, of course, a copy of the plan should be stored offsite.

Activities

1. List and describe the five types of backups.

    _____

    _____

    _____

    _____

    _____

    _____

    _____

    _____

    _____

    _____

2. Why is it necessary to conduct a full backup prior to performing incremental backups?

    _____

    _____

3. Describe the two common types of UPS systems.

    _____

    _____

    _____

    _____

4. What is meant by "fault tolerance?"

    _____

    _____

5. List and briefly describe all levels of protection offered by RAID technology.

_____

_____

_____

_____

_____

_____

_____

_____

_____

_____

Extended Activities

1. Using your favorite Internet search engine, find information on two vendors who supply tape backup systems for enterprise servers typically found in LANs. Summarize your findings in terms of storage capacities of these devices.

_____

_____

_____

_____

2. Using your favorite Internet search engine, find information about RAID as it pertains to software versus hardware RAID implementations. Contrast the two types with a brief description of each.

_____

_____

_____

_____

Summary

This unit reviewed the process of client/server communication, and provided an overview of the type of specialized servers that are commonly used in networks.

Many applications also reside on client machines, and use server resources only for file and print sharing. Other applications reside on a server and are accessed by many clients. The server computers that host these shared applications usually contain hardware features that are suited to the software they run.

When a client program requests a service across a network, APIs provide common interfaces for application programmers to make remote procedure calls. RPCs allow clients and servers to each specialize in particular tasks. Each remote procedure call invokes communications processes that build protocol headers used to transfer information across a network.

As more applications follow the client/server model, vital information and applications tend to be distributed throughout the network on both servers and user workstations. This means that the responsibility for backup and disaster recovery logically falls to the network administrative staff. Fortunately, a wide variety of storage products and utility applications is available to simplify this essential item of routine network maintenance.

Unit 6 Quiz

1. In a client/server arrangement, where are requests normally generated?

    a. Client

    b. Server

    c. Either client or server

    d. NIC

2. In a client/server environment, what is the software that determines the destination of a user's request for LAN services?

    a. Redirector

    b. Initiator

    c. IP

    d. IPX

3. Which of the following is the primary use of a redirector?

    a. Routes machine requests to hard drives and tape drives

    b. Directs traffic to a bridge or router

    c. Directs workstation requests to a WAN

    d. Directs workstation requests to a server

4. When a client application calls software routines that run on a server application, it is using which of the following?

    a. Remote protocol communications

    b. Remote procedure calls

    c. Redundant processing calls

    d. Remote processing connections

5. Which of the following is not a NOS?

    a. Windows NT

    b. Novell NetWare

    c. Banyan VINES

    d. Windows 98

6. When does it make sense to use a peer-to-peer NOS instead of a full-blown client/server NOS? When does it make sense to use a full-blown client/server NOS instead of a peer-to-peer NOS?

_____

_____

_____

_____

7. Name two common server types, and list their basic functions.

_____

_____

_____

_____

8. Where would an RPC be found (layer) in relation to the OSI model?

_____

_____

9. What is the difference between a VPN and RAS?

_____

_____

10. Why is file locking required for multiuser networked applications?

_____

_____

11. You configure your computer settings so that the OS performs routine hard disk maintenance during idle times. When you return from a coffee break one day, this maintenance is in progress, but it stops as soon as you resume working in your favorite application. What OS feature makes this possible?

    a. Preemptive multitasking

    b. Multithreading

    c. Spooling

    d. Multiprocessing

12. Jane can read and write to File A. John can read File A, but cannot write to it. What is the most likely cause?

    a. File access attributes

    b. A problem in John's NIC

    c. File locking

    d. Software bug

13. A binary bit that represents a value or its opposite is called which of the following?

    a. Marker

    b. Semaphore

    c. Flag

    d. Pointer

    e. a and d

    f. b and c

14. When a Web browser retrieves an HTML document from a Web server, this is an example of which of the following?

    a. Master/slave communication

    b. Client/server communication

    c. Virtual private network

    d. Remote procedure call

15. Web servers can be run on what platforms?

    a. Linux on Sun workstations

    b. Microsoft 2000 Server on Pentium III computers

    c. Mac OS on Apple G4 machines

    d. All of the above

16. You are the new corporate network administrator. As you become familiar with your new system, you discover that the entire network is sharing a single-user version of a popular word processor. When you ask about this, your boss says, "The last administrator tweaked a few settings, and it works like a charm. That was really clever of him." What should you do?

    a. Do nothing. If something is working, don't fix it.

    b. Quit before someone can blame you.

    c. Find out how the prior administrator did it.

    d. Immediately explain to management that the company must buy a multiuser license.

17. A university allows students to connect laptop computers to wall jacks in classrooms and libraries. The campus network is divided into six subnetworks, and each student moves through several subnetworks each day. Which of the following is the best technical solution?

    a. Assign each student six IP addresses

    b. Set up a DHCP server

    c. Use NAT

    d. Post the network number on a sticker on each wall jack

18. A company needs a fault-tolerant storage system that does not slow down its file access times. The best choice is which of the following?

    a. RAID 5

    b. RAID 0

    c. SLED 3

    d. RAID 6

19. A large retail catalog company receives orders 24 hours a day from its Web site and telephone lines. To ensure constant availability of its data system, which of the following should it have?

    a. UPS

    b. RAID

    c. Nightly backups

    d. Backup generators

    e. All of the above

Unit 7
The Novell NetWare Client/Server System

Novell was the forerunner of modern personal computer (PC) networking environments and maintains its presence today with NetWare 5.1, Novell Directory Services (NDS), integrated management, and numerous networking products. Novell has moved into the Internet solutions arena providing many key services and features designed specifically for the requirements of e-business. This unit outlines server and client environments, compares NetWare 5.1 services to previous versions of NetWare, looks at NDS and its management tools, and presents an overview of NetWare protocol stacks.

Lessons

1. NetWare Overview
2. NetWare Services
3. Novell Directory Services
4. NetWare Client
5. NetWare Protocols
6. NetWare Packet Structure

Terms

abend—Abend is short for "ABnormal END" and traditionally means a processing error that stops, or crashes, an OS.

bindery—In versions of NetWare earlier than 4.0, the bindery is a network database that defines entities such as users, groups, and workgroups. The bindery has been replaced by NDS.

block—A block is a small unit of physical disk space used to physically store files on a disk drive, usually configured in units of 4 KB, 8 KB, 16 KB, 32 KB or 64 KB. NetWare uses 64 KB by default. A block (sometimes called a "cluster") consists of several sectors, and is typically the smallest unit of storage that an OS can recognize. See sector.

client—The client portion of a client/server architecture is any node or workstation used by a single user. If multiple users share resources on the same workstation, it becomes a server. Examples of clients are Microsoft Windows NT Workstation and Windows 98.

firewall—A firewall is a controlled access point between sections of the same network, designed to confine problems to one section. A firewall is also a controlled access between a private network and a public network (such as the Internet), usually implemented with a router and special firewall software.

flat file—A flat file is the simplest type of database, which stores data in isolated tables that are not linked to each other. A box of paper file cards is essentially a flat file.

Internetwork Packet Exchange (IPX)—IPX is the Network Layer protocol Novell has adapted to be their protocol of choice, used for connectionless transport of packets. IPX appends addressing and routing information to data sent down from upper layers.

Java—Java is an interpreted, platform-independent, high-level programming language developed by Sun Microsystems. Java is a powerful language with many features that make it attractive for the Web.

Lightweight Directory Access Protocol (LDAP)—LDAP is a tree-structured directory format based on the X.500 standard. See X.500.

Link Support Layer (LSL)—LSL is part of Novell's ODI specification that provides routing for multiple protocols on one NIC.

NetWare Core Protocol (NCP)—The coding information used to request a service or process from a NetWare server is referred to as NCP. The server fulfills the request and responds with an NCP Reply.

NetWare Loadable Module (NLM)—NLMs are modular software components that expand the services provided by a NetWare kernel. They are loaded and unloaded on a server as necessary to free up memory and processor resources. NLMs also allow third-party vendors to develop products that run on NetWare.

Network Driver Interface Specification (NDIS)—NDIS is a Microsoft-developed specification that enables multiple protocol support for a NIC.

Network News Transport Protocol (NNTP)—Part of the TCP/IP Application Layer, NNTP is the protocol that supports USENET newsgroups.

Novell Directory Services (NDS)—NDS is a hierarchical database of information about users and network resources. NDS manages all network components through a single interface. NDS version 8 is available on other NOS platforms such as Microsoft, Sun Solaris, UNIX, and IBM.

Open Data Link Interface (ODI)—ODI is a Novell-developed specification that enables multiple protocol support for a NIC.

packet—A packet is a unit of information processed at the Network Layer. The packet header contains the logical (network) address of the destination node. Intermediate nodes forward a packet until it reaches its destination. A packet can contain an entire message generated by higher OSI layers, or a segment of a much larger message.

partition—Partition is the physical division of disk space set aside for use by an OS. A NetWare server typically has one bootable DOS partition, and one to three NetWare partitions.

public key encryption—Public-key encryption is a cryptographic system that uses two mathematically related keys: one key is used to encrypt a message, and the other to decrypt it. People who need to receive encrypted messages distribute their public keys but keep their private keys secret.

requester—A requester is a set of software modules that processes requests from a client application program and directs the request to either the local OS or a remote NOS.

RSA—The acronym RSA stands for Rivest, Shamir, and Adelman, the inventors of a widely used public-key encryption algorithm. The RSA encryption algorithm has become the de facto standard for industrial-strength encryption across the Internet.

sector—A sector is the smallest unit of physical disk storage. Most OSs combine several sectors into a block, and use the block as the smallest unit of file storage space. See block.

Secure Sockets Layer (SSL)—An application of both public-key and single-key encryption that secures an Internet connection between browser and server. Web page URLs that use SSL begin with "https://".

Sequenced Packet Exchange (SPX)—SPX is the connection-oriented transport protocol concerned with connection-oriented services, such as sequencing packets, and guaranteeing their delivery, which provides reliability for IPX communications.

server—A NetWare server is a system installed with a NetWare product that provides services to fulfill multiple client requests simultaneously.

Service Advertising Protocol (SAP)—SAP is a protocol that is part of the Novell Netware stack. A network device uses SAP packets to tell other devices about the services it can provide.

single-key (symmetric) encryption—Single-key encryption is a cryptographic system that uses the same key to both encrypt and decrypt a message. Single-key encryption systems require both the sender and receiver of a message to share the same key before using it to communicate.

volume—Volume is a logical area of disk space, configured in NetWare, and used to store a specific group of directories and files. For example, a NetWare server could configure a volume for system files, a volumes for data, and a volume for applications.

X.500—X.500 is an ITU-T standard for a global tree-structured directory that can provide a worldwide lookup service.

X.509—X.509 is an ITU-T standard for directory authentication services.

X Windows—X Windows is an early client/server system, with graphical user interface, developed for UNIX.

Lesson 1—NetWare Overview

NetWare was the first non-UNIX network operating system (NOS) to provide file sharing between PCs. Since then it has added a multitude of services and features to meet the demands of the technology industry. From basic file and print sharing to high-end security, World Wide Web (Web), and application services, Novell does it all. To begin with, a brief history of NetWare and an overview of the server will help set the stage.

Objectives

At the end of this lesson you will be able to:

*   Briefly detail the history of Novell and NetWare

*   Identify the key functions of a NetWare server

 **Key Point**

NetWare provides products and services for interoperability with other networks and technologies.

History of Novell and NetWare

NetWare began in 1983 as "Sharenet," a way to share files from PC to PC, at a time when only mainframes and minicomputers were available. It was the first of its kind to provide file and printing services to the growing PC desktop environment, moving away from "dumb terminals" and toward connectivity for DOS-based computers. Eventually, it added support for Windows, Macintosh, OS/2, and UNIX workstations.

NetWare versions 2.*x* and 3.*x* provided more network resources and management capabilities primarily centered around connection services, file access, mail systems, and print sharing. In those days, each server was its own stand-alone system, storing information about users, groups, and file access rights in a flat file database called a bindery. Each server had its own bindery. To access resources from one bindery to another, you had to have an account and log in individually to each one. There were many limitations to this scenario and, although it worked well at the time, Novell decided it was time for a big change.

In the spring of 1994, Novell released NetWare 4.0, the first version to include a new network resource management capability called NDS. NDS is a hierarchical, object-oriented, relational database that holds information about all network resources. InterNetWare, or NetWare 4.11, shipped in 1996. It patched the previous versions and enhanced NDS capabilities.

With complete refinement of NDS, the release of NetWare 5 in 1998 was a technology leap in the services and products available as part of the operating system (OS). Subsequent lessons outline the features of NetWare 5.

From its humble beginning, NetWare has evolved from file and print sharing of old, to the most diverse and expandable directory solution available. Today, Novell is the fifth largest international software vendor, and has an installation base of 4.3 million servers and 81 percent of the Fortune 500 companies globally. This number increases continuously as Novell provides new products and services that benefit and align corporate and Web-based enterprises with powerful networking solutions. Because of NDS, and many of the Web and Java capabilities of NetWare 5.1, the product has become a top choice for Internet-enabled businesses worldwide.

NetWare Server

In a Novell network environment, a server is the system that runs the NetWare OS and handles many simultaneous requests for services. It cannot be used as a workstation, and up until NetWare 5, all administration had to be performed from a client PC. NetWare 5 now offers a graphical user interface (GUI) on the server based on Microsoft Windows. A GUI is used to simplify installations, manage the file system, administer NDS objects, and access other servers remotely.

The hardware requirements to install NetWare 5.1 are very low:

- 128 megabytes (MB) random access memory (RAM)
- Pentium processor
- 1 gigabyte (GB) of disk space
- Video graphics adapter (VGA) monitor
- Compact disc and read-only memory (CD-ROM) and mouse

The NetWare architecture handles memory, processors, and network and disk access very efficiently, thereby preventing unnecessary reboots. NetWare supports up to 32 processors and provides preemptive processing, load balancing, multitasking, multithreading, and processor scheduling. New support has been added for memory protection and virtual memory that allows the system to swap cached information to disk.

Another feature protects the server from crashing if there is a critical problem. Abend (Abnormal End) protection and recovery is used by a server to stop an offending process while continuing to service requests. If the server cannot recover using this method, it will reboot itself, reconnect clients, and begin processing requests without human intervention. As an added feature, NetWare 5 provides Hot PCI, a utility that allows an administrator to shut down a protocol control information (PCI) slot, install a new network interface card (NIC) or disk controller, power up the slot, and provide the new resource, all without rebooting or affecting production.

NLMs

To provide services beyond the server kernel, a system uses NetWare Loadable Modules (NLMs). These provide access to configuration and monitoring tools; electronic mail (e-mail), Web, and applications services; protocol support; and many other service components. When an NLM is loaded, it uses memory and other server resources. When no longer in use, the NLM can be easily unloaded to free up memory without rebooting. NLMs make a system very expandable and allow third-party vendors to write additional products for NetWare. Some examples include Novell's partnership with Oracle for databases and Structured Query Language (SQL) support, IBM's WebSphere product for Web application services, and the Novell Netscape Enterprise Web Server.

TTSs

Transaction tracking service (TTS) is used by NetWare to prevent potential corruption. It is used by NDS and other databases, and keeps track of every transaction processed into that database. In the event the server encounters an unrecoverable error and reboots, TTS backs out incomplete transactions and returns the database to its previous state, preventing corrupted data from being added.

File Services

NetWare breaks the physical disk space of a partition down into logical storage areas called volumes. From there the directory and file structure is the same as any other system. To access a drive from a workstation, an administrator creates a drive mapping, which assigns a letter of the alphabet to a location on the disk, making it easy for users to find their information.

File security is implemented at two levels, through file system rights and attributes. File system rights assign the capabilities of read, write, create, erase, modify, file scan, and access control. The default assignment to any directory is read and file scan, allowing a user to view the files and read or execute a program. Attributes, on the other hand, are used to further protect the data. For example, a user may need to be able to erase files, but certain key data should never be removed, therefore the Delete Inhibit attribute can be added, which overrides the file system rights.

Block Suballocation

Block suballocation is the process used to efficiently store data on a disk. Before suballocation was available, each file had to be stored in its own block. The Novell File Sub-Block Allocation Scheme Diagram shows a 5-kilobyte (KB) file stored in 4-KB blocks, and then for efficiency, 16-KB blocks. Both scenarios waste a lot of disk space, and as more files are written, this really adds up. With block suballocation, a 64-KB block is used and broken down into 512-byte sub-blocks. Many files can be written to one block, filling it entirely and eliminating wasted space.

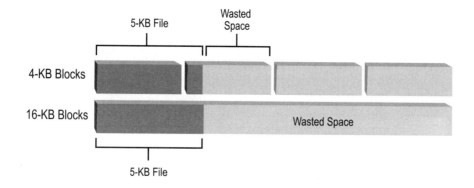

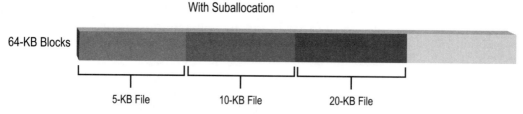

Novell File Sub-Block Allocation Scheme

File Compression

NetWare also uses file compression to further maximize disk use. By default, NetWare compresses data after it has not been touched for 14 days. This eliminates compressing and decompressing active files. The average compression ratio in a volume is approximately 63 percent. The process used for file compression follows:

1. NetWare reads and analyzes a file.

2. It builds a temporary file describing the original file.

3. NetWare determines whether any disk sectors can be saved by compressing the file. (Note: A gain of at least 2 percent [default] savings is required before a file is compressed.)

4. NetWare begins creation of the compressed file.

5. NetWare replaces the original file with a compressed file after performing an error-free compression of each file.

File compression is activated on all NetWare volumes but can be turned off at the subdirectory or file level for file types sensitive to compression. The compression process defaults to run at midnight everyday. If a compressed file is needed, it is decompressed. This allows file manipulation to continue without prolonged outage to the end user. The Novell File Compression Scheme Diagram shows a simplified view of the file compression process.

File Size Before Compression

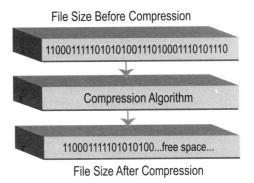

File Size After Compression

Novell File Compression Scheme

**Name Space
Support**

Name space support is offered to store UNIX, Windows, OS/2, and Macintosh files in their native file formats. Name space modules are loaded on a server for each client OS. The server then adds the appropriate name space information to the File Allocation Table and Directory Entry Table for each file and directory, respectively. When stored and accessed, a file is available in its native format without modification.

Activities

1. Within a partition, NetWare defines a logical disk storage area referred to as a _____.

2. NLMs are used for what purpose?

   _____

   _____

3. List and define two ways files and directories are protected in NetWare.

   _____

   _____

4. Define block suballocation.

   _____

   _____

Extended Activities

1. Go to **http://www.novell.com** and find the History of Novell document. Outline some of the product features from NetWare 3 to NetWare 5.

2. Go to Novell's knowledgebase support page at **http://www.support.novell.com** and locate the definitions of:

   a. Multitasking

   b. Preemptive processing

   c. Multithreading

   d. TTS

Lesson 2—NetWare Services

While maintaining all of NetWare's original functionality, Net-Ware 5.1 offers many new features for Web solutions and application services. Outside of OSs and NDS, Novell provides an extensive range of products and services. This lesson outlines the features of NetWare 5.1 and compares older versions of the product, which still make up a large share of the network environment. This lesson also describes other networking products offered by Novell.

Objectives

At the end of this lesson you will be able to:

• Describe the services and features provided by NetWare 5.1

• Describe and compare the features of NetWare 3, 4, and 5

• List additional products offered by Novell

 **Key Point**

NetWare 5.1 maintains all the original functionality, while adding a complete Internet-enabled business solution.

NetWare 5.1 Services and Features

The NetWare OS currently includes several services shipped with NetWare 5.1. These services go beyond standard file and print sharing and connection services:

• NDS—NDS is a distributed hierarchical database of information about all network resources managed through one interface. It can be extended to include new objects from third-party vendors, and has demonstrated its scalability with over one billion objects in one tree. Lesson 3 provides more information on NDS.

- eDirectory—Taken one step further, eDirectory applies the power of NDS to the Web environment. eDirectory stores information about clients, partners, suppliers, and customers around the globe, giving an administrator the capability to control security and access to Web environments. It offers Lightweight Directory Access Protocol (LDAP) capabilities, and a BULKLOAD utility to quickly import hundreds of users, and is managed through one interface.

- Novell Distributed Print Services (NDPS)—NDPS is the new printing environment that speeds print requests, eases administration, reduces Service Advertising Protocol (SAP) traffic on a network by registering printers in a database, and provides print driver downloads to a workstation. It includes several gateways in addition to Hewlett Packard and Xerox to create an enterprise-wide printing environment, and offers complete backward compatibility with queue-based printing in NetWare 3 and 4.

- High-capacity file storage systems and Novell Storage System (NSS)—File services is the foundation of NetWare, and NetWare 5 takes it one step further with NSS. NSS is an advanced system for storing and accessing up to 8 terabyte files and unlimited file storage. In addition, it requires no memory, offers instantaneous availability, and provides other capabilities like multiple NetWare partitions and fast CD-ROM access.

- Security—Novell offers a variety of security services to use individually or layered for the most secure system requirements. Novell's certificate server maintains secure transmissions using public-key cryptography. Other security products include Novell International Cryptographic Infrastructure, password encryption over Secure Sockets Layer (SSL), RSA private/public-key encryption, Secure Authentication Services (SAS), smart cards, and X.509v3 certificates. In addition, NetWare offers several alternate login methods using biometrics for finger print, face scan, and voice recognition.

- Dynamic Host Configuration Protocol (DHCP), Domain Name System (DNS), and Dynamic DNS (DDNS)—DHCP is used to assign Internet Protocol (IP) addresses and a multitude of additional information to a client system. DNS can provide name resolution configured as either a primary or secondary zone and is replicated using NDS synchronization processes. DDNS allows DHCP to deliver an address to a host, then updates the DNS table with the new information.

- Management Portal—This utility allows an administrator to change parameters and hardware settings, monitor system activity, modify NDS objects, manage applications and file systems, and reboot the server remotely from any Web browser. This utility revolutionizes system administration.

- Oracle 8i—Oracle 8i includes a five-user copy to provide client/server database access and design capabilities, and also Web publishing, INTTYPE file, and NET8 assistants.

- Zero Effort Networking (ZenWorks)—ZenWorks is used for desktop management, and incorporates policies, inventorying, application scheduling, distribution, and management. Additional ZenWorks products can be purchased for more workstation features, server management, or the network environment.

- Java support—This support is used to run and support Java applications at the server console, display them in a X Windows graphical interface, and deploy Java-based applets.

- Enterprise Web server—This service is used for hosting and securing Web sites and content. It can be used for Internet purposes or bound to a corporate NDS for a high-security intranet environment.

- IBM WebSphere—WebSphere represents a major partnership effort, which is integrated with NDS and provides a high-end, robust environment to manage and deploy Java applications through NetWare and the Web.

- News, multimedia, and File Transfer Protocol (FTP) services—These services provide access to or host news forums and discussion groups with the news service that uses Network News Transport Protocol (NNTP) for standard external communications. Multimedia services offer streaming video and sound files in Moving Pictures Experts Group 1, Layer 3 (commonly referred to as MP3), WAV, and RealVideo formats. FTP is the transport protocol used for fast transport of files between different hosts.

- Novell Internet Access Server (NIAS)—NIAS offers dial-in/dial-out capabilities for remote communications or Internet access, and supports multiple, simultaneous modem connections.

- Network Address Translation (NAT)—NAT allows companies to use private, nonregistered IP addresses internally, and makes the connection to the Internet with a public, registered IP address automatically.

- Storage Management Service (SMS)—Originally called SBACKUP, SMS is a new GUI-based utility that backs up servers, workstations, NDS, open databases, and the GroupWise e-mail system.

NetWare 3.*x*, 4.*x*, and 5.*x* Comparison

The Comparison of Principal NetWare 3, 4, and 5 Components Table compares the features offered by the different versions of NetWare. Although NetWare 4 and 5 are the main installation base because of improved performance and NDS, many NetWare 3.*x* and even NetWare 2.2 servers still remain. Many diehard administrators believe if it ain't broke, don't fix it.

Comparison of Principal NetWare 3, 4, and 5 Components

Category	Component	NetWare 3	NetWare 4	NetWare 5	Description
Operating system	NLMs	Yes	Yes	Yes	NLMs are the drivers, utilities, and applications that can be loaded to expand the NetWare servers' capabilities.
	Memory management	Multiple Pools	One Pool	One Pool	One memory pool provides more efficient distribution of memory among processes.
	Preemption	No	No	Yes	Allows the OS to switch processing to a higher priority task.
Operating system (continued)	Multiprocessing	No	Yes	Yes	Distribution of threads to additional processors for concurrent processing. Better distribution and load balancing is part of NetWare 5.
	Multithreading	Yes	Yes	Yes	Small elements of code that can be processed in parallel on the same processor. NetWare 5 allows these to be scheduled.

Comparison of Principal NetWare 3, 4, and 5 Components (Continued)

Category	Component	NetWare 3	NetWare 4	NetWare 5	Description
Transport	IPX/SPX	Yes	Yes	Yes	NetWare's preferred communication protocol.
	TCP/IP	Supported	Supported	Pure	NetWare 3 and 4 provide IP support by encapsulating it within IPX packets. NetWare 5 provides pure IP packet structure.
	ODI	Yes	Yes	Yes	Allows multiple protocols to be linked to a single NIC.
Transport (continued)	NDIS	No	Yes	Yes	Microsoft's implementation of ODI, Novell supports it for the Windows desktop environment.
	WAN	Minimal	Some	Full	WAN protocol support and configurable synchronization.
Services	Bindery	Yes	Supported	Supported	Predecessor to NDS, requiring individual login to each server. Bindery emulation offers backward compatibility.
	NDS	No	Yes	Yes	Allows all network resources to be managed from a single interface once authenticated. All resources are available without additional logins.
	Name space	Yes	Yes	Yes	Supports native file formats for long names used by OS/2 and Windows, MAC by Macintosh, and NFS for UNIX systems.

Comparison of Principal NetWare 3, 4, and 5 Components (Continued)

Category	Component	NetWare 3	NetWare 4	NetWare 5	Description
Services (continued)	Queue-based printing	Yes	Yes	Yes	Original printing environment of NetWare 3 and 4 (NDPS provides backward compatibility).
	NDPS	No	Available	Provided	Eases printing administration, reduces network traffic, and automatically downloads printer drivers to the workstation.
	Server manager	No	Yes	Yes	Allows network administrators to view and change the server configuration, also provides help for commands and sets parameters.
	Language	English	Many	Many	User-selectable language support.
	Remote console	Yes	Yes	Yes	NetWare 3 and 4 provide an IPX-based utility to access the server console from a workstation; NetWare 5 provides an IP, Java-based version as well as IPX.
	Java support	No	No	Yes	Support for Java applications at the server console and a GUI x-windows management console.
	Backup utility	Yes	Yes	Yes	SBACKUP provides backup and restore functions for the file system. The new SMS versions include GUI access, NDS, GroupWise, and database backups.
	FTP services	Available	Yes	Yes	Copies files between different OSs. Available in NetWare 3 with UNIX services.

Comparison of Principal NetWare 3, 4, and 5 Components (Continued)

Category	Component	NetWare 3	NetWare 4	NetWare 5	Description
Services (continued)	ZenWorks	No	Available	Provided	Automates many work-station management tasks and offers desktop policies.
	NAL	No	Yes	Yes	Used to deploy and manage applications for the desktop.
	NIAS	Yes	Yes	Yes	Previously called Net-Ware Connection in Net-Ware 3 and 4, offers dial-in/dial-out capabilities.

Additional products Offered by Novell

BorderManager   BorderManager is a suite of services administered through NWAdmin. A few of the services are as follows:

- Firewall—A firewall offers three levels of protection by providing packet filtering, a circuit-level gateway, and an application-level gateway. Firewalls keep the bad guys out and filter inside traffic to the Internet.

- Virtual private network (VPN)—This service allows physical networks to be securely connected logically through VPNs. This type of service is becoming more popular as the Internet is used as a network backbone alternative.

- Proxy and proxy cache services—Proxy service allows an administrator to determine appropriate Web site access and tracking. Proxy cache services provide Internet clients shorter access times to Web servers through memory caching of popular Web sites.

GroupWise   GroupWise version 5.5 incorporates full e-mail capabilities, such as standard mail delivery and browsing, calendars, busy search and appointment setting, task lists, workflow tracking, and news services. It also includes a library feature that allows people to share documents through the same interface, with cataloging, version numbers, indexing, security, and templates. GroupWise also provides support for:

- Simple Mail Transfer Protocol (SMTP)—SMTP transports mail to continuously connected or dial-up access clients.

- Multipurpose Internet Mail Extension (MIME)—MIME offers enhanced features over SMTP, such as multipart messages, attachments, multimedia support, and encoding schemes.

- Post Office Protocol version 3 (POP3)—POP3 is a transmission protocol used to download and read messages to POP3 clients, such as Netscape Communicator, Eudora Pro, PDAs, Telnet, and Microsoft Internet Explorer.

- Internet Mail Access Protocol version 4 (IMAP4)—IMAP4 also allows downloads and reads from third-party clients.

- Lightweight Directory Access Protocol (LDAP)—LDAP allows searches through address book information.

GroupWise's user interface allows mail browsing through a GUI GroupWise client, Outlook mail client, third-party mail client, or Internet browser. This allows end users to use their client of choice while maintaining only one e-mail system for administration. GroupWise also incorporates a fax interface to allow end users to send/receive faxes as easily as sending e-mail messages. Through additional messaging gateway services, GroupWise can be interconnected with other popular messaging systems, such as Lotus Notes, Exchange, cc:Mail, and MSmail.

ManageWise

Novell's ManageWise services provide complete network management for Novell networking environments. There are five components of ManageWise as follows:

- ManageWise console—This interface is used to view information collected with Simple Network Management Protocol (SNMP) traps. When a critical event takes place, such as a server reboots, a wide area network (WAN) connection is dropped, a virus is detected, and so on; SNMP traps information about a problem and alerts the management agent. This information is also stored in a database for future review.

- NetExplorer server—The NetExplorer server component uses NLMs to perform IP/Internetwork Packet Exchange (IPX) network discovery of SNMP network resources.

- NetWare server management NLMs—These NLMs create the management information base (MIB), offer configurable traps, and continuously monitor server statistics.

- Inventory and desktop management—This component keeps track of network resources by performing regular, automated physical inventories. Each client workstation is queried by an inventory server for information pertaining to the physical and logical configuration of the desktop.

- Virus detection and inoculation—This component provides an overall antivirus protection scheme for the network environment. Each Novell server is protected through continuous scanning of the server's volumes. Clients are protected through automatic scanning of their memory and local hard drives. In addition, periodic updating of antivirus signature files are performed directly to the server, and deployed out to the client workstations.

NDS for Windows NT

For companies with mixed environments, Novell offers NDS for Windows NT (discussed in detail in the next unit). This product redirects the Windows NT domain's SAM database into NDS for management. Users can be created or modified through either Novell's management tool (NWAdmin) or User Manager for Domains. Once in NDS, the domain structure looks like an organization unit container and allows the administrator to assign access to many different domains and their resources while eliminating the need for trust relationships. It provides single sign-on between domains and Novell authentication and creates a more secure NT environment because there are no hacking tools currently available that break the authentication process of NDS.

ZenWorks

NetWare 5.1 includes ZenWorks for Desktops, the starter pack which allows desktop environment policies, and application management and distribution all from NWAdmin. Additional ZenWorks for Desktop components include remote control capabilities and a help desk requestor providing information and tracking on help desk requests.

ZenWorks for Networks is a new product released to target monitoring and management of network traffic patterns. It prioritizes bandwidth in specific amounts or percentages to critical users and applications. It also allows remote performance tuning and configuration of routers and switches from 3Com, Cisco Systems, BayNetworks, Lucent, and Extreme through NDS. ZenWorks can be installed on either NetWare or Windows NT servers.

ZenWorks for Servers is also a new product used to standardize configurations and set parameters on servers throughout a network. In addition, it provides application deployment and installation pre-configuration to help in the standardization process. It also provides replication services for a file system from server to server, or a specified group of systems.

Activities

1. List and describe five services shipped with NetWare 5.1.

   _____

   _____

   _____

   _____

   _____

   _____

   _____

   _____

   _____

   _____

   _____

2. From the comparison discussion, identify three features that are only available in NetWare 4 or 5.

   _____

   _____

   _____

3. List and describe two additional Novell products.

   _____

   _____

   _____

   _____

Extended Activities

1. Go to Novell's Web site at **http://www.novell.com** and get more information about one of the following components: eDirectory, ZenWorks, BorderManager, GroupWise, or IBM WebSphere.

2. Also on Novell's Web site, search and review a document that has more information about one of NetWare's security products, including RSA, SAS, NICI, PKI, Certificate Server, Biometrics, Smart Card, etc.

Lesson 3—Novell Directory Services

NDS, released with NetWare 4, was a major advancement in the power of NOSs. NDS is a hierarchical directory structure that stores information about all network resources, provides secure access, and can be expanded to include many additional resources outside the Novell environment. NDS has demonstrated its scalability with over one billion objects that can be divided into smaller, manageable units and stored on other OSs, including Sun Solaris, Microsoft NT, UNIX, and IBM. It uses a comprehensive GUI to administer its database and is equally powerful in distributed or centralized administration environments.

Objectives

At the end of this lesson you will be able to:

- Describe NDS and the three classes of objects

- Describe NDS naming schemes

- Briefly outline partitioning and replication

- Identify the capabilities of NWAdmin and ConsoleOne

 **Key Point**

NDS is a database of all network resources stored on a server, and accessed from a workstation.

Overview of NDS

NDS became available as an integral part of NetWare 4. It was a difficult concept to understand, given the bindery environment that proceeded it. In the bindery, everything about users and groups was stored in flat file databases without any relationships or overall organization. Getting access to a network resource required logging into the server that managed the resource directly. This meant a user had a user account on numerous servers to provide all his or her network requirements.

NDS revolutionized this idea with the concept of the tree structure. It stored everything about an entire network in one database and then put copies of the database in several servers. A user now had one account and granted access to all resources at the time of login. This cut down dramatically on account management, password synchronization, and overall administration.

NDS is a hierarchical database of objects that includes information for every component in a network: users, groups, applications, workstations, routers and switches, servers, volumes, login scripts, files, licenses, e-mail components, and so on. The list goes on and on, because as new products are installed into NDS, new objects and properties are added for the products.

In addition to storing information and providing access to network resources, NDS is also a major component in network security. NDS provides real-time authentication, meaning a user is granted the appropriate rights and access at login; however, each time a resource is requested, the database is queried to validate his or her rights. This means users do not have to log out and log in to update their rights, and can be denied access instantaneously in critical situations. The Access Diagram shows the process that takes place when a user requests a network resource:

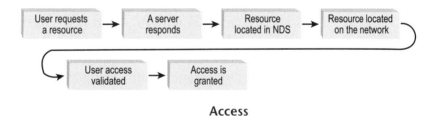

Access

1. User requests a resource—This could be a file, printer, login process, and so on.

2. A server responds—It does not matter which server responds, as long as it is a server holding a copy of the NDS database.

3. The resource is located in NDS—NDS is searched to find the physical location on a server or the network.

4. The resource is physically located on the network—The system goes to the physical location to provide the resource.

5. Authentication is checked—The system checks to verify whether the user has the appropriate rights to access the resource.

6. Access is granted—The user obtains access and uses the network resource.

NDS Structure

NDS is based on X.500 standards, which are objects representing people and resources organized hierarchically and stored in a database. The other three factors, which will be addressed later, are scalability, replication, and synchronization. To get an understanding of NDS, it is important to recognize its structure. There are three classes of objects in NDS:

- ROOT—The highest level in all NDS tree structures is ROOT. It is depicted as a globe and acts as a placeholder for the directory structure. ROOT is created at installation and cannot be deleted, renamed, moved, or changed. It can be equated to a file system, where root would be the same as the DOS C:\> prompt.

- Containers—These are objects used to organize the tree structure based on corporate requirements. The three Containers are Country, Organization, and Organization Unit:

  - Country—This optional Container is used for international companies to organize the directory by geographic location and corporate identity. If used, it is located directly under ROOT.

  - Organization—At least one organization is required, which depicts the name of the company. It holds all other objects within the tree.

  - Organization unit—These are used like a subdirectory in the file system to organize users and resources with similar requirements. For example, geographic areas or corporate departments and divisions are examples of organization units.

- Leaf—These objects are the lowest level of object within the tree structure. They represent and contain information about network resources and users. These objects are constantly being updated with information about last login, password changes, and requests for authentication to new resources.

The NDS Tree Structure Diagram illustrates an example of an NDS tree structure, including ROOT, Containers, and Leaf objects. This diagram will be referred to later in this lesson for NDS naming and object location examples.

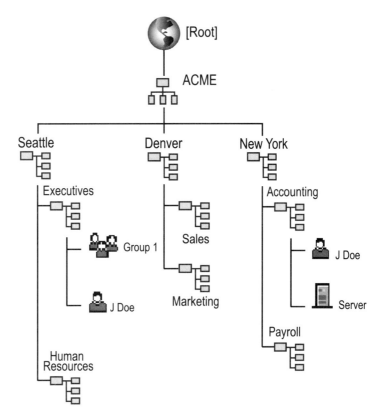

NDS Tree Structure

NDS Naming

Because NDS is built in a hierarchical structure, resources and users may have the same name as long as they are in different containers. Therefore, to locate an object in the tree and provide a unique name, a special naming scheme is necessary.

Distinguished Names

A distinguished name is made up of the common name of an object and all containers leading back to the ROOT. The idea is similar to the path for a file in the file system or the Uniform Resource Locator (URL) of a Web page. On the NDS Tree Structure Diagram, to log in or identify John Doe in accounting, the distinguished name would be:

.JDOE.ACCOUNTING.NEWYORK.ACME

For Jane Doe, an executive in Seattle, the distinguished name would be:

.JDOE.EXECUTIVES.SEATTLE.ACME

Each distinguished name is unique and completely identifies the location of the person, not only geographically but departmentally as well. The two key characteristics of a distinguished name are:

• A dot or leading period is used at the beginning of the distinguished name.

• The name includes all objects back to ROOT.

Relative Distinguished Name

A distinguished name is a lot of information for the average user to remember; however, and an administrator's job is to make the user environment more efficient. To do this, relative distinguished names are used. A relative distinguished name contains all the same information; however, a user provides some of the information and the system provides the rest. A workstation client is configured with the user's current context, meaning their location in the NDS tree. For example, in the above example, John's PC would have ACCOUNTING.NEWYORK.ACME and Jane's PC would have EXECUTIVES.SEATTLE.ACME. With this information already configured, the user simply has to provide the missing piece(s); in this case their user ID. Using a relative distinguished name, the current context is appended to the user ID and the name is complete. The characteristics of a relative distinguished name are:

• There is no dot (no leading period.)

• It contains only enough information to get to the current context (current context provides information back to ROOT).

Object Location

When accessing a resource or logging in, NDS looks at the distinguished or relative distinguished name from the end and works forward. In the previous example for John Doe, the systems would look at ACME, ACME would identify and locate NEWYORK, NEWYORK would locate ACCOUNTING, and finally JDOE would be located. If any of these pieces is missing, or too much information has been provided, an error will occur indicating "User not found in specified context." Thankfully, with the new workstation clients, this information no longer needs to be typed in; a browser can locate it within the GUI login interface.

Partitioning and Replication

As mentioned earlier, the other three factors in the X.500 standards are scalability, replication, and synchronization. NDS handles these requirements with partitioning and replication services.

Scalability and partitioning encompass the same basic concept. A very large NDS database is helpful because it provides uniformity and access to network resources in many locations. However, it needs to be able to meet the growing needs of a corporation and still be manageable. Partitioning takes a large database and logically breaks it into smaller pieces, storing the information on a local server.

For example, the ACME Corporation above could be partitioned for Denver, New York, and Seattle, and the information only stored at the designated site. This could be equated to the White Pages telephone book. If there was a telephone book listing names and numbers for the entire state, it would be too big to use, much less pick up. By breaking information down into local areas, however, the book becomes usable and manageable. A person still has access to call locations outside their telephone book, just as a user can access resources in other parts of the tree given the appropriate rights.

Replication and synchronization maintain all this information up to date. Replication stores multiple copies of the database on more than one server. By default, NetWare sets up three copies; however, an administrator can add more as necessary. Replicas are used to speed up access, because several servers hold the same information about network resources and can respond to the user's request. In addition, replication provides fault tolerance: if one server fails, another server holds the database to continue providing those services.

Synchronization maintains the replicas on different servers. The database is in a continuous state of modification, as administrators make changes, people log in and log out, and resources are accessed. This information has to be kept current for all databases; a process handled by synchronization. NetWare 5 added a service called WAN Traffic Manager to schedule synchronization across WAN links. This cuts down on traffic during high-use periods, but allows the database to still be maintained.

NetWare Administration Tools

Two GUI administration tools are available to manage NDS: NWAdmin and ConsoleOne. NWAdmin was the original management tool providing all administration capabilities; however, with NDS version 8 available on other platforms and NetWare's Web solutions directive, Java-based ConsoleOne is gaining popularity.

NWAdmin

NWAdmin is an IPX/Sequenced Packet Exchange (SPX)-based utility that allows for complete administration capabilities. It is available for Windows-based workstations, and can be used to:

- Create, modify, and delete containers and objects within the tree

- Create and edit login scripts for containers, profile groups, and users

- Configure and manage queue-based printing or NDPS

- Set up and monitor licensing of all NetWare products

- Monitor and manage disk space, volumes, directories, and files

- Setup login security requirements, file systems, and NDS access rights

- Configure and deploy applications to users, provide installations, and schedule application usage

- Manage and inventory workstations with policies

- Set up and administer e-mail systems, such as GroupWise, Exchange, and Lotus Notes

- Configure third-party products such as routers and switches

The NWAdmin Utility Screen Diagram illustrates how the GUI screen makes it easy to locate users and manage day-to-day administration.

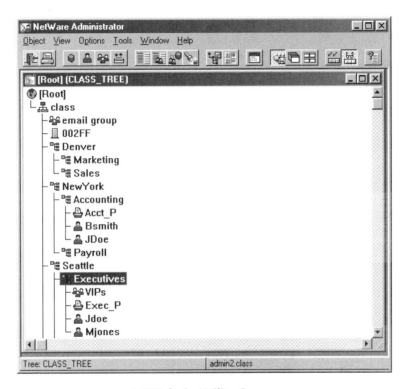

NWAdmin Utility Screen

ConsoleOne

ConsoleOne is a Java-based utility, available by means of IP. It runs on both a workstation and server to provide a common management interface in either location. ConsoleOne's benefits over NWAdmin are platform independence because it is Java-based, additional support for newer NetWare features, faster searching in large trees, and reporting capabilities. It provides virtually the same features as NWAdmin, with added capabilities to configure partition and replication, as well as manage NDS on multiplatforms such as UNIX, Microsoft, and Sun Solaris. ConsoleOne includes snapins for additional product management like ZenWorks, Certificate Server, and eDirectory. Other snapins are being developed to make ConsoleOne the only utility necessary for NDS management in the future. The ConsoleOne Screen Diagram shows the Java-based ConsoleOne interface; which is also used for daily administration tasks.

ConsoleOne Screen

Activities

1. Identify the following objects with a C for Container or L for Leaf object.

    a. John Doe a user _____

    b. Marketing printer _____

    c. Marketing department _____

    d. Acme Corporation _____

    e. UK, United Kingdom _____

    f. Data volume _____

    g. Database application _____

2. Describe the characteristics of a distinguished and relative distinguished name.

    _____

    _____

    _____

    _____

Extended Activities

1. Create a simple NDS tree structure with the objects from Activity 2 above.

2. Write a distinguished name for John Doe.

    _____

Lesson 4—NetWare Client

By definition, anything that makes a request from a server is considered a client. A workstation can become a client after a relatively small software program is installed over the workstation OS. The client works in tandem with the workstation's OS to provide additional services and redirect requests to the network that cannot be serviced locally.

Objectives

At the end of this lesson you will be able to:

- Identify which client and support services are available
- Define Open Data Link Interface (ODI) and Network Driver Interface Specification (NDIS)
- List the components of a typical client
- Identify the NetWare login screen and its associated files

 **Key Point**

NetWare provides client access for DOS, all Windows products, Macintosh, OS/2, UNIX, and Linux systems.

NetWare Client Services

The two clients available from NetWare that connect to NDS are the older DOS requester and Client 32. The DOS requestor is made up of numerous Virtual Loadable Modules (VLMs) that can be loaded individually or together to provide the appropriate services to the workstation. Their services were replaced by the 32-bit client that provides more robust and efficient network access. NetWare supports all the most popular workstation environments, providing a client that can be installed on each. The list includes DOS, all Microsoft workstation products from Windows 3.1 to Windows 2000, OS/2, Macintosh, UNIX, and Linux. The server provides not only a compatible protocol to communicate with these systems, but also supports storage of their file structures in native format through NetWare's name space support.

ODI and NDIS

Novell created ODI, which allows multiple protocols to be bound or communicate with a single network interface card (NIC). ODI is a Data Link Layer component and, for a NetWare client, allows both IPX and IP to be bound to the workstation's NIC. Before ODI, only one protocol could be active at a time, requiring reboots for connectivity to systems using differing protocols.

To achieve similar interoperability, Microsoft defined NDIS. For compatibility reasons, Novell enhanced ODI for Microsoft workstations with the development of the Open Data Link Interface Network Driver Interface Support Specification (ODINSUP). ODINSUP provides translation between the pure ODI format and the NDIS format expected by protocol stacks written for Microsoft workstation OSs. The interoperability of these interfaces for a NetWare client computer is illustrated on the ODI and NDIS Diagram.

User Application Programs

Requester			
ODI Protocol Stack		NDIS Protocol Stack	
		ODINSUP	
Link Support Layer (LSL)			
Ethernet	Token Ring	FDDI	Other Drivers
Physical Medium			

ODI and NDIS

Client Components

For simplicity sake, the following information outlines client configurations for Windows 95/98 and Windows NT. The Windows 2000 client is very similar to the Windows NT model. Besides NDIS, Microsoft supports IPX/SPX with its own protocol implementation called NWLINK. Other client-supported protocols include Transmission Control Protocol (TCP)/IP, Winsock, Named Pipes, Network Basic Input/Output System (NetBIOS), and SNMP.

A NetWare client coexists with a Microsoft client for Microsoft networks, allowing access to both NT domains and NDS simultaneously. The Workstation Diagram illustrates multiple layers of a workstation client.

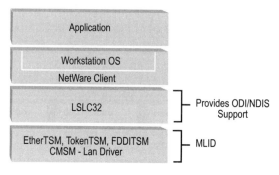

Workstation

The Application Layer on the Workstation Diagram provides application services, not application programs. Application services provide support for programs such as word processors, e-mail, and databases. These services include requesting file access, providing client/server processing for databases, and retrieving e-mail messages. NetWare Core Protocols (NCPs) are used to make these requests for network resources.

The client consists of numerous modules that, once installed on a workstation, provide request and redirection services. When using an application, these modules determine whether a request from an application can be serviced locally (on the same client computer), or requires use of the protocol stack to communicate with the NetWare server. For example, a word processor would not understand the R: drive to locate a file, or understand that a printer was available unless it was directly connected to the LPT port. If a server is required, the client will create a specific NCP request and send it through the protocol stack for processing. With NDS, any server holding a copy of the database will respond, locate the network resource, validate the user's rights, and then provide the requested service. The client, therefore, enhances the network capabilities of the workstation OS.

Below the client is the protocol support component LSLC32, which stands for 32-bit Client Link Support Layer. It is the software file that implements ODI/NDIS capabilities. Although ODI and NDIS allow multiple protocols to be supported, LSLC32 does all the work. Link Support Layer (LSL) acts as a router directing inbound IPX packets to the IPX protocol stack and IP to the IP protocol stack. It also applies header information based on the appropriate protocol for transmission of outgoing packets.

At the Physical Layer there are three client components: topology support modules (TSMs), C-based media support module (CMSM), and the local area network (LAN) driver. EtherTSM, TokenTSM, and FDDITSM are TSMs, which help determine the appropriate header information and network access methods. The LAN driver is the software component that allows communication directly to a NIC. Without this important component, network access is not possible.

For Windows 95 and 98, client services are started at each bootup with the NIOS.VXD file. This is a virtual device driver that loads the NetWare input/output (I/O) subsystem. It provides loader software and module launchers that become the actual interface between the client and OS once a successful login is complete. The modules loaded on the workstation are called NLMs as well, and like the server, they are loaded and unloaded as necessary by the system to free up memory resources.

For architecture and security purposes, the Windows NT client is loaded with NWFS.SYS and is simply used as a redirector/file system driver. It creates internal tables and services used to locate network resources and provide access. The final component is the NetWare Client Requestor or Client32.NLM, which tracks resources and provides autoreconnection and file caching.

NetWare Login

After a client has been properly installed on a workstation, and Client32 is selected as the preferred client, the system will provide a login screen upon bootup. If the NetWare splash screen appears, but the login screen does not, it means the service was started but the network or a NetWare server was not located. If this happens frequently, the client has a built-in feature to write the error condition to a log file for troubleshooting.

On a Windows 95/98 workstation, the file that executes the login process is C:\NOVELL\CLIENT32\LOGINW95.EXE. Because of Windows NT security, Novell replaces the MSGINA.DLL (graphical identification and authentication) file with one called NWGINA.DLL. This is the file that brings up the Ctrl+Alt+Del screen on a Windows NT system.

After the client is installed, the registry is changed to indicate the preference of NWGINA.DLL to provide login and authentication services to the network and the workstation itself. The Example Login Screen Diagram illustrates the interface that allows a user access to network resources. The user must enter a valid login ID and password, in addition to providing the name of the tree and their current context discussed earlier.

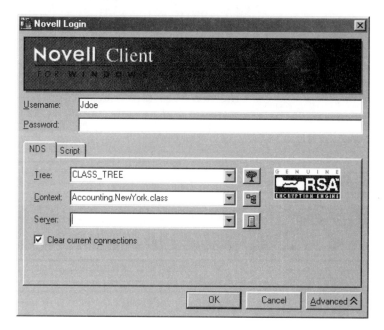

Example Login Screen

Activities

1. Explain the purpose of ODI/NDIS.

   _____

   _____

   _____

   _____

2. Describe how LSL fits in with ODI/NDIS.

   _____

   _____

   _____

   _____

Extended Activity

On Novell's support site at **http://www.support.novell.com**, locate and identify the latest client version available for download.

Lesson 5—NetWare Protocols

NetWare has always used the IPX/SPX protocol stack to transport information from server to workstation. It was originally developed by Xerox, but modified to become NetWare's proprietary protocol stack. This lesson outlines how IPX/SPX maps to the Open Systems Interconnection (OSI) reference model. However, the discussion would not be complete without including TCP/IP. NetWare 5 eliminates the need for IPX and uses IP as its default protocol to support its newest tools, applications, and Web capabilities. Finally, NetWare provides several features that optimize network performance and improve overall communications.

Objectives

At the end of this lesson you will be able to:

- Compare the NetWare server IPX/SPX protocol stack to the OSI model

- Compare the NetWare server TCP/IP protocol stack to the OSI model

- Discuss the features NetWare uses to optimize network communications

 **Key Point**

NetWare supports IPX and IP transport protocols and NCP to request services.

NetWare IPX/SPX Server Protocol Stack

The NetWare Server IPX/SPX Protocol Stack Comparison Diagram compares the NetWare server IPX/SPX protocol stack to the OSI reference model.

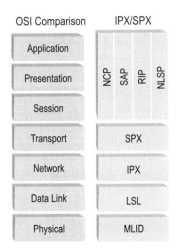

NetWare Server IPX/SPX Protocol Stack Comparison

The Multiple Link Interface Driver (MLID) and LSL of the NetWare server protocol stack map neatly to the OSI Physical and Data Link Layers. MLID is the component that allows multiple protocols to be bound or connected to the NIC. LSL is provided to route the information received from the MLID to the appropriate protocol stack; in NetWare, this would be IPX or IP at the Network Layer.

IPX

IPX was originally developed based on the Xerox Network Systems (XNS) protocol suite. It is used by the server and workstation to transport packets of information across the network. IPX appends addressing and routing information to the data sent down from the upper layers. It is connectionless and does not guarantee delivery. To use an analogy, IPX works like a delivery service. When we have something to send, we call a courier, put an address on the package, and it is picked up and put on a truck. At this point we hope it will get to the destination, and this is where SPX comes in.

411

SPX

SPX is an OSI Transport Layer function modified from a Xerox product called Sequence Packet Protocol (SPP). SPX is the component that makes IPX reliable. Where IPX provides the means to get a packet from point A to point B, SPX is concerned with connection-oriented services such as sequencing the packets and guaranteeing their delivery. In our courier analogy, SPX is the process that provides tracking for the package. For a little more money and, in the network sense, a little more overhead, the package can be tracked and signed for, or acknowledged, indicating it was properly delivered.

NCP

NetWare uses NCPs to communicate between workstations and servers. It provides connection control, packet level security, and service request encoding. NCP is part of the server kernel, and it is installed with the client software at the workstation. When a client requires a service that cannot be handled internally, it creates an NCP Request. The NCP Request contains a function code indicating the type of service needed. Some of the NCP services include file access, printer location, messaging, and login authentication or connection services. The server fills the request and sends back the appropriate information with an NCP Reply. After the client receives the NCP Reply and its request is fulfilled, it sends an NCP Destroy Service Connection Request to terminate its session with the server.

Upper Layer IPX/ SPX Protocol Suite

In addition to NCP, other services provided in the upper layers of the IPX/SPX protocol stack are SAP, Routing Information Protocol (RIP), and NetWare Link Services Protocol (NLSP). Servers and printers identify themselves on the network and let others know of their availability using SAP. RIP helps servers and clients determine the best path to transfer data. RIP and SAP broadcast every 60 seconds, which means they will always provide updated information but will also generate a lot of extra traffic on the network. NLSP is used to route RIP and SAP information efficiently across a WAN by only sending updated information instead of continuous broadcasts.

NetWare TCP/IP Protocol Stack

TCP/IP was developed in the late 1970s for the Department of Defense and has since become the standard for Internet access and communication between many different systems. As stated above, early versions of NetWare provided TCP/IP support, but they did this by encapsulating information into an IPX packet for delivery. It worked, but it was not the most efficient. TCP/IP is now the native and default protocol of NetWare 5, and is necessary for Web support and cross platform connectivity. The NetWare Server TCP/IP Protocol Stack Comparison Diagram shows a very simplified view of TCP/IP and some of its related protocols.

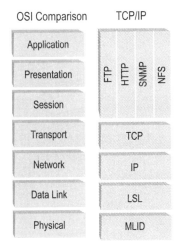

NetWare Server TCP/IP Protocol Stack Comparison

The MLID and LSL sections work exactly as they do in the IPX/SPX protocol stack. The rest of the layers are described below.

IP

IP has the task of addressing, sequencing, and routing information across a network. It is connectionless and does not guarantee delivery of the information it sends. In addition, it relies on other services, also at the Network Layer, to determine the best route to take. For example, Internet Control Message Protocol (ICMP) indicates where the collisions are and reroutes packets, RIP gets routing information, and Open Shortest Path First (OSPF) and Address Resolution Protocol (ARP) resolve addresses.

TCP

The better half of the pair is TCP, which is connection-oriented, and provides flow control, error-checking, acknowledgments, and guarantees delivery of the information. In flow control, TCP segments the information and provides sequencing numbers and tracking to ensure everything arrives at the destination and can be put back together. Error checking verifies information was received correctly and then acknowledges success or requests retransmission as appropriate.

Upper Layer TCP/IP Protocol Suite

There are many service protocols available at the upper layers, which could not be covered in one diagram. A few important ones include:

- FTP—For file transfer

- Hypertext Transfer Protocol (HTTP)—For files being sent to the Web

- SNMP—To gather and track information about network resources

- SMTP—To send e-mail by means of TCP/IP in basic format

- Network File System (NFS)—Used to transport and store UNIX files

Optimizing The Network

NetWare provides efficient network communications with three main components that go beyond either of the protocol suites: Packet Receive Buffers, Packet Burst, and Large Internet Packets (LIP).

Packet Receive Buffers

NetWare sets aside resources to handle requests from clients. It does not want to allocate too many resources, or other services may suffer. The Packet Receive Buffer is the area set aside for this purpose. It takes in requests from clients and holds them until the server can process the request. Packet Receive Buffers increase as necessary to hold more requests, preventing clients from having to retransmit data that might otherwise have been dropped if the server was too busy to respond immediately.

Packet Burst

NetWare also uses Packet Burst, which provides very efficient network communications. Without Packet Burst, a client sending data larger than one packet has to be acknowledged by the server for every packet. This would be similar to going to a restaurant and ordering only one bite at a time. The waiter brings it, you eat it, and ask for another. This becomes very time consuming and network-intensive.

Instead, with Packet Burst, when a client and server establish a connection they agree how many packets can be sent before an acknowledgement is made. The client can then send a number of packets together before the server responds. If a packet gets dropped, only that packet is retransmitted and the packet window is reduced for future sends to make sure the problem does not happen again. In our restaurant scenario, using Packet Burst allows you to get your whole meal, reply that it was good, and ask for a second helping.

LIP

In a network with routers, packets are automatically broken down into 512-byte packets, which are the lowest common size usable on any network topology. With NetWare LIP, the server recognizes this is not necessary and maintains the packet in its native size of 1,514 bytes for Ethernet or 4,202 bytes for Token Ring. This means these packets can be transmitted completely instead of broken up and reassembled later, reducing network traffic and system overhead.

Activities

1. Match the list below with the appropriate corresponding letter.

   Novell proprietary packet transport protocol _____

   Routes MLID information to multiple protocol stacks _____

   Helps determine the best path for data transfer _____

   Connectionless Internet protocol concerned with addressing _____

   Binds multiple protocols to a NIC _____

   Allows IP-based file transfer services _____

   a. MLID

   b. RIP

   c. FTP

   d. TCP

   e. IP

   f. IPX

   g. LSL

Extended Activity

How do Packet Burst and LIP make network communications more efficient?

_____

_____

_____

_____

Lesson 6—NetWare Packet Structure

Before a packet requesting services or transmitting data can be sent across a network, a lot of information is added to address, define, and establish a reliable communication link between a client and a server. This lesson provides an overview of an IPX/SPX packet structure used in NetWare.

Objectives

At the end of this lesson you will be able to:

- Describe the purpose of each field in an Ethernet 802.2 frame
- Explain the function of the NetWare SPX and IPX packet headers

Key Point

A data packet gets information added from every layer in the OSI model.

Ethernet Frames

The Ethernet 802.2 frame is the default frame type for NetWare 4 and 5 and is used for IPX/SPX connectivity. Numbers such as 802.2 refer to industry standards specifications, created by the consensus of professional committees such as Institute of Electrical and Electronic Engineers (IEEE) and other working groups. The frame type is the unit of data transmitted by a NIC on one computer to a NIC on another computer. The Ethernet 802.2 Frame Diagram is an example of a simplified Ethernet IPX packet.

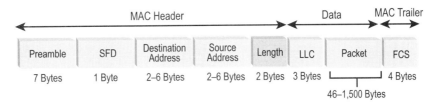

Ethernet 802.2 Frame

As information moves from the top to the bottom of the OSI model, additional fields are added to the data. For example, information about services being requested, addresses for routing, and error checking to make sure the packet is sent and received properly is added. As a result, the frame contains information from all layers of the OSI model built from the top down and the Medium Access Control (MAC), which is part of the Data Link Layer and is responsible for putting it all together before it is sent out on the network.

The MAC header and MAC trailer encapsulate the packet and, in the simplest terms, provide the necessary information computers need to successfully transmit the data packet from the source computer to the destination computer. A breakdown of the specific fields, or types of data, found within the MAC header and MAC trailer is presented below. Remember that the hardware, or MAC address, is the physical address assigned to the NIC in the computer.

The MAC header contains the following fields:

MAC Header

- Preamble and start frame delimiter (SFD) are bits that enable the receiver to synchronize with the transmitter.

- Destination addr is the hardware address of the computer to receive the packet.

- Source addr is the hardware address of the computer sending the packet.

- Length gives the length of the packet in bytes.

MAC Trailer

Frame check sequence (FCS) is an error-correction feature. The sending computer computes the FCS by applying an algorithm to all bits in the frame except the preamble and SFD. The receiving computer does the same, and if the results match, the packet is accepted. If not, the receiver may request a retransmission of the frame, or discard the frame, depending on the transport protocols being used.

Packet

The data section of the frame contains the packet, which is the data that has been passed down from the upper protocol layers, and the Logical Link Control (LLC) header. This is illustrated on the IPX/SPX Packet Structure Diagram. The LLC header contains information that channels the received packets up the protocol stack to correct layers on the destination computer. Remember that the LLC comprises the other sublayer of the Data Link Layer in the OSI model.

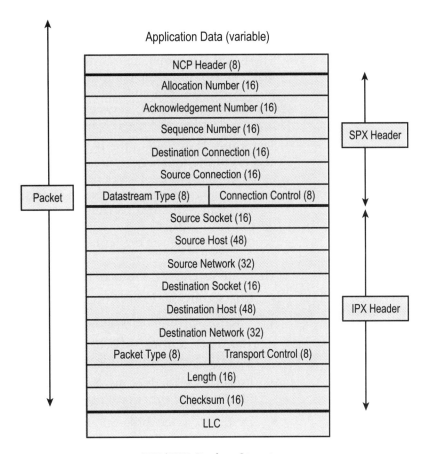

Application Data (variable)

NCP Header (8)	
Allocation Number (16)	
Acknowledgement Number (16)	
Sequence Number (16)	
Destination Connection (16)	
Source Connection (16)	
Datastream Type (8)	Connection Control (8)
Source Socket (16)	
Source Host (48)	
Source Network (32)	
Destination Socket (16)	
Destination Host (48)	
Destination Network (32)	
Packet Type (8)	Transport Control (8)
Length (16)	
Checksum (16)	
LLC	

IPX/SPX Packet Structure

The numbers in parentheses are the numbers of bytes in each field of each header.

Let us take a closer look at the packet within the frame. As we saw earlier, information in the packet is built from the upper layers of the OSI model. Application Layer information is at the top of the diagram followed by the NCP header, which contains Presentation Layer information. For example, if the server is responding to a client request, the packet will contain an NCP header that tells the client the result of the server operation on the request.

SPX and IPX Headers

Following the NCP header are the SPX and IPX headers, added by the SPX (Transport Layer) and IPX (Network Layer), respectively. These headers provide information that enables the frame to reach the destination computer (IPX address) and destination process on the computer (SPX address). Notice that some information is duplicated between the MAC header, which was described earlier, and the IPX header.

The Source Host field in the IPX header also contains the physical address of the source host. Some of these redundancies are useful because each protocol layer of the receiving computer strips off each layer of headers as it passes information up the protocol stack. Because the MAC header of the receiving computer strips off the MAC header of the frame, any information in that header is not available to the higher layers.

IPX Protocol Fields

There are several IPX protocol fields as follows:

- Checksum—Set to FFFF (hexadecimal) and is not used

- Length—Gives length of datagram (0 to 576 bytes)

- Transport control —Used to track the "hop count" as the packet travels through internetwork routers

- Packet type (defined by Xerox)—Contains values relative to RIP, NCP, and other options

- Destination network—Subnetwork address

- Destination host—Physical hardware address of destination node

- Destination socket (defined by Xerox)—Defines the process within the destination node such as error handling and routing information

- Source network—Assigned by network administrator

- Source host—Address of process within destination host

- Source socket—Address of the target process within the source host

SPX Protocol Fields

The SPX protocol fields are listed below:

- Connection control—Contains flags that control the data flow between source and destination

- Datastream type—Identifies the type of data within the packet

- Source connection ID—Identifies the connection within the source host

- Destination connection ID—Identifies the connection within the destination host

- Sequence number—Provides the packet number of the packet being sent

- Acknowledge number—Provides the number of the packet expected from the other node

- Application Data—Contains up to 534 bytes of data from the upper layers, such as NCP messages

Activities

1. What is the default frame type for NetWare 4 and 5?

   _____

2. What type of information does the MAC header provide?

   _____

   _____

   _____

   _____

   _____

   _____

3. What type of information does the MAC trailer provide?

   _____

   _____

4. Why is it necessary to duplicate information in multiple areas of the packet?

   _____

   _____

   _____

   _____

Extended Activities

1. Go to Novell's Web site and locate more information about NetWare 5's pure IP environment.

2. Based on the Web information discussed, diagram an IP packet including MAC header, LLC, and MAC trailer information in addition to the IP data packet itself.

Summary

This unit discussed all the features and functions of a NetWare server and client. It outlined many of the important services available and additional products that make NetWare a very robust and complete NOS. It also described NDS and the benefits provided by this structure. Finally, the unit reviewed Novell's implementation of the IPX/SPX and TCP/IP protocol stacks and packet structure.

Unit 7 Quiz

1. What is the difference between a server and client?

   _____

   _____

2. Describe NDS and its purpose in a network.

   _____

   _____

   _____

   _____

3. Describe what type of services are loaded with NLMs.

   _____

   _____

   _____

   _____

4. Describe the three classes of objects within NDS, and their location in the tree.

   _____

   _____

   _____

   _____

   _____

   _____

   _____

   _____

   _____

5. Identify the service that LSL provides for a client.

   _____

   _____

   _____

   _____

Unit 8
Network OS Software—Windows NT

Windows NT, Microsoft's 32-bit client/server operating system (OS), was first launched in July 1993. It was targeted at advanced business network environments and can be run on virtually every major processor including Intel, Alpha, and PowerPC. It also offered graphical administration utilities that made it easier to manage than the dominant NOS at that time, Novell NetWare.

Windows NT includes two products:

- Windows NT Workstation offers the same user interface as Windows 98/ME, but with enhanced stability and security features.

- Windows NT Server is a client/server OS designed for heavily used network servers. By running each application in a strictly separate memory space, this OS ensures that one application can crash without bringing down the others.

Windows NT is substantially more stable and reliable than the Windows 98/ME line of desktop OSs. Thus, in 2000 Microsoft used the latest Windows NT technology (version 5) as the basis for its next major departure in both desktop and server OSs. Microsoft's new Windows 2000 family of client and server OSs are all based on the more secure, more stable Windows NT technology.

But Windows NT servers are still common components of many networks, because administrators usually prefer to leave a system alone once it is running smoothly. Also, Windows 2000 is essentially the latest version of Windows NT. Thus, this unit will first present the concepts and components of Windows NT, pointing out any key differences between the technologies when necessary. Finally, we will present a brief overview of the essential features of the Windows 2000 product line.

Lessons

1. Windows NT Architecture
2. Windows NT Features
3. Windows NT Tools
4. Windows NT and NetWare Interoperability
5. Windows 2000

Terms

American Standard Code for Information Interchange (ASCII)—ASCII is one of the two most widely used codes to represent characters, such as keyboard characters (EBCDIC is the other). ASCII uses 7 bits for the 128 elements it represents. For example, the ASCII representation of the character "A" is decimal numeral 65, hexadecimal 41, or binary 100 0001. See EBCDIC.

bindery emulation—Bindery emulation is a process that allows a NetWare 4.x server to emulate the NetWare bindery (NetWare 4.x and above uses NetWare Directory Services, a different file system). Bindery emulation is necessary to allow a Windows NT server to access a NetWare 4.x server by using Gateway services for NetWare, which does not support NetWare Directory Services.

burst mode—Burst mode is a high-speed data transfer technique that uses special conditions to move data faster than normal. For example, a device may be allowed to monopolize control of a data bus, or memory access may automatically get the next memory address before it is requested.

C2 security—C2 is one level of security standards in a seven-level range defined by the U.S. Department of Defense. The C2 rating specifies the policies and practices necessary to achieve a level of computer security that is reasonable for most companies.

complex instruction set computer (CISC)—See reduced instruction set computer (RISC).

Extended Binary Coded Decimal Interchange Code (EBCDIC)—EBCDIC is the IBM standard for binary encoding of characters. It is one of the two most widely used codes to represent characters, such as keyboard characters (ASCII is the other). See ASCII.

interoperability—Interoperability refers to the ability of different types of computers, networks, OSs, and applications to work together effectively. An example of interoperability would be a TCP UNIX application using ASCII text files exchanging data with an EBCDIC IBM host.

Link Support Layer (LSL)—LSL is part of Novell NetWare's ODI implementation of the Data Link Layer. Novell designed this interface so drivers of various NICs, such as Ethernet and Token Ring, could communicate with any protocol stack. When a NIC driver is written according to the ODI specification, LSL handles communication between upper layer protocols and MLIDs, which are each unique to the underlying NIC and LAN medium (for example, Ethernet, Token Ring).

mail slots—Mail slots refer to a simple NOS service that transfers data between processes on different network computers. Unlike named pipes, a mail slot connection is created for a single data transfer, and then dropped. See named pipes.

named pipes—Named pipes is a NOS service that establishes a guaranteed virtual communication connection between processes on different computers on the network. After a named pipe connection has been created, it remains available until one of the nodes closes it. Therefore, the time to establish the connection is spent only once for each session of multiple data transfers. See mail slots.

name space—A set of OS rules that define the allowable length and format of a file name is referred to as the name space.

Network Basic Input/Output System (NetBIOS)—NetBIOS is a software system developed by Sytek and IBM that has become the de facto standard for application interface to LANs. It operates at the Session Layer of the OSI protocol stack. Applications can call NetBIOS routines to carry out functions such as data transfer across a LAN.

Network Driver Interface Specification (NDIS)—The NDIS standard was developed by Microsoft and 3Com to provide a common interface between NIC drivers and networking protocols. The functionality of NDIS is comparable to ODI.

NT File System (NTFS)—NTFS is one of the basic services of the Windows NT OS. NTFS is highly recoverable and secure because it is a transaction-based file system that logs all directory and file updates. In case of a system failure or power loss, the NTFS-logged information allows undo/redo operations to recover lost data.

reduced instruction set computer (RISC)—A RISC is a microprocessor that contains fewer instructions than traditional complex instruction set computer (CISC) processors, such as Intel or Motorola. As a result, they are significantly faster. RISC processors have been used in most technical workstations for some time, and a growing number of PC-class products are based on RISC processors.

Small Computer System Interface (SCSI)—SCSI is a high-speed interface for connecting peripheral devices, such as printers and disk drives, to computers.

Server Message Block (SMB)—SMB is the IBM PC LAN protocol used to communicate with devices located on a LAN. It uses NetBIOS at the Session Layer to communicate across a LAN. Functions requiring LAN support, such as retrieving files from a file server, are translated into SMB commands before they are sent to a remote device.

Transport Driver Interface (TDI)—TDI is the Windows NT interface layer between various transport protocols (SPX or TCP) and server or redirector software interfaces.

wizard—A wizard is an application that helps a user configure a computer's hardware or software settings. Wizards use a step-by-step interface that asks a series of questions and responds based on the user's input.

Lesson 1—Windows NT Architecture

Windows NT is a feature-rich network operating system (NOS) that includes a client component: Windows NT Workstation; and a server component, Windows NT Server.

Together, Windows NT Workstation and Server provide a 32-bit environment comparable in power to many mainframe or mini-computer environments. This capability lets us create a virtual environment that solves many of the problems of memory management, process control, and resource management imposed by earlier generation OSs. Windows NT also allows for reduced instruction set computing (RISC) and complex instruction set computing (CISC), and provides support for symmetric multiprocessor computers. It provides a scalable environment for an enterprise by integrating networking, print and file sharing, and application and security management capabilities.

Objectives

At the end of this lesson you will be able to:

- Sketch and describe the modular architecture of Windows NT

- Describe how redirection works with Windows NT

- Understand the basic steps for storing a file across a network

- Show where Transport Driver Interface (TDI) and Network Driver Interface Specification (NDIS) fit into the Windows NT protocol stack

Key Point

Windows NT was designed to be platform-independent.

Modules

The architecture of Windows NT is broken down into several modules, as shown on the Windows NT Architecture Diagram. Each module is an important component of Windows NT and is the same in both the Server and Workstation products.

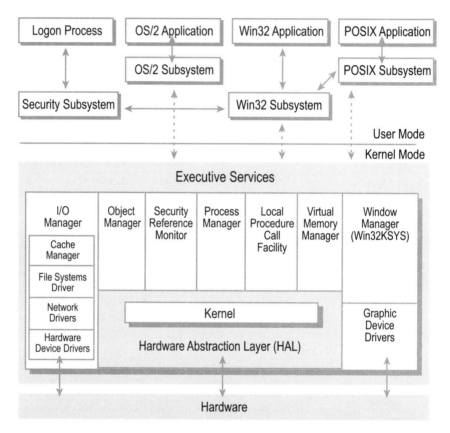

Windows NT Architecture

The module descriptions are as follows:

- The Hardware Abstraction Layer (HAL) creates virtual hardware interfaces. These virtual interfaces make Windows NT less dependent on any specific hardware requirements and allow for a more portable OS.

- The kernel is the core of the OS and manages the basic operations of Windows NT. Small and efficient, the kernel is also responsible for dispatching threads, synchronizing multiprocessors, and handling hardware exceptions.

- The executive provides a set of kernel-mode modules that perform basic OS services for the environment subsystems, such as the Win32 subsystem, Security subsystem, OS/2 subsystem, and Portable Operating System Interface for UNIX (POSIX) subsystem.

- The environment subsystems are user-mode services that run and support applications native to different OS environments. Each of these environment subsystems operates in a virtual environment, thus allowing for exception handling and simultaneous execution in different processes under Windows NT.

These modules are largely unchanged between versions 3.51 and 4.0, except for the Win32 subsystem and graphical user interface (GUI). Additional information on these subsystems, including how they interact, is available from the Windows NT Resource Kit.

Network Model and Interconnectivity

Windows NT uses a network model similar to the seven-layer Open Systems Interconnection (OSI) model. The OSI Model and Windows NT Diagram illustrates how Windows NT's network model compares to the seven-layer OSI model.

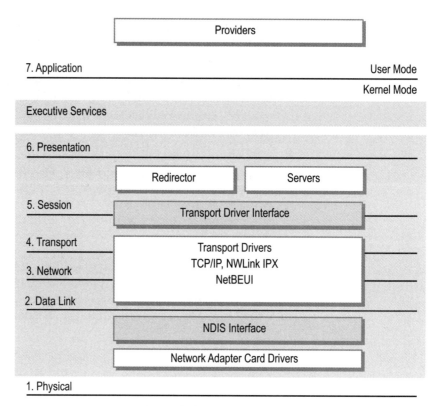

OSI Model and Windows NT

Workgroups and Domains

The Windows NT Server model is based on the concepts of workgroups and domains. The domain model is a conceptual and security model designed to support larger networks using Windows NT Server.

Workgroups

Workgroups are groups of computers linked to achieve a common purpose. A small company, or small department within a larger company, could be considered a workgroup. Workgroups are a way to manage small numbers of users, typically fewer than 20. Security and file access is controlled by each individual member of the workgroup, as is any sharing of applications or data. Access and security for each computer are defined by each user in a workgroup. Because individual users have so much power, the administration of a workgroup is highly decentralized.

The Sample Workgroup Diagram represents a typical small workgroup, interconnected by means of a LAN. The workstations in the workgroup can share data, as long as each user marks the files as sharable. If the files reside on Computer A, the owner of Computer A controls access to these files. If the owner of Computer A determines that a file or folder is not sharable, no other user can access the file. Computer B controls a printer; at the discretion of Computer B's user, the printer can be shared with the rest of the workgroup.

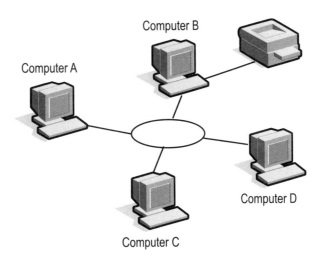

Sample Workgroup

Another example of a workgroup is the accounting department of a small business. The accounting system might include order entry, accounts payable, and accounts receivable software. The accounts database might reside on Computer A, but the reporting function may occur on Computer D.

These peer-to-peer workgroup environments require no servers or computers to act as dedicated controllers. Servers can be added for printing, applications, or other uses; however, they are not required in most cases. For example, if a small workgroup adds a mail server, workgroup members could share calendar information and electronic mail (e-mail) in addition to files and device access.

Domains

A domain describes a larger logical grouping of users. Domains are groups of servers that share common user account databases and security policies.

Security and domain accounts are enforced within each domain. A single LAN or wide area network (WAN) may include several domains, as long as each domain name is unique. Each domain must have a server that functions as its Primary Domain Controller (PDC), as shown on the Model of the Q Domain Diagram.

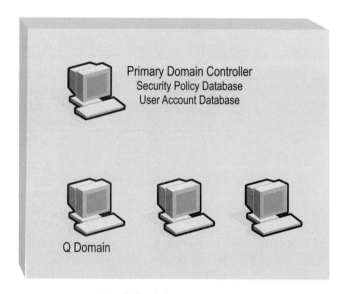

Model of the Q Domain

The PDC authenticates users and stores security and user account information. A Backup Domain Controller (BDC) can also be specified as a way to improve reliability. The BDC maintains copies of the user account and security information that are replicated on it. If the PDC is disconnected or fails, a BDC can be promoted to assume the role of the PDC.

The domain model provides a higher degree of centralization and easier management for larger numbers of users. In exchange for more centralized management, the domain model requires more sophisticated administrative support to take full advantage of the capabilities of the domain. Domains can also be interconnected, as in the case of an enterprise WAN.

BackOffice Considerations

Microsoft BackOffice is a suite of applications and services that includes Microsoft Exchange, Systems Management Server, System Network Architecture (SNA) Server, Structured Query Language (SQL) Server, and Internet Information Server. Windows NT Server is usually the primary platform on which BackOffice products operate.

As the name implies, the "BackOffice" is where most heavy-duty work occurs. BackOffice applications are typically shared by multiple users. These products provide much of the connectivity between networks and tend to become mission-critical over time. For example, when a LAN depends on Microsoft Exchange for mail support, any failure in Exchange has far-reaching consequences for the enterprise. Other examples of BackOffice products are data servers and network servers. BackOffice systems are generally more complicated and usually have multiple layers of services and activities that need to be monitored and tuned.

Each BackOffice product has additional memory, storage, and processor requirements beyond those of Windows NT Server. These server products allow Windows NT Server to fulfill many information systems requirements. However, you must carefully consider memory and storage requirements to ensure adequate response time and service levels.

Server Concepts

In general, a server is a computer that provides resources to network users called clients. In a Windows NT Server domain, a server is a computer that receives a copy of the domain's security policy and domain database, and authenticates network logins. Windows NT Server is designed to provide both the networking foundation and client-server platform that make it possible to integrate current and future technologies.

Object Model

Architecturally, Windows NT was designed using an object model. This means that most of the services and resources provided by the OS files, such as directories and printers, are represented as objects. By using an object model, Windows NT provides a modular approach to the OS. Therefore, the various components operate independently, and they can be modified without breaking the entire system. The Windows NT Architecture Diagram illustrates this design.

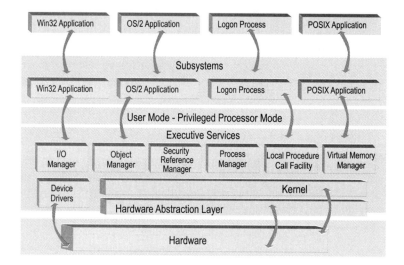

Windows NT Architecture

Windows NT moves beyond the 640 kilobyte (KB) limit of MS-DOS, using a flat 32-bit memory model. Each application is allocated a 4-gigabyte (GB) virtual memory space.

Protocol Stack

Networking is built into Windows NT, including both client and server capabilities. This allows any Windows NT computer to participate in a network in either capacity. Windows NT networking architecture includes both peer-to-peer and server-based networking. With no additional software required, Windows NT can interoperate with the following networks:

- Microsoft networks
- Novell NetWare

- TCP/IP, including UNIX hosts
- AppleTalk (Windows NT Server only)
- Remote access clients

As with other portions of the OS, Windows NT networking architecture is based on a modular component design. This modular approach enables modification and extensibility of the various components with minimal effect on the other components. The Windows NT and OSI Model Diagram illustrates the modular approach to these networking components.

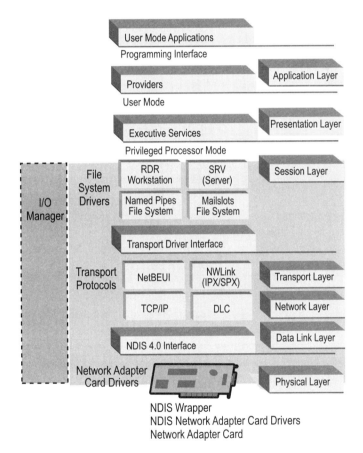

Windows NT and OSI Model

The networking components are described as follows:

- The network adapter card drivers that connect Windows NT to the related network adapter card are located at the Physical and Data Link Layers of the OSI model. These layers also include Remote Access Service (RAS) drivers that allow remote network access.

- Above these drivers are the NDIS 3.0/4.0 Interface, as well as low-level portions of the various transport protocols.

- The transport protocol drivers reside in the Network and Transport Layers of the OSI model. On top of these drivers, in the Transport Layer, is the TDI.

- The transport protocols pass data to the network adapter card drivers through the NDIS Interface, and communicate with the redirector by means of the TDI.

- Two software components, redirectors and servers, reside at the Session Layer of the OSI model. These components are implemented as file system drivers, which enable client applications to call a single applications programming interface (API) to request file access, without knowing whether the file is local or remote. Redirectors handle client-side functions, whereas servers handle server-side processing. Redirectors and servers communicate with the protocol stacks to which they are bound by means of the TDI. Additional redirectors are necessary to communicate with non-Microsoft networks.

- At the Presentation Layer of the OSI model reside the various executive services of the OS. The executive services include the input/output (I/O) manager, object manager, virtual memory manager, and other services. The Windows NT Architecture Diagram (previously shown) presents the various executive services.

- The Application Layer of the OSI model encompasses software called clients, or providers. A provider is a component that enables Windows NT to communicate with the network. Windows NT includes providers for Windows NT networks, client services for NetWare, and gateway services for NetWare (Windows NT Server). The various network vendors supply provider software necessary to connect Windows NT to their networks.

On top of the various provider components sits a multiple provider router (MPR). An MPR provides a single API for applications, and ensures that file requests are sent to the appropriate file systems or redirectors as necessary.

Client Access and Redirection

When a user process wants to open a file, it passes the request to the I/O manager executive service. The I/O manager then recognizes that the file physically resides on another computer and passes the request to the redirector. The redirector then uses the TDI to pass the request down to the network adapter card and on to the appropriate server computer for processing.

An example of how redirectors work is shown on the Windows NT Redirector Diagram.

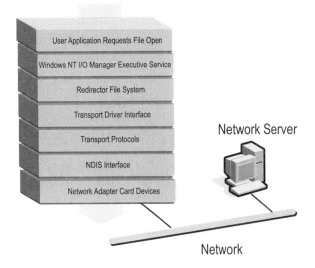

Windows NT Redirector

Windows NT includes two important interfaces in its networking model:

- NDIS 3.0/4.0 Interface
- TDI

These interfaces isolate the layers of network component software, so that each adjacent component can be written to a common programming interface. This allows the various components to be portable and interchangeable. For example, network interface card (NIC) drivers are written to the NDIS 3.0/4.0 Interface. Therefore, each NIC driver does not need a specific programming code to access the various transport protocols. This access is handled by the NDIS 3.0/4.0 Interface and related transport protocol drivers.

441

Server components handle requests from client-side redirectors, and allow access to the local resources of the server computer. The Windows NT Server Diagram illustrates a typical file read request passed from a client redirector. When a client redirector passes the file read request to the remote computer, the low-level network drivers receive the request and pass it to the server driver. The server driver passes the request on to the appropriate local file system driver, which retrieves the data from the disk drive and passes it back to the server driver. The server driver then forwards the data to the low-level network drivers for transmission to the client computer.

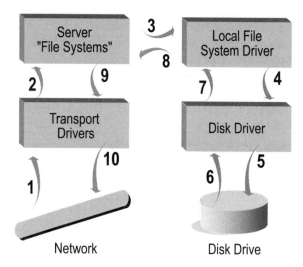

Windows NT Server

Activities

1. What is the purpose of using an object model for Windows NT?

   _____

   _____

   _____

2. What advantages does a 32-bit OS have over a 16-bit OS?

   _____

   _____

   _____

3. What protocols are supported by the TDI?

   _____

   _____

   _____

4. What is the purpose of the NDIS interface?

   _____

   _____

   _____

5. How does Microsoft's NDIS compare with Novell's ODI speci-fication? Do they achieve the same goal functionally?

   _____

   _____

   _____

6. Why is a layer of software needed between NIC drivers and transport protocols?

   _____

   _____

   _____

7. Why is a layer of software needed between transport protocols and file system drivers?

_____

_____

_____

8. Describe what happens when a client accesses a file from a local workstation.

_____

_____

9. Describe what happens when a client accesses a file from a server attached to the same physical network.

_____

_____

10. Describe what happens when a client accesses a file from a server attached to a network located on a remote network.

_____

_____

Extended Activity

1. As directed by your instructor, perform the following labs:

   a. Network protocols

   b. Installing Windows NT Server

   c. Domain membership management

   d. Managing disk partitions

   e. Managing NTFS

   f. Directory replication

   g. Creating user accounts

   h. Hardware Compatibility

   i. Hard Disk Partitions

   j. File Systems

Lesson 2—Windows NT Features

Windows NT includes a rich set of features for both network communication and resource management. Both the Workstation and Server components provide multitasking and security capabilities, as well as support for multiple hardware platforms and network protocols. Advanced disk management facilities include support for multiple file systems.

In addition, Windows NT Server provides disk fault tolerance features, centralized user management, and greater support for Novell NetWare. This lesson presents the main features of the workstation and server components, shown on the Windows NT Feature Comparison Diagram.

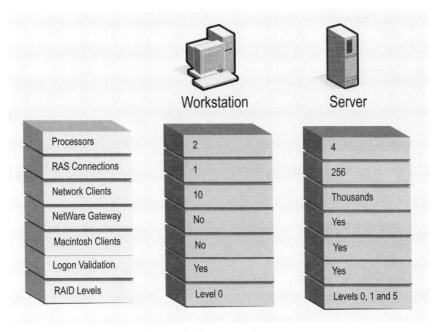

	Workstation	Server
Processors	2	4
RAS Connections	1	256
Network Clients	10	Thousands
NetWare Gateway	No	Yes
Macintosh Clients	No	Yes
Logon Validation	Yes	Yes
RAID Levels	Level 0	Levels 0, 1 and 5

Windows NT Feature Comparison

Objectives

At the end of this lesson you will be able to:

- Describe the key features of Windows NT
- Name key file services offered by Windows NT
- Explain the basic concepts of disk mirroring and striping

 **Key Point**

Windows NT features enhance reliability and fault tolerance.

Multitasking

Windows NT is a full 32-bit preemptive multitasking OS. Processes are executed in separate memory spaces, preventing any one process from crashing the OS. Each process can run multiple threads of execution. Each thread is scheduled for processing on the processors available to the OS.

Symmetric multiprocessing (SMP) allows Windows NT to operate on systems with more than one central processor. Out of the box, Windows NT Workstation supports two processors, and Windows NT Server supports four processors. Some original equipment manufacturers' (OEM) implementations of Windows NT Server support up to 32 processors. When multiple processors are available to Windows NT, the OS is capable of executing process threads simultaneously, which can significantly increase system throughput.

Multiple Hardware Platform Support

Versions of Windows NT are available for the following hardware platforms:

- Intel Pentium, Pentium Pro
- Digital Equipment Corporation (DEC) Alpha

Windows NT was designed with platform portability as a central feature, using a hardware abstraction layer to isolate physical hardware from the OS. Therefore, portability to future hardware platforms is virtually ensured, although Microsoft has chosen to halt the development of NT on future, non-Intel-compatible platforms.

Support for Multiple Network Protocols

Network protocols are services that allow computers to be interconnected in a network. Windows NT supports three common transport protocols:

- NetBEUI is a LAN transport protocol developed by IBM in 1985 to operate underneath NetBIOS. NetBEUI is a small, efficient networking protocol for LANs of 20 to 200 workstations. Windows NT supports an enhanced protocol called NetBEUI Frame (NBF) protocol, which is compatible with LAN Manager and MS-Net installations. Windows NT supports NetBIOS under MS-DOS, 16-bit Windows, and Win32 subsystem environments.

- NWLink is a set of protocols that allow for connection to Novell NetWare environments. Protocols compatible with IPX/SPX can be connected by means of remote procedure calls (RPC), Windows Sockets (WinSock), Novell NetBIOS, and NWLink installed with Windows NT.

- TCP/IP is the primary protocol suite for interconnected networking and the Internet. TCP/IP is commonly used on UNIX-based systems; however, it is supported by most computer manufacturers and network software. TCP/IP is the recommended enterprise networking and connectivity tool on Windows NT computers.

Windows NT also supports a number of other proprietary networking transports, such as DECnet, AppleTalk, Vines, and Xerox Network System (XNS). Third-party software and hardware manufacturers also support a number of other protocols.

Windows NT Server adds support for Macintosh clients and gateway services for NetWare. Gateway services allow clients on the Windows NT network to access file and print resources on NetWare networks, without having to run the IPX/SPX protocol and the NetWare client. File and print services for NetWare allow NetWare clients to access file and print resources of the Windows NT Server, making the it visible to NetWare clients.

The Windows NT Server protocols allow for a variety of interconnectivity. However, implementing them requires some forethought. For example, if you are installing TCP/IP as part of your networking protocols, you need to know the existing IP addresses, server addresses, and additional information about other users in the TCP/IP environment. Changing these settings may disrupt services for those users.

Support for Multiple File Systems

Windows NT supports two file systems designed to meet the needs of varying audiences:

- File Allocation Table (FAT) system
- NT File System (NTFS)

The FAT system, a carryover from MS-DOS, has existed for more than 20 years and is still the file system used in Windows 95, Windows 3.1, and Windows for Workgroups 3.11. FAT initially had a limitation of 32 megabytes (MB) of data per volume. Later versions of MS-DOS and Windows 95 allow for larger disk volumes. The FAT 32 file system used by Windows 98 is not supported by Windows NT, but is supported by Windows 2000.

NTFS is designed for large, multiple-volume disk configurations and derives the most benefit from faster, more modern disk drives. NTFS also provides full access to the security capabilities of Windows NT. NTFS was announced with the release of Windows NT 3.1 and is the file system of choice for most server applications. Long file names are allowed on all of the supported file systems.

You should choose between NTFS or FAT based on your security and compatibility requirements.

Although the FAT system is supported for compatibility with MS-DOS and Windows 95/98, NTFS is the file system of choice due to its recoverability and security. NTFS is a transaction-based file system, which logs all directory and file updates. In case of a system failure or power loss, the NTFS-logged information allows undo/redo operations that can recover lost data. NTFS also allows for full security support. For example, unauthorized users cannot bypass security on an NTFS system by booting from a floppy disk. FAT file systems are DOS compatible and allow for dual-boot capability.

Hard Disk Storage and Partitioning

Windows NT Workstation provides enhanced disk management ability. Volume sets allow noncontiguous areas of free space, on one or more hard disks, to be combined into a single logical drive. Stripe sets allow identically sized areas of free space on multiple hard disks to be combined into a single logical drive. Both volume and stripe sets are used to accomplish the same goal of combining unused disk space into single logical drive units. When used with NTFS, a volume set can be extended to include additional disk space without the need to reformat the existing volume.

The system partition must have a minimum of 160 MB for RISC-based systems. Pentium-based systems must have a minimum of 124 MB of disk space available on the system partition. If installing Windows NT Server on computers with Intel processors, you can choose between NTFS and FAT; however, NTFS provides the best security and performance. RISC system partitions must be configured with at least a 2-MB FAT partition for the Windows NT boot files (OSLOADER.EXE, HAL.DLL, and *PAL files for Alpha). Windows NT Server cannot be installed to a FAT compressed disk. Additionally, the maximum size of a FAT partition is 4 GB.

Security

Windows NT includes the following sophisticated security features to control access to system resources:

- Certified C2-level security, subject to user configuration
- File- and directory-level security with NTFS
- Local desktop security (Windows NT Workstation); user login required for access
- Centralized management of network logins (Windows NT Server)
- Account lockout capabilities to prevent unlimited login attempts

Windows NT uses a resource/permission model for security, whereby users (or groups of users) are given permission to access various system resources.

Windows NT Server security is built around the centralized domain model. The security subsystem is an integral subsystem, not an environmental subsystem, because it affects the entire OS. Windows NT Server can perform one of three primary security roles in a domain:

- PDC maintains the master copy of the domain account database.
- BDC keeps backup copies of the domain account database.
- A member server is any Windows NT server that does not store a copy of the domain database. In other words, a member server is not a PDC or BDC.

Each domain is allowed only one PDC, although multiple BDCs can exist. During installation, you must choose which server will be the PDC; a PDC must be configured for a new domain to exist.

Member servers can be added to any network; however, they will not be added to a domain unless a PDC has already been created. When you add a BDC to a domain, you must have administrative privileges.

Note: Under Windows 2000 Server, there is no longer a PDC. A server may either be a Domain Controller (the only one, or one of several) or a member server.

Remote Access

For remote network connectivity, RAS enables both inbound and outbound connections by means of Integrated Services Digital Network (ISDN), X.25, and standard phone lines and virtual private networks (VPNs) over the Internet. With RAS, Windows NT computers can dial out to connect to remote servers and allow dial-in connections from other workstations. Windows NT Workstation allows one connection. Windows NT Server allows up to 256 simultaneous RAS connections.

Fault Tolerance

FAT file systems can sometimes be repaired using MS-DOS or Windows 95 recovery utilities.

NTFS supports Redundant Array of Inexpensive Disks (RAID) level 1, which is a standard for fault tolerance that includes disk mirroring or disk imaging. RAID level 5 defines disk striping with parity, currently the most fault-tolerant file system available on Windows NT Server. If you choose NTFS, you must select either RAID level 1 or RAID level 5 to be able to recover data in the event of corruption. You should use RAID level 5 in server installations to provide the most reliability.

Windows NT Server has the following fault tolerance capabilities:

- Disk mirroring (RAID level 1)
- Disk striping with parity (RAID level 5)
- Sector sparing (both workstation and server)

Disk Mirroring
Disk mirroring maintains a backup copy of part or all of your disk. Mirroring requires a minimum of two hard disks. It is an inexpensive way to add fault tolerance and data redundancy to a Windows NT system. However, because mirroring requires duplicate disks, it is not the most cost-effective method. Additionally, disk duplexing may be used, which uses additional disk controllers. This has the benefit of increased performance and guards against controller failures as well as media failures.

Disk Striping with Parity
Disk striping with parity writes disk data across an array of disks and maintains parity information. If a disk in the array fails, the system can recover the lost data from the remaining disk data and parity information. Although read performance is typically very good, write performance is slower due to the need for writing to an array of disks. Also, in case of a failure, read performance slows because the system must recover the lost data using the remaining valid data. Because striping with parity is a software-based solution, it is not as fast as a hardware-based disk array.

Sector Sparing
Sector sparing is used in addition to RAID technology, and is generally available with small computer systems interface (SCSI) disks. When Windows NT detects a bad sector on a disk, it attempts to move the data to a good sector, rebuilding it from the redundant copy if necessary. The disk driver then requests the hardware to map out the bad sector. If the process is not successful, the administrator is notified through a system event message.

Activities

1. SMP allows Windows NT to operate on systems with more than five central processors. True or False

2. According to this lesson, what is the maximum number of processors some OEMs will configure Windows NT to support?

3. Name at least two networks that Windows NT will support.

   _____

   _____

4. List at least five key features of the Windows NT OS.

   _____

   _____

   _____

   _____

   _____

5. Discuss advantages and disadvantages of the fault tolerance solutions covered in this lesson, including:

   a. Disk mirroring

      _____

      _____

   b. Disk striping with parity

      _____

      _____

   c. Sector sparing

      _____

      _____

6. List and compare the file systems supported by Windows NT.

_____

_____

_____

_____

Extended Activities

1. Research each level of RAID and list the specification for each level.

2. As directed by your instructor, perform the following labs:

   a. NT Network Environment

   b. NT Server Roles

   c. Licensing Modes

   d. Server Requirements

Lesson 3—Windows NT Tools

The Windows NT Server programs provide many tools that help monitor and troubleshoot networks, including the following:

- Event Viewer
- Performance Monitor
- Task Manager
- Network Monitor
- Registry Editor

This lesson reviews the basic features of these tools.

Objectives

At the end of this lesson you will be able to:

- Name the most common Windows NT tools and describe their functions
- Explain how you would typically use each type of tool

 **Key Point**

Windows NT provides many tools for network analysis.

Event Viewer

Windows NT records events using three kinds of logs:

- A system log contains events logged by Windows NT Workstation system components. For example, the failure of a driver or other system component to load during startup is recorded in the system log. The event types logged by system components are predetermined by Windows NT.

- A security log contains valid and invalid logon attempts, as well as events related to resource use, such as creating, opening, or deleting files or other objects. For example, if we use User Manager to enable logon and logoff auditing, attempts to logon to the system are recorded in the security log.

- An application log contains events logged by applications. For example, a database program might record a file error in the application log. Application developers decide which events to monitor.

System and application logs can be viewed by all users; security logs are accessible only to system administrators. Event logs consist of a header, description of the event (based on the event type), and optionally, additional data. Most security log entries consist of a header and description.

Event Viewer displays events from each log separately. Each line shows information about one event, including date, time, source, event type, category, event ID, user account, and computer name. The Windows NT Event Viewer Screen Diagram illustrates this type of tool.

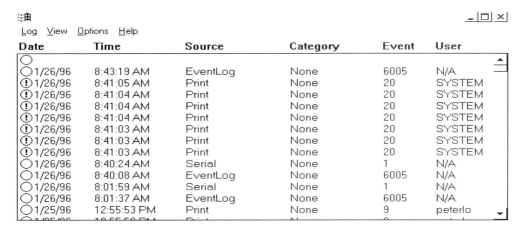

Date	Time	Source	Category	Event	User
1/26/96	8:43:19 AM	EventLog	None	6005	N/A
1/26/96	8:41:05 AM	Print	None	20	SYSTEM
1/26/96	8:41:04 AM	Print	None	20	SYSTEM
1/26/96	8:41:04 AM	Print	None	20	SYSTEM
1/26/96	8:41:04 AM	Print	None	20	SYSTEM
1/26/96	8:41:03 AM	Print	None	20	SYSTEM
1/26/96	8:41:03 AM	Print	None	20	SYSTEM
1/26/96	8:41:03 AM	Print	None	20	SYSTEM
1/26/96	8:40:24 AM	Serial	None	1	N/A
1/26/96	8:40:08 AM	EventLog	None	6005	N/A
1/26/96	8:01:59 AM	Serial	None	1	N/A
1/26/96	8:01:37 AM	EventLog	None	6005	N/A
1/25/96	12:55:53 PM	Print	None	9	peterlo

Windows NT Event Viewer Screen

Performance Monitor

Windows NT Server and Workstation editions include the Performance Monitor (perfmon) tool that allows administrators to view and analyze the performance of Windows NT operation. In addition to real-time charts of resource utilizations, Performance Monitor provides a way to log and replay the statistics, view them as a report, or send alerts if metrics (performance criteria) exceed or fall below preset thresholds. Using Performance Monitor, Windows NT Workstation or NT Server can monitor performance metrics on remote Windows NT systems, even across a wide area. You can also export a chart for use by external tools, such as Microsoft Excel.

Task Manager

Task Manager is an integrated tool for monitoring applications, tasks, and key performance metrics of a Windows NT system. Task Manager provides detailed information on each application and process running on the workstation, as well as memory and central processing unit (CPU) usage. Task Manager also allows for easy termination of applications and processes that are not responding, improving system reliability.

Network Monitor

An essential part of administering a distributed network is the ability to analyze and maintain the integrity of the network itself. The Network Monitor tool provides the network administrator with the means to do this through identifying traffic patterns, testing networks, and pinpointing network trouble spots.

Network Monitor works by monitoring a network's data streams (all information transferred over a network at any given time). Individual frames can be copied, as they are sent across the network, to a capture buffer. The captured frames are then displayed dynamically through the Network Monitor window.

Typically, it is not necessary to examine all captured frames. When it is necessary to record only a segment of network data, a capture filter can be designed to do this. Like an inventory query, a capture filter collects only the network traffic of interest. For example, a capture filter can be used to copy only frames sent between two specific computers.

Network Monitor also allows remote capturing of information, by using the Network Monitor agent. The agent gathers statistics from a remote computer and sends them to a local computer, where they are displayed in a local Network Monitor window. Network Monitor allows troubleshooting of LANs and WANs running RAS.

To have a capture respond to events on a network as soon as they are detected, a capture trigger can be designed. A capture trigger performs a specified action, such as launching a program, when Network Monitor detects a particular set of conditions on the network. Captured frames can be edited and retransmitted to generate network activity to simulate specific test conditions.

Network Monitor is limited to the data it can see on the network port (NIC) of the machine running it. In a switched Ethernet environment, for example, the network administrator may have to take extra steps to ensure that Network Monitor can actually see the traffic of interest.

Registry Editor

The registry is a centralized database of configuration maintained by Windows NT. In concept, it replaces all .INI and .SYS configuration files of earlier versions of Microsoft Windows. To a large extent, user interaction with the registry is behind the scenes. The various Control Panel applications and other configuration utilities perform most tasks needed to configure the registry.

In those rare cases when the registry must be edited directly, Windows NT provides a program called Regedit (and Regedt32). Regedit, or Registry Editor, is activated from the Start menu by selecting Run, then typing Regedit (or Regedt32) as shown on the Run Dialog—Regedit Dialog Box Diagram.

Run Dialog—Regedit Dialog Box

The registry is a hierarchical database of information, and is structured in the form of subtrees, keys, and their values. Keys can also contain subkeys. When a discrete body of keys, subkeys, and values is saved as a file, it is called a "hive."

HKEY_ values are all subtrees. The + signs to the left of the subtrees indicate the subtrees contain keys. The Registry Editor—CurrentControlSet Screen Diagram shows the Registry Editor expanded to display the HKEY_LOCAL_MACHINE subkey, with its SYSTEM hive displayed.

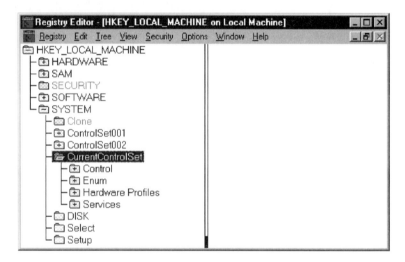

Registry Editor—CurrentControlSet Screen

As a general rule, the registry should not be directly edited. This cannot be over-emphasized. In almost all cases, a registry entry should be modified indirectly by means of the Control Panel or Windows NT setup.

Improper editing of a registry could render a system unusable. Therefore, if it is necessary to edit the registry, first run the RDISK application to update the Emergency Repair Disk. This application updates or creates a copy of the registry files, and is critical for recovery of a system if there is a problem while editing the registry.

Activities

1. List each tool presented in this lesson and describe the purpose of each.

   _____

   _____

   _____

   _____

   _____

   _____

2. Describe a situation in which you would use each of these tools in a network.

   _____

   _____

   _____

   _____

   _____

   _____

3. What precautions should be taken before editing the Microsoft Registry?

   _____

   _____

   _____

Extended Activities

1. As directed by your instructor, perform the following labs:

   a. Windows NT Tools: Event Viewer

   b. Performance Monitor

   c. Task Manager

Lesson 4—Windows NT and NetWare Interoperability

Windows NT provides software products and services to allow Windows NT servers to work in a NetWare environment. Windows NT can emulate a NetWare server, as well as provide services to NetWare clients. In general, there are three levels of NetWare interoperability:

- Basic connectivity

- Gateway services for NetWare

- File and print services for NetWare

This lesson reviews each of these Windows NT services used to provide connectivity to NetWare.

Objectives

At the end of this lesson you will be able to:

- Describe how Windows NT and NetWare interoperate

- Explain the concept of a NetWare client

- Describe how Gateway Services for NetWare operates

 **Key Point**

Windows NT provides services for emulation and connectivity to NetWare.

Basic Connectivity

Basic NetWare connectivity requires installation of the following components on either a Windows NT Workstation or Server computer:

- NWLink (IPX/SPX-compatible transport protocol)

- Client services for NetWare

NWLink is Microsoft's 32-bit IPX/SPX-compatible protocol. It supports NetBIOS and remote procedure call (RPC) (on top of SPX). NWLink is routable, allowing Windows NT systems to communicate with each other through IPX routers. Use of NWLink also allows NetWare clients to run the server portion of client/server applications, such as SQL Server, on a Windows NT computer.

Client services for NetWare (CSNW) is a 32-bit, native NetWare redirector for Windows NT. It includes a service and device driver, as well as the following functions:

- Windows NT user access to NetWare file and print servers

- NetWare application support

- Support for NetWare Core Protocol (NCP) and Burst Mode

- Long file name support (when NetWare is running the OS/2 name space)

The Windows NT and NetWare Interoperability Diagram presents a list of connectivity options for Windows NT and NetWare clients.

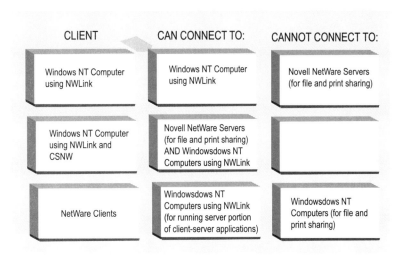

Windows NT and NetWare Interoperability

461

Gateway Services for NetWare

Gateway services for NetWare (GSNW) is available only on Windows NT Server. By installing this service, the Windows NT Server computer acts as a gateway for its clients, allowing them to use resources available on the NetWare network. Unlike CSNW, Microsoft network clients do not need to run the NWLink protocol and Client Services for NetWare to access the NetWare server file and print resources, as illustrated on the Windows NT NetWare Gateway Services Diagram.

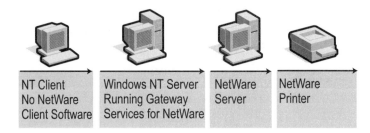

Windows NT NetWare Gateway Services

As with basic NetWare connectivity, the NWLink protocol must be installed on the server. GSNW is compatible with file and print services on NetWare versions 2.*x* and 3.*x* servers and NetWare version 4.*x* servers running bindery emulation. NetWare 4.*x* Novell Directory Services (NDS) is not supported.

GSNW is intended as an occasional-use router, because all Windows NT client users are accessing the NetWare network through one NetWare connection. Excessive access to the NetWare network through the Windows NT gateway could cause performance to suffer.

File and Print Services for NetWare

File and print services for NetWare (FPNW) is an extra cost service that allows NetWare clients access to Windows NT Server. Essentially, FPNW allows Windows NT Server to act like a NetWare version 3.12 file and print server. NetWare clients can then access file and print resources of Windows NT Server. FPNW is a critical tool to allow the integration of Windows NT Server into an existing NetWare 3.12 network. The connectivity is illustrated on the Windows NT File and Print Services for NetWare Diagram.

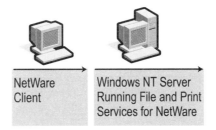

Windows NT File and Print Services for NetWare

Specifically, FPNW supports the following functions:

- File access and management using NetWare tools
- Creation and management of user accounts
- Printing and print queue manipulation
- Remote administration
- Secured logins

Activity

Using the Windows NT and NetWare Interoperability Diagram, draw a mixed network, including all connectivity.

Extended Activity

1. As directed by your instructor, perform the following lab:

   a. Installing NWLink

Lesson 5—Windows 2000

The Windows 2000 product line is essentially the latest version of the highly respected Windows NT NOS. Thus, an administrator can migrate a Windows NT Server network to Windows 2000 without changing the fundamental organization of the network. This lesson introduces some of the most significant enhancements and differences in the Windows 2000 suite of OSs.

Objectives

When you finish this lesson you will be able to:

- Explain the difference between Windows 2000 Professional, Server, Advanced Server, and Datacenter Server

- Describe the key difference between domains in Windows 2000 and Windows NT

- Explain the concepts of clustering and load balancing, and describe the environments in which they would be necessary

 **Key Point**

The Windows 2000 products are all new versions of Windows NT technology.

One Client, Three Servers

The Windows 2000 family includes four OSs:

- Windows 2000 Professional is a client OS for individuals and businesses of all sizes. It can also be used as a stand-alone desktop OS or to build peer-to-peer networks.

- Windows 2000 Server is for Web servers or office servers in small- to medium-sized businesses.

- Windows 2000 Advanced Server is for larger business servers, especially those that host large databases.

- Windows 2000 Datacenter Server is designed for the very largest corporate databases (called data warehouses) and other applications requiring high-speed computation and large data storage.

Windows 2000 Professional

Like the Windows 98/ME OS it replaces, Windows 2000 Professional serves as the client component of the client/server architecture, and can also be used to create peer-to-peer networks. However, Windows 2000 is based on Windows NT, so it brings the stability of NT to the client desktop.

For example, if an application becomes unstable under Windows 98, it often corrupts the memory it shares with other applications. The user's best choice is usually to reboot the computer. But Windows 2000 executes each application in its own protected memory space, so a misbehaving program can be shut down without affecting the others.

Windows 2000 Professional has added many user-friendly features to the foundation of Windows NT, but the most notable are the enhanced security and power-management features designed for laptops. Some of these mobility features include:

- Offline files and folders—Server-based documents can be copied to the client machine. When the user returns to the office, a Synchronization Manager updates the server files with the user's changes.

- Encrypting File System—This extension to NTFS can use public key encryption to protect selected files or folders. Thus, if a laptop computer is stolen or lost, confidential information remains safe.

- Power management—On computers that comply with the Advanced Configuration and Power Interface (ACPI), users have a new range of "hot pluggable" features. They can dock and undock laptops, or swap hardware modules, without shutting down the computer first. Power-saving utilities can also suspend most computer activity, while preserving the current state of all work in progress. This "hibernation" feature conserves battery power and reduces wear on disk drives.

- Improved hardware management—Windows 2000 supports a wide range of new hardware standards. Improved Plug and Play features, and better hardware configuration wizards, make it easier to install or remove devices.

Windows 2000 Server Products

All three of the Windows 2000 server OSs offer the same core features, but each one is tailored for a different level of user traffic and reliability. In other words, Server is the "standard" product, Advanced Server is "heavy duty," and Datacenter Server is "industrial strength."

For example, all three systems use the symmetric multiprocessing (SMP) that was central to Windows NT. But Windows 2000 Server supports SMP up to 4 processors, Advanced Server up to 8, and Datacenter Server up to 32.

Windows 2000 Server products use most of the same architectural concepts as Windows NT. An administrator can preserve existing NT Server settings and preferences during an upgrade to 2000 (though many prefer to do a "clean" installation of an OS on a reformatted hard drive).

Core Features

There are many new features and enhancements in the suite of server products, but the following are a few of the most significant:

- Reliability—The key changes to the 2000 server line are designed to enhance reliability and uptime. Fewer configuration tasks now require a server reboot, and improvements to protected memory make it easier for an administrator to shut down an offending application. When a setup task does require a reboot, the system now starts up faster.

- Simplified administration—Windows 2000 Server products have added new tools and wizards that simplify desktop administration and make it easier to set up new servers. Improved Plug and Play support simplifies the process of installing new hardware.

- Client backup to the network—The IntelliMirror feature can back up a client computer to the network, and preserve all administrative policies and user preferences. Administrators can use this feature to quickly restore a user's desktop system.

- Support for FAT32—Windows 2000 supports the FAT32 file system, so hard disks larger than 2 GB can be formatted as a single drive.

Domains

Windows 2000 handles domains and domain controllers slightly differently than Windows NT. Under Windows 2000, a server can have one of three roles in a domain:

- Domain controllers contain matching copies of the user accounts and other Active Directory data in a given domain.

- Member servers belong to a domain but do not contain a copy of the Active Directory data.

- Stand-alone servers belong to a workgroup rather than a domain.

The main difference is that Windows 2000 has no PDC or backup domain controller (BDC). Each domain must have at least one domain controller, and should have more than one to provide fault tolerance. But all domain controllers function as equal peers.

When a Windows NT network is upgraded to one of the Windows 2000 server OSs, each PDC becomes a domain controller. Each BDC becomes either a domain controller or a member server (the administrator chooses). Member servers and stand-alone servers keep the same assigned roles.

Advanced Server and Datacenter Server Features

Advanced Server and Datacenter Server add features that support very high-performance servers, as well as configurations of multiple servers. The following are the most important of these features:

- Large-scale memory—If a server platform is configured to use Intel's Physical Address Extension (PAE) memory, Advanced Server can support more than 4 GB of physical RAM. Datacenter Server can use up to 64 GB of physical RAM.

- Clustering—A cluster is a group of up to four servers that appears to clients and applications as a single logical device. If one server in a cluster fails, its workload is automatically shifted to the other members of the cluster. This process, called "failover" can ensure very high availability of Web sites and other mission-critical systems.

- Network Load Balancing (NLB)—Load balancing spreads the total workload evenly across all servers and processors in a cluster. For example, Advanced Server can load-balance across up to 8 processors in the same cluster, while Datacenter Server can spread the work across 32 processors in one cluster.

Activities

1. Name the Windows 2000 product that is best suited to each of the applications listed below.

   a. A traveling executive's laptop computer

   b. A Web site with load balancing across four servers

   c. An office server with 50 clients

   d. One of that office's client desktop computers

   e. A worldwide hotel reservations system

2. How many processors can each of the Windows 2000 server OSs support?

   _____

   _____

3. When a Windows NT network is upgraded to Windows 2000 Server, what happens to the PDCs?

   _____

   _____

4. Explain the relationship between clustering and load balancing.

   _____

   _____

   _____

   _____

Extended Activity

On the Web, research the level of availability called "five nines." How much downtime per year is allowed if a network has five nines availability? Can any of the Windows 2000 Server products achieve this level?

Summary

The Windows NT NOS provides many functions and capabilities for computer networks. This unit reviewed many of these but only scratched the surface of the features of Windows NT.

Windows NT is a multitasking NOS that provides a great deal of network support and troubleshooting tools. It provides services that allow for communication with other NOSs such as Novell NetWare, UNIX, and AppleTalk. It also provides support for many different types of clients, such as Windows, Macintosh, and UNIX.

With regard to protocols, Windows NT can dynamically provide a number of different protocol stacks for a given situation. In small LANs, Windows NT can communicate with an efficient NetBEUI, or may use TCP/IP to communicate in a larger network or across the Internet. Interface software such as NDIS and TDI provide flexibility in building and accessing multiple protocol stacks.

Most of the key features of Windows NT are preserved and enhanced in the Windows 2000 suite of OSs. Windows 2000 Professional replaces Windows NT Workstation as the client component of the system. Windows NT server has been replaced by three products. Depending on their levels of traffic and fault tolerance requirements, companies may choose Windows 2000 Server, Windows 2000 Advanced Server, or Windows 2000 Datacenter Server.

Unit 8 Quiz

1. What is the main advantage of Windows 2000 Professional over Windows 98?

   a. User interface

   b. Reliability

   c. Graphics rendering

   d. Speed

2. Windows 2000 Server is a new version of what OS?

   a. UNIX

   b. Windows Millennium Edition

   c. Windows NT

   d. Linux

3. How many CPUs can Windows 2000 Server support?

   a. 4

   b. 8

   c. 16

   d. 32

4. The core functionality of Windows NT is contained in what software component?

   a. Core

   b. Kernel

   c. Code base

   d. Layer 1

5. Under Windows NT, when one application fails or becomes unstable, what happens to the other applications?

   a. Nothing

   b. They also become unstable

   c. They stop processing, repair damaged memory, then continue

   d. They take over the workload from the failed application

6. What does Windows NT have that Windows 2000 Server doesn't?

   a. Domains

   b. Workgroups

   c. PDCs

   d. Domain Controllers

7. Windows 2000 Professional may be used as:

   a. A stand-alone desktop OS

   b. Part of a peer-to-peer network

   c. A client of Windows 2000 Server

   d. All of the above

8. Gateway Services for NetWare functions at what layer of the OSI model?

   a. Presentation

   b. Application

   c. Data Link

   d. Translation

9. What is the main service of NDIS?

   a. Support for NetWare

   b. Support for multiple transmission media

   c. Support for multiple NICs

   d. Support for UNIX applications

10. On which of the following does a redirector reside?

    a. A client

    b. A server

    c. A PDC

    d. A hub

11. What is the feature that allows Windows NT to use multiple processors?

    a. Parallel processing

    b. Symmetric multiprocessing

    c. Asymmetric processing

    d. Multitasking

12. What Transport Layer protocol does Windows NT not support?

    a. NetBEUI

    b. TCP

    c. NWLink

    d. PPTP

13. Most administrators choose what file system for a Windows NT Server?

    a. FAT32

    b. FAT

    c. NTFS

    d. NFS

14. Which statement about hard disk storage is true?

    a. A volume is the same as a partition.

    b. A partition is a physical section of a hard disk.

    c. A hard drive may have only one partition.

    d. The OS is installed in the system volume.

15. The most fault-tolerant file system for Windows NT is:

    a. RAID 1

    b. RAID 0

    c. RAID 5

    d. RAID 10

16. What tool is used to view security logs?

    a. Event Viewer

    b. Performance Monitor

    c. Network Monitor

    d. Log Viewer

17. On Windows NT, what tool would you use to shut down a malfunctioning application?

    a. Registry Editor

    b. Task Manager

    c. Application Manager

    d. KillApps

18. What tool does Windows NT provide to analyze network traffic patterns?

    a. Traffic Manager

    b. Traffic Monitor

    c. Network Monitor

    d. Performance Manager

19. What is the worst thing that can happen if you make an error while using the Registry Editor?

    a. You'll lose your personal settings

    b. You must reboot the computer

    c. The OS becomes unusable

    d. You must reconfigure the computer's IP address

Unit 9
Analysis of LANs

Network professionals follow the same general process, whether they build a new local area network (LAN) from the ground up, or upgrade a network by adding new features. The essence of this development process is objectively deciding whether a particular data communication system, existing or proposed, meets the needs of a business and its users.

Network design and development is a complex subject that is beyond the scope of this course. However, this unit will explain the key concepts of network development and introduce the types of network analysis tools that you will use as you evaluate the performance of an existing LAN.

Lessons

1. Overview of the Network Development Process
2. Working with Binary and Hexadecimal Numbers
3. LAN Analysis and Testing Tools

Terms

Address Resolution Protocol (ARP)—ARP is the protocol used by IP (as in TCP/IP) for address resolution. Address resolution refers to the ability of a station to resolve another station's MAC (hardware) address given its IP address.

availability—Availability refers to the amount (or percentage) of time a given network or component in a network (such as a host or server) is available to carry out its intended task.

baseline—A network baseline is a "snapshot" of activity and performance at a given time. A baseline is used to measure changes in network performance.

binary—The base 2 numbering system used by computers to represent information. Binary numbers consist of only two symbols: 1 and 0. In a binary number, each position is two times greater than the position to its right.

cyclic redundancy check (CRC)—CRC is the mathematical process used to check the accuracy of data transmitted across a network. Before transmitting a block of data, the sending station performs a calculation on the data block and appends the resulting value to the end of the block. The receiving station takes the data and the CRC value, and performs the same calculation to check the accuracy of the data.

Data Link Control (DLC)—DLC is a generic term that refers to a protocol (such as Token Ring or Ethernet) used to transfer information across a single link.

expert system—An expert system is a sophisticated computer application that attempts to solve problems by analyzing data according to a set of rules designed by human experts.

hexadecimal—Hexadecimal is the base 16 numbering system used to represent binary information in a condensed format. Hexadecimal numbers consist of 16 symbols: 0 through 9, plus A through F. In a hexadecimal number, each position is 16 times greater than the position to its right.

Packet Internet Groper (Ping)—Ping is a TCP/IP utility used to verify that a computer's IP software is running properly and to verify the connectivity between computers. Ping transmits a test message to a destination host, and asks that host to reply.

promiscuous mode—Promiscuous mode is a setting that forces a NIC to process every frame it receives. For example, the NIC in a network analyzer is set to promiscuous mode.

systems development life cycle—Systems development life cycle is the process of creating a new system, or changing an existing system, from concept to completion.

traffic—Traffic refers to the amount of information traveling across a network. It includes both user data and network-related information.

uninterruptible power source (UPS)—An UPS provides battery backup in the event a power failure occurs.

utilization—Utilization refers to the amount of bandwidth being used at a given point in time or over a period of time. For example, if a 10-Mbps Ethernet LAN is running at 40-percent utilization, it is using 4 of the 10-Mbps bandwidth available.

Lesson 1—Overview of the Network Development Process

This lesson introduces a five-phase network development process that is similar to the phased approach commonly used in software development and engineering. Each phase of the network design process forms a logical sequence of events called the systems development life cycle. This step-by-step process is beneficial for both new networks and upgrades of existing networks.

The network development process describes the general tasks that must be accomplished when building or changing a network. However, each project has its own unique needs that may require a different process with different tasks.

Objectives

At the end of this lesson you will be able to:

- List and describe the typical phases of a network development process

- Explain the importance of a requirements analysis

- Explain the difference between a logical design and a physical design

- Discuss the relationship between requirements and baseline measurements

 **Key Point**

A given LAN design represents a balance of elements, based on user needs and business requirements.

Process Phases

The phases of a process break a large project down into understandable, manageable pieces. If you think of a project as a long list of tasks, these phases are simply task categories. In other words, each phase includes certain jobs that must be performed to prepare the project to move to the next phase. The life cycle of a typical network design project consists of the following phases, as illustrated on the Network Design Process Diagram:

1. Requirements Gathering

2. Analysis of the Existing Network

3. Logical Design

4. Physical Design

5. Installation and Maintenance

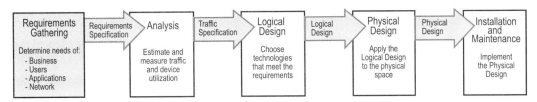

Network Design Process

The process only defines the phases of a systems development life cycle: thus it can apply to life cycles that use either a waterfall or a spiral approach. The decision whether to complete each phase before starting another (waterfall), or work through several iterations of the process in one life cycle (spiral), is up to each organization.

Deliverables

You can also think of a project in terms of what it is trying to produce, its "deliverable." For example, if someone asks, "What is the project's deliverable?" you could answer, "upgrading from Ethernet to Fast Ethernet." However, to get to the final goal of a faster network, the development team must produce many supporting products, such as design documents, estimates, or reports. Each phase produces its own deliverables that become the input to the next phase.

Like the invisible foundation of a building, these deliverables form a strong structure that strengthens the overall design. Therefore, all documentation that records your design assumptions, technical alternatives, customer information, and management approval should be retained for easy access and future reference.

Of course, not all projects require all of these phases or deliverables. Smaller projects may skip some phases or combine them. Once you understand the reason for each phase, task, and deliverable, you can decide how much of this formal process is necessary for each of your development projects.

Phase 1: Requirements Gathering

This is the most crucial phase in the development process, because requirements provide the target your network design must hit. Although Requirements Gathering is fundamental to the network design, it can often be a challenge to collect and organize information gathered from many sources.

Gathering requirements means talking to users, managers, and other network personnel, then summarizing and interpreting the results. Often, it means resolving conflicting needs and desires among user groups. However, network personnel are sometimes distanced from the users, and might not have a clear idea of what they want or need.

Requirements Gathering is time-consuming, and it may appear to produce no immediate results. On the contrary, requirements analysis helps the designer to better understand how the new network should perform.

Requirements for All Types of Needs

Just as different types of users have different networking needs, each aspect of the organization has its own requirements. Depending on the type or size of a project, it may be necessary to gather requirements for:

- The business or organization as a whole
- Users
- Applications
- Computing platforms
- The network itself and the network staff

Qualities of Good Requirements

Good results depend on gathering good requirements that are both user- and business-centered, as well as detailed and specific. The Requirements Gathering phase is a chance to define, as precisely as possible, what users want and need.

Designers must deliberately postpone any technical decision-making, and focus instead on discovering what factors make a real difference to users. Do they have enough storage space? Do their applications perform well? Are people waiting too long for print jobs? Is the security system understandable and usable? Do any network problems really get in their way?

Network designers cannot be expected to understand the jobs of system users. However, users often assume that certain essential features will be part of a network, even though they never explicitly ask for them. Thus, it is often helpful to directly ask users what they think about the current network, and what features they would most like to have. A simple survey, such as the User Requirements Matrix (as shown below), can gather good information without taking much of a user's time.

User Requirements Matrix

Category	Ratings: 1 = Good 5 = Unacceptable	Comments
Availability of Printers	NA 1 2 3 4 5	
Quality of Printers	NA 1 2 3 4 5	
Ease of Use of Mail System	NA 1 2 3 4 5	
Internal Network Speed	NA 1 2 3 4 5	
Internet Access Speed	NA 1 2 3 4 5	
Overall Network Stability	NA 1 2 3 4 5	
Overall Network Availability	NA 1 2 3 4 5	
Access to Network from Home	NA 1 2 3 4 5	
Computer System (PC or Mac)	NA 1 2 3 4 5	
Work Space	NA 1 2 3 4 5	

The network designer must formally record the requirements in a Requirements Specification document that describes exactly what the organization and users need from the network. This document should not propose solutions or designs (that will come later). Instead the Requirements Specification should clearly and specifically summarize the needs and desires of the organization and users.

Phase 2: Analysis of the Existing Network

When a network design project upgrades or enhances an existing network, it is essential to analyze the existing network architecture and performance. The Analysis phase complements the Requirements Gathering phase; requirements show you where you need to be, and analysis tells you where you currently are.

The effectiveness of a new network design depends on whether the current computing infrastructure can support the new requirements. The existing network installation and its supporting systems may be an asset to the new development, or a liability. Therefore, after the Requirements Specification has been written, but before the design process begins, the design team must thoroughly analyze the existing network and any other resources the new network may depend on.

A thorough analysis should gather both qualitative information (such as user estimates of storage and traffic) and quantitative data (such as traffic measurements and network management statistics).

The process of measuring traffic and gathering statistics is often called "baselining" because it provides a snapshot of the network's performance. As time goes on, the network staff can compare later measurements to this baseline, to see whether the network is still meeting its requirements. It is also important to take baseline measurements when users report performance problems and after you implement a solution. By comparing the two sets of performance measurements, it is easier to see whether the solution was effective.

A Traffic Specification Document is created during this phase of the design, and is considered a formal deliverable before proceeding to the Logical Design Phase. The Traffic Specification Document should include:

- Logical diagram of the current topology

- Estimated traffic volumes and patterns that describe the network capacity required for each application, each network segment, and the network as a whole

- Detailed statistics, baseline measurements, and any other direct measurements that describe the network's current level of performance

- A report on the quality of service provided by suppliers of Internet connections or wide area network (WAN) links

- A list of design constraints, such as the need to use existing cabling or devices

Phase 3: Logical Design

The Logical Design describes what the network must do and how it must perform to meet the requirements. A Logical Design specifies how data flows through a network, not where particular network elements are physically located (that comes in the next phase).

The designer creates a logical network structure based on the Requirements Specification and results of the network analysis. If the current hardware or software cannot meet the needs of the new network, they must be upgraded. If current systems can be reused, the new design can integrate them. If not, the team can find new systems, and test them to confirm they meet the requirements.

This phase should produce a Logical Design document that identifies the services, equipment, network architecture, and addressing structure necessary to create a network that satisfies its requirements. This document should include:

- Logical network diagrams

- Addressing strategy

- Security scheme and general services

- Specification of new hires or training for the network staff

- Initial cost estimates for hardware, software, services, personnel, and training

Phase 4: Physical Design

The Physical Design shows how to make the Logical Design work in the real world. In this phase, the network designer creates a detailed specification of the hardware, software, links, services, and cabling necessary to implement the Logical Design.

The Physical Design guides the equipment procurement and installation, thus the Physical Design document must be as specific and detailed as possible, often including:

- Physical network diagrams and to-scale wiring plans

- Detailed lists of equipment and parts

- Cost estimates for hardware, software, and installation labor

- Installation schedule that specifies the time and duration of physical or service disruptions

- Post-installation testing plan

- User training plan

Phase 5: Installation and Maintenance

Installation   A smooth installation is the reward for thorough work in the first four phases. When network developers are disciplined enough to invest real effort in the earlier phases, they find that they have already solved or prevented many common installation problems. Of course, the main output of the Installation phase is the network itself. However, a good installation should also produce:

- Updated diagrams (logical and physical) that include all last-minute changes

- Cabling, connections, and devices that are clearly labeled

- Any notes or documents that can simplify later maintenance or troubleshooting, such as test results or new traffic measurements

Any necessary hardware or software must be purchased and tested before installation can proceed. In a broader sense, any resources the network needs before its final deployment should also be arranged. New employees, consulting services, training, and service contracts are all resources that may need to be in place.

The procurement of these resources should always occur before installation begins in earnest. If a total system cannot be procured and tested prior to installation, a complete or partial redesign may be necessary. Although painful, it is better to deal with it before the network staff has already dismantled sections of the existing network.

The objective of the whole design process is to answer questions, make decisions, and discover problems before the installation phase begins. However, nobody is perfect, and the best plans cannot always prevent unexpected problems. Therefore, it is important that the designer participate in the network's installation.

Maintenance   After the network has been installed, the network staff shifts its focus to getting input from the user community and monitoring the network itself for potential problems. As each set of additional requirements arises, the network development life cycle repeats.

Activities

1. Name the phases of the network development process, in order.

    _____

    _____

    _____

2. Why is it important to invest a lot of time and energy in the Requirements Gathering phase?

    _____

    _____

3. What is the difference between a logical design and a physical design?

    _____

    _____

    _____

Extended Activity

In class, discuss other industries (such as construction or manufacturing) and discuss how their development processes are similar to the network design process. How important is a formal process to those types of work?

Lesson 2—Working with Binary and Hexadecimal Numbers

You must learn to handle binary numbers because computers do. Many common network processes and tasks are much easier to understand when you use binary numbers, and some jobs are impossible to do without them.

For example, Internet Protocol (IP) subnet masks are represented in a dotted decimal format, like this: 255.255.240.0. Each decimal number represents an 8-bit binary number or octet. When you convert each decimal number to binary, the pattern of the 32-bit subnet mask is easy to see. But in its dotted decimal format, the mask pattern is not apparent at all.

Conversely, when you design a subnet mask, you will work the bit pattern out in binary. But to communicate that pattern to people and computer applications, you must convert the binary value to dotted decimal.

You will not learn the details of subnet masking in this course; however, we will use subnet masks in our examples, because it is one of the most common reasons to convert between binary and decimal.

Objectives

At the end of this lesson you will be able to:

- Convert decimal numbers to binary
- Convert binary numbers to decimal
- Convert binary numbers to hexadecimal
- Convert hexadecimal numbers to binary

 **Key Point**

The decimal numbering system is base 10. Binary numbering is base 2, and hexadecimal is base 16.

Decimal to Binary Conversion

The decimal numbering system is a base 10 system. Each position has a placeholder value represented by a power of 10. Each position may contain one of 10 symbols: 0 through 9. For example, the decimal number 1,234 has the following placeholder values:

Placeholder Value (Decimal)	10^3 (1,000's place)	10^2 (100's place)	10^1 (10's place)	10^0 (1's place)
Symbol	1	2	4	8
Resultant Place Value	1,000	200	30	4

The binary numbering system is a base 2 system. In binary, each position has a placeholder value represented by a power of 2. Each position may contain one of two symbols, 0 or 1. For example, the above number represented in binary looks as follows:

Binary Placeholder Value	2^{10}	2^9	2^8	2^7	2^6	2^5	2^4	2^3	2^2	2^1	2^0
Decimal Value	1,024	512	256	128	64	32	16	8	4	2	1
Symbol	1	0	0	1	1	0	1	0	0	1	0
Resultant Decimal Place Value	1,024	0	0	128	64	0	16	0	0	2	0

Summing the resultant place values results in the original decimal number:

$$1,024 + 128 + 64 + 16 + 2 = 1,234$$

The Divide by Two Process

How did we make the conversion from the original decimal number to binary? One method we can use for performing this conversion is the divide by two process.

In the divide by two process, we lay out our conversion problem as follows:

Decimal number/base = quotient + remainder

Quotient/base = quotient + remainder, and so on

Using the above example, the decimal to binary conversion process is as follows:

1. Divide the decimal number 1,234 by the base, 2.

   1234/2 = 617, remainder 0

2. Next, divide the quotient, 617, by the base, 2.

   617/2 = 308, remainder 1

3. Continue on, dividing the results by the base. Here is how the whole process looks, step by step:

   1,234/2 = 617, remainder 0

   617/2 = 308, remainder 1

   308/2 = 154, remainder 0

   154/2 = 77, remainder 0

   77/2 = 38, remainder 1

   38/2 = 19, remainder 0

   19/2 = 9, remainder 1

   9/2 = 4, remainder 1

   4/2 = 2, remainder 0

   2/2 = 1, remainder 0

   1/2 = 0, remainder 1

4. Stop the process when you divide 1 by 2.

5. List the final remainder as a whole number.

6. Carry down the remainders, starting from top to bottom, arranging them from right to left. The right most remainder character becomes the binary number's least significant bit (LSB) and the left-most character becomes the most significant bit (MSB). The resulting binary number looks like this:

10011010010

Therefore, the binary value 10011010010 is equivalent to the decimal number 1,234.

Binary to Decimal Conversion

The simplest way to convert binary to decimal is to sum the decimal representation of each binary place value. To convert the binary number 1100011001 to decimal, we express each binary bit position as its decimal equivalent value:

Binary Placeholder Value	2^9	2^8	2^7	2^6	2^5	2^4	2^3	2^2	2^1	2^0
Decimal Value	512	256	128	64	32	16	8	4	2	1
Symbol	1	1	0	0	0	1	1	0	0	1
Resultant Decimal Place Value	512	256	0	0	0	16	4	0	0	1

Then we add all of the decimal values:

512 + 256 + 16 + 8 + 1 = 793

Converting a Dotted Decimal Address to a Binary Value

A subnet mask is a binary bit pattern that indicates what bits of an IP address identify the network, and what bits identify each individual host. A 1 in the mask means that the corresponding bit position in the address is part of the network number. A 0 in the mask means that the corresponding bit position in the IP address is part of the host number.

Your network's subnet mask is 255.255.192.0, and you want to know how many bits identify the network. To do this, you must convert each of the four decimal numbers to their binary equivalents.

Convert First Octet   1.   First decimal number: 255

255/2 = 127, remainder 1

127/2 = 63, remainder 1

63/2 = 31, remainder 1

31/2 = 15, remainder 1

15/2 = 7, remainder 1

7/2 = 3, remainder 1

3/2 = 1, remainder 1

1/2 = 0, remainder 1

First octet: Decimal 255 = 11111111

Convert Second Octet   2.   Second decimal number: 255

This is easy, because this number is the same as the first.

Second octet: Decimal 255 = 11111111

Convert Third Octet   3.   Third decimal number: 192

192/2 = 96, remainder 0

96/2 = 48, remainder 0

48/2 = 24, remainder 0

24/2 = 12, remainder 0

12/2 = 6, remainder 0

6/2 = 3, remainder 0

3/2 = 1, remainder 1

1/2 = 0, remainder 1

Third octet: Decimal 192 = 11000000

Convert Fourth Octet   4.   Fourth decimal number: 0

This is the easiest conversion of all, because zero is the same in any numbering system. However, in binary, we always include the leading 0s as placeholders; thus the binary result is always 8 characters.

Fourth octet: Decimal 0 = 00000000

Combine the Binary Numbers

To see the pattern of our IP subnet mask, we now list each binary number from left to right, in the same order as the dotted decimal representation:

255	255	192	0
11111111	11111111	11000000	00000000

Now the subnet mask is apparent. In this network, the first 18 bits of each node's IP address identify its subnet. The remaining 14 bits identify the node itself.

Converting a Binary Value to a Dotted Decimal Address

You have determined that your network needs the following subnet mask:

11111111   11111111   11110000   00000000

When you configure your network, the operating system will ask for this value in dotted decimal format. Thus, you must convert each of the eight octets to its decimal equivalent. To do this, you sum the decimal representation of each binary place value.

First octet = 128 + 64 + 32 + 16 + 8 + 4 + 2 + 1 = 255

Second octet = 128 + 64 + 32 + 16 + 8 + 4 + 2 + 1 = 255

Third octet = 128 + 64 + 32 + 16 = 240

Fourth octet = 0

Thus, the dotted decimal form of this subnet mask is 255.255.240.0

Hexadecimal Numbering

Network professionals and programmers use systems such as dotted decimal because humans have a hard time keeping track of long strings of binary digits. However, decimal is not always the best way to express a binary value.

For example, a network interface card (NIC) address is 48 bits long. The decimal equivalent of a 48-bit number can be as high as 2^{48}, or 281,474,976,710,656. That is almost as hard to work with as the binary number.

Computer professionals use the hexadecimal system to represent many types of binary values. Network analysis tools, such as protocol analyzers (explained later in this unit), generate a lot of hexadecimal notation. Thus, it is important to understand how this system works.

Hexadecimal Values

Hexadecimal is a base 16 numbering system. Each position is a power of 16, as shown in the Hexadecimal Numbering Table.

Hexadecimal Numbering

Hexadecimal Placeholder Value	16^1 (16's place)	16^0 (1's place)
Symbol	2	5
Resultant Decimal Place Value	32 (2 x 16)	5 (5 x 1)

For example, in the decimal system, we can count in the first position (ones place) up to nine. When we reach 10, we put a 0 in the first position and start over with a 1 in the second position (tens place). In hexadecimal, we can continue counting up to decimal 15 in the first position, as you can see in the Decimal and Hexadecimal Symbols Table.

Decimal and Hexadecimal Symbols

Decimal	Hexadecimal
0	0
1	1
2	2
3	3
4	4
5	5
6	6
7	7
8	8
9	9
10	A
11	B
12	C

Decimal and Hexadecimal Symbols (Continued)

Decimal	Hexadecimal
13	D
14	E
15	F

We use the symbols A through F to represent the additional numerical values beyond decimal 9. Thus, the most obvious difference in hexadecimal notation is the symbols it uses. An old computing joke explains that it is easy to count in hexadecimal, just use all of your fingers, and six of your toes.

Hexadecimal for Condensed Binary

In networking, hexadecimal is most often used as a shorthand numbering system that condenses 4 binary bits into one of 16 symbols, as shown in the Decimal, Binary, and Hexadecimal Symbols Table.:

Decimal, Binary, and Hexadecimal Symbols

Decimal	Binary	Hexadecimal
0	0000	0
1	0001	1
2	0010	2
3	0011	3
4	0100	4
5	0101	5
6	0110	6
7	0111	7
8	1000	8
9	1001	9
10	1010	A
11	1011	B
12	1100	C

Decimal, Binary, and Hexadecimal Symbols (Continued)

Decimal	Binary	Hexadecimal
13	1101	D
14	1110	E
15	1111	F

When we use hexadecimal in this way, each 4-bit chunk of a binary address is separately represented by its corresponding hexadecimal value. In other words, we do not convert an entire 8-bit binary number to its equivalent hexadecimal number. Instead, we evaluate each 4-bit section separately. For example:

binary 1111 = hex F

binary 0000 = hex 0

11110000 = F0

10101111 00000101 = AF 05

To make them easier to read, binary octets and pairs of hexadecimal numbers are usually separated by a space. Of course, the computer processes binary numbers in a continuous stream.

Converting Binary to Hexadecimal

When we use hexadecimal as a condensed notation system, not a true numbering system, it is easier to convert between binary and hexadecimal. That is because we only need to work with 4 bits at a time. Thus, let us convert the binary string 1011001001 to a hexadecimal value:

1. Break the binary number into groups of 4 bits, starting at the right.

   10   1100   1001

2. If the left most value has fewer than 4 bits, add enough leading zeroes to make 4 bits.

   0010   1100   1001

3. Convert each 4-bit binary value to decimal, using the method you learned earlier. Soon, you will not need to sum the numbers but will simply recognize the decimal value of each 4-bit group.

   2   12   9

4. Convert each decimal number to hexadecimal.

2 C 9

5. If you have an odd number of hexadecimal values, add a zero to the left. Then group the hexadecimal values in pairs.

02 C9

Converting Hexadecimal to Binary

To convert a hexadecimal value to a binary number, we simply reverse the process you just learned. Here is how to convert the hexadecimal value 56 F2 C1 to binary:

1. Convert each hexadecimal value to decimal.

5 6 15 2 12 1

2. Convert each decimal value to binary.

0101 0110 1111 0010 1100 0001

Activities

1. In the grid below, enter the decimal value of each binary position.

2. What is the decimal value of the character 1 in the binary number 0010?

    _____

3. What is the decimal equivalent of the binary number 0010 1001?

    _____

4. What is the binary equivalent of the decimal number 127?

    _____

5. What is the binary equivalent of the decimal number 492?

    _____

6. What is the hexadecimal equivalent of the binary number 1101 0001 1001?

    _____

7. What is the binary equivalent of the hexadecimal number CC F0 9D E8?

    _____

Extended Activities

1. Convert the following IP addresses from dotted decimal to binary.

   a. 192.44.168.93

   _____

   b. 10.0.12.3

   _____

   c. 127.0.0.1

   _____

   d. 172.168.153.255

   _____

   e. 36.244.45.199

   _____

2. Convert the following binary addresses to dotted decimal.

   a. 10000010 10101010 10100110 11110000

   _____

   b. 00010100 01110001 01010010 11001110

   _____

   c. 01100111 10011001 00001100 00011010

   _____

   d. 00111110 10111100 11000100 11111111

   _____

   e. 11011000 00111100 10110100 01111100

   _____

Lesson 3—LAN Analysis and Testing Tools

Every LAN administrator should understand basic analysis and testing concepts, because basic analysis tools are essential for keeping a network functioning smoothly. As the network grows, those tools can also predict the need to replace overworked components before they fail, or before performance suffers too much.

Network analysis tools generally focus on finding faults in a physical medium or analyzing patterns in data flow. Some tools specialize in one or the other, while others combine these functions.

This lesson introduces the most common types of LAN testing tools. We do not explain exactly how to use them, because each of these categories includes many different products. Also, to effectively use these products to analyze or troubleshoot a real network, you will need a deeper understanding of the way various protocols operate. Later courses will give you that knowledge.

Objectives

At the end of this lesson you will be able to:

- Describe the function and purpose of a network baseline
- Identify key fields of a frame header in a network trace
- Name the tools used to detect problems in physical media

 **Key Point**

Special hardware and software are used to monitor LAN performance and troubleshoot problems.

Baselining

Baselining, also called benchmarking, is the process of measuring and documenting the capacity and operating efficiency of a network. A network baseline is a snapshot of activity and performance, as depicted on the Baseline Capture Screen Diagram.

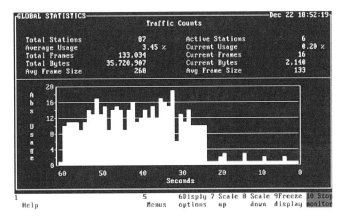

Baseline Capture Screen

A baseline report should include graphs and tables of network operating parameters over time. It should also include a summary of anomalies, trends, and suggestions for threshold alarm configuration and monitoring.

When you regularly measure your LAN's activity, and compare those measurements with your baselines, you can detect important problems and trends before they can interfere with users' work. For example, on the LAN Segment Utilization Table, utilization measurements have been compared to baseline data to show how traffic has increased over a six-month period.

LAN Segment Utilization

Network Segment	Segment Type	Utilization (percent)	Percent Increase in Past Six Months
Corporate Hub Workgroup 1	10-Mbps Shared Ethernet	55	15
Corporate Hub Workgroup 2	10-Mbps Shared Ethernet	50	12
Corporate Hub Workgroup 3	10-Mbps Shared Ethernet	42	8
Corporate Hub Workgroup 4	10-Mbps Shared Ethernet	57	18
Corporate Switch	10-Mbps Switched Ethernet	66 (Port from corporate switch to backbone switch)	15
Server Room Switch	10-Mbps Switched Ethernet	70 (Port from corporate switch to backbone switch)	18
Classroom 1 Hubs	10-Mbps Shared Ethernet	5 to 10 on average	0 (Traffic has remained flat over the past six months.)
Classroom 2 Hubs	10-Mbps Shared Ethernet	5 to 10 on average	0 (Traffic has remained flat over the past six months.)
Classroom Switch	10-Mbps Switched Ethernet	10 to 20 on average	0 (Traffic has remained flat over the past six months.)
Corporate Back-bone Switch to Internet	10-Mbps Switched Ethernet	20	20
Internet Router	CPU	75	20

It is also good to take a baseline measurement when unusual network activity is occurring, such as high-bandwidth utilization. However, baseline measurements should not be taken at a specified regular interval. A baseline taken at the same specified interval or time of day could result in the same results over time. It is better to baseline each subnet of a network at random times throughout a normal business day.

Software Tools for Baselining and Testing

LAN baselining and analysis requires special software tools. Some are provided with network operating systems, and others are offered by third-party vendors. Some even require dedicated hardware. Most network testing tools are expensive, but the cost of an analysis tool is usually justified by faster repair times.

Built-In NOS Utilities

Most NOSs have built-in software components that measure server CPU utilization and other network statistics. Measuring network utilization, in conjunction with a given traffic load, can provide valuable insight into the operation and capacity of a network.

Protocol Analyzers (sniffers)

Protocol analyzers detect patterns of network operation by capturing and reading frames. For example, a protocol analyzer can identify a device that is sending out too many broadcast frames, or one that is consistently transmitting damaged frames.

To understand what a protocol analyzer does, let us take a look at a typical ARP request contained in an Ethernet frame traveling between two NICs. If we could actually see the data, it would appear as a stream of binary bits, 1s and 0s, flowing down the wire. But because people do not handle binary as well as machines do, we will represent this bit stream in hexadecimal notation:

```
FF FF FF FF FF FF 00 00 C0 48 8C 11 08 06 00 01
08 00 06 04 00 01 00 00 C0 48 8C 11 80 01 00 02
00 00 00 00 00 00 80 01  00 01 00 00 00 00 00 00
00 00 00 00 00 00 00 00  00 00 00 00 ...
```

This is still pretty confusing, but you already know enough to figure it out. As you have learned, an Ethernet frame uses the following format, which we can use to decipher this data:

- Destination hardware address: 6 bytes

  The first 6 bytes are FF FF FF FF FF FF, or all binary 1s. This is a broadcast address; thus this frame is being sent to all nodes on the network.

- Source hardware address: 6 bytes

  Each NIC address uses the first three bytes to identify the manufacturer, and the second three bytes to identify the card itself. Thus, 00 00 C0 is the manufacturer's code, and 48 8C 11 is the card's address number.

- Type: 2 bytes

  08 06 is a code that identifies the type of data carried in this frame. In this case, it is an ARP request.

- Data: 46 bytes minimum, padded if necessary

The encapsulated data is an ARP request message; thus the ARP header begins at this point. We could then use an ARP request diagram to figure out the rest of this trace. But you can already see that this is a very slow and tedious way to analyze network data.

Types of Protocol Analyzers

Because computer protocols were designed to be understood by machines, it is a lot faster and easier to let machines, called protocol analyzers, work with them. These tools tend to fall into two main categories:

- WAN analyzers capture data on external links, such as Point to Point Protocol (PPP), Frame Relay, ATM, and others. It uses special interface cards to read frames off a WAN connection. Additionally, WAN analyzers are typically connected to the wide area line with a "Y" connector. This allows the monitor to capture traffic as it flows normally across the link.

- LAN analyzers capture and display frames from LAN protocols such as Ethernet, Token Ring, and FDDI. These analyzers are connected to the LAN segment by means of a hub or a switch, just like any other node. However, when a protocol analyzer is connected to a switch port, it will only capture information directed to the switch port it is connected to. For that reason, certain switches allow us to designate a monitor port and an analyzer port. In that case, all traffic appearing on the port that is being monitored will be copied to the analyzer port.

Components of a LAN Protocol Analyzer

A LAN protocol analyzer has two components:

- Hardware may be a dedicated portable computer temporarily connected to the LAN, or a computer that is permanently part of the LAN. The key hardware element is a NIC that is set to operate in "promiscuous mode." That simply means that the NIC eavesdrops on all traffic on its segment. It copies and processes all frames, not just those addressed to it.

- Proprietary software interprets frames and packets, and detects useful trends and patterns.

Popular protocol analysers include Network Associates' Sniffer, Hewlett-Packard's LAN Advisor, Novell's LANalyzer, NetXray's Sniffer Basic, Shomiti Systems' Surveyor, and the freeware Ethereal protocol analyzer (distributed under the GNU General Public License). Sniffer originally dominated the analyzer market, thus many network professionals use the word "sniffer" to refer to any protocol analyzer.

Protocol Analyzer Traces

One of the simplest services of a protocol analyzer is to translate data streams into a neatly formatted report, called a trace, that humans can understand. For example, the following trace shows the same ARP request we saw above. However, this format makes it a lot easier to understand:

```
DLC:  ----- DLC Header -----
DLC:
DLC:  Frame 1 arrived at 23:33:39.6638; frame size is 60 (003C hex) bytes.
DLC:  Destination = BROADCAST FFFFFFFFFFFF, Broadcast
DLC:  Source      = Station WstDig488C11
DLC:  Ethertype  = 0806 (ARP)
DLC:
ARP:  ----- ARP/RARP frame -----
ARP:
ARP:  Hardware type = 1 (10Mb Ethernet)
ARP:  Protocol type = 0800 (IP)
ARP:  Length of hardware address = 6 bytes
ARP:  Length of protocol address = 4 bytes
ARP:  Opcode 1 (ARP request)
ARP:  Sender's hardware address = WstDig488C11
ARP:  Sender's protocol address = [128.1.0.2]
ARP:  Target hardware address = 000000000000
```

```
ARP:  Target protocol address = [128.1.0.1]


ADDR  HEX
ASCII
0000  FF FF FF FF FF FF 00 00  C0 48 8C 11 08 06 00 01   .........H......
0010  08 00 06 04 00 01 00 00  C0 48 8C 11 80 01 00 02   .........H......
0020  00 00 00 00 00 00 80 01  00 01 00 00 00 00 00 00   ................
0030  00 00 00 00 00 00 00 00  00 00 00 00               ............
```

As you can see, the protocol analyzer has helpfully identified both the frame header (Data Link Control [DLC] header) and the encapsulated ARP request. It also includes the data in hexadecimal format. The numbers at the beginning of the hexadecimal lines simply identify each line of that part of the trace. To the right of each line of hexadecimal is the ASCII representation of the hexadecimal. When the application data is in ASCII format (such as word processor text or e-mail), this display makes it easy to read.

Protocol analysis tools offer many other sophisticated services, beyond simple trace generation. Many display network statistics in a user-friendly "dashboard" format that shows overall network health at a glance. Network administrators can configure some analysis packages to monitor the network, and sound an alarm if key statistics exceed a defined threshold. The most sophisticated analyzers even include expert systems that detect broader trends and suggest likely problems.

The Dark Side of Protocol Analysis

The same tools that keep your network running smoothly are also used by criminal hackers (crackers) who want to disable your network or steal valuable data. Some crackers use protocol analyzers to learn passwords and important network addresses that can be used to further penetrate the network. To do this, the cracker must have physical access to the network's cabling (or wireless channel). This can be as difficult as tapping into wiring that runs through walls or ceilings, or as simple as plugging a notebook computer into a hub when no one is watching.

Simulation Tools

Network designers often use general rules of thumb and rough estimates to create or upgrade a LAN. Simulation software can also be used to model the behavior of a LAN under a given load. These tools allow a picture of a LAN's performance, given a certain number of users, applications, and telecommunications links. These tools can be very helpful when designing a large or complex network. However, simulators do not always provide an accurate picture of actual activity.

Examples of these types of tools include:

- Network mapping tools
- Physical network management tools
- Network design tools
- Network planning and simulation tools
- Network management tools

LAN traffic simulation packages (as well as Sniffer and LAN Advisor) generate actual LAN test traffic. By varying the size and frequency of the test traffic, the effect on the LAN is measured. Progressive degradation of LAN performance can be gauged as a function of client activity, using just a few personal computers (PCs). The activity of each LAN device (such as servers, bridges, and routers) can be monitored to determine the delay within each component. One client can simulate many workstations.

Testing Physical Media

A common cause of problems in data networks is the cabling, connectors, and other transmission media that link every network device.

Damaged or poorly installed wiring can scramble the frames it carries. Higher software layers must then request retransmission of that damaged data, which degrades network performance. This problem is generally called a cyclic redundancy check (CRC) error, because CRC is the method used to detect frame errors.

Protocol analyzers can provide statistics on CRC errors but may not be able to determine their cause. Different hardware may be necessary to detect problems specific to each type of physical medium. In addition, a technician often needs special training and experience to correctly use these devices.

Copper Cables

Copper cabling problems are often caused by broken wires (open circuits), bad connections, short circuits, too-long segments, or excessive crosstalk between one pair of wires and another.

A time domain reflectometer (TDR) detects wire damage by sending a controlled electrical signal down a cable. It analyzes the changes in that signal to detect problems with the circuit. Like radar, the TDR measures the distance to the end of a cable or to the site of wire damage by calculating the time necessary for a signal to travel down the medium and reflect back.

Crosstalk is a specific type of noise, caused by an electrical signal in one cable that induces a voltage fluctuation in an adjacent cable. In telephone lines, crosstalk allows you to hear someone else's faint conversation in the background. In data lines, it is detectable as errors. Crosstalk is typically described as near end crosstalk (NEXT), and is measured by injecting a known signal on one line and measuring the strength of the induced signal on an adjacent line.

Optical Fiber

Problems with fiber optic cables often are caused by a broken fiber, bad connections, or stress on the fiber that causes light to escape through the cladding and weaken the signal.

An optical time domain reflectometer (OTDR) can detect all of these problems. It sends a pulse of light down a fiber, then measures the time it takes for a light pulse to reflect back. In a fiber optic cable, light reflects back from the end of the fiber (a splice) or a crack or break in the fiber. Because the speed of light is constant, the OTDR can calculate the distance to the location of cable damage.

An OTDR can also determine whether light signals are being scattered within the fiber. This symptom can indicate milder forms of damage, such as too-tight bends.

Wireless LANs

Wireless LAN performance suffers if transmitted signals are too weak or if signals are being disrupted by a source of interference such as a microwave oven. A spectrum analyzer is a smart tunable radio receiver that can analyze the quality of the signal transmitted by devices such as access points, and may reveal the presence of an interfering radio source. However, spectrum analyzers cannot detect whether a wireless device is correctly receiving a radio signal.

Activities

1. What is a protocol analyzer used for?

   _____

   _____

2. Why is it important to baseline a network?

   _____

   _____

3. How do traffic simulation tools help a network manager?

   _____

   _____

4. Using the hexadecimal detail located in the lesson, identify the following key portions of the ARP request:

   a. Sender's IP address

   b. Sender's hardware address

   c. Destination IP address

Extended Activities

1. Using a Web search engine, research at least three products that can be used for baselining a network, such as network mapping tools, protocol analyzers, or traffic simulation tools. List each product and its major features.

   _____

   _____

   _____

   _____

   _____

   _____

2. Using Windows NT Network Monitor, take a trace of traffic traveling between a Windows NT Server and client.

3. The following trace shows a Token Ring frame from a client to a server. Review the details and list the headers contained in this trace.

_____

_____

_____

_____

```
DLC:  ----- DLC Header (Token Ring) -----
DLC:
DLC:  Frame 2 arrived at  15:57:04.871; frame size is 67 (0043 hex) bytes.
DLC:  AC: Frame priority 0,  Reservation priority 0,  Monitor count 1
DLC:  FC: LLC frame,  PCF attention code: None
DLC:  FS: Addr recognized indicators: 00, Frame copied indicators: 00
DLC:  Destination = Station IBM    0033BF
DLC:  Source      = Station IBM    002FEB
DLC:
LLC:  ----- LLC Header -----
LLC:
LLC:  DSAP = E0, SSAP = E0, Command, Unnumbered frame: UI
LLC:
IPX:  ----- IPX Header -----
IPX:
IPX:  Checksum = FFFF
IPX:  Length = 50
IPX:  Transport control = 00
IPX:          0000 .... = Reserved
IPX:          .... 0000 = Hop count
IPX:  Packet type = 17 (Novell NetWare)
IPX:  Dest   network.node = 00001111.10005A0033BF (NETWARE-XT), socket = 1105 (NetWare
      Server)
IPX:  Source network.node = 00001111.10005A002FEB, socket = 16385 (4001)
IPX:  ----- Novell Advanced NetWare -----
IPX:  Request type = 2222 (Request)
IPX:  Seq no=62   Connection no=1    Task no=2
IPX:
NCP:  ----- Read File Data Request -----
```

```
NCP:   Request code = 72
NCP:   File handle = 0000 AC08 0200
NCP:   Starting byte offset    = 166
NCP:   Number of bytes to read = 4
NCP:
NCP:   [Normal end of NetWare "Read File Data Request" packet.]


ADDR   HEX   ASCII
0000   18 40 10 00 5A 00 33 BF   10 00 5A 00 2F EB E0 E0   .@..Z.3...Z./...
0010   03 FF FF 00 32 00 11 00   00 11 11 10 00 5A 00 33   ....2........Z.3
0020   BF 04 51 00 00 11 11 10   00 5A 00 2F EB 40 01 22   ..Q......Z./.@."
0030   22 3E 01 02 00 48 00 00   00 AC 08 02 00 00 00 00   ">...H..........
0040   A6 00 04                                                          ...
```

a. Where does the frame begin and end in the hexadecimal detail?

_____

_____

b. Where does the packet begin and end in the hexadecimal detail?

_____

_____

c. Where does the message begin and end in the hexadecimal detail?

_____

_____

d. What is the purpose of this client request?

_____

_____

4. As directed by your instructor, go to the Ethereal Web site (**http://www.ethereal.com**) to get a copy of this freeware protocol analyzer. Follow Ethereal's instructions for downloading and installing the appropriate binary distribution file for your computing platform.

   After successfully installing the Ethereal Analyzer, explore it by capturing different types of traffic. Here are a few suggestions to get you started.

   a. Capture a Ping command to the IP address of another node on your network.

   b. Capture a Ping command to a node outside of your network, using a name instead of an IP address. Observe that a Domain Name System (DNS) request was issued to determine the destination IP address. Set a display filter to only display the DNS information.

   c. Capture a session to a Web server, either on or off your network. Set a display filter to only display HTTP messages.

Summary

The same five-phase network development process can guide you as you create a new network, or as you upgrade an existing system. The key of this process is its focus on business and user needs. Rather than adjusting the operation of the business to some preferred technology, a good network professional first defines what an organization needs, then determines what technology will best meet those needs.

A network must be upgraded when it no longer meets the needs of the organization. A wide range of analysis and testing tools can help you objectively measure the difference between how a LAN is currently performing and how it should be performing to satisfy its users.

Some of these analysis tools are included with NOS software, while others are separate systems from third-party vendors. Most of them, however, monitor a network's traffic, then analyze that data for patterns that can reveal problems. To use these tools well, a network professional must have a thorough understanding of the protocols and applications that operate on each LAN.

Those systems are constantly evolving, just as an organization's business needs are always changing. Thus, both the LAN and its administrative staff must always be in a continual process of improvement.

Unit 9 Quiz

1. What is the main benefit of the phased network development process?

   a. It keeps the developer focused on user requirements

   b. It minimizes the cost of the system

   c. It prevents errors and installation problems

   d. It ensures that the logical and physical designs are identical

2. Your CEO complains that his network performance has become very slow in the past few weeks, and demands to know what you are doing about it. You have a good set of test tools available. What do you also need before you can determine whether the problem is occurring network-wide or just at the CEO's desktop?

   a. Traces on every network segment

   b. Network baseline data for comparison

   c. Average performance statistics for all desktop computers

   d. Help desk records showing past complaints by the CEO

3. What is the purpose of requirements gathering?

   a. To see if users can adapt to the chosen technology

   b. To find out how much money is available for the project

   c. To tell users what features they can and cannot have

   d. To find out what features users most need and want

4. What is the most effective way to gather user requirements?

   a. Analyze networks at similar organizations

   b. Ask management what they think the users need

   c. Ask the users what they need

   d. Brainstorm requirements with the network staff

5. You find a network diagram that shows what devices and applications work together. There are notes on the boundaries of broadcast domains and the network's IP addressing scheme. The diagram does not show the shape of the office space. What type of diagram is this?

    a. Logical

    b. Physical

    c. Matrix

    d. Conceptual

6. Your network development process is almost complete, and it is time to get three bids from cabling installation contractors. What diagram do the contractors need to prepare their estimates?

    a. Logical

    b. Physical

    c. Matrix

    d. Conceptual

7. Binary is what type of numbering system?

    a. Base 2

    b. Base 8

    c. Base 4

    d. Base 16

8. Convert this address to binary: 198.64.255.1

9. Convert this binary value to hexadecimal notation:
   10100010 11000101

10. Convert this hexadecimal value to binary: CF 80 4E

11. Your subnet mask is: 11111111   11111111   11100000 00000000. What do you enter into the Subnet Mask field of a network setup dialog box?

     _____

12. Write the decimal number 145 in binary.

     _____

13. Your local grocery store owner only understands hexadecimal. How do you tell him that you want a dozen eggs?

    a. C eggs

    b. C0 eggs

    c. 1100 eggs

    d. 0.0.0.12 eggs

14. In the hexadecimal number FC, what is the decimal value of the F?

    a. 15 x 10, or 150

    b. 16 x 16, or 256

    c. 15 x 16, or 240

    d. 15 x 15, or 225

15. What is the key hardware component of a protocol analyzer?

    a. Multiple NICs, one for every segment in the network

    b. A NIC in stealth mode

    c. A TDR

    d. A NIC in promiscuous mode

16. What does a computer criminal need to be able to use a sniffer against your network?

    a. A user's logon ID and password

    b. Physical access to the cabling

    c. The IP address of the hub

    d. A spectrum analyzer

17. What tool can test a network's logical design before the network is built?

    a. Protocol analyzer

    b. Traffic simulation application

    c. VPN

    d. VLAN

18. What does a TDR measure?

    a. The speed of light through a fiber

    b. The distance to a break in a copper cable

    c. Interference on a radio channel

    d. The strength of a transmitted signal

19. One of your company's workgroups is suddenly complaining of poor wireless LAN performance. What tool can tell you whether the access point is malfunctioning or if the new microwave oven is to blame?

    a. Wireless TDR

    b. Spectrum analyzer

    c. An FM radio receiver

    d. A laptop with a standard wireless NIC

COURSE QUIZ

1. On a tour of a colleague's network equipment room, you see three MAUs. What type of Data Link protocol does this network use?

   a. Token Ring

   b. Ethernet

   c. FDDI

   d. It is impossible to say, because all networks use MAUs

2. If you could only study two NOSs, what two would you be most likely to encounter on the job?

   a. Windows NT/2000 and Banyan VINES

   b. Novell Netware and 3Com

   c. Novell Netware and Windows NT/2000

   d. Windows NT/2000 and LANtastic

3. What is the function of NDIS?

   a. Map Network Layer protocols to physical media

   b. Map Network Layer protocols to Data Link Layer protocols

   c. Map Data Link Layer protocols to physical media

   d. Map Transport Layer protocols to Network Layer

4. What type of device is used with UTP cabling to create a star network configuration?

   a. Router

   b. Gateway

   c. Hub

   d. Bridge

5. What category of UTP cable supports both 10-Mbps and 100-Mbps Ethernet using twisted pair?

   a. Category 3

   b. Category 4

   c. Category 5

   d. Category 3E

6. What does NIC stand for?

   a. Network interface control

   b. Network interface card

   c. National Institute for Communications

   d. Network interface carrier

7. Which of the following best describes the function of a MAC layer address?

   a. Transmits a frame to the destination NIC

   b. Transmits a packet to the correct port

   c. Transmits a frame to the final destination

   d. Transmits a frame to the correct socket

8. Which of the following is not a MAC layer protocol?

   a. FDDI

   b. Ethernet

   c. Token Ring

   d. IPX

9. What is FDDI commonly used for in a corporate network?

   a. Wireless configurations

   b. Router connectivity

   c. Bridge connectivity

   d. Backbone connectivity

10. A hub functions as what logical topology?

    a. Bus

    b. Mesh

    c. Ring

    d. Layer

11. Why would you replace a hub with a switch?

    a. Provide WAN connectivity

    b. Provide Internet connectivity

    c. Increase LAN performance

    d. All of the above

12. Why would you use a patch panel in an Ethernet network?

    a. Simplify connections between network devices

    b. Repair broken connections

    c. Patch server software

    d. Remotely monitor a network

13. What is the most widely installed LAN technology?

    a. Ethernet

    b. Token Ring

    c. ARCnet

    d. FDDI

14. In a client/server arrangement, where are requests normally generated?

    a. Client

    b. Server

    c. Either client or server

    d. NIC

15. What Transport and Network Layer protocols are proprietary to a Novell NetWare network?

    a. TCP/UDP

    b. SPX/IPX

    c. PU/LU

    d. Ethernet and Token Ring

16. Which LAN link architecture is deterministic?

    a. Ethernet

    b. Token Ring

    c. Star

    d. LLC

17. What layer of software is normally loaded on a NIC?

    a. Physical

    b. Data Link

    c. Network

    d. Transport

18. When you upgrade Windows NT Server to Windows 2000 Server, what happens to your PDC by default?

    a. It becomes a domain controller

    b. It becomes a backup domain controller

    c. It becomes a member server

    d. It remains a primary domain controller

19. UNIX ships with which of the following protocols?

    a. TCP/IP

    b. SPX/IPX

    c. VIP/IP

    d. SNA/DECnet

20. In a client/server environment, what software determines the destination of a user request for LAN services?

    a. Redirector

    b. Initiator

    c. IP

    d. IPX

21. Which of the following is not true of Ethernet?

    a. Ethernet (CSMA/CD) becomes more efficient as traffic increases

    b. Ethernet can use 10Base5, 10Base2, and twisted pair at the Physical Layer

    c. MAC frames are transmitted across the physical media

    d. It is also referred to as the 802.3 standard

    e. None of the above (all statements are true)

22. What is the primary reason an Ethernet NIC transmits a jamming message?

    a. To warn other stations that a collision has been detected.

    b. To corrupt the preamble of the incoming MAC frame.

    c. To resynchronize all stations on the local Ethernet.

    d. A jamming message is the same as the MAC preamble.

    e. To ensure that all remote stations have received the previous frame.

23. How are frames and packets different?

    a. Frames travel from NIC to NIC, packets travel from end to end.

    b. Frames have both headers and trailers, but packets have only headers.

    c. Packets are carried within frames.

    d. All of the above

24. Which of the following is not a 100-Mbps technology?

    a. CDDI

    b. 100VGAnyLAN

    c. FDDI

    d. ATM

25. What is the purpose of a redirector?

   a. Route machine requests to hard drives and tape drives

   b. Direct traffic to a bridge or router

   c. Direct workstation requests to a client

   d. Direct workstation requests to a server

26. What is the most likely candidate to replace standard 10-Mbps Ethernet in a LAN?

   a. 100 Mbps Ethernet

   b. 100 Mbps FDDI

   c. Gigabit Ethernet

   d. 622 Mbps ATM

27. What common information is found in both Ethernet and Token Ring headers?

   a. Source and destination addresses

   b. Port numbers

   c. IP addresses

   d. Socket numbers

28. What does the RI port of a Token Ring MAU provide?

   a. Connection from a monitor

   b. Connection from another MAU

   c. Connection to a router

   d. Connection to a bridge

29. When an LLC process receives information from a MAC layer process, what will it most likely do?

   a. Transmit the information across the physical link

   b. Respond to the sending IP process

   c. Respond to the sending application process

   d. Send the information to the Network Layer process

30. What is the primary advantage of an Ethernet switch over an Ethernet hub?

    a. Management capabilities

    b. Cost

    c. Increased bandwidth of connected devices

    d. Increased distances between devices

31. Which of the following is not a NOS?

    a. Windows 2000

    b. Novell NetWare

    c. Banyan VINES

    d. Windows 98

32. What does it mean if a NOS is said to be peer-to-peer only?

    a. Dedicated server is not used

    b. Dedicated server is used, but only for printer sharing

    c. Dedicated server is only used for e-mail

    d. Dedicated server is not used except for Internet access

33. What is the Windows NT equivalent to the ODI?

    a. LSL

    b. MLID

    c. NDIS

    d. MAC

34. What is the Windows database that stores configuration information?

    a. Domain

    b. NT File System

    c. Registry

    d. NWLink

35. What bus is most commonly shipped in desktop PCs?

    a. EISA

    b. MCA

    c. PCI

    d. PCMCIA

36. What is the difference between the Ethernet version 2 frame format and IEEE 802.3 frame format?

    a. Length of the frame

    b. Length field in the frame

    c. Length of the padding

    d. Length of the cabling

37. Which of the following statements is not true regarding Ethernet?

    a. Ethernet is the predominant MAC standard being used in LANs.

    b. The Ethernet frame type is the same for Fast Ethernet and 10 Mbps Ethernet.

    c. Ethernet speeds range from 10 to 1,000 Mbps.

    d. Ethernet can only be used with Category 5 UTP.

38. Which is not a MAC layer standard?

    a. Ethernet

    b. Token Ring

    c. CDDI

    d. UTP

39. Why is it important to baseline a network?

    a. To provide a basis of comparison with later performance measurements.

    b. To help you recognize a developing problem before it becomes critical.

    c. To justify requests for network upgrades or support.

    d. All of the above

40. You come in to work late one night and discover that your janitor has plugged a laptop computer into your hub. She explains that she's a college student, and likes to play Internet games during slack times at work. What should you do?

    a. Challenge her to a game

    b. Immediately escort her and her computer out of your office, then ask management to hire a different janitor

    c. Advise her to not download any software to your network

    d. Scan her computer for viruses

41. You are designing a new network for a startup company. You have detailed information about the number of users and type of applications that the network must support. What is the most cost-effective way to test your design?

    a. Build a prototype network, then monitor network traffic as temporary workers use the applications.

    b. Use a traffic simulation tool to model the network's operation in software.

    c. Ask three experienced network designers how they would do it, then average their responses.

    d. Don't test. Install the bare minimum, then gradually upgrade until users stop complaining.

42. A software development firm is moving into new offices. Each programmer needs two networked computers, plus a telephone. How many Category 5 UTP cables must you run to each work area?

    a. One. A Cat 5 cable has four wire pairs, and each device needs one pair.

    b. Two. A Cat 5 cable has four wire pairs, and each device needs two pairs.

    c. Three. Each device needs its own cable.

    d. None. Copper UTP is obsolete

43. In a typical Ethernet network using Cat 5 UTP, what are the blue and brown wire pairs for?

    a. They provide automatic failover if the green or orange wires are damaged.

    b. They are used for network control signaling and monitoring, while the other pairs carry data.

    c. They are unused by the network but may be used by other devices.

    d. They absorb crosstalk interference from the green and orange wires.

44. A Cat 5 cable is terminated on an RJ-45 connector, according to the TIA/EIA 568A standard. What wire colors are connected to the two center pins?

    a. Brown and white brown

    b. Blue and brown

    c. White green and orange

    d. White blue and blue

45. When the NIC of a sending Ethernet node receives a packet that is only 12 bytes long, what does it do?

    a. It adds a frame header and trailer to the packet and transmits it.

    b. It drops the packet because it is too short.

    c. It sends the packet back up to the Network Layer and asks it to resend the data in a longer packet.

    d. It adds extra bits to the end of the packet to lengthen it to 46 bytes. Then it adds a frame header and trailer to the packet and transmits it.

46. One of your company's top executives is always the first to own the latest and fastest new technology, which he insists on ordering himself. But when his new laptop arrives, its wireless NIC won't connect to the wireless access point he has used for two years. Existing computers in the area have no difficulty. What is a likely cause of this problem?

    a. The wireless card uses the 802.11A standard, but the access point uses 802.11B.

    b. There is a new source of radio interference in that area.

    c. His NIC is using Ethernet Version 1, and the access point is using Ethernet Version 2.

    d. His NIC is using CSMA/CD, but the access point is using CSMA/CA.

47. If LAN cable is installed within air ducts, it must be plenum grade. Why?

    a. Electrical reliability

    b. Fire safety

    c. Network security

    d. Cost

48. The previous network administrator made his own patch cables and crossover cables but did not mark them in any way. How can you tell them apart?

    a. Patch cables use two RJ-45 connectors, but crossover cables use one RJ-45 and one RJ-11.

    b. Both ends of a crossover cable use the same pinout configuration, but each end of a patch cable uses a different configuration.

    c. Patch cords use only two pairs of a Cat 5 cable, but a crossover cable uses all four.

    d. Both ends of a patch cable use the same pinout configuration, but each end of a crossover cable uses a different configuration.

49. Of the following Physical Layer media, which is the most inherently secure?

   a. UTP

   b. Coaxial

   c. Optical fiber

   d. Wireless

50. Most of your company is highly satisfied with your Fast Ethernet network. However, the research and engineering departments want ATM in their areas, because they run high-bandwidth real-time applications. Upper management has agreed to this, because "all we need to do is run some new fiber for the engineers." What is your answer?

   a. "Yes, that's true. You'll have it next month."

   b. "We can do it, but we'll also need ATM switches."

   c. "We can do it, but we'll also need ATM switches, as well as LAN emulation software and network staff training."

   d. "No, this is impossible. You cannot connect ATM and Ethernet. "

51. As the new network administrator, you are asked to evaluate the existing cable plant and recommend any upgrades you feel are necessary. The previous network staff did not prepare physical diagrams of the network wiring. How can you determine the lengths of key cable segments that are concealed in walls or ceilings?

   a. Use a TDR

   b. This is impossible.

   c. Use a harmonic resonator

   d. Track down the original cable installer, and hope the diagrams are there

52. What system manages users and resources across an entire NetWare network?

   a. PDC

   b. NDS

   c. NLM

   d. NDPS

53. Why has Category 5 twisted pair become the predominant physical media in today's LAN environments?

_____

_____

_____

54. If you were going to implement a NOS in a 20-employee company, which NOS would you use and why? What topology and wiring structure would you use?

_____

_____

_____

55. When is it appropriate to locate servers within departmental workgroups instead of on a corporate backbone?

_____

_____

_____

56. Name at least two common server types, and explain their basic functions.

_____

_____

_____

57. List the protocol of each of the listed NOSs responsible for transmitting a packet (or datagram) of information across a network.

    a. NetWare

    _____

    b. UNIX

    _____

    c. Windows NT/2000

    _____

58. What is the most common protocol stack, from Physical Layer to Transport Layer, used in today's networks? Draw the protocol stack.

_____

_____

_____

GLOSSARY

100VG-AnyLAN—100VG-AnyLAN is a 100-Mbps Ethernet technology standard that directly competes with 100BaseT Ethernet. The IEEE 802.12 committee is currently investigating this technology. The access method used by this standard is different than the CSMA/CD method used by 10-Mbps Ethernet and Fast Ethernet; however, the MAC frame format is the same. The new access method is called "demand priority."

abend—Abend is short for "ABnormal END" and traditionally means a processing error that stops, or crashes, an OS.

adapter—An adapter is a term used to identify the computer card that fits into the computer bus. One type of adapter is a NIC. A NIC provides a connection (interface) to the networking media for sending information across a network.

Address Resolution Protocol (ARP)—ARP is the protocol used by IP (as in TCP/IP) for address resolution. Address resolution refers to the ability of a station to resolve another station's MAC (hardware) address given its IP address.

American National Standards Institute (ANSI)—ANSI is a national voluntary organization that develops and publishes standards for data communications, programming languages, magnetic storage media, the OSI model, office systems, and encryption.

American Standard Code for Information Interchange (ASCII)—ASCII is one of the two most widely used codes to represent characters, such as keyboard characters (EBCDIC is the other). ASCII uses 7 bits for the 128 elements it represents. For example, the ASCII representation of the character "A" is decimal numeral 65, hexadecimal 41, or binary 100 0001. See EBCDIC.

AppleTalk Filing Protocol (APF)—AFP is the protocol used in Apple networks for retrieving and storing files across a network.

application programming interface (API)—In general, an API consists of computer processes used by applications to carry out lower level tasks performed by a computer's OS. In networking, an API provides applications with a consistent method of requesting services from a network. One of the most common APIs used in networking is NetBIOS.

ATM Forum—The ATM Forum is an international industry organization that promotes the use of ATM by facilitating a rapid convergence of interoperability specifications.

attempt counter—An attempt counter is a value that records the number of times an Ethernet NIC has attempted to transmit the same frame. The NIC discards a frame after 16 consecutive collisions occur for the same transmission attempt.

attempt limit—An attempt limit is the maximum number of times (16) that an Ethernet NIC will attempt to retransmit a frame after a collision.

availability—Availability refers to the amount (or percentage) of time a given network or component in a network (such as a host or server) is available to carry out its intended task.

backbone—The backbone of a network is the portion that carries the most significant traffic. It is also the part of the network that connects many LANs or subnetworks together to form a network. Bridges are often used to form network backbones. In this configuration, bridges often limit local traffic from the backbone to reduce congestion and isolate problems.

backoff time—When a collision occurs on an Ethernet segment, all transmitting nodes "back off" and do not transmit for a random length of time before attempting to transmit again. This is referred to as the backoff time. This random time interval reduces the likelihood that both stations will attempt to retransmit at the same time.

backplane—The backplane is the "motherboard" of a device that provides the device's basic functionality. The backplane's design determines the basic features of a hub, switch, bridge, or router. Modules plug into the backplane to provide port interfaces or additional features. If the backplane architecture is Ethernet, Token Ring, or FDDI, it is referred to as a shared-bus backplane, because Ethernet, Token Ring, and FDDI are all shared-media protocols.

bandwidth—Bandwidth is the amount of data that can be transmitted in a fixed amount of time. For digital devices, the bandwidth is usually expressed in bps or bytes per second. For analog devices, the bandwidth is expressed in cycles per second, or Hz.

baseband—Baseband is a form of modulation where signals are placed directly on the transmission media and take up the available bandwidth of the entire communication channel.

baseline—A network baseline is a "snapshot" of activity and performance at a given time. A baseline is used to measure changes in network performance.

binary—The base 2 numbering system used by computers to represent information. Binary numbers consist of only two symbols, 1 and 0. In a binary number, each position is two times greater than the position to its right.

bindery—In versions of NetWare earlier than 4.0, the bindery is a network database that defines entities such as users, groups, and workgroups. The bindery has been replaced by NDS.

bindery emulation—Bindery emulation is a process that allows a NetWare 4.x server to emulate the NetWare bindery (NetWare 4.x and above uses NetWare Directory Services, a different file system). Bindery emulation is necessary to allow a Windows NT server to access a NetWare 4.x server by using GSNW, because GSNW does not support NetWare Directory Services.

block—A block is a small unit of physical disk space used to physically store files on a disk drive, usually configured in units of 4 KB, 8 KB, 16 KB, 32 KB or 64 KB. NetWare uses 64 KB by default. A block (sometimes called a "cluster") consists of several sectors, and is typically the smallest unit of storage that an OS can recognize. See sector.

bridge—A bridge is a hardware device that connects LANs. It can be used to connect LANs of the same type, such as two Token Ring segments, or LANs with different types of media such as Ethernet and Token Ring. A bridge operates at the Data Link Layer of the OSI reference model.

bridge/router (Brouter)—A brouter is an internetworking device that combines the functions of both a bridge and a router. See router.

Broadband-Integrated Services Digital Network (B-ISDN)—ISDN line rates are available in two basic varieties: basic (primary) and broadband. Basic, primary, or "narrow" ISDN consists of two bearer (B) channels and a data (D) channel. Each bearer channel can carry one voice conversation or data at a transmission rate of 64 Kbps. The ISDN-PRI is similar to T1 signaling, and consists of 24 channels, including 23 channels (64 Kbps each) that carry voice, data, and video; and 1 data channel that carries signaling information. B-ISDN (also called wide ISDN) offers multiple channels above the primary rate (A, C, and H series of channels).

broadcast—The term broadcast is used in several different ways in communications and networking. With respect to LANs, the term refers to information (frames) sent to all devices on the physical segment. For example, a bus topology, in which a common cable is used to connect devices, is considered a broadcast technology.

Another common use of the term broadcast relates to frames. Broadcast frames contain a special destination address that instructs all devices on the network to receive the frame.

burst mode—Burst mode is a high-speed data transfer technique that uses special conditions to move data faster than normal. For example, a device may be allowed to monopolize control of a data bus, or memory access may automatically get the next memory address before it is requested.

C2 security—C2 is one level of security standards in a seven-level range defined by the U.S. Department of Defense. The C2 rating specifies the policies and practices necessary to achieve a level of computer security that is reasonable for most companies.

cable categories—There are several cable categories used to describe the different types of twisted pair networks as follows:

- Categories 1 and 2 are used for low-speed data transmission and voice.

- Category 3 is the most common type of network cabling in use today. It is used for 4-Mbps Token Ring and 10BaseT networks.

- Category 4 is used for voice and data transmission rates of 16 Mbps.

- Category 5 is used for voice and data transmission rates up to 100 Mbps. It is the most popular type of network cabling being used in new installations. Category 5E (enhanced) provides data rates up to 200 Mbps through more precise manufacturing techniques.

carrier sense multiple access with collision detection (CSMA/CD)—CSMA/CD is set of rules determining how network devices respond when two devices attempt to use a data channel simultaneously (called a collision). Standard Ethernet networks use CSMA/CD. This standard enables devices to detect a collision. After detecting a collision, a device waits a random delay time and then attempts to retransmit the message. If the device detects a collision again, it waits twice as long to try to retransmit the message. This is known as exponential backoff.

central processing unit (CPU)—A CPU controls the operation of a computer. It interprets and executes instructions to carry out computer-related tasks.

channel—Channel refers to the physical link that provides connectivity between communicating devices. Channel and link are often used interchangeably.

checksum—The number of bits in a transmitted unit of data is referred to as the checksum. A checksum is appended to the data unit as a simple error-detection method. The receiving node counts the data bits and compares the result to the checksum, to see whether all bits have arrived. If the numbers match, the transmission was probably complete.

circuit switching—Circuit-switched networks establish a physical connection between two nodes, and all packets in one transmission are passed between the same nodes by "switching" them through intermediate points (other nodes or a host computer). Circuit switching guarantees that all packets in the same transmission will sequentially travel over the same physical transmission path. However, each transmission is limited to one path, and cannot achieve greater transfer speed by using multiple parallel paths.

class of service (CoS)—In general, CoS (also called quality of service, or QoS) measures different characteristics of a transmission service. In the context of the OSI reference model, users of the Transport Layer specify QoS parameters as part of a request for a communication channel. These parameters define different levels of service based on the requirements of an application. For example, an interactive application that requires good response time would specify high QoS values for connection establishment delay, throughput, transit delay, and connection priority. However, a file transfer application requires reliable, error-free data transfer more than it needs a prompt connection, thus it would request high QoS parameters for residual error rate/probability.

client—The client portion of a client/server architecture is any node or workstation used by a single user. If multiple users share resources on the same workstation, it becomes a server. Examples of clients are Microsoft Windows NT Workstation and Windows 98.

client/server—Client/server (or client server) is a model in computer networking where individual PCs can access data or services from a common high-performance computer. For example, when a PC needs data from a common database located on a computer on a LAN, the PC is the client and the network computer is the server.

cluster controller—A cluster controller is an IBM device used to control communications between an IBM mainframe and a terminal device (IBM 3270 or ASCII terminal). It is also referred to as a communications controller.

coder/decoder (codec)—A codec is a hardware/software device that takes an analog video signal and converts (codes) it to digital format for compression and transmission. On the receiving end, the digital signal is put back (decoded) into the original analog signal. See PCM.

collapsed backbone—Collapsed backbone is a network topology that uses a multiport device, such as a switch or router, to carry traffic between network segments or subnets. This dif-

fers from the original Ethernet backbone, which consisted of a single common bus cable to which nodes and subnets are connected.

collision—A collision occurs in an Ethernet network when two frames are put onto the physical medium at the same time and overlap fully or partially. When a collision occurs, the data on the physical segment is no longer valid.

compiler—A compiler is a software program that takes source code from a programming language such as C++, and converts it into machine readable, executable code to be run on a computer.

complex instruction set computer (CISC)—See reduced instruction set computer (RISC).

Copper Distributed Data Interface (CDDI)—CDDI is a version of FDDI that runs on copper wiring such as twisted pair.

co-processor—A co-processor is a secondary computer processing chip that is optimized for a particular type of operations, such as graphics rendering or mathematical computation. If an application has been written to take advantage of a co-processor, then those operations can be processed there instead of the main CPU.

cross-connect—The term cross-connect refers to a high-speed switch that does not error check frames, but simply passes them to the appropriate destination.

crossover cable—A crossover cable is a UTP cable with RJ-45 connectors at both ends, designed to directly connect the NICs of two computers. The pins on each connector are attached to different wires, thus signals flow from the output of one NIC to the input of the other, and vice-versa. See patch cable.

cyclic redundancy check (CRC)—CRC is the mathematical process used to check the accuracy of data transmitted across a network. Before transmitting a block of data, the sending station performs a calculation on the data block and appends the resulting value to the end of the block. The receiving station takes the data and the CRC value, and performs the same calculation to check the accuracy of the data.

daisy chain—A daisy-chain network is created by linking multiple devices by means of a cabling system. In an AppleTalk network, the daisy-chain topology is created using PhoneNet connectors and twisted pair wiring (regular phone wire). A daisy-chain configuration must be terminated at both ends using terminating resistors.

Data Exchange Interface (DXI)—DXI is an ATM interface that converts variable-length network frames to fixed-length ATM cells. ATM DXI converts LAN frames to the variable-length DXI frame format. The ATM CSU/DSU then converts the DXI frames to fixed-length ATM cells. This two-step conversion simplifies processing on the ATM CSU/DSU, because it only needs to convert one type of frame.

Data Link Control (DLC)—DLC is a generic term that refers to a protocol (such as Token Ring or Ethernet) used to transfer information across a single link.

data service unit/channel service unit (DSU/CSU)—The hardware required to connect a common carrier connection (leased line) to a router is referred to as the DSU/CSU. Frame relay service requires one DSU/CSU, whereas private line service requires two DSU/CSUs.

datagram (packet)—A datagram is a unit of information processed by the Network Layer of the OSI reference model. The packet header contains the logical (network) address of the destination node. Intermediate nodes forward a packet until it reaches its destination. A packet can contain an entire message generated by higher OSI layers, or a segment of a much larger message.

detector—A detector is a device that receives optical signals and converts them into electrical signals.

direct memory access (DMA)—DMA is the type of memory access that does not involve the main processor in a computer to transfer data directly from memory to a peripheral device, such as a hard drive or NIC.

Distributed Queue Dual Bus (DQDB)—DQDB is the IEEE 802.6 standard for MANs. See SMDS.

Domain Name System (DNS)—DNS is an Internet service that translates domain names into IP addresses. Because domain names are alphabetic, they are easier to remember. The Internet however, is really based on IP addresses. Every time you use a domain name, a DNS service must translate the name into the corresponding IP address. For example, the domain name www.example.com might translate to 198.105.232.4.

Dynamic Host Configuration Protocol (DHCP)—DHCP is a proprietary approach from Microsoft that simplifies IP network management by dynamically assigning IP addresses to logical end-stations for fixed periods of time.

Electronic Industries Association (EIA)—EIA is a national trade organization that publishes hardware-oriented standards for data communications. EIA-232-D is an example (corresponds to RS-232).

encryption—Encryption is the process of scrambling data by changing it in a series of logical steps, called an encryption algorithm. To increase security, an encryption algorithm uses a numerical pattern, or "key," to guide the scrambling process. Different algorithms and keys will each produce data scrambled, or encrypted, in different patterns.

error correcting code (ECC)—ECC memory tests the accuracy of data as it passes in and out of memory.

Ethernet—Ethernet technology, originally developed in the 1970s by Xerox Corporation in conjunction with Intel and DEC, is now the primary medium for LANs. The original Ethernet has 10-Mbps throughput and uses the CSMA/CD method to access the physical medium. Fast Ethernet (100-Mbps Ethernet) and Gigabit Ethernet (1,000-Mbps Ethernet) are later technologies based on the original approach.

expert system—An expert system is a sophisticated computer application that attempts to solve problems by analyzing data according to a set of rules designed by human experts.

Extended Binary Coded Decimal Interchange Code (EBCDIC)—EBCDIC is the IBM standard for binary encoding of characters. It is one of the two most widely used codes to represent characters, such as keyboard characters (ASCII is the other). See ASCII.

Extended Industry Standard Architecture (EISA)—EISA is a 32-bit computer bus specification introduced in 1988. It provides additional features beyond that of the ISA bus standard.

FDDI II—FDDI II is an incompatible extension to FDDI that provides better support for constant bit-rate applications such as voice and video transmission. FDDI II divides its 100-Mbps bandwidth into 16 circuits that can be allocated to various types of traffic; those circuits can be further divided into 96 channels per circuit.

FDDI Follow-On LAN (FFOL)—FFOL is a proposed 2.4-Gbps standard that could eventually replace FDDI.

feeder—A cable that connects a single-floor network segment to a building backbone or multistory trunk is referred to as a feeder.

Fiber Distributed Data Interface (FDDI)—A LAN standard specifying a 100-Mbps token-passing network using fiber optic cable.

Fibre Channel—Fibre Channel is a very high-speed fiber optic data transfer interface based on the ANSI FCS. FCS can carry multiple existing protocols, including IP and SCSI.

firewall—A firewall is a controlled access point between sections of the same network, designed to confine problems to one section. A firewall is also a controlled access between a private network and a public network (such as the Internet), usually implemented with a router and special firewall software.

flat address space—Flat address space refers to a system of one-part, unique addresses, not arranged into a hierarchical organization.

flat file—A flat file is the simplest type of database, which stores data in isolated tables that are not linked to each other. A box of paper file cards is essentially a flat file.

frame—A frame is a unit of information transmitted across a data link. Ethernet frames, for example, are frames generated by an Ethernet NIC.

frame check sequence (FCS)—FCS is a 4-byte CRC value used to check for damaged frames. CRC is a mathematical process used to check the accuracy of data being transmitted across a network. When a block of data is about to be transmitted, the sending station performs a calculation on the data block and appends the resulting CRC value to the end of the data block (frame). The receiving station performs the same calculation on the data. If the CRC values match, the data is transmitted without errors.

frame relay—A frame relay is essentially an electronic switch. Physically, it is a box that connects to three or more high-speed links and routes data traffic between them. Frame relay is intended only for data communications, not voice or video. Transmission errors are detected but not corrected (the frame is discarded).

freeware—Freeware is software that does not require a license fee, because its copyright is in the public domain. In other words, the creators of the software give it away. The source code is also freely distributed, so any developer may modify or add to it (fees may be charged for those added components). Periodically, the best modifications become part of the next "official" release of the core software. Thus, freeware, or open source software, benefits from the best ideas and approaches of the worldwide software development community. The Linux OS and the Apache Web server are two of the best-known examples of freeware.

Front-end processor (FEP)—A FEP is a device used in IBM mainframe networks that provides connectivity between networking devices and a mainframe. A FEP is also referred to as a communications controller.

hexadecimal—Hexadecimal is the base 16 numbering system used to represent binary information in a condensed format. Hexadecimal numbers consist of 15 symbols: 0 through 9, plus A through F. In a hexadecimal number, each position is 16 times greater than the position to its right.

hub—Also referred to as a wiring concentrator, a simple hub is a repeater with multiple ports. A signal coming into one port is repeated out the other ports.

hypermedia—Hypermedia takes hypertext to another level, and includes images, sounds, and video with links that can be selected and viewed.

hypertext—Hypertext is computer information containing text that can be linked with selected phrases. The links point to other documents or files. Hypertext is basically the same as regular text, however, it contains connections within the text to other documents. The links in the text are called hyperlinks.

Hypertext Transfer Protocol (HTTP)—HTTP is the Transmission Control Protocol/Internet Protocol (TCP/IP) Application Layer protocol used to request and transmit HTML documents. HTTP is the underlying protocol of the Web.

IBM 3172—An IBM 3172 is a type of protocol converter (gateway) that translates traffic between a LAN (Token Ring or Ethernet) and an IBM mainframe. It is also referred to as a LAN gateway.

index of refraction—The index of refraction is the ratio of light velocity in a vacuum to its velocity in another transmission medium. See refraction and total internal reflection.

input/output (I/O)—I/O is the process of moving data to and from a computer CPU to a peripheral device. Input devices include such things as keyboards and mice. Output devices include monitors and printers. Some devices are used for both input and output, such as a disk drive or NIC.

insertion loss—Insertion loss is the reduction in signal strength caused by cutting an optical fiber cable to attach a node or monitoring device.

Institute of Electrical and Electronic Engineers (IEEE)—IEEE is a professional organization composed of engineers, scientists, and students. Founded in 1884, IEEE publishes computer and electronics standards, including the 802 series that defines shared-media networks such as Ethernet and Token Ring.

insulation displacement connector (IDC)—An IDC is a type of electrical connection device that strips away a wire's insulation as the wire is pressed down (punched down) into an electrical contact point. Punchdown blocks, patch panels, and RJ-45 connectors are types of IDC.

intelligent hub (smart hub)—An intelligent hub is a hub that has been enhanced with additional hardware to support multiple media types and media access methods (Data Link protocols), such as Ethernet, Token Ring, and FDDI. Smart hubs can provide additional internetworking functionality through plug-in bridge and router modules and network management.

interference—Interference is any energy that interferes with the clear reception of a signal. For example, if one person is speaking, the sound of a second person's voice interferes with the first. See noise.

interframe gap—An interframe gap is the minimum time interval between Ethernet frames. After a node detects the end of a frame, it must wait this amount of time before attempting to transmit.

International Telecommunication Union-Telecommunications Standardization Sector (ITU-TSS)—ITU-TSS is an intergovernmental organization that develops and adopts international treaties and telecommunications standards. ITU was founded in 1865 and became a United Nations agency in 1947. ITU-TSS was formerly the Consultative Committee for International Telephony and Telegraphy (CCITT).

Internet Engineering Task Force (IETF)—IETF is a large, open, international community of network designers, operators, vendors, and researchers concerned with evolution of the Internet architecture and smooth operation of the Internet.

Internet Protocol (IP)—IP is a Network Layer protocol responsible for getting a packet (datagram) through a network. It is the "IP" in TCP/IP.

Internetwork Packet Exchange (IPX)—IPX is NetWare's proprietary Network Layer protocol.

interoperability—Interoperability refers to the ability of different types of computers, networks, OSs, and applications to work together effectively. An example of interoperability would be a TCP UNIX application using ASCII text files exchanging data with an EBCDIC IBM host.

Java—Java is an interpreted, platform-independent, high-level programming language developed by Sun Microsystems. Java is a powerful language with many features that make it attractive for the Web.

latency—The transmission delay created as a device, such as a bridge or router, processes a packet or frame is referred to as latency. It is the duration from the time a device reads the first byte of a packet or frame, until the time it forwards that byte.

light-emitting diode (LED)—An LED is a device that converts electrical signals into light pulses.

Lightweight Directory Access Protocol (LDAP)—LDAP is a tree-structured directory format based on the X.500 standard. See X.500.

Link Support Layer (LSL)—LSL is part of Novell's ODI specification that provides routing for multiple protocols on one NIC.

Logical Link Control (LLC)—LLC is a Data Link Layer protocol used to control the flow of information across a physical link. LLC is often used in Ethernet networks that use the IEEE frame type, which does not include a type field.

mail slots—Mail slots refer to a simple NOS service that transfers data between processes on different network computers. Unlike named pipes, a mail slot connection is created for a single data transfer, and then dropped. See named pipes.

Medium Access Control (MAC)—MAC is one of the media-specific IEEE 802 standards (802.3, 802.4, and 802.5) that defines the protocol and frame formats for Ethernet, Token Bus, and Token Ring. It is the lower sublayer of the Data Link Layer of the OSI model.

microsegmentation—Microsegmentation is the practice of increasing usable bandwidth by subdividing networks into smaller and smaller segments.

mode—A mode is an independent light signal traveling through an optical fiber.

multidrop—Multidrop refers to a data communication configuration where multiple terminals, printers, and workstations are located on the same media, and only one can communicate with the "master" at a given time. Multidrop is a form of unbalanced communication.

multimode fiber—Multimode fiber is a fiber optic cable thick enough to transmit several different optical signals simultaneously. Each signal is separated by the others by being reflected at different angles within the fiber. See single-mode fiber.

multiplexer (MUX)—A MUX is a device that allows multiple signals to travel over the same physical medium. See TDM and STDM.

multiprocessing—In a multiprocessing environment, multiple computers are used to process a single application.

multistation access unit (MAU)—A MAU is a device used in Token Ring networks to provide connectivity between individual workstations. It is also referred to as a Token Ring hub.

multistory trunk—A multistory trunk is a bundle of cables installed vertically in a multistory building to provide a medium for network backbones that connect network segments on multiple floors.

multitasking—The ability of a computer to execute multiple processes and applications. Although a computer with a single processing unit can only execute one instruction at a time, a multitasking OS can load and manage the execution of multiple applications by allocating computer processing cycles to each application in sequence. The perceived result is the simultaneous processing of multiple applications or tasks. There are two kinds of multitasking: preemptive and cooperative. With preemptive multitasking, the OS is in charge and manages system resource allocation and task scheduling. With cooperative multitasking, applications are in charge and share resources.

multithreading—A thread is a process within an application that executes a specific operation. A computer capable of multithreading is one that supports multiple threads, essentially allowing applications to multitask within themselves.

name space—A set of OS rules that define the allowable length and format of a file name is referred to as the name space.

named pipes—Named pipes is a NOS service that establishes a guaranteed virtual communication connection between processes on different computers on the network. After a named pipe connection has been created, it remains available until one of the nodes closes it. Therefore, the time to establish the connection is spent only once for each session of multiple data transfers. See mail slots.

nanometer (nm)—A nanometer is one billionth of a meter, or 10^{-9}. See wavelength.

NetWare Core Protocol (NCP)—NCP is the proprietary protocol used by the NetWare OS to transmit information between clients and servers. NCP messages are transmitted by means of IPX.

NetWare Loadable Module (NLM)—NLMs are modular software components that expand the services provided by a NetWare kernel. They are loaded and unloaded on a server as necessary to free up memory and processor resources. NLMs also allow third-party vendors to develop products that run on NetWare.

Network Basic Input/Output System (NetBIOS)—NetBIOS is a software system developed by Sytek and IBM that has become the de facto standard for application interface to LANs. It operates at the Session Layer of the OSI protocol stack. Applications can call NetBIOS routines to carry out functions such as data transfer across a LAN.

Network Driver Interface Specification (NDIS)—The NDIS standard was developed by Microsoft and 3Com to provide a common interface between NIC drivers and networking protocols. The functionality of NDIS is comparable to ODI.

Network File System (NFS)—An NFS is a file management system commonly used in UNIX-based computer systems.

network interface card (NIC)—A NIC is an expansion board that is inserted into a computer so the computer can be connected to a network. Most NICs are designed for a particular type of network, protocol, and media, although some can serve multiple networks.

Network News Transport Protocol (NNTP)—Part of the TCP/IP Application Layer, NNTP is the protocol that supports USENET newsgroups.

network operating system (NOS)—NOS is the software that manages server operations and provides services to clients. The NOS manages the interface between the network's underlying transport capabilities and the applications resident on the server.

noise—Noise is any condition, such as electrical interference, that destroy signal integrity. Noise can be caused by many electromagnetic sources, such as radio transmissions, electrical cables, electric motors, lighting dimmers, or bad cable connections.

Novell Directory Services (NDS)—NDS is a hierarchical database of information about users and network resources. NDS manages all network components through a single interface. NDS version 8 is available on other NOS platforms such as Microsoft, Sun Solaris, UNIX, and IBM.

NT File System (NTFS)—NTFS is one of the basic services of the Windows NT OS. NTFS is highly recoverable and secure because it is a transaction-based file system that logs all directory and file updates. In case of a system failure or power loss, the NTFS-logged information allows undo/redo operations to recover lost data.

Open Data Link Interface (ODI)—ODI is a Novell-developed specification that enables multiple protocol support for a NIC.

open source—See freeware.

Open Systems Interconnection (OSI)—OSI began as a reference model, that is, an abstract model for data communications. However, now the OSI model has been implemented and is used in some data communications applications. The OSI model, consisting of seven layers, falls logically into two parts. Layers 1 through 4, the "lower" layers, are concerned with the communication of raw data. Layers 5 through 7, the "higher" layers, are concerned with the networking of applications.

operating wavelength—The wavelength of an optical signal (mode) is referred to as an operating wavelength. Wavelength determines the color of visible light, although network signals in optical fiber use infrared wavelengths that are invisible to the human eye.

optical carrier (OC)—OC is one of the optical signal standards defined by the SONET digital signal hierarchy. The basic building block of SONET is the STS-1 51.84-Mbps signal, chosen to accommodate a DS3 signal. The hierarchy is defined up to STS-48, that is 48 STS-1 channels, for a total of 2,488.32 Mbps capable of carrying 32,256 voice circuits. The STS designation refers to the interface for electrical signals. The corresponding optical signal standards are designated OC-1, OC-2, etc.

packet—A packet is a unit of information processed at the Network Layer. The packet header contains the logical (network) address of the destination node. Intermediate nodes forward a packet until it reaches its destination. A packet can contain an entire message generated by higher OSI layers, or a segment of a much larger message.

Packet Internet Groper (Ping)—Ping is a TCP/IP utility used to verify that a computer's IP software is running properly and to verify the connectivity between computers. Ping transmits a test message to a destination host, and asks that host to reply.

parity—Parity checking is a common error-checking method for data communications and storage devices. In parity checking, a parity bit is added to a small unit of data (usually 7 bits).

The parity bit is set to 1 or 0 to make the total number of set bits in the data unit either odd or even. For example, if two devices are communicating with "even" parity, the sending device checks each data unit before transmitting it. If the 7 bits contain an even number of 1s, the parity bit is set to 0 (to maintain the even number). If the 7 bits contain an odd number of 1s, the parity bit is set to 1 (to create an even number). The receiving device then checks incoming bytes to see whether each one contains an even number of set bits. An odd number indicates a transmission or storage error.

partition—Partition is the physical division of disk space set aside for use by an OS. A NetWare server typically has one bootable DOS partition, and one to three NetWare partitions.

patch cable (patch cord)—A patch cable is a UTP cable with RJ-45 connectors at both ends, designed to connect a computer's NIC to a port of a hub or switch. On both connectors, each pin is attached to the same wire, thus signals flow straight through the cable. See crossover cable.

peer-to-peer—Two programs or processes that use the same protocol to communicate and perform approximately the same function for their respective nodes are referred to as peer processes. With peer processes, in general, neither process controls the other, and the same protocol is used for data flowing in either direction. Communication between them is referred to as "peer-to-peer."

Peripheral Component Interconnect (PCI)—PCI was introduced by Intel to define a local bus system for a computer. PCI allows up to 10 expansion cards to be installed in a computer. PCI technology is capable of transferring data across a PC bus at very high rates.

permanent virtual circuit—A path through a packet-switching or cell-switching network that behaves like a dedicated line between source and destination endpoints is referred to as a permanent virtual circuit.

photodiode—A photodiode is a semiconductor device that converts light into electrical signals.

plenum—A plenum is a duct for building heating or air conditioning, often found above suspended ceiling tiles or in raised floors. Plenum-grade cable meets fire codes because the cable coating is fire-resistant and does not emit toxic fumes when burned.

point-to-point—A network connects nodes, some of which are hosts to which terminal nodes attach, in two different ways: point-to-point and broadcast. Point-to-point networks fall into two classes: circuit-switched networks, in which a connection is formed between the nodes, as in a telephone network; and packet-switched or connectionless networks, in which packets of data, or datagrams, are passed from node to node until they reach their destination, like telegrams.

print server—A print server is a LAN-based computer that provides users on a network access to a printer. Multiple users, therefore, share the printer.

promiscuous mode—Promiscuous mode is a setting that forces a NIC to process every frame it receives. For example, the NIC in a network analyzer is set to promiscuous mode.

protocol—Data communications involves the transfer of data between computer programs. Just as humans must share a common language to communicate, programs must have a common protocol. A protocol defines the format and meaning of the data that programs interchange.

public key encryption—Public-key encryption is a cryptographic system that uses two mathematically related keys: one key is used to encrypt a message, and the other to decrypt it. People who need to receive encrypted messages distribute their public keys but keep their private keys secret.

pulse code modulation (PCM)—PCM is a method of converting an analog voice signal to a digital signal that can be translated accurately back into a voice signal after transmission. The device that converts an analog signal to PCM is a codec. The codec first samples the voice signal at several thousand samples per second. Each sample is converted to a binary number that expresses the amplitude of the sample in a very compact form. These binary numbers form the digital bit stream that comes out of a codec. The receiving codec reverses the process, using each successive binary number to control a digital/analog circuit that generates the required analog wave form on the voice output channel.

quality of service (QoS)—See class of service.

random access memory (RAM)—RAM is the memory of a computer that can be read from or written to by computer hardware components such as a CPU.

random backoff—See backoff time.

reduced instruction set computer (RISC)—A RISC is a microprocessor that contains fewer instructions than traditional complex instruction set computer (CISC) processors, such as Intel or Motorola. As a result, they are significantly faster. RISC processors have been used in most technical workstations for some time, and a growing number of PC-class products are based on RISC processors.

refraction—Refraction is the tendency of a light ray, or electromagnetic signal, to be deflected from a straight path when it passes obliquely from one medium into another medium that has a different index of refraction. See index of refraction and total internal reflection.

remote access service (RAS)—The term RAS is normally used in the context of Windows NT, and the ability to access Windows NT and LAN services from a remote location.

remote procedure call (RPC)—RPC is a call made by an application program for services across a network connection, usually to a server.

repeater—A repeater is a Physical Layer device that connects one cable segment of a LAN to another, possibly connecting two different media types. For example, a repeater can connect a thin Ethernet cable to a thick Ethernet cable. It regenerates and boosts electrical signals, thus a repeater can be used to lengthen a network segment. Because a repeater reproduces exactly what it receives, bit by bit, it also reproduces errors. However, it is very fast and causes very little delay.

Request for Comment (RFC)—RFC is one of the working documents of the Internet research and development community. A document in this series may be on essentially any topic related to computer communication, and may be anything from a meeting report to the specification of a standard.

requester—A requester is a set of software modules that processes requests from a client application program and directs the request to either the local OS or a remote NOS.

RJ-45 connector—RJ-45 is a snap-in connector for UTP cable, similar to the standard RJ-11 telephone cable connector. The RJ-45 connector can terminate up to 8 wires.

router—A router is a Layer 3 device with several ports that can each connect to a network or another router. The router examines the logical network address of each packet, then uses its internal routing table to forward the packet to the routing port associated with the best path to the packet's destination. If the packet is addressed to a network that is not connected to the router, the router forwards the packet to another router that is closer to the final destination. Each router, in turn, evaluates each packet and then either delivers the packet or forwards it to another router.

RSA—The acronym RSA stands for Rivest, Shamir, and Adelman, the inventors of a widely used public-key encryption algorithm. The RSA encryption algorithm has become the de facto standard for industrial-strength encryption across the Internet.

sector—A sector is the smallest unit of physical disk storage. Most OSs combine several sectors into a block, and use the block as the smallest unit of file storage space. See block.

Secure Sockets Layer (SSL)—An application of both public-key and single-key encryption that secures an Internet connection between browser and server. Web page URLs that use SSL begin with "https://"

semaphore—A semaphore, or a flag, is a binary bit set to indicate use of a shared system resource, such as a file. For example, if a file semaphore is set to 1, the file is in use and cannot be accessed by another user. In general, a flag can represent any value or its opposite.

Sequenced Packet Exchange (SPX)—SPX is the connection-oriented transport protocol concerned with connection-oriented services, such as sequencing packets, and guaranteeing their delivery, which provides reliability for IPX communications.

server—A NetWare server is a system installed with a NetWare product that provides services to fulfill multiple client requests simultaneously.

server farm—A server farm is a collection of departmental servers located in a data center, where they can be provided with consolidated backup, uninterrupted power supply, and a secure operating environment.

Server Message Block (SMB)—SMB is the IBM PC LAN protocol used to communicate with devices located on a LAN. It uses NetBIOS at the Session Layer to communicate across a LAN. Functions requiring LAN support, such as retrieving files from a file server, are translated into SMB commands before they are sent to a remote device.

Service Advertising Protocol (SAP)—SAP is a protocol that is part of the Novell Netware stack. A network device uses SAP packets to tell other devices about the services it can provide.

signal reflection—Signal reflection refers to the situation where part, or all, of an electrical signal bounces back from an improperly made cable connection. This effect creates signal noise that can be misinterpreted as frame collisions.

Simple Network Management Protocol (SNMP)—SNMP is a network management protocol based on the manager/agent model, in which a complex central manager directs simple device-based agents to supply information or change configurations. The original version of SNMP was derived from SGMP, and was published in 1988.

single-key (symmetric) encryption—Single-key encryption is a cryptographic system that uses the same key to both encrypt and decrypt a message. Single-key encryption systems require both the sender and receiver of a message to share the same key before using it to communicate.

single-mode fiber—Single-mode fiber is a thin fiber optic cable that can transmit only one optical signal. Because there is no chance the signal can interfere with any other signal, single-mode fiber can transmit signals over much longer distances than multi-mode fiber. See multimode fiber.

Small Computer System Interface (SCSI)—SCSI is a high-speed interface for connecting peripheral devices, such as printers and disk drives, to computers.

source code—Source code is human-readable instructions written in a programming language, such as C++. Before an application can be run on a computer, the source code is converted to machine-readable binary codes by an application called a compiler.

start of frame delimiter (SOFD) —An SOFD is a byte that ends with two consecutive bits, which serve to synchronize the frame-reception portions of all stations on a LAN.

statistical time-division multiplexing (STDM)—STDM is a multiplexing technology in which each port competes for access to the bus based on need. Bandwidth is not wasted on unused time slots, which sometimes happens in TDM. STDM is good for bursty traffic. See MUX and TDM.

Structured Query Language (SQL)—SQL is a standardized language used to retrieve data from a database.

super server—A super server refers to large-capacity computing hardware that handles huge transaction loads or giant databases, and functions as a server in a client/server architecture. Some organizations, such as those hosting heavy e-commerce traffic, are converting mainframe systems to function as super servers.

switch—A switch is a device that operates at the Data Link Layer of the OSI reference model. A switch can connect LANs or segments of the same media access type. A switch dedicates its entire bandwidth to each frame it switches.

Switched Multimegabit Data Service (SMDS)—SMDS is a connectionless service used to connect LANs, MANs, and WANs to exchange data. SMDS is cell oriented and uses the same format as the ITU-T B-ISDN standards. ITU-T has standardized a connectionless Broadband Network Service (I.364) that will primarily be offered by local telephone companies as a MAN service. Internal SMDS protocols are referred to as SMDS Interface Protocol-1, -2, and -3 (SIP-1 through -3). They are a subset of the IEEE 802.6 standard for MANs, also known as DQDB.

switching hub—See switch.

Synchronous Digital Hierarchy (SDH)—SDH is an international standard for synchronous data transmission over fiber optic cables; SONET is the U.S. implementation. The standard SDH transmission rate, referred to as STM-1, is 155.52 Mbps. This is equivalent to SONET's OC-3.

Synchronous Optical Network (SONET)—SONET is the U.S. optical transmission standard that is part of the international SDH. The basic building block of SONET is the STS-1 51.84-Mbps signal, chosen to accommodate a T3 signal.

synchronous—Synchronous refers to data communication that is controlled by the microprocessor clock; signals are permitted to start and stop at particular times. To use synchronous communication, the clock settings of the sending and receiving systems must match.

Synchronous Transport Signal (STS)—STS is a term that describes a SONET data transfer rate. For example, STS-1 is 51.84 Mbps, STS-3 is 155.52 Mbps, STS-12 is 622.08 Mbps, and STS-48 at 2.488 Gbps. The STS designation refers to the interface for electrical signals. The optical signal standards are correspondingly designated OC-1, OC-2, etc.

systems development life cycle—Systems development life cycle is the process of creating a new system, or changing an existing system, from concept to completion.

T3, E3—T3 is one of the T-carrier multiplexing standards. It operates at 44.736 Mbps, the equivalent of 672 voice circuits. E3 is the European equivalent of T3, operating at 34.368 Mbps.

T-carrier—T-carriers are one of several hierarchical systems for multiplexing digitized voice signals. The first T-carrier was installed in 1962 by the Bell system. The T-carrier family of systems now includes T1, T1C, T1D, T2, T3, and T4 (and their European counterparts E1, E2, etc.). T1 and its successors were designed to multiplex voice communications. Therefore, T1 was designed such that each channel carries a digitized representation of an analog signal that has a bandwidth of 4,000 Hz. It turns out that 64 Kbps is required to digitize a 4,000-Hz voice signal. Although current digitization technology has reduced the requirement to 32 Kbps or less, a T-carrier channel is still 64 Kbps.

Thicknet—Thicknet is also known as 10Base5 or Yellow Wire. Thicknet can carry a signal 500 m before a repeater is required. The maximum number of nodes allowed in a trunk segment is 100. The maximum number of trunk segments allowed in an Ethernet network is five, of which only three may be populated with nodes. Thicknet is no longer installed in computer networks.

Thinnet—Thinnet (or 10Base2) can carry a signal 185 m before a repeater is required. The maximum number of nodes that can be connected to a Thinnet trunk segment is 30.

time-division multiplexing (TDM)—TDM is multiplexing technology that guarantees each port a fixed amount of bandwidth on a rotating basis. TDM is suited to constant bit-rate traffic. See MUX and STDM.

topology—Topology refers to the specific physical configuration of a network or a portion of a network. Ring and star are examples of different network topologies.

total internal reflection—Total internal reflection occurs when a light ray traveling in one material hits another material and reflects back into the original material without any loss of light. In optical fiber, total internal reflection occurs for two reasons. First, the core has a higher index of refraction than the cladding; this difference causes the light to refract, or bend. Second, the light signals enter the cable at a shallow angle; an overly steep light angle will cause some or all of the light to enter the cladding instead of reflecting back into the core. See refraction and index of refraction.

traffic—Traffic refers to the amount of information traveling across a network. It includes both user data and network-related information.

transceiver—A device that can both transmit and receive optical signals is referred to as a transceiver.

Transmission Control Protocol (TCP)—TCP is a Transport Layer protocol used to send messages reliably across a network. It is usually paired with IP.

transparent bridging—Transparent bridges enable frames to move back and forth between two network segments running the same MAC-layer protocols. This type of bridging is referred to as "transparent" because the source station transmits a frame to the destination station as if it were on the same physical network segment, that is, the bridge is "invisible." Transparent bridges typically connect Ethernet network segments. However, transparent bridging may also be used with Token Ring and FDDI networks.

Transport Driver Interface (TDI)—TDI is the Windows NT interface layer between various transport protocols (SPX or TCP) and server or redirector software interfaces.

twisted pair—In twisted pair cabling, pairs of conductors are twisted together to randomize possible cross-talk from nearby wiring. Inadequate twisting is detectable using modern cable testing instruments.

uninterruptible power source (UPS)—An UPS provides battery backup in the event a power failure occurs.

unshielded twisted pair (UTP)—UTP is the most common type of network cabling, and is used extensively in telephone networks and many data communication applications. UTP can carry a 100-Mbps digital signal 100 m using twisted pairs of cable without requiring that the signal be repeated.

utilization—Utilization refers to the amount of bandwidth being used at a given point in time or over a period of time. For example, if a 10-Mbps Ethernet LAN is running at 40-percent utilization, it is using 4 of the 10-Mbps bandwidth available.

virtual channel connection (VCC)—VCC refers to the endpoints of a one-directional ATM VC. A VCC is a point at which the ATM cell payload is passed to, or received from, a VC.

virtual LAN (VLAN)—A VLAN is a group of computers in a large LAN that behave as if they are connected to their own small private LAN. VLANs are created using special switches and software, so computers can be assigned to different VLANs without changing their physical configuration.

virtual private network (VPN)—VPN is a connection, over a shared network, that behaves like a dedicated link. VPNs are created using a technique called "tunneling," which uses encryption to transmit data packets across a public network, such as the Internet or other commercially available network, in a private "tunnel" that simulates a point-to-point connection.

volume—Volume is a logical area of disk space, configured in NetWare, and used to store a specific group of directories and files. For example, a NetWare server could configure a volume for system files, a volumes for data, and a volume for applications.

wavelength—The distance between one crest of a wave and the next is referred to as the wavelength. Light wavelengths are measured in nanometers (nm), or billionths of a meter. Each nanometer is 10^{-9} meter.

wizard—A wizard is an application that helps a user configure a computer's hardware or software settings. Wizards use a step-by-step interface that asks a series of questions and responds based on the user's input.

World Wide Web Consortium (W3C)—W3C is an independent industry organization that works to develop technically sound open standards for the Web. W3C (www.w3c.org) is the chief standards organization for HTTP, HTML, XML, DHTML, and many other Web-based technologies. It cooperates with the various Internet organizations.

X Windows—X Windows is an early client/server system, with graphical user interface, developed for UNIX.

X.25—X.25 is a packet-switching network, public or private, typically built upon the facilities of public telephone networks (leased lines). In the United States, X.25 is offered by most carriers and VARs, such as AT&T, US Sprint, Ameritech, and Pacific Bell. The X.25 interface lies at OSI Layer 3, rather than Layer 1. X.25 defines its own three-layer protocol stack.

X.500—X.500 is an ITU-T standard for a global tree-structured directory that can provide a worldwide lookup service.

X.509—X.500 is an ITU-T standard for directory authentication services.

INDEX

Numerics

100VG-AnyLAN 204
10Base2 52
10Base5 52

A

Abend 372
Adapter board 290
Address
    broadcast 125
    logical 25 to 28
    multicast 125
    physical 25 to 28
    Resolution Protocol (See ARP)
American National Standards Institute
    (ANSI) 47, 83
API 310
AppleTalk Filing Protocol (APF) 310
Application
    components 326
    network 347
    Programming Interface (API) 310
    server 346
Architecture, ATM 239, 244
ARP 106, 204
ASCII 428

ATM
    architecture 239, 244
    bandwidth 215
    case study 256
    connection-oriented mode 218
    deployment 295
    devices 272
    fixed-length cells 220
    flow control 220
    forum 204
    growth 224
    interfaces 240
    LAN 263
    layer 249
    limitations 235
    migration 298
    network 241
    overview 212
    physical layer 246
    preparing for 299
    routers 283 to 285
    scalable solution 234
    segmentation 225, 232
    switches 273 to 282
    vs. STM 213
    vs. traditional networking 215
Attempt 106

B

Backbone
    collapsed 230
    distributed 228
    FDDI 229
    switched 155, 157
    token ring 187
BackOffice 437
Backoff time 106

547

Overall Course Evaluation Survey

Congratulations on completing this course! We hope you enjoyed your learning journey.

This survey will help us identify where we can focus our strengths and improve our weaknesses. As a token of our appreciation for your time in completing this, we will send you a Certificate of Appreciation (if you tell us who you are!).

Introduction to Local Area Networks

Course # (see book cover): _____

Location of course: _____

Instructor-led ☐   Self-paced ☐

Did you use the CD?   Yes ☐   No ☐   Comments: _____

Did you access the online course?   Yes ☐   No ☐   Comments: _____

Did you use the Web board for support?   Yes ☐   No ☐   Comments: _____

Did you visit the student Web site?   Yes ☐   No ☐   Comments: _____

What are this course's strengths? _____

What did you like best? _____

What are this course's weaknesses? _____

What did you like least? _____

Would you be interested in other titles from this publisher? _____

If so, what specific topics would you like to see addressed? _____

Optional (must provide this information if you would like a Certificate of Appreciation):

Name: _____

Occupation/Title: _____

Company: _____

Address: _____

City/State/ZIP: _____

Country (if outside USA): _____

E-mail address: _____

Gender: Male ☐   Female ☐

Age: Under 25 ☐   26-40 ☐   41-60 ☐   61+ ☐

Please return this survey to: WestNet Learning Technologies, Attn: Executive Vice President, 5420 Ward Rd., Suite 150, Arvada, CO 80002 USA

Or fax to: 303-432-2565

BUSINESS REPLY MAIL

BULK RATE MAIL   PERMIT NO. 83   ARVADA CO

POSTAGE WILL BE PAID BY ADDRESSEE

WestNet
LEARNING TECHNOLOGIES

5420 WARD ROAD STE 150
ARVADA CO 80002-9929